Go To Heaven!

Don Hockamudel

9/24/10

ODYSSEY TO LIFE

An Autobiography and Abortion Analysis

by

Don Hochanadel, Sr.

ISBN 1-58597-348-3

Library of Congress Control Number: 2005904855

LEATHERS
PUBLISHING

4500 College Blvd.
Overland Park, KS 66211
1/888/888/7696
www.leatherspublishing.com

The life of a little baby is priceless.

The life of an unborn baby is even more priceless.

The eternal soul of both is the epitome of priceless.

— *Don Hochanadel, Sr.*

FOREWORD

WHEN I FIRST started writing this book, it was a form of therapy for me. I had just lost the biggest case of my legal career, the "retirement" case, as it is called in the legal profession. I had worked on it for six years, had an eight-week trial in federal court in Wichita, and the jury ruled in favor of the defendant. When I returned to my office in Overland Park, my practice was in shambles. I had very few cases, and there was really not much work to do. I worked each case to the smallest detail, but by the end of that work there were still hours left in the day.

However, I was determined not to just sit around. I needed something to keep me productive. I had always dreamed of writing a book, and this looked like the time to start on it. The daily plan was first to do all the law work until there was no more I could do, then work on the book. Then came the hard decision as to what to write. I learned a long time ago that you should only write about the things that you really know about. If you didn't, then you were dead in the water, because readers are just like a jury. Both are very perceptive, and if you try to fool them, then you lose. They know when a writer is trying to hustle them.

When I asked myself what I knew the most about, I first considered something centered around law. But unfortunately, there were so many lawyers writing books that I felt I wouldn't be able to compete. And I wanted a book that would have some real value and the public enthusiastically embraced. It was then that I realized the one thing I knew the most about was … me. I don't mean that egocentrically. It's just that I have had an extremely interesting life, have felt the worst disasters you can imagine, have overcome so many difficulties, and have been blessed so many times, and have such a very strong moral message that the public may be interested in some real substance for a change. Additionally, I really knew nothing about my grandpa and not very much about my own dad in the years before I reached the ability to remember things.

Then the realization set in that I needed to write about my life for the very best of reasons – my kids and their kids. Along with my life, they were the centerpiece of my life, and at some time in their lives, probably after I was gone, they would get around to wondering what it was like when Dad or Grandpa was a kid, etc. So an autobiography was the only choice.

I considered various methodologies, but finally arrived at a very somber conclusion. The book had to be brutally true and honest, no matter how embarrassing or thrilling it was for me. I am a 25-year dry alcoholic and learned in AA that honesty is the cornerstone of sobriety.

The next question was format. After a lot of attempts to adopt some kind of organization, I finally decided to just start writing, and when I reached a point where a stage had been completed, or something new started, then I ended that chapter and started on a new one. For some reason, this worked out beautifully. Out of deep respect for my wife Joy, since she was and is the biggest part of my life and we have experienced so many things together, I gave her each chapter as it was written. Since there are ups and downs in everyone's life, I absolutely didn't want to put anything in the book that made her uncomfortable; she had absolute veto power over what went into the book on things about her. Happily, she was as completely honest as I intended to be, and although she wanted some things excluded, she was very understanding and supportive.

I hope that those who read this book get a sense that life can deal some very devastating blows as it did to me. And I hope that perhaps in some small way the reader can get a sense of strength to deal with his or her own calamities. And I also hope that they get to experience the moments of supreme delight that I have enjoyed in my life. But most of all, to my wife and kids, who know that I love them very much, I hope that their love for "the ole man" is as deep as his love for them....

CONTENTS

1

WHY I WROTE THE BOOK AND EARLY CHILDHOOD

(Welcome to Life)

I WENT TO my office the following Monday morning, dragging my heels. I made a cup of instant coffee with hot tap water, as I always did first thing in the morning, then sat at my desk, leaned back and took a long, pensive look at my situation. I hit the CD button on my remote, and the soothing, almost sorrowful music of Enya filled my office with the soft, relaxing smoothness of her music. It seemed to fit the mood. I took an inventory of my cases, and their number was woefully thin. My practice was a shambles because of the time devoted to the big case we had just lost. The bad part was that there were no "quick fixes." Almost all of my business resulted from either referrals from other attorneys, or by word of mouth by satisfied clients. Some of the cases took up to two years from the time I was retained until there was a recovery. And I wasn't getting any fees until the recovery was made and the money paid to us.

I knew I couldn't just run out and manufacture clients. I abhorred any type of advertising, such as TV or big yellow page ads, and even if I didn't abhor it, I lacked the funds to purchase it. I could see dark days ahead. There was rent both on the office and home, Michael's tuition was over $3,000 a year, paid in 10 installments of $300. There was insurance and utilities, and *food.* With five of us at home, the food bill was out of sight, even though we didn't eat like kings. The only fast track I could see to generate quick income was to get on the phone to as many Missouri lawyers as I could and see if they needed a Kansas lawyer to act as co-counsel on their Kansas cases. It was demeaning and humiliating, because most lawyers would sense fairly quickly by virtue of my call that I needed business. That itself was a tacit admission that I wasn't doing too well and, therefore, couldn't be much of a lawyer. But that was a risk I'd just have to take. I had a family to feed. Unfortunately though, most of these lawyers were already "married" to a Kansas attorney or had someone in their own office who had a Kansas license. After about a week of this with no luck at all, I realized this wasn't going to help.

Then I started going through each case I had and made sure that everything I could do right up to that minute was done. Most of the cases were fairly current, because that is just the way I operated. I took representing someone as a sacred trust and duty, regardless of their color, intelligence, or what else. Every person deserves the best a lawyer has to give. It made me feel productive to go through each of the few cases I had and make sure nothing was lacking. Soon, I was through all my cases, and there just wasn't any more work I could do on them. Now I had tons of time on my hands.

As I contemplated my situation, I recalled that all my life I had wanted to be an author. Maybe this was a situation that the Lord simply "created." That's when the idea dawned on me that it would be useful to fill the vacant time with writing a book. At least, I would be doing something productive. I didn't have delusions of grandeur, thinking that I could crack the "big time" as another John Grisham. No, I knew that wouldn't work. But I felt that to write a good book, I had to write about something I knew well. I knew that if I tried writing about something I didn't know too much about, I'd lose the reader in the first few pages. Readers, in a way, are the ultimate jury. If you can't keep their attention, then you may as well pack your bags and head for home.

For some reason, I started pondering in depth over everything that had happened to me in my life. I recalled my childhood, the years in the seminary, in Wichita, in the Army, then my marriage to Joy, and losing two babies. Richard's adoption crossed my mind, and then the other four sons. I recalled all the years of struggling to raise the kids, the ups and downs, and wondered when was it going to cease. I remembered the comment a stranger made to me years ago, sitting in O'Hare airport with a long wait between connections, after we had traded life stories. He looked at me with eyes of quiet admiration and said that after all that I had been through, I must have had the patience of Job. The more I thought of it, the more I realized that the only thing I probably knew the most about was me, myself and my life.

Then I thought, who am I? Who would ever be interested in the life of a guy who grew up in the Midwest and was a nobody? Besides that, I knew nothing about writing a book, book marketing, editing, publishing, etc., etc. But a couple of things impacted my thinking. First, even if the book were never published, it should be a great boon to my kids as they got older, and then to their kids, and then, hopefully, to their kids. As I thought about this, I realized I knew next to nothing about my grandfather, the man who had raised my father, the one man above all men for whom I had the deepest affection. I wished I knew more about him, about his times, about his philosophies on life, about his early life before I was born and old enough to start remembering, and other things like that.

The second consideration was the times we were living in. As I looked at the values, or rather the lack of values today, I felt that perhaps the public might be refreshed with a book about an average person, his failures, his successes, his tragedies and his joys. It was clear that I had been around, had been through my share of misery, and still I could hold my head high, had a good family, was sober, and still had a strong bond with God and a constant, positive outlook on life. Perhaps the public was looking for someone ordinary, like themselves.

So I decided to write my autobiography. Little did I know how great an influence this would have on my life. Little did I know the long locked doors this would open, the long forgotten feelings that had been repressed and would now be felt again. It would prove to be almost like living your life all over again and then asking yourself, for what purpose? Sure, raising a family is an enormous fulfillment. But is there more? As I went from chapter to chapter, I felt certain feelings start to rustle and begin polarizing. Writing the book itself was and is an arduous odyssey. It was a journey through old feelings and experiences, and the birth of some new feelings and thoughts.

I was born on February 1, 1937 in Russell, Kansas. Not too long after I was born, my parents, Lawrence and Maurine Hochanadel, moved to Hoisington, Kansas, a small town about 30 miles southeast of Russell, Kansas. I was my parent's fifth of what would eventually become a total of 12 kids. (I know "children" is "proper," but that's just not me). What is remarkable is that, although my dad was broke all his life, nevertheless, among his six sons are two lawyers, a doctor of education, a petroleum engineer, a successful businessman and a high school teacher. Among his six daughters are a hospital lab supervisor, an X-ray technician, a respiratory therapist, a business clerk, and two registered nurses. But what is *most impressive* is that all 12 kids married, and are *still* married to their original spouses. And the youngest marriage is 30 years! Together, that adds up to over four-and-a-half centuries of married life!

My earliest memory was when I was in kindergarten. It was at the Catholic school, a block from St. John's Church in Hoisington. We lived a few blocks from the school and the church, and, of course, walked to school each day. Anyhow, this happened on the playground by the school. The school had a typical metal merry-go-round on which we played. At recess one day everyone was outside playing. Since my two older brothers, Dave and Max, were also in grade school, they were outside at recess as well. Dave was in the fourth grade, and Max in the third grade. Teresa was in the first grade.

While we were playing near the merry-go-ground, a kid was being mean to the rest of the kids, including me. It had happened before, and my older brothers told me that if it happened again, I was to hit this kid square in the mouth with my fist. I really wasn't an aggressive kid and usually didn't initiate any fights. In fact, I was the opposite. If I could avoid a confrontation, that was my first objective. So this kid and I got into a squabble, and eventually he hit me. I remembered the advice that my brothers gave me, and I hauled off and smacked him right in the mouth, just like they said. He immediately started bleeding and spit out a tooth. I had actually knocked out one of his teeth! My brothers came over to us, and were they ever proud! All the other kids had looks of admiration in their eyes. I was the king of the hill! I didn't even get into trouble with the sisters, since this kid admitted he hit me first. They just lectured me on not fighting. Needless to say, from then on no one messed with me.

I don't remember much more about living in Hoisington, but I do remember that while I was still in kindergarten, my parents decided to move to a small town 10 miles west of Hoisington, a German town, named Olmitz. Olmitz was really a quaint town, with a population of about 400. It was actually a settlement of Germans who had come over from Germany many years before. A lot of the residents still couldn't speak English. It was located off an asphalt county road, but all the streets in town were sand and gravel. I understand there is a sister town in Germany or Austria by the same name. There were many such German settlements, such as Schoenschen, Otis, Liebenthal, and on and on, all within miles of Olmitz.

Olmitz had two general stores for groceries and other items, two pool halls, a big Catholic church, a school for grades through the grade eight, and a Knights of Columbus Hall, which was brand new. The K of C Hall was built after we arrived, because I remember that when people got married, they had a wedding dance that evening, and they had these dances in another, older building. At these dances the local band was made up mostly of the farmers and people living in town, who could play accordions and other instruments. They would play polkas and dance and drink beer well into the night.

Olmitz also had a blacksmith shop, whose owner was the mayor, a filling station for gas, and Meitner's auto repair shop. The filling station had one of those old red pumps where you took a handle that was vertical to the ground and pulled it back and forth. This pumped gas up into a glass tank at the top of the pump. You pumped until you had the amount of gas you wanted to buy pumped into the glass tank at the top; then you stuck the nozzle into your car's gas tank, and let the gas drain by force of gravity into your tank. Gas was 14 or 15 cents a gallon back then.

My first memory of Olmitz was of a small white schoolhouse on the southeast side of town. I was finishing up kindergarten after our family moved from Hoisington. Our playground abutted a gravel street across from which were wheat fields and farm lands. I remember I didn't like the idea of leaving Hoisington and the kids I knew there, and then being thrown into a new school where I didn't know anyone. I was an outsider, and the kids in Olmitz treated me that way. It was really rough for a while and I was homesick for Hoisington. I just didn't like it. I was, and felt like, a complete stranger. To make matters worse, we had hot lunches at school. That was okay, but someone on the staff had this thing about whole baked apples, and none of us liked whole baked apples. Yet, we had whole baked apples at almost every meal. God, did we hate them! When I finally had all the baked apples I could take, rather than eat mine (and the sisters generally checked to make sure that our trays were cleared), I smuggled mine outside. I sneaked out to the ditch at the end of the playground and threw the apple into the ditch. Unfortunately, one of the nuns saw me do it. She retrieved the apple from the ditch and brought it back into the school. They had me dead to right. Boy, was I in trouble! I got a stern lecture from the sisters about throwing away food. Oddly enough though, we didn't have too many whole baked apples after that.

That's all I can remember from the years prior to the first grade, and I suppose many of these experiences aren't earth-shattering. But they do set the table for the next chapter, and I think you will enjoy it immensely.

2
GRADE SCHOOL AGE
(The Golden Years)

I CALL THIS period the Golden Years, because they were completely free from the pressures of adolescence and the strenuous responsibilities of adulthood. It was a period when I was not shackled with long term concerns and, as is typical with young kids, was mostly concerned about today, and only today.

After the first school year in Olmitz my childhood really started getting into gear. There were four of us kids all about the same age. In addition to myself, there was my younger brother Tony, Don Crowell (whose dad was the local bootlegger), and Jerry Linenberger. There wasn't much to do in such a small town, but what we did do, the four of us did together. These are some very fond memories. We lived right across from the school, and behind our house was a full baseball diamond. On many week ends some team from the next small town would come over and play our local team, made up from the men living in and around Olmitz. My dad was the catcher on the team and we were so proud to watch him play.

We were enterprising young kids, and these games gave us a chance to make some money. Our garage was very near the ball diamond and many of those who came to the game had to walk or drive right by it. We borrowed enough money from mom to buy a few cases of pop and ice, put the ice in a metal tub and iced down the pop. Then we set up a concession stand in our garage and sold the pop to the people who came to the game. We bought the pop for a nickel a bottle and sold it for a dime. There was some good pop in those days. I remember a sweet tasting small bottle of grape pop called "Grapette" and "Dad's" root beer. We also had the good old 8 oz. reusable bottles of Pepsi and Coca-Cola. We also had a chocolate pop and "Nesbitt's" orange drink. Boy, was it good when it was ice cold. That was just about the extent of the pop selection that was available in those days. I remember when the Negro teams came over to play us. Some of our patrons were disappointed that we weren't selling beer also. Obviously, as minors we couldn't.

The garage where we sold the pop was a typical small town garage. It was made of corrugated sheet metal nailed to a simple wood frame on a concrete slab. Kansas is known for its tornadoes, and the sides of the garage were riddled with holes where rocks had been picked up by tornados and whipped into the sheet metal with such force that they completely penetrated the walls, leaving holes about the size of a nickel to a quarter. I mention this, as while we were living there, mom came to know some family who was passing through and were down on their luck. She allowed them to live in our garage until they could get back on their feet. It was summer, and this family had one or two small kids. For beds they laid blankets on the concrete floor and slept on them.

One day I overheard the wife of this family tell my mom that she was going to take a bath. Now, we didn't have any inside showers. In fact, we had to use the out house if we wanted to go to the toilet. So I knew that she would have to take her bath in the garage in one of our metal wash tubs. I bided my time until I knew she was inside the tub, taking her bath. Then I snuck up to the back of the garage and peeked through a tornado hole. That was when I got my first look at a real, live naked woman. As I watched her, I realized that if she looked over my way she could see that there was no sunlight coming through the holes I was blocking with my eyes and body. Guilt and fear had begun setting in, so I eased myself away and headed out across the baseball diamond and went on about playing. I never got caught and boy did I ever get an eyeful.

My dad was a "rig builder," a breed of oil field worker that was quickly becoming extinct. It was about 1942 when we moved to Olmitz, and the oil boom had long ago struck in Kansas. There were quite a few shallow oil wells, about 3400 feet deep and some natural gas wells especially in Southwestern Kansas around Liberal and in the Oklahoma panhandle. In the early days they built steel derricks over the area they wanted to drill. The rig builders would start at the bottom and bolt the metal beams together with large bolts and keep adding one tier after another until they had reached the desired height. The rigs had to be tall enough, since once the drill bit had drilled down so that the end of one section of pipe gradually came down to the drilling floor level, they had to add another section of drill pipe. The derricks had to be high enough to hold up the next section of pipe, lift it up, and place the bottom of that section in the top end of the section sticking out of the derrick floor. They screwed the new section into the bottom section, and continued drilling.

If the well came in (struck oil), they left the permanent derricks standing, and set up a "horse head" pump that did the pumping of the oil. The heads had a strong cable fastened to them which, in turn, was fastened to the pump rods that went down into the well. The pump was powered by a motor so that the pump head went up and down. On the up swing they would pull up the oil from the bottom of the well, and on the down swing, drop down and get another load of oil to pull up through the well casing to the surface, and on into the storage tanks, called tank batteries.

They soon replaced these permanent derricks with mobile derricks that they could move on trucks from one well site to another. Once the mobile derrick trucks were on site, then they pulled up the derricks so that they were standing vertically over the spot they wanted to drill the well. The mobile derricks made the permanent derricks obsolete. But long before the mobile derricks came along, there were literally hundreds of these permanent derricks still standing, even after the wells had petered out or were pumped dry. To this day you can still see an occasional such derrick still standing in parts of Kansas.

My dad worked for Jack Murray, a man in Hoisington who owned and operated a liquor store. He ran this rig business on the side, where Mr. Murray contracted to tear down or dismantle these old steel derricks. My dad and his crew of three other men would go to the well site, climb the derrick, and, with their wrenches, loosen the bolts, dropping the metal cross beams to the ground. They would start at the top and work down until they had disassembled the entire derrick. They were so good at it that they could dismantle an entire rig in one day.

Dad had a black metal lunch box with the rounded lid that held his thermos bottle of coffee. His lunch was placed in the bottom half, then the top lid closed over the bottom, and snaps held it closed. All of the men took similar lunch boxes, so dad had his nickname, "Lonk," painted in white on his lunch box; in this way it wouldn't get confused with the others. He got the nickname from his co-workers, who called him "Lonk" instead of Lawrence.

One of Dad's favorite jokes was about lunch boxes. It seems that one of the workers at lunch break would complain every day about always getting bologna sandwiches for his lunch. Finally one of his co-workers had enough of his complaining, and told him to tell his wife to make him something else. To which the worker replied: "I can't." When his co-worker asked why not, he replied: "Because I make my own lunch." Silly, but I heard dad tell that joke a hundred times.

As you can imagine, this kind of manual work required good agility, strength, and a lot of safety concern. Too many people were injured or killed. The weather had a dominant effect on whether they worked. If it rained, they didn't work. Wind was another detrimental factor. If the wind was blowing too hard, then the men simply couldn't climb the derricks. There was no health insurance, so if you got hurt, you paid your own bills. And if you didn't work, then you didn't get paid. And my dad had a lot of kids to feed and clothe. God only knows how often he went out and worked in highly dangerous conditions, just so he could feed his family. Eventually he was seriously injured but that will be covered later.

We could only afford one car, and that had to be kept in good running condition, because if Dad didn't make it to Hoisington on time, the crew would leave without him, and he would miss a day's work. I think that is why we moved to Olmitz right across from the school, and one-half block from the church and two blocks from the grocery stores. In looking back, I realize that *for his entire life* my dad's paycheck was spent long before he got it. This has caused me to have a lot of deep affection for my father because he never really had a dime to his name. All of his life he was broke. And I know it hurt him not to be able to put new clothes on his kids, and knew that most of us had to wear hand-me-downs that the older kids had grown out of, and that were practically worn out. Many were the times that we had to stick cardboard inside the bottoms of our shoes because there were holes in the soles, and we didn't have enough money for a new pair of shoes, or even decent hand-me-downs. To this day, I feel almost cheated, since I don't think I got a fair shot at really knowing my dad. I was fifth in a line of 12 kids, and there just wasn't enough of him to go around for all of us.

Once I got up into the second, third and fourth grades, my life expanded considerably and I could do more things. We lived in Olmitz from before my first grade until after my sixth grade, and I guess I can best describe these years as very happy years, with a few episodes of, shall we say, disappointing events. I'm not sure at which point these experiences occurred, so I will just relate what they were and you can keep them within the time frame of the first-through-sixth grade period.

I mentioned that my folks had 12 kids. I clearly remember when Dianne, the 12th, was born. Many homes in Olmitz didn't have telephones. To make a call we had to go about a block and a half north to a house where the town's main phone was installed. We then asked the woman who lived there and ran the phone service to make the call. Dad was at work that day, July 1, 1948. I was 11 years old and in the sixth grade. This was also the birthday of my older brother, Max. Apparently Mom was going into labor, and someone had to get the message to Dad to come home and get Mom to the hospital. I must have been the only one home, because I was chosen to get on the bike and get to the town phone as quickly as possible.

However, the bike didn't have a pedal on the left side, and the pedal on the other side was broken off except for the bar that stuck out. What made matters worse was that I was also barefooted. So here I was, trying my best to pedal the bike as fast as I could, with just a partial pedal on one side, in my bare feet, with the admonishment from Mom to hurry as fast as I could. I got there and told the woman to call my dad, etc. I then walked the bike home and we waited for Dad, hoping he would get there on time. After what seemed like forever, we could see his car coming from the north on the county road like a bat out of hell. He took the corner coming into town at break-neck speed, came out of the turn spinning his wheels and threw up a tornado of dust, as he came in on the sand and gravel road to home. He rushed Mom to the hospital, and fortunately, they made it on time. Wow, what a day!

There was another time that they called upon me at a very early age to perform a truly adult duty. We either purchased a new gas stove, or Dad discovered that we had a gas leak beneath the house. It had to be fixed. The problem was, there was not enough room for Dad or any grown-up to crawl between the 2" x 10" wood beams under the house to get to the point where the natural gas pipeline came into the house. Since I was slender and wiry, Mom selected me to take the wrench and crawl under the house between the wooden beams to the line. It was too dark to see, so Tony had to follow and hold the flashlight. I got the wrench around the pipe coupling and tightened it as much as possible. As an added precaution, we put some tar or heavy grease around the coupling.

But then came the scary part. We had to know if there was even the slightest of leaks. If there was, it could gradually build up and blow up the house. The only way to be sure was to go down there again and light a match right at the coupling. If there was a small leak, then it would light up like a pilot light on a stove. I was selected to go alone for this job. Tony got to stay behind. I crawled to the coupling, sniffed as hard as I could and, smelling no gas, struck the match. Ah, no explosion! But I still had to move it along the pipe to the coupling. I did, and to my great relief there was no explosion or fire, and the house didn't blow up. God, what crazy things we did!

I want to tell you a little bit about my friends. As I mentioned before, there were four of us who got into a good share of mischief. Jerry Linenberger lived about two blocks away. He also came from a very large family, and his parents couldn't speak good English yet. Something happened to him that he never really lived down. In those days no one had inside toilets. We all had outhouses. In fact, your status was somewhat determined by the number of seat holes your outhouse had. If you only had one hole to sit on, then you were in the lower class. But if your outhouse had two or even three, then you were in the upper class. Isn't that a terrible way of determining status?

One of the favorite Halloween tricks for us kids was in the dark of the night to move the outhouses back off their holes so that if someone came out late at night in the dark to go to the toilet, hopefully they would fall into the holes which were full of you-know-what. We would either do that or simply push them over. We had to be discreet and careful because everyone in town knew that was one of the favorite pranks, and some of them set counter-pranks. And there was no police department, so we didn't have to worry about police officers patrolling.

Getting back to Jerry, what happened to him was everyone's worst nightmare. He apparently was using the outhouse and had accidentally dropped something that he really wanted to keep down through the toilet hole. Whatever it was, it didn't sink. So, being somewhat young and oblivious of the risks, he reached down through the toilet hole to try to retrieve his lost article. And, you guessed it, he fell through the hole into the liquid mass below. Now some of these holes were a good six to seven feet deep. You might say he was in deep shit. At any rate, he was eventually rescued and was given a succession of outside baths. He said it was a week before he could get all the smell off himself. God, did we laugh!

The other member of our foursome besides my brother Tony (who was exactly one year, one month, one week, and one day younger than I) was Don Crowell. His dad was the town bootlegger. He lived about a block east from the church, in a typical small town house. But his dad had a storage shed in his back yard, and the floor of the storage shed was earthen. To hide his contraband, he simply dug a hole in the floor of his shed, then slid a wide flat cover over the hole and put some of the floor dirt on top of the covering. It looked just like the rest of the floor. It was a little difficult to find, and without local police, the only way to control it was for the sheriff of Barton County to come over from Great Bend, some 15 to 20 miles away. But the sheriff usually had bigger fish to catch, so we rarely saw him in town.

In fact, there were only two occasions that I ever heard of the sheriff or his deputies coming to Olmitz. Once was to confiscate some slot machines from one of the taverns and to arrest the owner. (Some poor loser must have complained). And the other time was when a grown man, Edwin Bahr, got into an argument outside the pool hall with my oldest brother, Dave, who I think was in the eighth grade at the time. This full-grown man actually hit Dave with his fist, giving him a huge black eye. That really upset mom, and she called the sheriff, who sent a deputy over. The deputy arrested and handcuffed the man and hauled him off to jail. It's a good thing Dad wasn't around, because I know he would have beat the hell out of him.

Growing up in a small town, there wasn't much opportunity for us kids to make any money. Lord knows our folks didn't have any. And there weren't too many people who didn't mow their own yards. We literally had to beg to get to mow yards and got maybe two or three dollars for the effort. And we had to use the old two-wheel mowers with the revolving curved blades that were turned by the wheels that rolled along the ground. They were strictly push movers. No one had power movers, let alone self-propelled mowers. It was a lot of work, but we were desperate.

As a result of being broke and having few lawns to mow, we kept an eye out for when the delivery trucks came to town. From our house and yard we could easily see them arrive on the county road coming into town. We knew they were headed for either the general stores or the taverns, so we ran down there as fast as we could. Then we asked the delivery man if we could help him unload. Although usually they didn't need the help, I think they let us help out of pure generosity. The pop trucks were usually the best. They usually gave us each a quarter or a bottle or two of pop for helping carrying in the cases of pop. However, every now and then we would run into a cheap driver. He would let us help him, but then didn't give us anything. What a way to treat young kids!

But we had a way of dealing with this kind of delivery man. Usually they pulled into the dirt alley along the side the taverns to make their deliveries. If they didn't pay us, then we hid a little bit down the alley and, as the pop truck drove by, two of us would hop on the rear of the truck where the driver couldn't see us; then we started pitching bottles of pop into the ditch, as the truck went down the alley until he got to the street. There we hopped off, made sure the driver wasn't coming back, went back to gather up the bottles of pop, and headed for our secret clubhouse. This was an old abandoned woodshed near the grain elevator that no one cared about. Once there, we pulled up boards in the floor and hid the pop. Then the four of us would laugh and gloat over getting the best of the evil driver. He would have actually saved pop if he had just given us a couple of bottles.

But sometimes we pressed our luck too far. There was a tobacco truck that came to town to deliver cigarettes. Desperate for making any kind of money, we even tried to help them. But they really didn't reward us too much. On one occasion, as this truck was parked just off the street in the alley, with the end of the truck toward the street, I helped the driver fill an order to take inside. The truck doors swung around to the side of the truck, so that you could get up into the truck; then there was a narrow space you could walk down the center of the truck and pull cartons of cigarettes from the shelves and into a box. This time I had a rather sullen driver, and I could tell there would be little, if any, reward for helping. So I waited until the driver had his back to me; then I slipped a whole carton of cigarettes off the shelf, leaned out the back of the truck and tossed it into the grass along the sidewalk away from the tavern. The only problem was that a man was walking along the sidewalk, and I hadn't seen him. But he saw me, picked up the carton, handed it to the driver, and wow, did I ever get a chewing out! I'm still smarting from that.

But there was one experience that finally broke me from having "sticky" or "long" fingers. This happened as I was getting closer to the fifth grade. I was helping a candy truck unload at Fred Nuss' general store. Fred had a storeroom on the ground floor level. He and his family lived on the upper floor, so his wife was always there. If they were upstairs when a customer came in, the door had a bell on it that would ring when the customer came in. While I was putting away the candy in the storeroom, I couldn't resist sticking two Hershey bars into my pocket, thinking I could easily slip away without being noticed. However, I didn't know that the Nusses had a small glass window in the wall of the store that allowed them to look into the storeroom. Nor did I know that Mrs. Nuss had watched me the entire time I was in the storeroom. So when I came out, she asked me if I had anything in my pocket. I denied it, of course, but then she reached into my pocket and pulled out the candy bars. Not only was I now a thief, but also a liar. This episode had a lasting mark on me. I decided right then that a life of crime just wasn't worth it. That frightened me into complete honesty.

Long before this, my friends and I had pulled off enough stunts that it is really amazing we didn't eventually wind up behind bars. For example, Tony, Don, Jerry and I had formed our own little club and decided that one of our secret objectives was to get inside every building in Olmitz, except homes. This presented some interesting challenges. There was an old empty, red brick bank building right across from the pool hall, where we hung out. This was about our fourth or fifth grade years. We could pry open some boards in the back and sneak in. There really wasn't much to the bank, just some old dusty floors and empty rooms.

The most difficult challenge was a building about a half a block away from the old blacksmith shop. This building was a huge mystery to us. None of us even knew anyone who had ever been in the building, or who had even heard about what was in the building. The problem with this building was that the only way to get into it was through the front. And, although the front opened into the alley, the other side of the alley was an open lot. We scouted the backs and sides of the building, and there were no doors or windows that we could get open. So we knew we had to go in through the front. But this was risky, because the blacksmith shop across the street from the lot had a clear view of the front of the building. Still, we were consumed with curiosity. We picked a time of day that we felt was the safest, then brought our tools, hammer, screwdrivers, etc., and worked on the front door. We hurried as much as we could, but it seemed like it was an eternity. Finally we pried some nails loose and got the door open. We slowly peered into the building and saw junk stored everywhere.

We were just about to make a more thorough investigation, when our spotter at the door sounded the alarm. The owner of the blacksmith shop, Olmitz's mayor, was halfway across the lot, heading our way. We all hit the door and lit out like a bunch of scared rabbits. There was no way the mayor could catch us, because we all split up and went in different directions. He just couldn't chase all four of us. But sadly, the small-town syndrome got us. Living in such a small town, the mayor knew each one of us. He contacted our parents, and we were in deep trouble over this. We really got reamed out good, and getting caught really scared us. But at least we could now say we had been in every building in town.

Ray Schugart ran the pool hall across from the old bank building. We spent a lot of time there, especially in the summer. There just wasn't much else to do. As long as we behaved ourselves, no one was bothered by us being there, despite our age. As you entered the pool hall, there was the traditional bar down the left side, behind which were the typical coolers for the bottles of beer and pop. They also had a freezer where they kept five-gallon cartons of ice cream, sold by the cone. My favorite was the chocolate swirl; I'd almost kill for one of those, and they only cost a dime. Maybe that's why they let us kids come in.

Across from the bar, they had tables where the farmers and patrons would play pitch or dominos. Toward the back of the bar there was a pool table, and at one time along the wall across from the bar they had a shuffleboard. I remember that quite well, because they had shuffleboard tournaments from time to time. My oldest sister Rita got to be very good at shuffleboard, mainly because she worked there as a waitress for a while.

If you had to go to the toilet, you had to go to the rear of the tavern, through a door leading into the storage room, where they stored the empty and full cases of pop and beer. From there you walked out the back door of the storage room to the outside, and finally about 20 steps to the outhouse. Boy, did it stink! The pool hall also had a small ice house next to it where they sold ice for those who still had the old ice boxes, which some people still had in those days. The owner of the pool hall had punch boards which were illegal, but kept them hidden under the bar. You spent a dollar or two to punch out a tightly wrapped paper. You smoothed out the paper, and it told you if you won anything and how much.

We played a lot of pool when the table was clear and the owner let us, and we also did a few other things as well. You must remember that we were only in the fourth, fifth and sixth grades during these times, in the years 1945 to 1949. We were regularly exposed to drinking and drunks, watched the gambling, the card-playing for money, pool being played, and other things as well.

In those days you didn't have *Playboy* magazines. But other such items were available. Some of the favorites were the decks of playing cards, each card with a picture of nude couples in various forms of sexual intercourse. And there were times that we were able to get these decks of cards, and thoroughly looked them over right there in the pool hall.

Since the owner let us spend a lot of time at the pool hall, we developed a sense of when various people had too much to drink, those to stay away from, those who were friendly, and those who might buy us a pop or an ice cream cone. One day Maury Nemblewell, who lived about a block from the pool hall, had been drinking pretty heavily and was obviously drunk. I noticed that when he bought his last beer, he stuck his change into his left front pocket, leaving a dollar bill partially sticking out. Well, what an opportunity! I managed to saunter up and stood as close as I could next to him. I waited until I thought everyone was otherwise occupied, then slipped the dollar bill from his pocket and put it into mine. He didn't notice it. A few moments later when all was quiet,

I silently left via the front door.

I waited until I was about a block away, then I pulled out the dollar bill. But it wasn't a dollar. *It was a ten-dollar bill!* This was more money than I'd ever seen in my life! That's when I really got scared. I just knew that Mr. Nemblewell would figure out what happened and come after me. That made the $10 hotter than hell, and I knew I had to get rid of it. I furiously racked my brain for a place to hide it, finally settling on a place I thought was safe — the old bank building. It was brick, and in some places the old concrete between the bricks was loose. I worked a piece of this concrete out and slipped the $10 in, then replaced the concrete. Now I was safe. If they accused me, I would let them search me and, of course, they wouldn't find it.

I left the $10 there for a day or two until I felt it was safe. Then I told my buddies about it. They couldn't believe it. So I took them down and showed them the $10. Then we went on a spending spree. I bought all of us pop and candy, even some for my little brothers and sisters. We were in treat heaven. But somehow word got to Mom. I was summoned home, and Mom grilled me on where all this money had come from. In desperation, I told her that I had found $5 and wanted to spend it on all of the kids. I don't think I ever completely convinced her, but since I wouldn't admit to stealing it, she just had to live with my story.

We got to be very brazen in some of the things we did. Spending so much time in the pool hall, we knew all about the storage room where they stored the beer. One day we decided to steal some beer. So we got our wagon and went down one side of the street pulling the wagon, trying to look like we were looking for pop bottles in the ditches. As we passed in front of the pool hall, we tried to look as inconspicuous as possible. Then we went down the street, along the side of the pool hall where there were no windows. When we got to the back of the pool hall, we snuck into the storage room and got four quart bottles of Storz beer. We laid them in the wagon, placing a gunny sack over the top of them, then boldly pulled our wagon back around to the front of the pool hall, walked right by the front doors, and got away. We took the beer to our club and had a great time drinking the beer.

Tony and I did another thing that is another example of our ornery youth. Occasionally we stayed a little late at the pool hall, so that it was dark when we left. To get home from the pool hall, we had to go two blocks dead west, then a half a block south. There were sidewalks the entire distance. We decided to see if we could pee all the way home. One of us would pull our pecker out, then start peeing, while walking as fast as we could. The first one of us would pee a line on the sidewalk until he went dry. Then the other would take over and continue the line down the sidewalk. Eventually we got to where we could pee all the way home.

Mom and Dad had charge accounts at both the grocery stores. And since Mom didn't have a car and usually had one or two babies all the time, she frequently sent one of us kids to either Nuss' or Chief Mayer's store to get groceries. Well, we felt they should compensate us for making the trip (a whole two blocks and back!). So we sometimes added a pound of sugar wafers to the order and stuffed ourselves with them on the way home. Then we ate a full supper, too. At times food was scarce at our house, so if we had the chance to eat, we didn't miss it.

As I am writing this, I realize that so far all I have been telling you about were some of the mischievous things we did. So that you don't draw an inaccurate opinion that I grew up to be a completely unconscionable kid, I should tell you that we also did some "good" things. Our mother was a very religious Catholic woman. And she was very domineering. We lived half a block from the church, and we went to church as a family every Sunday. She also insisted that we walk right down the aisle and sit in the front pews. I think she was proud of her family, and this may have been her way of showing us off to the rest of the community. After all, kids were all she had.

Tony and I were servers for Fr. Meyers at his masses. Good old Fr. Meyers — if we didn't do something right or got into trouble, he would grip our ear and then jerk it down hard to punish us. And that really hurt. During school there were a lot of servers, because all the farmers brought their kids to school. But the summer was another thing. There weren't too many kids living in town to serve Father's masses. Those of us who did live in town usually took turns serving a week at a time. That's not so bad except father said his mass at *6:00 a.m.!* Can you imagine kids our age getting up during the summer in time to go over to the church and get into our server's outfit and be ready at that ungodly hour? And I recall one summer when kids either got sick or were out of town, and I had to serve 6:00 a.m. mass *six straight weeks!* So we had our good sides, too.

But even at church we still managed our share of mischief. One of the chores of the server was to put away everything after mass. This included removing the cruets or little bottles of water and wine that were left. There were doors on each side of the altar. The one on the left went into the sacristy where they stored all the supplies, and the one on the right went into another room. These two rooms were joined behind the altar by a narrow hallway. So we watched to see if Father drank all of the wine from the cruets, and he usually didn't. When he left some wine, then when we removed the cruets, we left the altar via the *right* side. As we were walking down the narrow hall behind the altar, we drank whatever wine was left. Eventually Father caught onto this, and it was ear-pulling time again.

We disliked Fr. Meyers so much that one day Tony and I got some galvanized tar paper nails that had rather large heads on them, and took them over to the gravel driveway of Father Meyers. He had a long driveway that was difficult to see from his house or the church. We set a bunch of these nails up with the points sticking up, and spread some of the sand and gravel over the heads, concealing them. Thus, later when Father drove out of the driveway, he got two flat tires. He was really upset, but never found out who did it.

Olmitz is in the middle of the wheat belt. So, like every other small Kansas town, Olmitz had a grain elevator. A grain elevator is a building for the receiving and storing of wheat brought to town by the farmers during harvest time. It also could load the wheat into rail cars for shipment. As Tony and I got older, Jake Ochs hired us to help around the elevator during the harvest season. Each loaded wheat truck drove on the long scale in front of the elevator office and was weighed.

Mr. Ochs then went out to the truck with a special can and got a sample of the wheat on the truck. He then weighed this sample inside to determine its specific gravity. Some wheat was more moist that other, and thus the weight was considered in determining the number of bushels on the truck. The truck then drove into the elevator until its front wheels were on a lift. The driver then got out of his truck and opened the tailgate so the wheat would start falling out of the truck. The lift, operated by air pressure, would lift the front end of the truck up so that the wheat would run out the back end of the truck.

Our job was to make sure all the wheat was out of the truck, and then to make sure all of the wheat was shoveled and swept through the bars in the floor into the bin below. An auger system then moved the wheat into the large tall storage silo that was part of the elevator. Mr. Ochs had to keep close watch over how much wheat he had, because if he had too much, then he had to ship it out on rail cars. After we unloaded each truck, then we replaced the tailgate, and the driver drove the empty truck back on the scales where they again weighed it. They subtracted this weight from the loaded weight, and thus they determined how much wheat had been on the truck. The farmers were issued receipts for their wheat, but they generally consigned the wheat to the elevator. They waited until they either needed money or until the price of wheat was favorable, then they sold it.

Mr. Ochs also used Tony and me in the office/store part of the elevator to help wait on customers. Generally, these farmers were in a terrific hurry to get unloaded and back out to the fields. They had to get their wheat cut while the weather was good, so they didn't waste any time. They might quickly buy a couple of items in the store area, then hit the road. At the end of the day, Tony and I would clean up the store and around the elevator. However, we always felt that Mr. Ochs didn't pay us enough. We thought he was cheap. And we figured out a way to "make things right." At the back of the store part of the elevator was a high window about five feet off the floor. It had a latch at the bottom, and when you unlatched it, it would swing in and up. So to "make things right," we occasionally left that window unlatched. Later, when it was dark we sneaked into the store, opened the register and took enough change so that we felt we were properly "compensated." We never considered for a minute that this was breaking and entering, burglary, etc. But we never got caught.

A scary thing happened one summer when my brother, Tony, was working at the elevator. There was a deep storage bin below the elevator that Mr. Ochs couldn't use because water had seeped into it. The water was about six to eight inches deep. One day Mr. Ochs decided to try and get all the water out of that bin. He set it up so that Tony climbed down the ladder into the bin and used a wheat scoop shovel to pick up water and pour it into a bucket. Another worker waited at the opening at the top of the bin, and when the bucket was full, he hoisted it up and took it away to dump it.

What no one knew, though, was that there was an old underground gas tank that developed a small leak. This gas eventually found its way into the bin where Tony was working. No one knows for sure what happened, whether Tony simply didn't smell the gas, or just didn't pay didn't pay attention to the odor. After Tony's partner had returned from emptying the bucket, he yelled down to Tony, but got no response. He shined the flashlight down and saw that Tony had passed out. He screamed for Mr. Ochs and started down the ladder to help Tony. He was completely unconscious. In desperation, they tied a rope around him and then pulled him up. Fortunately, once they got him to the top they were able to revive him. Tony was very sick, and Mr. Ochs was white as a sheet. He had almost killed him. The thought of how close I came to losing one of my brothers was very scary. On one hand, I was really happy that he survived, but on the other, I was mad as hell at Mr. Ochs. After all, he was a grown-up, and he should have known about the gas. To this day, I still believe he suspected there was gas down there, but just took a chance anyhow.

One summer when I was in the fourth grade, one of the farmers asked my Mom if one of us kids could work for him during harvest, leveling the wheat in the combine's storage tank. As they combined the wheat, it was funneled into a storage tank on the combine until the tank was full. Then the wheat truck came alongside and the wheat was loaded from the combine into the truck. Unfortunately, sometimes the truck got delayed at the elevator, or was late for some reason. Well, with a kid in the combine's open tank, it could continue cutting if the kid would use his hands to level out the wheat into the four corners of the tank. This would allow the combine to continue cutting wheat, in case the truck was delayed. I agreed to do it, but the farmer said I had to spend the harvest nights at his farm. Well, I didn't see this as a problem, although I had never spent a night away from home. Everything went fine the first day until the work was done and we had supper. Then I was struck with a colossal case of homesickness. I spent my time outside the farm house just petting their dog on the verge of tears. The farmer noticed this, and after awhile he came out, knelt down, and in a fatherly tone asked me if I wanted to go home. I eagerly nodded my head; then he said: "Come on," and took me home. I was embarrassed, but was I ever glad to be home!

Tony and I did a lot of things with Dave and Max. We had our favorite swimming hole, a cow pond out on Schugart's farm. We went there a lot. In fact, that is where we learned to swim, although it was in a very unorthodox manner. At the side of the pond was this small watering tank that had in the past been used for watering the cows. We tested it to see if it would float, and surprisingly it didn't leak. So now we had a boat. One day, all four of us were in the boat, and we were at the deep end of the pond where the water was way over our heads. Dave and Max felt it was time for us to learn how to swim. So they just pitched both of us over the side and told us to either sink or swim. We weren't too far from shore, and we managed to beat the water long enough to make it to shore. We were scared, but at least we now knew we could save ourselves from drowning, and as time went by our swimming improved.

Occasionally Tony and I would go rabbit hunting with Dave and Max. One day, we were out in the country, and we chased this cottontail into a large hole in the side of a hill. In reality, it was a badger hole. Now, a badger is nothing to fool with. We knew it was one of the most ferocious animals around. But somehow we got too caught up in the drive to get this rabbit. Or at least Dave and Max did. We stood around the badger hole and studied it. This part of the country was also known for rattlesnakes. And we knew they were deadly. As we were standing around figuring out how to get that rabbit, I noticed Dave and Max looking at me in an odd sort of way. At this time I was a small, wiry kid. It suddenly dawned on me that they were trying to figure out if I could fit down into the hole. Oh, no! I wasn't having any part of this. But they talked and talked and promised to hold on to my ankles so they could pull me out if there was something down there. If there wasn't, then maybe we could get the rabbit.

Despite all my protests, they finally talked me into it, and I started down the hole, which was more like a very small cave in the side of a hill. I stuck my hands out in front of me so I could feel anything ahead. I wiggled further in, at any time expecting a rattlesnake to slash out at my hand, or a vicious badger to rip into me. I wiggled further until my entire body was now inside the hole, and Dave and Max could barely hold on to my ankles. Then suddenly I felt something furry. I froze. Then I felt a little further and felt some kind of animal's leg. I slowly wrapped my hand around the leg and tightened my grip. Nothing bit me! Then I yelled at Dave and Max to pull me out. As I finally saw daylight and could see what I had, I could tell it was the rabbit! God, was I relieved! Some things kids will do!

When I was in about the fourth grade, I developed a toothache, and the tooth definitely had to be pulled. The problem was, Dad had the only car and had to use it to go to Hoisington to work. And the nearest dentist was in Hoisington, 10 miles away. I could ride with Dad to Hoisington in the morning, but had no way of getting back. Mom and Dad decided they had no choice but to have me walk the 10 miles back by myself. Thanks a lot! So I rode with Dad the next morning, walked to the dentist's office and waited on the curb for him to open up. When he did, he placed me in the dental chair. I don't remember if he gave me any painkillers or even what the procedures were in those days. All I know is that it hurt, and then I had this long tortuous 10-mile hike in the hot sun, across fields and over barbed wire fences, to get home. But did I ever really have any choice? I trudged on through fields, feeling nauseous; then finally I saw the trees that told me I was near Olmitz. I plodded on and began to feel safer once I made the outskirts of Olmitz. I finally got home, my jaw killing me, and tired as hell. I dropped on the sofa, and Mom was really relieved that I had made it home safely. I know she really felt sorry for me and felt guilty that this was the way it had to be. But it was comforting, because this also told me she loved me. And besides, this was quite an ordeal and I had survived. In fact, I was more than a little bit proud.

Tony and I did a lot of things together. We were more than brothers; we were true friends. We were always together, and if someone messed with one of us, he had the other to contend with as well. We were inseparable. We hunted together, fished together, played a lot of sports together, did everything together. He was my closest brother. We frequently hiked to Walnut creek right near Bahr's farm to go fishing. That was a good five miles away, so when we went, it was an all-day affair. We used chicken livers or worms for bait. We'd catch catfish, carp, some blue gill, snapping turtles, and occasionally a soft-shelled turtle. These were really weird-looking animals, but in no way as dangerous as the snapping turtles. When we caught a snapping turtle and could get him on land, we pulled on the hook in his mouth, thus pulling his head out of his shell. Then we cut his head off, because they ate the fish we were trying to catch, or those on our stringers.

I recall one day (with some chagrin) when we decided to hike to Walnut Creek to fish. But we didn't have a stringer on which to keep the fish we hoped to catch. Anything would have worked. All we needed was a fishing line with a short stick on both ends. You stuck one stick in the mouth and out of the gill of the fish, so he couldn't get away. The other end was on a bigger stick that you then stuck into the ground, anchoring it. But this day we just didn't have any extra line. I noticed an old car seat out by the garage and found what appeared to be a strong string built into the seat. I pulled it out, and it looked okay, so off we went.

It was a hot day, and it seemed like it took forever to get there. At last, we made it and settled down, expecting to catch all kinds of big fish. But it just wasn't a good day for fishing. Tony and I fished all up and down the creek and never had one bite. It was well after noon, and we were about to chuck it to 'em. As I glumly watched my bobber, it appeared to be slowly moving against the ripples that the gentle breeze caused on the water. I studied the ripples to make sure they weren't fooling me; then I pulled on my cane pole, and I had a bite! At last! And it was a good one! I pulled the line in and landed one of the biggest channel catfish I had ever seen! I knew this would bring some wows from the kids back in town and from our older brothers. I very carefully made the stringer out of the car seat string and strung my prize catch on it. I lowered the fish into the water and made sure I anchored it well on the bank. Then I sat back, proud. This was the way we dreamed of it happening. Encouraged, we decided to continue fishing. We fished another hour or two and never got another bite. So we decided to head home. We rolled our lines up on our poles, got our bait together, and then I went to pull in my prize fish. But when I pulled on the stringer, there was no tugging on the other end. This was strange, because fish always put up a fight. I kept pulling until, to my complete horror, the line ended, and there was nothing on the end! My fish had escaped! God, what a blow! Then it dawned on me that the seat string must have been very old, and the longer it was in the water, the weaker it got, until it easily broke and the fish swam away. Believe me, walking back was twice as long as it took getting there.

But on to other things. German wedding dances were always a lot of fun. The beer flowed freely, the polkas were loud, and everyone let their hair out. It was fun for us kids, because many of our farmer classmates got to come to town also. And we didn't get to see too much of them during the summer months. So it was party time, and we had our own way of partying. I supplied the cigarettes. My dad bought *Lucky Strike* cigarettes by the carton and kept them in his top drawer. I sneaked a pack when I had the chance. So we had cigarettes. Don Crowell sneaked a pint of whisky or brandy from his dad's shed, and away we went. We smoked those cigarettes and sipped on the liquor until the dance was over. A problem developed, however, when my older brothers, Dave and Max, caught on to what we were doing, and started following us around. Finally, they confronted us in front of the old bank building. *They* wanted the booze and cigarettes and threatened to tell Mom and Dad. But we didn't flinch. They could get their own stuff. We wound up in a scuffle, and the bottle dropped on the sidewalk and shattered. What a shame! We really had to be careful after that.

Another form of entertainment was the occasional Saturday night movie. There was no theater in town, so the local merchants arranged for someone to come to Olmitz on Saturday night and set up a projector outside the K of C Hall. They put a big screen on the side of the building and ran the movie. We all had our home-made pop corn and Kool-Aid and sat on blankets. After each reel of film we had a brief intermission while they rewound that reel and put the next one on. It was crude, but better than nothing.

I've just about cleaned out my memories of Olmitz. But there are still a few things I should tell you about. As a kid, Christmas was not a very happy time for me. We never had much. We rarely got more than one gift, and generally it was something we needed like a new pair of overalls. And we could sense that Mom and Dad felt bad that they couldn't do more for us. We had rich relatives in Texas who were kind enough to send us a crate of various kinds of fruit — oranges, apples and grapefruits. A lot of the gifts were hand-made.

When I was in the sixth grade I had my first real date with a girl. It caught me completely by surprise. I was home one evening when a car full of kids pulled up outside our house, and they wanted to talk to me. Me, of all people. They were going to a movie in Hoisington, and one of the guys had to cancel out at the last minute. So rather than there being three girls and two boys, they decided to see if I could go. I went in and asked Mom. She scraped up enough money for the movie, and I got to go.

I felt a little strange, because I didn't have any time to prepare for this. So I did the best I could. We went to the movie, watched it and started driving back. I was sitting in the back seat along with my date and the second couple. On the way back, this other couple was kissing and smooching up a storm, but I tried not to notice it. Finally, my date whispered in my ear, "Look at what those two are doing." I looked and acknowledged it, and it dawned on me that this girl wanted to do the same with me. But I was just simply too bashful to do it. I had never smooched with a girl before. I was frozen into inactivity. There are some things in life that you wish you had as "overs," and this is one I wish I had over. But who knows, maybe that would have changed the course of my life a smidgeon. It's just something I'll always remember.

I should tell you about the house where we lived. It had a full unfinished second floor. Mom and Dad slept downstairs. The stairs came up in the center of this single huge room, the size of the entire second floor, where the beds were all double beds, two kids to a bed. The order of birth of us kids was Rita, Dave, Max, Teresa, myself, Tony, Rosalie, Judy, Mark, Gery, Mary and Diane. So in bed we paired up as follows: Rita and Teresa, Dave and Max, Tony and I, Mark and Gery, Rosalie and Judy, and Mary and Dianne. At any rate, I will never forget this one night. We talked after we went to bed, and the later it got, the more static we got from Mom to shut up and go to sleep. And every night all of us had to yell downstairs to Mom and Dad and say: "Good night, Mom and Dad, we love you." This night we must have been louder that usual, because after a few warnings from Mom that we didn't pay attention to, Dad came stomping up the stairs. We all knew we were in deep trouble now. Dad stopped on the landing, and that allowed all of us to see him from about the waist up. He stopped and the silence was deafening. Then he pointed his finger at us and in a very serious voice said: "I've just got one thing to say to you kids." He paused, and we all knew that his belt was going to come off, and it was spanking time. Instead, he let the loudest fart I've ever heard in my life! He busted out laughing, and then so did we. We roared. God, did we love him for that!

That's one thing I'll always love about Dad. He had a great sense of humor. I'll just tell you one of his favorite jokes, the one about the two boys sitting on a log, fishing. They were very quiet so as not to scare the fish. Finally, one boy leaned over to the other and whispered: "My rear end's asleep." The other leaned over to him and said: "I know, I heard it snoring." Dad had a lot of those jokes. And what made them so much fun was that he laughed at them himself each time he told them, no matter how often he had told them. I guess as hard a life as he had, he had to have a good sense of humor, just to survive.

The other thing about our house was, of course, there was no inside plumbing. The back porch was fully screened. Under it was a cistern, complete with a pump handle to pump water up when we needed it. This was convenient, as it partially protected us from the elements in cold weather. From time to time the cistern ran low. When that happened, Dad jacked up the rear of his car, took the tire off, wrapped a long belt around it, then wrapped the other end around a wheel on the water well out in our back yard. He then put the car in gear and the wheel turned, pumping water from the well into the cistern. When the cistern was full, he disassembled everything, and we had a full cistern.

Then there was our outhouse. I can remember one summer day when Tony and I had some cigarettes and chose to smoke them in the outhouse. We were careless, though, and flicked the ashes on the concrete floor. When we left, we left the door open so the smoke would dissipate. But my sister Teresa had to use the toilet not much later and saw the ashes on the floor. She went right in and told Mom. Mom called us in and we 'fessed up to the smoking. Now, our mom was a real disciplinarian. When we did something that was really bad, she laid us down on the bed with our pants and shorts pulled down. We then got a bare-ass spanking. And sometimes, rather than using a leather belt she used a rubber hose. If she did that today, I am sure Social Services would have taken us away from her. We got a hell of a spanking that day.

We had a healthy fear of Mom. In fact, I can remember one day when Rita, who was in high school, got into an argument with Mom. They were going at it first in the kitchen, then in Mom and Dad's bedroom. Eventually, Rita must have said something that really set

Mom off. Mom had a coffee mug in her hand and flat-out hit Rita right on the top of her head. Rita went down and was actually knocked unconscious for a couple of minutes.

I'm telling you this, because the very next day Tony and I went out into the outhouse and smoked cigarettes again. This time Rita came out later, saw the ashes and marched right in and told Mom. Mom got us right back in the house and demanded to know if we were smoking again. This time we knew our lives were on the line. We talked for all we were worth. We told Mom that those were the ashes from the day before. And we must have created just enough doubt, because she decided not to do anything, although grudgingly. Man, did we ever sigh with relief!

I'm really embarrassed to tell you about this next event, but I promised to be completely honest. One night, late, right before bedtime I had to have a bowel movement. But I was scared of the dark and wanted someone to come out to the outhouse with me. No one would do it, not matter how much I pleaded. I was getting desperate. Finally, when it was obvious that no one would come with me, and with my fear of the dark being so great, I snuck into the pantry and took a small pan out to the screened-in back porch and did my duty in the pan. Only I forgot to get rid of it.

The next day Mom wanted to know who pooped in one of her pans. Well, the other kids remembered me asking them to go with me out to the outhouse, so they told Mom it had to be me. She confronted me and I denied it. And no matter how much pressure the rest of the family put on me to get me to admit it, I wouldn't budge. So the day wore on and Dad came home from work. We sat down to eat, and the subject of the pan came up again. Everyone said that Don had to be the one who did it. Dad turned to me, and in a quiet voice asked me if I did it. Without blinking an eye, I admitted it. Dad was one person that I simply could not lie to. And you know what? All he said to me was not to do it again. Then he lectured the other kids about not going out to the outhouse with me. I really loved my dad, as he was as fair a man as there was in my eyes, and I knew deep down that he cared a lot for us.

One of the big daily events for us kids was to hike down the county road to meet Dad coming home from work. Sometimes three, four or five of us would walk south on the county road as much as a mile to wait for him. I wonder how it made him feel to see us so far from home, just waiting for him. We were pretty young at the time, but I can't help feeling now that this had to be a sight that made him feel proud and made his load a lot lighter. Once, he tried to act like he hadn't seen us until he got just past us. Then he slammed on the brakes so hard that he broke one of the springs in his car and had to get it fixed. We really loved our dad. The only problem was that we never had the opportunity to get enough of just plain Dad. There were 12 of us kids, and he just couldn't spend much time with each of us, one on one.

Mom's mother visited us for a lengthy stay and taught us kids how to play canasta. It was a fun game, and we learned it easily. Grandma had pure white hair, was up in years, and was a bit obese. She was the typical grandmother. What I remember most about her was that, while we were playing cards, she would occasionally lean over to one side and say, "Oh, dear." A few seconds later the air was pungent with the terrible odor of the air she had passed. Boy, they were bad!

There were four kids in our class at school. The others were Don Crowell, Marietta Ohnmacht and Mary Riedel. The school was taught by Catholic nuns, one of whom was Sister Alphonsa. Boy, was she a tough one! As we sat in our seats, we faced the teacher. Behind the teacher was the cloak room, which was a long hall the width of the room with hangers, so we could hang our coats up in the winter. Once, when Sister Alphonsa had her back to me, I took the corner of a folded sheet of paper and reached up and scratched the top of her head. I was trying to show off to the rest of the kids that I was really brave. The problem was that I didn't know what was under the back veil on the top of her head. I soon found out that it was her head, because she turned around with a look of total disbelief that anyone would be so stupid as to do such a thing. Well, it was knuckle-rapping time again, and did I ever have sore knuckles when she finished with me.

One lunch recess someone had a plug of chewing tobacco. We tried to act big by biting a piece off and acting like the big kids. Only I made the mistake of swallowing mine. I started feeling queasy, but passed it off. Recess ended, and we all headed into our classrooms. Just as we were in the cloak room hanging up our coats, I couldn't contain it any further. I puked my guts out. And it came so suddenly that it shot out of my mouth and all over this kid in front of me. It was on the wall, on the floor, everywhere. Since I lived across the street, Sister just sent me home. But, boy, did I ever feel sorry for that other kid!

I did another thing back then that was so bad it still scares me to this day. Don Crowell sat in the desk in from of me. I used to take my ruler and flick the hair at the back of his head, just to bother him. He'd jerk his head back to try to get me to stop. Now, each desk had a slot across the front top of the desk, where you could set your pencil and it wouldn't roll off the desk. So one day I had this bright idea. I took my compass with the sharp metal point aimed toward the back of Don's head. I propped the other end in the pencil slot and held it there so it wouldn't move. Then I took the ruler in my other hand and started tickling the back of Don's hair. Sure enough, he jerked his head back to make me stop. But this time his head jerked into the compass's metal point. He was both hurt and furious, I don't know which was greater. The Sister wasn't watching, so she never found out. I shudder to think what would have happened if that point had pierced his scull and entered his brain. I still get the shivers over that to this day.

In 1949, the summer after my sixth grade, our family moved to a farm about five miles west southwest of Hoisington, called Schneider's farm. The older kids were now in high school in Hoisington, and Dave had his own car, so he was our ride to and from school. I remember Dave driving and playing his harmonica, while all of us kids were jammed into the seats. On the way back he would stop a mile from home, and Tony and I got out and ran the last mile to improve our running and athletic ability.

The farmhouse was a typical wood frame house, with a central coal and wood stove on the first floor and no heat for the bedrooms upstairs. Winters were very cold, with temperatures well below zero. Tony and I had an upstairs bedroom. The window had been knocked out, and Dad either didn't have the time or money to fix it, so we went through the whole winter with that window out. Before going to bed, we placed bricks on top of the stove to get them hot. We then wrapped them in newspapers just before we went to bed. We then placed the bricks at the bottom of the bed, so we could put our feet against them and keep them warm. Another way we kept warm was that we literally had to snuggle up to each other so our bodies could keep each other warm as well. The only blanket Tony and I had was a horsehide blanket. It was actually the hide of a horse with a liner sewed inside it. It was barely big enough to cover the two of us, as long as we had our knees drawn up, and snuggled next to each other. It was cold, but we lived through it.

I don't remember much about the seventh grade, just that it was back in the same school where I had spent kindergarten. It was the Catholic school, taught by nuns, and I guess it took me about a year to get reacquainted with the other kids. Here I was, an outsider again.

Tony and I did all we could to improvise sports. We didn't have a basketball, so we knocked the bottom out of a basket and nailed it to the side of the barn. Then we used the football to play basketball. We got to the point where we could dribble somewhat with it, and then shoot. The biggest battles were over the rebounds, and they sometimes led to fights. Although we were close, we were also very competitive, which led to some knock-down, drag-out fights.

In one of them Tony got so mad that he picked up a huge metal bolt and came at me with every intention of smacking me in the head with it. In self-defense, I picked up a rock-hard dirt clod, and before he could get me with the bolt. I hit him as hard as I could in the nose with the clod. It's a wonder I didn't break it. All it did was give him a severe bloody nose, and that stopped the fight. We had to go into the house to get his nose taken care of, and Mom found out. Boy, was she mad, but when she saw the size of the metal bolt, she realized I didn't have any choice. So she didn't punish either of us; she just lectured us about fighting. Tony was bigger and stronger than I, even though he was younger. But I, on the other hand was wiry and cat quick. I could always beat Tony in a fight, because I was so much quicker.

This was when I became a true blue Brooklyn Dodger fan. Many a night I stayed up late, listening to them on the radio in the kitchen after everyone else went to bed. They were in Brooklyn then, and I hated the Yankees. I recall one night when it looked like my Dodgers were going to lose by one run. It was the bottom of the ninth with two outs. But the next batter got a hit, then so did the next batter. Then, when the next batter got a single tying the game, I was thrilled to death. And, sure enough, my Dodgers won the game in the bottom of the tenth. That's when I guess I started learning that you just never give up. You just keep trying, no matter what.

There were 12 of us kids by that time, most of us in either grade or high school. I attended St. John's school which was one block east of St. John's church, where the family attended mass. I sang in the choir with the girls, even though I was the only boy, because I had a decent voice, enjoyed singing, and Mom also wanted me to sing. Sunday masses were a ritual. Mom made sure we were all dressed as best we could, with enough time for us to walk as a family to church. Only it wasn't a walk. It was a forced march. We went in formation, with the two youngest in front, then the two next oldest, and finally, Mom and Dad. So there were seven sets of two, and we marched two blocks to the church, in the front door, down the middle aisle, and sat right up in the front pews. After a while the other parishioners more or less accepted the fact that the front pews were reserved for us, because they were always vacant. That's where I heard the best sermon in my life from Fr. Leahy, an Irish priest. It was midsummer, temperatures above 100, no air conditioning, and everyone was sweltering from the heat. When it came time for the sermon, Father Leahy ascended the pulpit and said: "It's very hot today. There is another place that is a lot hotter than this. Don't go there." Then he descended the pulpit and continued with the mass. What a sermon!

The eighth grade was more enjoyable than the seventh. I was now in the top class, and the smartest boy in the class, if not the smartest kid overall. I found out the year before that the student with the best graduation marks got a $25 savings bond. So all year long I set my sights on winning it, and I did. That year was a lot of fun for me. I had some new friends, Tony and Ken Drees. Tony Drees must have been all of 180 lbs., and the rest of us were well under 100. When we played football at recess, instead of having to tackle him, which no one could possibly do, the ball was down at the point where we just crashed into him. We'd just bounce off him and the play was called dead.

It was about this time that I started noticing girls. There was a girl in our class named Barbara Gilstrap. She was a rather pretty brunette, who lived a few blocks from the school. But what really stood out was her chest. She was really built, and I know she wished she didn't have so much because it drew a lot of attention, and she just wanted to be an average girl. And she had a really nice personality. I'm sure I'm not the only one who noticed her.

I'll end this chapter with probably the single most important time in my life at that time, when my dad went well beyond the call of duty just for me. I don't know why, but I really had my heart set on graduating from the eighth grade dressed in a suit. It was the only time that I let my parents know that something was extremely important to me. However, no one in the family had the money, about $40. Still, I think Dad sensed that he never really had any choice. He knew he had to get it done. And I will never forget my dad going downtown to one of his friends and borrowing the $40, just so I could have the charcoal black suit I wanted. I was very proud the day I graduated, not only to be graduating, but knowing how much Dad cared for me.

3

HIGH SCHOOL IN THE SEMINARY

(What Am I Doing Here?)

I MENTIONED BEFORE that my mother was a very staunch religious person. Now, I don't know what precipitated this, but in 1947, the summer after Dave graduated from the eighth grade, for a period of one or two weeks, he wanted to be a priest. Then he changed his mind. But ... it was too late, the damage had been done. Mom became obsessed with the idea of having a son who was a priest. From that summer on, when discussion arose about what her sons were going to do, Mom launched into a passionate dissertation about how special being a priest was, etc., etc., etc. That is all we heard.

That may well be what helped Max decide to become a priest. Max was 14 when he graduated from the eighth grade, and in early adolescence. After summer he left home to attend the seminary in Epworth, Iowa. From then on, for the next two years, all I ever heard from Mom was how proud she was that she had a son who was going to be a priest! Consequently, when the eighth grade ended for me in 1951, I felt really I had no choice. Off to the seminary I went. And the following year, Tony went. Then Mark went. And, finally, Gary, *MOM'S BABY BOY,* followed. We sons were never really given a choice. Mom never told us that we could decide whatever we wanted for a career. I never felt I had an option. Perhaps this experience has influenced me so much, that when I had my own sons later, I tried my best to make sure that what they wanted to do, was *their* choice. I was available for consultation, but I vowed I would never tell them what they should choose.

Perhaps it was poetic justice, but in the end Mom never got her wish. Max lasted in the seminary for 10 years, I went six, Tony went five, Mark went two, and, finally, Gary went one year or so. But who knows what would have happened to each of us, had we not gone to the seminary? As it turned out, I received a great education, including six years of Latin, five years of German, four years of Greek, and tons of English and speech. Besides that, you really can't get into too much trouble in the seminary.

But on with life in the seminary. At the end of summer in 1951, Max and I climbed on the train in Great Bend, Kansas, to make the trip to Holy Ghost Seminary in East Troy, Wisconsin. It was my very first train ride, and I really enjoyed the experience and the scenery. We were met at the train by one of the Brothers who were actually religious, in the sense that they took the three vows of poverty, chastity, and obedience. They dedicated their lives to performing religious manual labor. At the time Max was a senior and I, of course, a freshman. But I was accorded a little extra status, since I had an older brother in the seminary.

There are just a couple of items in my freshman year that stand out in my mind. One was athletics. With no girls to distract us, we spent plenty of energy in sports. We had a new basketball gymnasium, and for the first time in my life I could play some serious basketball in a real gym. It became the year-round sport. We played football in the fall, but our school wasn't part of any league, so we formed teams among ourselves. We had the traditional freshman versus sophomore game on Thanksgiving and got out butts kicked. It seems we had a rather weak class of athletes (myself excluded, if I may humbly say).

Another athletic event that stands out had to do with the traditional freshman versus sophomore softball game. It occurred within the first few months after the start of school. By now, it was obvious that I was a fairly decent player, so I wound up in the short stop position. In those days that was the position where you placed your quickest and most agile athlete. We had also developed a fairly good idea of who the better athletes were among the sophomores. They had one kid who was a terrific athlete. He was as fast as greased lightning, could hit, run — he had it all. I was at short stop when he came up to bat. I could sense that he was going to try to drive the ball just to the right of second base into center field. I'm not saying he was trying to avoid me, or anything like that. But I could tell from his stance that he was going to try to hit it there, away from me.

This was slow pitch softball, so there was a lot of time between when the ball left the pitcher's hand until it got to the batter. As soon as the ball was out of the pitcher's hand, I started shifting from my short stop position over toward the right field side of second base. The batter, of course, was focused on the ball and was intent on driving it to the right of second base. And he did just that. However, I was already on the move to that spot. He hit a line shot ground ball that took off like a bullet. I was already in motion and dove to my left with my glove extended as far out as I could get it. I was literally in mid-air, parallel to the ground, when the ball got there. I had my mitt in the right spot, caught the ball and fell to the ground. I'll never forget the look on that batter's face as he was running to first base, and could he run fast! He just couldn't believe I had made the play. I got to my knees to make the throw to first base, and I knew it would still be a close play. Unfortunately, because I was off balance, my throw was wild, and the runner was safe. We lost the game, but that one play stood out, and it gave a us freshmen a grain of respect. The whole sophomore team was lavish with their praise for that play. That was really the first spark of the athletic ability that I would later learn I had.

Athletics took up the lion's share of our free time. We had a number of handball courts and became quite adept at playing that game. In the interest of avoiding a lengthy and probably boring explanation of the game, I won't go into it. You had to wear a leather glove because you slapped the hard rubber ball so hard you needed the protection. And it really improved your game if you were ambidextrous. I remember playing handball for many long hours.

We played all the other traditional sports: basketball, football, baseball, volleyball, and in the winter, ice hockey. Our school was on the edge of Lake Beulah, a beautiful, mile-wide, crystal clear lake. This gave us the ability to swim, fish, boat and do all the water sporting activities. It was really beautiful, especially in late spring and in the fall. When the lake was warm, we spent a great deal of time with water sports, especially swimming. One of everyone's goals was to swim completely across the lake. Many of us were eventually able to do it. We always had someone accompany us in a rowboat in case someone got tired or ran into trouble. Frequently, we swam both across and back. We had a saying that if anyone drowned, they were expelled from school.

The other event I recall, and this, with a great deal of embarrassment, happened in late November. This being the seminary, there was a very strong emphasis on religion, especially Saturday nights. Sounds antisocial, doesn't it? Well, every Saturday night we had what they called "Silence." We were free to read or study, or do things of this nature. But there could be no sports activity, no basketball, and there could be *no talking*. There had to be silence.

One Saturday night, I was in the empty study hall with another kid who for some reason was wearing a cap. Being young and immature, I decided to have a little fun with this kid. At just the right time I grabbed his hat and took off running down the aisles between the desks. He was hot on my tail. I rounded the corner at the end of a row of desks, heading for the door into the hall, when suddenly it opened. I slammed on the brakes and found myself looking up to a very stern-faced Father Dudink. Father Dudink was our Prefect. The Prefect was basically the equivalent of a Principal. He was the "main man." He was the disciplinarian, and everyone dreaded being called to his office. It usually meant we were in trouble. He nailed me on the spot.

But he didn't dole out any penance right then. He made me wait overnight to find out what my penance would be. The next day I was called into his office with my knees trembling. He decided that for my penance I had to memorize a religious poem of about 15 stanzas. The poem was about the baby Jesus. He gave me a week to get it memorized. I had to memorize it in addition to keeping up with all my other studies. At the end of the week I appeared at his office to recite the poem from memory. Trembling, I started through the poem and managed haltingly to get through it. I breathed a huge sigh of relief when it was done, but Father Dudink had this pensive look on his face. He looked at me kind of oddly, then looked out the window, thinking. By now I was starting to get really worried. I had performed my allotted punishment. What else could he want?

Finally he turned to me and said that the school put on an annual Christmas pageant for the parents who lived close enough to attend, and for the people living around the seminary. They held it the last Saturday night before all the students went home for Christmas. He said he wanted to include my recitation of this poem in the pageant. Oh, no! I thought I was done. But did I have any choice? How could I turn down the *Prefect?* There was no way out, and I agreed to do it. He told me, however, that I had a lot of polishing up to do. So, over the next few weeks he and I had a number of one-on-one sessions in his office working on the poem. He taught me about voice inflections, when to raise my voice as if in a question, when to lower it at the end of the sentence, when to be loud, and when to be soft. We worked hard on it and finally got it to where he was comfortable putting it into the pageant.

The night of the pageant came, and everyone was nervous, as was to be expected. I was in the choir, dressed in my white surplice over a black cassock. The choir had also practiced long and hard, so we could sing beautiful Christmas music. They held the pageant in the gymnasium. Folding chairs were set up for the audience. We didn't use the stage for the pageant, but set up the big crib off to the right side, with the choir set up over on the left side. The guests started arriving, and we were filled almost to capacity.

The pageant began. I don't recall everything that was in the pageant, but do vividly recall the part where I was to recite my poem. The choir finished a beautiful piece of Christmas music; then all the lights in the gymnasium were dimmed except for a gentle spot light on the crib. I quietly left the choir, walked over to the crib and knelt down in front of it. It was very quiet. The audience was straining to witness what was going to happen next. I looked at the statue of the baby Jesus in the crib, waited until it was very quiet, then started my poem. The first stanza went off beautifully. The audience was in utter rapture. Then my mind went completely blank. I could not remember a single word of the rest of the poem. I knelt there, stunned, right out there in front of everyone! God, how embarrassing! Fortunately, Father Dudink picked up pretty quickly on what had happened to me, and as quickly as he could, he got the choir singing the next song. I got up and slowly and sheepishly returned to the choir. I tried to hide myself as far back as I could. I thought Father was going to kill me. But he must have known how embarrassed I felt, because all he said was that it happens to everyone, and don't worry about it. But I did, and I will never forget that.

The rest of my freshman year had no other significant memories that I can recall. Max and I took the train back to Great Bend for Christmas, and then back after Christmas. The winter was a lot heavier there than down in Kansas, so we had to spend more time inside. That meant spending more time playing basketball. Little did we know that this was the foundation that years later ultimately led to the greatest basketball upset of all time.

I touched on the excellent education I received in the seminary. We generally had a full schedule of, I think, seven classes a day, the same for all students. There were no electives, no choices; it was all laid out for us. We had one study hour, then were released on our own until the supper meal at 6:00 in the dining room. Father Dudink or his assistant always ate at the small raised head table at the front of the dining room. The meals were cooked by a few SVD nuns, and they were hearty. Each table had a jar of home-made jelly, and we frequently added a jelly sandwich to our regular meal. The meals would always begin and end with a prayer led by the dining room "senior" who was usually an upperclassman.

Our society was called the SVDs, or Societas Verbi Divini. That translates to the Society of the Divine Word. It was a religious (we were eventually going to take the three vows of poverty, chastity and obedience), missionary (many of us would be sent all over the world to the missions) society. In addition to those of us who studied to become priests, the society also had an order of nuns, who in addition to going to the missions, provided support such as cooking at the seminaries. We also had an order of brothers, who had a vocation to perform manual labor, also in the missions, and around the seminary and the farm we owned right next to our seminary. They were the real workers. At the farm they raised many items we ate at our meals, such as apples, pears, etc. As a result, we had a lot of apple sauce, apple cider, jellies and other farm staples.

The first Sunday of each month was visitors' Sunday. On that day relatives were allowed to come after the noon meal and visit the students. We drew a lot of seminarians from the Chicago and Milwaukee area, and so there were some classmates who regularly had visitors. Usually, they brought with them a parcel of goodies that the students could keep in their lockers and eat later. It was a disappointment that no one from our family ever visited us on visitors' Sunday. Mom and Dad lived so far away and were so poor, with so many kids, that they just didn't have the money or time to make the trip. And in those days it would have been a long trip. Those were lonely days for me.

My freshman year passed, and Max and I caught the train home. I was now 15. By this time my parents had moved out to Joe Finger's farm about five miles west northwest of Hoisington, a short distance from Blood Creek. Mr. Finger just charged us $10 a month rent, really out of charity. He just wanted us to keep the grass cut and prevent the property from deteriorating. Rita was now about 21, in college, and Dave was in the Navy in Okinawa, I think. Teresa had just graduated from high school and was not getting along well with Mom. Rita was the apple of Mom's eye. I can still remember Mom yelling at Teresa and asking her why she wasn't as good and smart a daughter as her older sister, Rita. Mom was really brutal doing that, and this awareness never really sunk into me until years later. I really have a lot of empathy for Teresa, because she may never really have deserved this. I'm not saying Teresa was perfect. She just didn't need to have Rita thrown in her face all the time. I think this is what influenced the way I tried to raise my kids later. I decided that I would never compare one of my sons to another. I vowed never to tell one of my sons to be like another son. I felt that all that did was promote friction, maybe even hate, between brothers.

By now I was older and could help the farmers with their field chores. I remember driving a 1929 McCormick-Deering tractor plowing the fields. To me, it was as big as a house and could pull a barn if we wanted it to. Tony and I also helped at baling hay. It was while doing this that I had my first serious encounter with a rattlesnake. We had a system where one man mowed the hay one day, then we followed the next day with the baler that scooped up the hay, pounded it into compact rectangular blocks and tied two strings of cord around it to keep it together. The baler then pushed the finished bale out of the end of the baler to the ground. We followed the baler with the flat wagon or truck, grabbed the two cords, lifted the bales to our chest, then shoved them above our heads onto the trailer or truck.

We were in the process of loading the bales in the field one day when we all heard it at the same time ... and froze. If you've never heard a rattlesnake, then you need to know that it is not properly named. It doesn't rattle. It shakes its rattles so fast that the sound it makes is really a buzz. We froze, because a rattlesnake's buzz is its way of warning you to stay away from it. We couldn't flinch until we found out where the snake was. Then one of the adults spotted it. It was far enough away so that he could go to the truck and get a long metal bar. He had to kill the snake for all our safety. He chased the snake down into a wide, dry crack in the ground. This posed a dangerous problem. No one knew how far along the crack the snake crawled. Finally we spotted him and the farmer managed to kill him.

But that is just the prelude to the really scary experience. Sometimes the baler snatched up a rattlesnake and trapped it inside a bale of hay. This presented the added problem of watching out for rattlesnake heads sticking out of the bales. They couldn't rattle, but they might still be able to bite.

The next day we were back in the field again. We were a little more nervous now, because we knew that rattlesnakes traveled in pairs. So where was the second one? Maybe it was this awareness that saved my life. To pick up a bale, I planted my left foot right next to the bale, then bent over, grasped the cords with my hands, and hoisted up the bale. You had to plant your foot to get the leverage you needed. I approached the next bale I wanted to lift, and was just about to plant my foot next to it, when I noticed a slight movement right in front of the bale. I backed off, and to my horror, there was a rattlesnake coiled to strike! But why hadn't he rattled? I called over to the farmer, and he ran over, clearing us all away. He then got the metal bar out and killed the snake. It was only after he killed him that we found out that the snake's rattles had been cut off by the mower the previous day. That's why the rattlesnake couldn't rattle his warning! And if I hadn't caught the slight glimpse of movement, I would have stepped right on that deadly snake! That was very scary!

We did other things to occupy ourselves in the summer months between school years. We had a 17 shot .22 caliber rifle. It was the first rifle on which Tony and I learned to shoot. I remember once when I was hunting out in the pasture behind our house. Kansas is known for its huge jack rabbits that are quite a bit larger than the ordinary cottontail rabbit. The jack rabbit is an easily spooked rabbit, and when spooked, it simply puts on its afterburners and never quits running. It blazed away with terrific speed for a half a mile or so, until it felt safe. The cottontail, on the other hand, used deception as a defense. It ran a short distance and suddenly stopped next to a fence post or something similar, hoping its pursuer failed to detect it.

We hunted cottontail for food, since they were very tasty. The jack rabbits, on the other hand, were far too tough to eat, so we gave them to the dogs to eat. Anyhow, as I was walking in the pasture, I saw a jack rabbit take off about a hundred yards away and was running like a bat out of hell. But it was running in a line parallel to me. So I pulled up the .22 and started taking shots. I could see puffs of dirt kicked up by my bullets, and with each shot they kept getting closer to the rabbit, until I saw it do a complete flip in mid-air and fall to the ground. I ran up to the rabbit and saw that my last shot had nailed it right at the shoulder. I was really proud of that.

I think it was the summer of 1953 when Howard Boyle, who had a farm a half mile south of us, got a television set. This was big news. It was like having a movie screen in your own home. And the programs went on and on! Fortunately, the Boyles were nice enough to occasionally let us kids come down and watch. Up to that point all we had was a radio, and in the evenings we laid around on the floor in the living room and listened to shows like "I Love a Mystery, "The Shadow" and "Nick Carter." It's a shame today that kids have so much TV, movies and VCRs that they stifle their imaginations. When we listened to those old shows, our imaginations would run wild, trying to keep up with the stories.

Mr. Finger kept a few cows on our farm, with a bull named "Rupert." He was huge, and we all avoided him whenever we could. We had a Guernsey cow named "Daisy" that we milked for our milk and cream. We all learned how to milk on that one cow, and to this day I marvel at how patient she was. Even Mary and Dianne, who were the youngest two girls, also learned how to milk. Mom almost fainted one day when Mary, who couldn't have been more than five at the time, came in the house and asked her why she couldn't get any milk out of Rupert. She had actually been out trying to milk this huge bull! Mary was lucky to be alive.

Sundays were Mass days. We all put on our best clothes and climbed into the car, piled one on top of another, to go to church. Our Sunday meal generally was always the same. We raised chickens, so when we returned from church, we changed clothes and headed out of the house. We took a wire clothes hanger or similar piece of wire with a wedge on one end, so that we could stick it under a chicken, then pull it and catch the chicken's leg in the wedge. We usually caught around six chickens. Then we laid them down on the ground, placed a stick over their necks, put one foot on each end of the stick, then pulled on the chicken until we pulled off its head. Then we tossed the chicken away from us, because its body jumped and jerked until it was finally dead. Then we dipped the chickens in hot water, which made it easy for us to pull out the feathers. The next step was to de-gut them, and finally, Mom singed the hairs off them by holding them over the stove's fire. She then cut them up and started frying them. Later in the afternoon if we were lucky, we scrounged up enough money to go to town and buy a five-gallon container of ice cream. That was a real treat, and with all the kids, the whole container was gone in no time flat.

During cold weather our house was heated by a single stove in the center room of the house. It was a wood and coal stove, but we generally burned coal, as it burned longer. In winter that one stove had to keep the whole house warm. We loaded it with coal before going to bed, but by morning the fire was out, and the first one up had to get the fire started. Those were some cold mornings. We didn't have running water either. In fact, poor Mom had to wash the clothes out in a little wash shed behind the house. She had to heat the water on the stove, then take it by bucket out to the wash shed. With all her kids, it seemed like washing the clothes and cooking was all she had time for. She really did have a rough life. Fortunately, there weren't any babies in diapers.

The sophomore and junior years in the seminary went by quickly. I sang in the choir, learned Gregorian chant, and we put on a number of plays, such as "The Pirates of Pinzance," "Everyman," the passion play, and others. I made good grades, saw classmates gradually drop out, realizing they didn't have vocations to the priesthood. I now realize that I hadn't ever really asked myself if becoming a priest was what I really wanted to do. I guess I felt with all of the pressure from Mom, I really didn't have a choice. It was just expected of me.

We couldn't do our own laundry at the seminary, nor would anyone else do it for us. That really would have been too big a project, because the clothes would get mixed up. So each of us had these reusable mail boxes with straps attached to them. When our dirty clothes piled up, we mailed the box of dirty clothes home for Mom to wash. Mom washed them and sent them back to us. We knew about when they were due to arrive and started watching for the Brother who went into town to get the mail. When the box finally came, we hurried and opened it, hoping that Mom might have included a couple of bucks, or some cookies, home-made candy, or even a letter. Too many times there wasn't anything but clean clothes. That really hurt.

My senior year was the most fun of the four years I spent at East Troy. By now I was pretty well established as one of the leaders in the senior class. I was probably the best athlete in the school, made good grades, was made the work senior, dining room senior and captain of the football team. I had a lot of things going for me.

September and October of my senior year started with football. This was in 1954. Since we were not in a league, the Prefect simply split the alphabet down the middle. Students with last names starting with A-K were on one team, and L-Z were on the other team. That put both my brother Tony and me on one team. Now, by this time Tony had gown into a big, strong kid. He didn't have a lot of speed, but he made a great fullback. As to myself, I must honestly, yet humbly, tell you I was fast, cat quick, and tough as nails. I went both ways, quarterback on offense, and middle linebacker on defense. Father scheduled a series of three games to decide the champs, and the winners of two out of three won the school championship.

Saturday rolled around and we suited up for the first game. Our team had good size, but their team had blazing speed. They had two kids, Wagner, who was a short, but well-built German kid, and was easily the fastest kid in school, and Symkowiak, a squat, very strong Polish kid, and probably the second fastest kid in school. During the game we designed a lot of plays as we went along. Since Tony was very strong, I would frequently call a play with him busting into the line for three or four yards. Then I would carry the ball and get a few yards. I avoided carrying the ball as much as I could because they were keying on me. I was pretty well shut down by their defense. The score at half time was 0-0.

Late in the second half, still in a scoreless tie, I had been calling a lot of running plays so that the defensive backs were cheating closer and closer to the line of scrimmage. I picked up on this and designed a play that I felt would cross up the defense. We usually ran a "T" formation, where the quarterback was under the center, and directly behind him was the fullback, with a halfback on each side of the full back. From above it looked like a "T," hence the "T" formation name.

There were a lot of options we ran out of that basic formation. On a long count all four of us in the back field would shift one step to either the left or right side, and the center would snap the ball back to the halfback who was now directly behind the center. This usually meant a sweep to the strong side, so when the backfield shifted like that, the defensive backs came up even closer to the line, as they were sure it was a running play coming their way.

It was now time to spring my new play. I called a left shift, so that the right halfback would get the snap. I told our right end to take off for the left corner of the end zone as soon as the ball was snapped. But I also told the right halfback to run a few steps to his left, as if it were a sweep with blockers in front of him. I hoped this would pull the defensive backs up to the line. Then I had the halfback stop and pass the ball to our right end, who was a kid by the name of John Doohen from Sioux City, Iowa. The right halfback about filled his britches when I called this play because he had never thrown a pass before. So, up to the line we came. I started calling the numbers, then we did the left shift, then called "Hut." The ball was snapped to the halfback, who started around the left side. Then he pulled up and blindly threw the ball where he thought the right end was supposed to be. The pass was as flat as a lame duck, and Doohen had to come back to catch it. But the play had faked out the whole defensive backfield so badly that he walked into the end zone for the touchdown. We made the extra point and led 7-0. This was the first actual use of what they now call the "halfback pass," and this play is sometimes used today by every level of football. I don't know if I was the first to ever call it, but we did design it on the field.

Now the other team had the ball and was marching down the field, about to tie the score. Their speed was just killing us. As time was running down, I felt that they would go exclusively to their speed merchant, Wagner. So, from my middle linebacker position I decided to key on him. They were down to their last series of plays, and it was third down. They had two plays left in which to score. From my middle linebacker slot I cheated up to the line of scrimmage, and as soon as the ball was snapped, I blitzed and was able to get through the line and got to Wagner just as he got the ball. I nailed him for a four-yard loss.

It was now fourth down, and the whole game was riding on this last play. I knew the ball was going to Wagner, as he was their only hope. He was the right halfback, so I moved into the line left of our nose tackle. This would give me a clear shot at him. But to my horror, they shifted their backfield to their left, so that they centered the ball directly to Wagner. I knew he would be going to his left, away from me, and if he ever got around the end, he was gone. As soon as the ball was snapped, I took off like a bullet. But the ball got to Wagner well before I did, and he started to his left away from me. I had no chance of catching him, so I dove with all I had, with my hands stretched out front, grasping for anything I could get. I could just get one hand around his ankle, and it was just enough to barely trip him up, and down he went. The game was won! Wagner came over to me after the game and told me that those two plays killed them and complimented me profusely on them. I don't know, but that may have been the birth of the blitz.

The L-Z team managed to win the second game 7-0. So now we were tied at one game apiece. But I was injured. I had torn a muscle in the left side of my back and couldn't raise my left arm above the shoulder. I'm not bragging, but without me, we were dead, so I had no choice but to play injured. It was a hard-fought game. I decided to keep the plays as simple as possible and kept running Tony into the line for the usual three or four yards. When we finally got down to their one or two-yard line, I called a quarterback sneak and carried the ball into the end zone for the first touchdown of the game. I felt bad about that, as Tony had done the bulk of the work and I got to score the touchdown. But it was the safest play, since there were no hand-offs that might cause a fumble.

But we hadn't won the game yet. It was late in the game and the L-Z team was driving toward our end zone. On one play, their big fullback, Jim Schmitt, also a senior, came busting through a hole in the line. I grimaced, as I knew from the way we were positioned that I had to tackle him with my injured left shoulder. Nonetheless, I hit him right above the knees just as hard as I could. My tackle dropped him in his tracks for no gain, and when he got up, the look he gave me told me the tackle either hurt him badly, or he was tacitly saying, "There's no way you can hit me that hard with your hurt shoulder." I met his gaze, but wasn't about to let him know that my shoulder hurt so badly from the hit that I was on the verge of passing out.

Somehow they managed to keep their drive alive, and right before time ran out in the game, they were able to punch in a touchdown. We were now ahead 7-6, and the try for extra point was coming up. They decided to go for two points by running the ball into the end one. It was a good call on their part, as they had the speed to get to the outside quick. The quarterback started calling signals, then they shifted left. This told me that they were probably going around their left end. I decided to gamble on that being their play. So I cheated up to the right side of our nose tackle, and as soon as the ball was snapped, I blitzed through the line. Symkowiak got the ball and started around his left end. He didn't get more than four steps and I was on him, diving with a picture-perfect tackle that took his legs right out from under him. He went down like a ton of bricks, three yards short of the end zone. Time ran out, and we won 7-6. This time both he and Wagner came over and congratulated me on the play. They just couldn't believe I got through the line as fast as I did. Sometimes you simply have to gamble to win.

For some reason sports seem to take up a great part of my memory during this period. Perhaps subconsciously I never really wanted to be a priest, and as a family we were near the poverty level. I don't know. But as I write about myself during this period, there was no memory of a deep religious "happening" or experience of that nature. I do recall that I started developing a strong devotion to the Blessed Mother. My reasoning was that most men have a soft spot for their moms. And if I really wanted something from the Good Lord, then the smartest way to get it was through his mother. That devotion has never left me to this day, and I feel very strongly about this.

But back to the sports. Both Tony and I were later convinced that, had we gone to a public high school, we probably would have wound up in one of the professional sports. During winter we did a lot of ice-skating in our free time and on weekends, and played a lot of hockey, too. One of the brothers drove a tractor down to the lake from the farm and plowed the snow off the top of the ice, creating our hockey rink. Although I was from Kansas, I became fairly adept at this sport, too. I hope I'm not bragging too much, but I recall one game in which Fr. Dudink himself was the referee. I got the puck down in our end of the rink and started skating up the ice with the puck toward the opposing goal. I guess I pushed it pretty hard, as I went around three or four defensemen, darted in front of the goalie and slammed the puck in the net. This was no big deal to me, because that was what we were supposed to do. But the reason I mention this is that Fr. Dudink went bonkers over this play. He skated up and down the ice telling all the other players "That's the way to do it! That's the way to do it!" I was actually a little embarrassed.

Largely because of my older brother, Max, I became interested in trapping. About two miles from the seminary was a very marshy lake, Army Lake, where there was strong evidence of muskrats. Tony and I had accumulated about 15 or 16 spring traps, designed to catch animals about the size of muskrats and mink. When cold weather had set in and the muskrats had thick fur, Tony and I went over to Army Lake on a Sunday afternoon and set up all our traps. We set them all at strategic places where it seemed small animals traveled through the marsh, or at places where it appeared there were entrances to muskrat holes at the water's edge.

The trap line had to be checked daily, and the first thing in the morning was the best time. Otherwise a trapped muskrat might be seen by someone else or even a predator. Our problem was that we had very little time between breakfast and the first class of the day. But we had a solution. At the time I was the dining room "Senior." That meant that I led the prayers for all the students before breakfast. As soon as the prayer was over, I shoveled down my food, told my assistant to lead the prayers after breakfast, then rushed to my locker. There I changed into my rough hunting clothes, put on my heavy navy jacket and jogged as fast as I could over to Army Lake to start checking our trap line.

I jogged with a lot of anticipation, wondering what, if anything, we had caught. I had my ax handle club with me, just in case. As I got near the place where we had set our first trap, I heard some kind of thrashing about. But when I got to the first trap, I discovered that the trap was gone! Was someone stealing our traps? What was going on? Then I heard some movement in the thick marshy reeds. Something was in there! Cautiously I went in after the noise. Soon I came upon a huge raccoon! And it was dragging our trap along, trying to elude me. When it heard me approaching, it must have with one last desperate pull jerked the stake out of the ground and took off, dragging our trap with it. I crept close enough so that I could club it behind its head, breaking its neck and killing the raccoon. I then reset the trap, left the dead raccoon there and hurried off to check the other traps.

I was excited as I checked the rest of the traps. This was great. We actually caught something on the very first day! We had nothing in the rest of the traps, so I picked up the raccoon by the tail, slung him over my shoulder, and started the long jog back. I think I had about 25 minutes' time from breakfast until I had to be back, changed into my school clothes, and was ready for classes. As I came across the football field toward the school, the other students had finished their breakfast and were milling around outside getting some fresh air before classes. They soon saw me and saw that I had caught something. The nearer I got, the prouder I got. I jogged by them with my chest stuck out a mile, when suddenly they all started laughing. Now, this made no sense to me. Then they started pointing at my back. I couldn't figure out what was so funny about a dead raccoon. I put it down, and they kept laughing and pointing to the back of my coat. Hurriedly, I took it off. Now I knew why they were laughing. During my run back from Army Lake, the raccoon had a bowel movement all over the back of my coat, and it was yellow, just like a baby's. How disgusting and humiliating! And here I was, the great white hunter. I meekly hurried into the building, washed off the coat, changed clothes and still made it to class on time. Nonetheless, I was still proud.

When the trapping season was over, we ended up with about 14 muskrats, the raccoon and one mink. To preserve them, we skinned them by cutting the fur around each rear leg and the tail. Then we cut a slit from the legs to the tail. The next step was simply to pull the skin from the tail of the muskrat to the head. It came off very easily. Next, we slid the skin, inside out, over a strong wire stretcher, and hung it in a shed at the farm to dry out. We sent them to a tanning company and made a few extra bucks.

Probably our main sport, though, was basketball. We had a brand new gym, no girls, long weekends and long winters, so we spent a lot of time in the gym shooting baskets. Little did I know that we were laying the foundation for what was to be the greatest basketball game ever played. I developed into a point guard, mainly because of my quickness and agility. I guess I had super peripheral vision because I started learning what today they call "no look" passing. A "no look" pass is one made to a certain point, when you are not looking at that point. Generally, a defender is watching your eyes, hoping they will telegraph your pass. But I could see exceptionally well out of the very corner of my eye and made passes that the defenses weren't expecting. I didn't get to score a lot, but the men I passed to were generally wide open for easy shots, and the name of the game was scoring and winning.

I should mention another item about the seminary. As a member of the senior class, they also made me the "work senior." We didn't have custodians, as you find in most high schools today. We students were assigned the tasks of sweeping, mopping, waxing and buffing the floors. We had to vacuum the carpets in the church and other custodial type work. It was my job to develop a list of what workers were to do what, and to see to it that the work was done properly, and in the short time that we had to it. In looking back, I can see that I was starting to exhibit the early signals of leadership and proper planning. It seems that all my life I have focused on getting the job done. I started developing a sense for what the desired result was, then worked backward to plan what had to happen before that result was reached. Occasionally, it took some good planning and coordination, because I frequently had three or four different jobs going on at the same time. I've never really been afraid of big jobs or difficult odds, whether it is in work or in sports. Both Tony and I simply never gave up, no matter what. Sure, we would fail, sometimes frequently, but never, ever because of lack of effort.

Being in the seminary didn't necessarily mean that I was a "saint." I still managed to get involved in enough ornery escapades. We managed to get gallon jugs of apple cider from the farm, took them out into the woods and concealed them in hollow trees, then let them ferment long enough so that eventually we had our own supply of wine. Late in our senior year we planned nocturnal escapades such as midnight trips down to the lake for swimming, or building carbide guns, using small bolts for bullets.

We soon discarded the carbide guns, though, as we could see that they could be really dangerous. If just to maintain our sanity or self-respect, we had to have some semblance of anti-establishment attitudes, or we just couldn't live with ourselves.

One of the most difficult things for me during the four years at Holy Ghost was the sleeping arrangement. We had two large dormitories, one for the freshmen and sophomores, and the other for the juniors and seniors. In our dormitory the beds were metal cots with a wire woven base on which was placed a thin mattress, very similar to an Army cot. They lined the beds up in rows, also similar to an Army barracks. In addition to our cots, we had either a chair or a small table next to the head of the bed. We had lockers along the wall where we had our clothes and sparse toiletries. In those days we didn't have deodorant or "worldly" aftershave lotions. I don't know if they just didn't exist or, if they did, they did not permit us to have them.

But my big problem was with sleeping. After they turned out the lights, we were all supposed to go to sleep. However, I always had a hard time getting to sleep. In this open area, if someone snored, the whole dormitory heard it, and that just drove me up the wall. I don't know how many hours and hours I spent, just trying to get to sleep. If someone snored, even with my pillow over my head, I couldn't sleep. Eventually I would have to get up, go over to the snorer and hold my fingers over his nose to stop the snoring. I never really learned to tolerate the snoring and suffered this problem throughout the entire four years.

Just before summer in my senior year in 1955, the school held its annual "Field Day." This was a three-day affair in which every student participated in all of the track and field events. Since it included all classes which obviously created an unfair advantage for the more developed upperclassmen, the participants were divided into three classifications: heavies, mediums and lights. Each participant then competed against all those in his weight classification. Points were assigned to the top three winners in each event and in each weight classification. Tents were set up out on the fields, pop and treats were provided, and it was a very fun event.

We had to participate in all of the usual track and field events. We actually had more events than the decathlon. We did the mile run, 100-yard dash, 100-yard hurdles, standing long jump, running long jump, hammer toss, shot put, discus, javelin toss, high jump, pole vault, and I may have left out some others. The points were then totaled, and a little brochure of results printed for everyone entitled, "Field Day Jive for Fifty-Five." The last part of this brochure listed everyone according to total points. I suppose I should tell you that I won first place. And to confirm that athleticism ran in our family, my brother, Tony, came in second. Tony and I often reflected that, had we went to a public high school, we probably would have gone on to play some form of pro sports. But, unfortunately, we'll never know.

In looking back at the four years I spent at Holy Ghost Seminary in East Troy, I'm probably most grateful for the excellent basic education I received: four years of Latin, three years of German, two years of classical Greek, English and speech. I'll never know and often wonder what path my life would have taken had I gone to a public high school instead of the seminary. Probably the greatest deficit was that I really was deprived of developing a healthy social relationship with females during those adolescent years. I simply had no exposure to them and, as a result, both socially and emotionally, didn't quite know how to deal with them later. In this sense my social development was stunted. One lesson I had already learned by this time, though, was never to look back. You simply can't change the past and only have the future to work with. So I was always looking to the future.

4

TWO-YEAR SEMINARY NOVITIATE

(Heavy Metal Religion and the Greatest Basketball Game Ever Played)

IN THE FALL of 1955 I took the train to Techny, Illinois, a very small town north of Chicago. Techny was the "home office" of the SVD society in the United States. This facility housed the novitiate, the major seminary, the printing presses of the society, the related support personnel, housing for the priest-teachers, the Provincial, and everything needed to run a major seminary. The novitiate consisted of first and second year novices, and its purpose was to instill a very deep religious consciousness and self-denial, through long periods of meditation and cloture from the worldly distractions. This was done to prepare the novice for taking the three vows of poverty, chastity and obedience at the end of the two years. Each of us wore black cassocks and the Roman collar. We looked just like priests. We also had the 4" wide black cloth belts, or cinctures, with the tassel down the side, and the three-winged biretta, which was a hat that went with the cassock.

After the novitiate, the novice then graduated into the major seminary. Here the emphasis was on scholarly development, philosophy, theology, languages, etc. They sent the cream of the crop of the major seminarians to Rome for even further academic studies. While the novices were preparing for the three vows, the seminarians were preparing for ordination to the various orders of sub-deacon, deacon, and finally the priesthood. Since our society was also a missionary society, the religious personnel, be it priest, brother or nun, were also being prepared to travel all over the world to work in the missions. In many respects this society, though not extremely well known in some circles, was ranked at about the same level of the Jesuits, who were also a religious missionary order with very heavy emphasis on education.

The religious and missionary priests differ greatly from the priests that you find in the Catholic parishes today. The ordinary parish priest generally does not take the three vows, is trained to deal with the challenges of a parish, and generally is not required to reach the educational requirements of, say, the Jesuits or the SVDs. I'm not trying to put down the parish priest, just pointing out that the respective vocations are entirely different, and the preparation time and emphasis are entirely different.

But about the novitiate. In my first year we had eight or nine first year novices in my class. Combined with the second year, we had a total of about 20. We were housed in one wing of a huge four-story building constructed with a very large interior patio. Standing in the patio, you were surrounded by continuous sections of the building, except for one corner, where there was a breezeway to the area outside the building. The southern section running east and west was the enormous church that could house virtually everyone at Techny, and many visitors for the major feasts and ceremonies such as ordinations, Christmas, Easter, etc. It was really more like a cathedral than a church. In the back of the church up in the balcony was one of the largest pipe organs in the country. Brother Roman was the organist, and he could not only play the most delicate of music, but he could also make the whole building thunder from the force of the organ. We all stopped and listened with delight when he practiced. It was really breathtaking.

The novitiate was headed by the Magister, Father Glorious, born in 1890, so he was 66 at the time I was there. His eyes could look right through you with the hardness of tempered steel, or kindle you with the gentleness of a loving father when it was appropriate. He was tough as nails and demanded the same out of us. There are some who believe he was a saint, and when he was killed in 1966 while walking across the highway in front of Techny, some of the Sisters came out and wiped up his blood in reverence. I still remember today many of his favorite sayings such as: "Start where you are, take what you have, and make something out of it." He would also warn us not to be like "dishrags," rags that are stiff when they are dry, but completely limp when they got wet. In other words, you must be stiff and strong at all times.

In the wing where we were quartered we had our own classrooms, a small private novitiate chapel and our own dormitory. They tried as much as possible to seclude us from the rest of the world, so that our focus could be very religious, and thus the preparation for the vows more successful. They took those vows very seriously and wanted us to do so also.

In the dormitory they gave us a bit more privacy than at Holy Ghost, although we were all still in a large, one-room dormitory setting. Here we had cubicles that consisted of curtains around our bed and locker, similar to the sliding curtains that you see in hospitals. Once in your cubicle, you could pull all the curtains closed, and you then had some semblance of privacy. My only problem was that, if anyone snored, it blew my sleeping. And with all of this religious and educational intensity, I really needed to be able to get a good night's rest. Unfortunately, those nights were not very frequent, and this problem tormented me throughout my novitiate.

Our routine was rigorous. Silence was the order of the day. They did not permit us any conversation with anyone as we rose in the morning, shaved and dressed. We went to mass in our private chapel, then had about five or ten minutes to walk in the patio to get some fresh air before classes. Classes went until noon, when we went to our small private dining hall. We were not permitted talking or "colloquium," as it was called, during our meals. Instead, we listened to religious readings read by a novice from a podium. We had two readers at breakfast, three at lunch and three at dinner. After lunch we had a short break again until classes resumed. At about 3:30 classes ended; then we reported to our work details.

The novices had a great deal of manual labor to perform. I think it was all part of our training to instill the necessary humility they felt we needed for the three vows. It was our job to dust, sweep, mop, wax and buff not only the main church, but all the hallways throughout the entire facility. I can tell you that I have a healthy respect for custodians, because I know the work they have to do. At the same time I will also tell you that I can probably outwork any custodian alive, and can make that mop spread its strings like a peacock spreading its tail. That requires experienced wrist action. We covered a lot of halls quickly.

South of the main chapel was the novitiate's own private secluded park. It consisted of a couple of acres of crushed stone paths, bushes, beautiful green lawns, and a small grotto of the Blessed Virgin. It was completely surrounded by a row of thick, tall trees on the sides where there were no buildings. They completely cut us off from the outside world. Since it was our park, we also had to take care of it. We had to keep the lawns mowed, the bushes trimmed, and took special care that the grass didn't gradually grow over into the crushed stone paths. Every so often we had to mix an acidic chemical and pour it into a metal container that could be pressurized by a hand pump. Then we went along the path and sprayed where necessary on grass growing into the paths to keep the paths even and neat. We had to be very careful with this chemical, because it could eat right through your clothes. We had other work duties of a more minor nature, but I won't go into them, because the point is that we had a lot of manual labor to do after classes.

After the day's work was finished, we were permitted our one hour of recreation. That's it. One hour per day during the week days. On weekends we had more, but during the week, that's all we got. During warm weather we played all of the outside sports. Our football was limited to tag football, because there simply wasn't time for conditioning, and sports were a very low priority in our novitiate regimen. Remember, we were preparing for the vows, not to be star athletes. We played a lot of baseball, softball, soccer, and even invented a game that was a cross between soccer, football and basketball. As you took the ball down the field, you could carry it with your hands, but you could only take two steps before you had to pass it off. It was somewhat akin to rugby without the smashing tackling. In the winter months we played basketball in the gym, or went ice skating on the small pond in the major seminary's park north of the buildings. It was large enough so we could play some hockey, too.

Most of these sports were played in the summer months when school was out and we had considerably more time for recreation. We had an outdoor swimming pool that was completely surrounded with booths for changing into our swimming suits. On top of the booths was a roof that stuck partially out beyond the booths over the pool. In one corner was the diving board. We spent a lot of time diving, and that is where I learned to do a "butt" dive that I did on occasion for most of the rest of my life. It was a bit comical, so we had a lot of fun doing it. To do it, I walked out to the end of the diving board, stood very still until the board settled down, then you deftly kicked both feet out in front of me. I then landed on the end of the diving board on my butt, the board bent down, then spring back, flipping me back up and out over the water. As I was being flipped out over the water, I kicked my legs up, so that I made a smooth, head-first entry into the water. This was a rather dangerous dive, as we learned first-hand. If you landed too far out to the end of the board, you landed on your tail bone. Occasionally we did that, and it hurt for a long time, so we learned to do it right.

You might find what I am about to tell you to be totally unbelievable. However, it is completely true. I was there. And we did it. After awhile, we got bored with the usual dives off the diving board. Someone brought an inner tube to the pool one day, and we started exploring with it. At first, we tried to dive off the board and through the center of the inner tube. We found that if you missed and hit the tube, it never hurt much. You'd just slide off into the water. Pretty soon that got to be routine. Then someone got the bright idea of trying to dive through the tube *after* doing a complete *360-degree forward flip* off the board. This took a lot longer, and you had to have someone in the pool to position the tube just right. After quite a bit of practice, we mastered this to the extent that we could do it about two out of every three tries.

Then someone really came up with the craziest idea. We got up on the roof and found that it came far enough out that with the right leap you could land on the end of the diving board and dive into the water. Since you were leaping both out and down, it didn't put as much stress on the diving board as you'd think. Soon we were able to do this with ease. And it was really fun. Then came the real crowning idea. How about leaping off the roof, bouncing off the diving board, doing a complete 360-degree forward flip *and then diving through the tube?* So we started practicing diving from the roof, off the board, doing the flip, and then into the water. After we got that down pat, then we added the element of tube. We had reached the point where we could actually do it successfully about every one out of three tries. Then one of the priests dropped in for a swim, saw us doing it, got scared as the dickens, and told us to never again dive off the roof. And that was the end of that.

As a general rule, we were not allowed to compete in any sports with the major seminarians. However, on Christmas day each year we held the only basketball game between the novitiate and the major seminary. This was a traditional game every year, and every year the major seminary normally clobbered the novitiate. True to form, they did so as usual on Christmas Day, 1956, my first year in the novitiate. After all, they had over 200 vigorous athletes from the ages of 20 to 30 to pick from. Little did we all know, though, that the greatest basketball game of all time would be played exactly one year later.

But back to our routine. After the hour of recreation, we returned to our quarters, donned our cassocks and proceeded to dinner. After dinner, we generally had about 15 minutes or so to walk in our park. During this time we were allowed to mingle about and have conversations with each other. We then returned to our wing and spent the rest of the evening studying or praying.

Just before retiring, we went to our chapel for Vespers, a short series of evening prayers. On occasion we attended Vespers with the major seminarians in the main chapel. After Vespers we retired to our dormitory and got ready for bed. We were not permitted to talk to others during this time. In fact, the only time we were permitted to talk to the other novices was for a few minutes after breakfast, a few minutes after lunch, during recreation hour and for a few minutes after supper. Other than that, silence was the order of the day.

We were not allowed to go home at any time during these two years. When summer rolled around, we had much more recreation time. Since there were no classes, we occasionally hiked about six miles over to Lake Michigan, where we examined the ruins of the McCormick mansion. Rumor had it that a McCormick had built this huge mansion for his bride, and shortly after their marriage they had a terrible falling-out, and he literally destroyed it. We played a lot of sports, and on some weekends were permitted visits by our families. I remember Mom and Dave coming up once, but since my family lived so far away, those visits were not very frequent.

I guess we still had a streak of orneriness in us, even in the novitiate. With the Roman collar and cassocks, we were dressed exactly like the priests. On the days that visiting was permitted, and there were outside visitors allowed on the premises, sometimes we would be approached by cute little girls and boys, who had just purchased new rosaries. They frequently came up to us and asked, "Father, would you please bless my new rosary?" Well, we weren't priests, but we didn't want to turn down the cute little kids. So we took the rosary in our left hand, and with our right hand we made the sign of the cross, while saying out loud, *"Quod non habeo, non possum dare."* The little kids then ran to their mothers, telling them that they just had their rosaries blessed. Little did they know that what we had actually said in Latin was, "What I don't have, I can't give." Somehow, I've always felt a little guilty about that.

At the end of our first year we had a 30-day retreat. For those of you who do not know what a "retreat" is, it is similar to a few days jammed with sermons, meditations, religious readings, and with no recreation or conversations with each other. Again, silence was the order of the day. Just dead silence. But this one was the granddaddy of them all. It went for 30 long, grueling days. We were allowed one free day per week, when we were permitted to have recreation, talk and act like normal human beings. But after that, it was back to the retreat. They were determined to shape us into saints, long before we died. And I really don't have any argument with that. If you believe in something and are committed to it, then you may as well go all out. At the end of the 30-day retreat, we were promoted to the second year of novitiate.

I started the second year of novitiate in the fall of 1957. Tony had graduated from East Troy and had now joined me. Although I didn't realize it at the time, this would prove to be a very hard year for me for many reasons. In fact, it was such a difficult time for me that I have to push myself to finish writing about this part of my life. On the positive side, I got to play in the greatest basketball game of all times, which I will tell you about later.

As I mentioned before, we had a relatively small class of eight or nine. So there weren't too many of us to provide real leadership to the first year novices. I don't know why, and it is something that I will never understand, but somehow Fr. Glorious loaded me down with extra responsibilities that I am sure many of my classmates could have handled just as easily. For example, I was made the work senior. That meant I was in charge of coordinating virtually all of the manual labor of the novices. I've told you about the custodial and park work. It was a nightmare having enough men and equipment assigned to each job and estimating when they would be done, so I could be there and move them on to other tasks without any dead time. I had to maintain all the mopping equipment, the lawn mowers and park equipment, and have sufficient supplies of soap, etc.

Father Glorious also put me in charge of the readers at the meals. That meant I had to plan, type and post the readers' names for each meal on a weekly basis, following the list of books that Father Glorious selected. Each morning after breakfast that day's readers gathered around the podium and reviewed the readings they had for that day, looking for difficult words, etc. I had to listen to each of them read a small portion, to make sure that they read well enough so we could get the most benefit from the readings. If that was not enough, Father Glorious called me to his office and told me that he had chosen me to be the one to make the ciliciums and the flagellums.

Ciliciums and flagellums. What memories they conjure. A

cilicium was a wire mesh-like apparatus that had about 40 short blunt wire ends on one side. We wrapped these around our arms just above the elbows with the ends pointing inward, so that they were pressed into our flesh. The idea was to tighten them enough so that they were causing pain, but not enough to cause the metal ends to puncture the skin. We were told to wear them under our cassocks as often as we could at discreet times, but the amount of time that we wore them was up to us. We could always tell when one of our friends was wearing one, if we accidentally bumped into his arm, and he would involuntarily wince with pain. There were times when they did pierce your skin.

The flagellum was a braided whip that was given to each of us. We were told to use this whip on ourselves on our bare backs in private as often as we could, but were warned not to attract attention. The idea was for us to beat our bodies into submission through physical pain, thus allowing religious matters to be more in control. When supplies of the ciliciums and flagellums ran low, I went up into a very small, secluded room, way up in the attic, and made enough of each of these to fill the needs. I had a spool of wire that I cut into certain lengths, bent them with a manual machine so that the ends were bent down about a half an inch, then hooked each of the wires to the last one until I finished the cilicium. I made the flagellum from a spool of twine that I braided in strips that were then attached and bound into a handle at one end. When one of the novices needed one of these, they were told to see me.

That's why this was a very hard year for me. In addition to the normal load of studies in Latin, German, Greek, math and the normal load of praying and self-studying and working on my faults (few as they were), I had the additional load of work senior, park senior, reading senior and these other little odd jobs. It was just more than I could handle.

Another job I had, but really enjoyed, was in the morning at mass. Behind our small private chapel was a wall, behind which were two very small altars. With so many priests at Techny, they had to have plenty of altars, so that each of them could say mass every day.

So, while our mass was being held in our novitiate chapel, there were also two private masses being said on the other side of the wall. And the SVDs loved to sing. Since I had been in the schola, or choir, at East Troy, I got to sing solo high masses at these small private masses. I had to sing very quietly to avoid interfering with the mass next to me or the mass going on in our chapel. I really loved doing that.

We also had the "Chapter of Faults." About once a month we gathered in the chapel. Each of us had been secretly assigned the name of one of our fellow novices a week in advance. We then had to discreetly keep a watch on him so that, as we knelt in the Chapter of Faults, we could verbally tell him the three main faults that he had, as we saw them. And give examples. Then each of us would tell everyone else what we thought our three main faults were. This was a very somber, serious ceremony, and we all did it while kneeling on the hard floor. Again, it was designed to cleanse us of our faults in preparation for the vows. The emphasis was on humility and the elimination of self-will.

As I had mentioned, my brother, Tony, had finished at East Troy and was a first year novice. I loved Tony. We had been through a lot growing up together, had been at East Troy together for three years, and we frequently leaned on each other when we needed to. I sure miss him. He passed away a few years ago. Perhaps he made my load a little lighter during the seminary days, as sometimes he and I visited while walking in the park, talking about home and things like that. When he first arrived, he told me all about the latest music and a new star called Elvis Presley, whose music was supposed to be "dirty." I had not been allowed to go home for the summer of 1956, so I missed out on all of these "worldly things." Tony made the fall of 1956 easier for me, even though I didn't sense it at the time. He was a pretty good basketball player himself. He was both taller and bulkier than I was. I think I was 6" and he was 6'1" or 6'2". He had improved considerably in the year that he had been at East Troy. So this brings us to ...

THE GREATEST BASKETBALL GAME OF ALL TIME

It was Christmas Day, 1956. This was the day of the annual

novitiate versus major seminary basketball game. It was a very long tradition, and the novitiate had never won. This year the seminarians fully expected to continue their domination. After all, there were only about 20 in the whole novitiate, and many of them didn't even play basketball. On the other hand, there were over 200 seminarians, all aged 21 and up. They had the advantage of considerably more practice time, whereas the novitiate only had one hour of recreation a day. It appeared to the seminarians that it was just going to be another easy victory.

But there were a lot of things they didn't consider. They didn't take into consideration that these novices had practiced at that beautiful new gym up at East Troy, and all of us had four years there, playing lots of basketball. So our basketball skills were sharp. And the first year novices provided us with three starters, Tony, at what is now called the off-guard, and two 6'3" forwards, Paul Bergen and Norman Bohl. From the second year starters came our center, big 6'4" Jim Schmitt, and myself, the 6' point guard. I was now almost 20, and my quickness and agility had sharpened considerably. Furthermore, we went into the game thinking we had a good chance of beating them. We were not going to lay down and take another defeat. But I had a problem - no basketball shoes. I was able to scrounge around and borrow a pair from someone, but they were a little too big for me.

The seminarians were loaded with talent, starting with their big center, 6'6" Joe Noble, and Ernie Brandewie, an excellent athlete. I don't recall the names of their other players, but they had some very good athletes. We had a lot of respect for them, because we had either watched them play in other sports or had played against them in other sports during the previous summer. They must have had 12 players suited up. We only had six, and the sixth was just for show, in case one of our players fouled out.

Finally, warm-ups were over, and the game was ready to start. This was the only "action" of the morning, so many of the seminarians were there, as were a lot of the priests. Father Glorious didn't place much emphasis on sports, so he never came. After breakfast, he jokingly asked us who was going to win, and when we told him we were, he laughed outright. Can you believe that? He laughed! But why shouldn't he? His novices had never won. So he never showed up to watch. You have to remember that he was a very religious person, and sports simply were a distraction to him. I'm not putting him down. He was just a very holy man and knew what was important.

We lined up for the tip-off. The ball went up and Noble easily swatted it to one of his players. We went into the standard two-three zone defense. For those of you who don't know what that is, the two guards set up just about at the free throw line, about two arms lengths apart. Big Jim Schmitt set up in the center, just in front of the basket. The two tall forwards, Bohl and Bergin, set up on both sides of the center, a few arms lengths away. As the ball moved from one side to another, the zone of five shifted over in order to prevent a shot from being taken close to the basket. The idea of this zone defense was to force a long outside shot, where the shooting percentages are a lot less than shooting from closer to the basket.

The major seminary scored first and were able to keep about a four-point lead throughout most of the first half. All during the first half I was having problems with my shoes. They were too big, and when I stopped or cut very abruptly, my shoes kept slipping, slowing me down and cutting down my efficiency. Once I literally ran out of my shoe. My older brother, Max, who was in the major seminary at the time, saw this, and at halftime scrounged up a pair of basketball shoes that actually fit me. That first half turned out to be very important to us because we now knew that we could play with them. We now knew we were competitive at their level. All those years in the gym at East Troy was starting to pay off.

My peripheral vision was really sharp. I never scored much, but as my teammates were weaving in and out and back and forth to get open, I could see them open out of the corner of my eye. I also had extremely quick reflexes. I could drill a pass past a defender before he could react. As a result, I hit a lot of open men with bullet-like passes, and they made many easy baskets. It never bothered me not to score; I got as much thrill getting a sharp pass to the open man for the score, as if I scored myself.

Halftime came, and the major seminary was up by four points. Both teams huddled to go over their second half strategies. We knew the seminarians were thinking that they would blow us out in the second half. We, on the other hand, were telling each other that we were holding our own, and that with a few breaks, we might even pull off the ultimate upset. Our confidence was high and growing. We no longer feared them and no longer felt dominated by them. I now had on a pair of shoes that fit, so now I had some good "wheels," as they say in sports jargon today. We were determined. We were not going to be denied. Our resolve had hardened.

The referee blew the whistle to start the second half. I could see the intensity in the eyes of my teammates. I could see that they looked to me to get them the ball, and they were determined to get it in the hoop. The second half started, and the battle thickened. We were able to tie the score late in the third quarter, and that stunned the major seminary. This can't be! They were supposed to blow the lowly novices out! But the novices wouldn't roll over and give up! You could just see the seminarians grit their teeth and kick their resolve up a notch. They were not going to let us beat them. They put all the pressure they could muster on us to grind us down. Every time they scored a basket, the huge crowd of seminarians erupted into a roaring cheer. We hung on and the third quarter ended with us trailing by two points. It was going to come down to the last quarter.

We really needed the rest between the third and fourth quarters. We hadn't made a single substitution the whole game, and we had all played with more intensity than at any other time in our lives. We looked at each other, tired, proud, hearts pumping like pistons. I told my teammates that we were going to win. I told them that all we needed to do was to win this last quarter. I told them that we had proven to ourselves that we were at least as good as the seminarians, and if we could take this quarter, then we were better. The whistle blew for the start of the fourth quarter. We stuck our five hands together and looked into each other's eyes, silently telling each other, "Let's do it." Then we walked out on the floor to take up our positions for the final tip-off, our tails dragging. The seminarians also came out, and they had the air of soon-to-be winners about them. They had made many substitutions during the first three quarters, and their starting five were back in the game; they were sure they had us worn out. They were poised for the kill.

The fourth quarter started out furiously. They wanted to put us away quick. But a funny thing happened. I seemed to catch my second wind; then all of my teammates seemed to catch their second wind. The pace of the game was unbelievable! Players were diving for loose balls, and our big boys were battling hard for each rebound with elbows flying. It's a shame so few people got to watch this display of players playing their hearts out against impossible odds. The seminarians would score, then we would come back, work the ball around, and I'd spot an open man under the basket and drill him the ball. We were locked into a basket-for-basket battle. Then came the play.

It was late in the quarter, and we were up by two points. Suddenly, one of their guards made an unbelievable steal of the ball and started racing down the court for an easy lay-up. With the steal, the major seminary crowd jumped to their feet with their arms in the air and their fists clinched. There was no doubt that it was going to be an easy two points. Everyone in the building knew that, including myself. I knew I couldn't catch him in time to block the shot. But knowing that sometimes players miss an easy shot, I poured on the speed and blazed down the court, leaping at full speed. But he didn't miss the shot! At the peak of my leap, the ball came down through the net for their score. As pandemonium erupted in the stands, in mid-air I ripped the ball out of the net with both hands, and twisted my body so that I landed out of bounds with the ball in my hands and I was facing the opposite end of the court. It was as if some force had taken over my body and was controlling me.

I instinctively looked up court, paying no attention to the roar of the crowd. I spotted a teammate under the seminarian's basket, and another teammate way over in the left-hand corner. But there was a seminarian about halfway between them. He was close enough to both of them so that he could easily intercept a full court pass to either one if I tried it. Without thinking, I stared straight at the teammate in the corner as if I hadn't see the seminarian. In the same instant I unloaded a full court pass before the rest of the seminarians court get back on defense. The lone seminarian focused on my stare, and as soon as I launched my pass, he followed my eyes and broke for the corner to intercept it. But while I was staring at the player in the corner, I launched my pass to my teammate under the basket. I had completely faked him out. When the ball was at half court, the seminarian realized he had been faked out and slammed on his brakes, desperately trying to get back to intercept the pass. But he was too late. Like a bullet the pass went the full length of the court right into the hands of my wide open team mate, who calmly dropped it in for an easy basket.

The seminarians both on and off the court were stunned. They just stood there. In one instant they had stolen the ball and got what they thought was a game-breaking basket. However, before they could even fully absorb that, I had the ball back to the other end of the court, and we got that basket right back. That one breakaway play that they made, that almost broke our back, turned out to be followed immediately by our play, that proved to break their back. Time had almost expired. We managed another basket, and the final score was Novices - 54, Seminarians - 50. We had done it. We had beat the seminarians, the one and only time that the novices had ever beat them. It is a shame that so few witnessed what had to be the greatest game ever played. That game further imbedded in me the conviction that, no matter what the odds are, you can still prevail. Just don't ever give up.

After the game and showers, Max was besides himself with pride. As we walked along the basement corridor, I will never forget him slapping me on the back time and again, saying, "Your passes were unbelievable! Where did you learn that?" and, "How could you pass without looking first?" He was not a great sports fan to speak of, and this was the most excited I had ever seen him over a sporting event.

When we assembled in our small dining room for dinner, Father Glorious jokingly asked who won. When we told him we did, he wouldn't believe it. He just would not believe it. He seriously thought we were all putting him on. So, when we met for supper, he told us right after prayers that he had confirmed that we won, and, as a reward for winning, he dispensed with the religious reading and permitted talking during the meal. I will never forget that day.

Winter eventually gave way to spring, and then the school year ended, and summer took over. During the summer we had much more time to walk in the park, because there were no classes the next day, so no studying. One evening Tony sought me out after supper, and we walked out into the novitiate park. As we strolled along, I could tell he was worked up over something. Finally, he told me that he had made up his mind to leave the seminary. As soon as he told me that, I felt both stunned and proud. Stunned, because all of us boys were supposed to become priests. Proud, because he had the backbone to make such a decision on his own, knowing what Mom's reaction would be. Yes, I was very proud of him. I told him I supported him completely, that if he didn't feel he had the vocation, then the seminary was the wrong place to be. I could see that this was a relief to him, as he must have worried considerably about my reaction. I guess he may have overlooked the biggest factor, that we were brothers and that I loved him very much. If that was what he wanted, then by all means that was what I wanted for him. It took a few days for him to wrap up the loose ends, and then he caught a train home. He was gone.

Tony probably never realized what effect his decision had on me. Besides being my closest brother, he was the best friend I have ever had in my life. Even I didn't fully realize the effect of his decision on me until I started writing this book. See, his leaving the seminary opened up an entirely new horizon for me. Up to that time, I didn't realize that I myself had any choice as to whether or not I wanted to be a priest. Mom's obsession with having a son become a priest, and the pressure she put on all of us at a very early adolescent age of 14, suppressed my own desires as to a vocation. That, combined with the heavy emphasis of self-denial in the novitiate, worked to blind me to any possibility other than being a priest.

But Tony's decision changed that. I started to realize that maybe I myself had some say as to what I wanted to do. And for the first time, I started asking myself, "Do I really want to be a priest?" The first time that I squarely addressed that question was right after Tony left. After about two weeks of soul-searching on this issue for the first time and praying, I realized that I never really wanted to be a priest. I realized that what I was doing was something that I was told I should be doing. Not once had either of my parents ever asked me if I really wanted to be a priest. It was evident to me that I was living a false life in the sense that I was living a life that someone else designed for me. The conclusion was simple and logical. I really didn't belong in the seminary. It was someone else's dream. So I made the decision to leave, and in a few days I also was on the train home.

I don't harbor any deep resentment over Mom's domineering. I do have some resentment, though, as I was deprived of the chance to develop some of the social skills that I needed later in life. I had no real interaction with girls, so this hampered me for a very long time. I missed the chance to excel in sports, something that I loved dearly. But on the other hand, I really got a terrific education, six years of Latin, five years of German, four years of Greek, speech, English, composition, math, you name it. And that education has helped me all my life. Still, I wish Mom would have given me the choice.

5

THREE YEARS FOLLOWING NOVITIATE

(Freedom!)

IT WAS NOW the summer of 1957 and Mom and Dad were living in Hoisington again. I remember coming home from the seminary, walking into the house, and Dad was resting in his bedroom. I felt I should go in and tell him that I was back. I went in, sat down on the edge of his bed and said, "Dad, I'm home." He didn't even get up and was just lying on top of the covers, fully clothed except for his shoes. I never thought of it until just now, but he never even got up out of bed to welcome me home. I suppose the burden of trying to raise all those kids might have been wearing him down. Still, I felt I needed to go direct to him, to give him the chance to say or ask anything he wanted.

This was the first major decision I'd made in my life on my own, and after all he had done for me, I guess I wanted to make sure he wasn't upset with me. He just asked one question, "Are you sure you don't want to be a priest?" I said, "Yes," and all he said was, "Okay." I knew then that he supported my decision and was not upset with it. I don't even recall ever having a discussion with Mom as to why I left the seminary. It would seem that I should have been really concerned about her, but I honestly cannot remember even worrying about it. Dad was the one that I was worried about. I cared a lot for him, and did not want him upset with me.

So, I was home, 20 years old, and had to figure out what I wanted to do. Dave had returned home from the Navy and had just finished his freshman year at Hutchinson Junior College, the closest college to Hoisington. He was studying to become a petroleum engineer, since he had done some rig building with Dad years earlier before he went into the Navy. Tony was also home, and since Dad was in the oil business as a rig builder and Dave was going to be a petroleum engineer, Tony and I felt we wanted to be petroleum engineers, too. Here we go again, following the footsteps of an older brother. However, thinking for ourselves was still something completely new to us. So, Hutch Juco it was. Dave agreed that Tony and I could stay with him and the three of us would share the rent and groceries. Dave was on the GI Bill, so he had a monthly check from the government. Tony and I would have to find part-time jobs. So, off we went.

The complete freedom was a drastic shock to Tony's and my social systems. We just were not accustomed to doing what *we* wanted to do *when* we wanted to do it. We were short on books and tuition money, so we looked up the track coach and told him some of our times and stats at East Troy. He was impressed enough that on the spot he gave us our books free as part of a scholarship. That got us over the hump and school started. Later we had to drop track, because we had to work part-time.

Most of the subjects were pretty easy for me because of the great education I had in the seminary. In fact, our speech teacher held a speech contest sponsored by an insurance company where the winner won $25 and got to give his speech on the local television station. I wish I could say the competition was ferocious, but there were only about five of us entered, and I won easily. I also had to attend a dinner where the check was formally presented. I then went to the Hutchinson TV station and gave my speech live. Mom could see it in Hoisington, so I told her in advance and she was pretty proud. Me, just give me the money, because I was on a very limited income.

One of the required courses for pre-engineering was geology. We had a teacher for this course whose name was "Sleepy" Jones. We gave him that nickname for a reason. He is the only teacher I have ever heard of who could actually go to sleep while standing in front of the class, talking to the class. It was an afternoon class, and he started out standing behind his desk, then he backed up to and leaned against the blackboard. Finally, he rested his head against the blackboard, and in a minute or two he'd fall completely asleep. That was great with us, because he was very boring anyhow. So we left him that way until the bell rang at the end of the class, waking him up, and the class was dismissed.

Chemistry was the worst course for me. We had no high school preparation for this subject, and I'd have to say it was pure Greek to me, except I knew Greek. So I'll say it was pure Egyptian to me. Of all the courses I took at Hutch Juco, that was the most difficult, and I had to take it both semesters. I never studied more on a subject all the time I was there. I eked out a C both semesters and was happy as hell to get it. The rest of the subjects were fairly easy.

As time passed, Tony and I started enjoying our newfound freedom. It wasn't long before we started cutting classes where we had safe grades, so we could hang out in the student lounge. After all, we had some "social development" that we needed to address. There were some mornings when we spent most of the time in the lounge.

It was probably inevitable that we had conflicts with Dave. He was four years older, had spent four years in the Navy, had done a lot of partying in the Navy, and was now mature enough to start getting serious about a career. On the other hand, Tony and I were like babes in the woods socially. Naturally, we were inclined to do the things that were fun, rather than study or look for a job. In addition to that, I am sure that Dave, as our oldest brother, felt he should "guide" us. It was when we didn't want to be guided that the friction developed. But Dave was stubborn. And did he ever have a temper! We made him so mad once that in a fit of anger he took his coffee cup and threw it as hard as he could across the living room, coffee flying everywhere. Tony and I dove for cover. We expected to hear shattering glass when the cup hit the wall. But all we heard was a muffled "thump." We cautiously looked up, and found that the cup had just stuck in the wall, bottom first. It didn't break. It was just stuck about halfway into the plaster wall. It was so completely unexpected that we all started laughing, and the situation was diffused.

I know we were probably a burden on Dave, because we were so socially naive, and just simply had a lot to learn. Dave was probably very instrumental in helping Tony and me in that first year. We knew we were socially behind most of the others our age, and the only way to catch up was to dive in and try. We went to the school sock hops, not knowing how to dance, but got out on the floor and tried. After the first few dances, it got difficult to get girls to dance with us, but eventually we learned how to dance and we were over that hump.

Part of our social development included introduction to alcohol in its various forms. Tony and I started to develop a taste for beer, and usually every weekend we scrounged together enough money to get a quart or two of beer. One of our favorite pastimes with our friends was to get a couple quarts of beer, hide them inside our trousers with our jackets pulled over them, and go to the local movie theater. The theater we went to was kind of a second-class theater with the floors slanting down toward the front, and had no carpet. This was important, because when we finished drinking a quart, we set the empty bottle on the floor. As the movie went on, we sometimes forgot about the bottle on the floor and accidentally kicked it. When that happened, the bottle inevitably started rolling down the concrete floor toward the screen, making the loudest of noises as it banged into the metal seat legs, paused, and then continued rolling. We all busted out laughing. The doorman would hear it and come down the aisle trying to find out who did it. There were generally so many of us that he really didn't try too hard. After awhile we started doing it on purpose just for the fun of it.

I had a lot of different part-time jobs while at Hutchinson. For some time I worked for J.S. Dillon, a grocery store chain, washing their trailers and trucks next to a service station. I was really impressed with Dillon, as I thought that they were spending a lot of money just to have clean equipment. Another job I had was doorman at the main downtown theater. I was doorman when the movie "Ten Commandments" came out. The movie was so long that there was an intermission about halfway through the movie. The crowds were so huge that the people just physically couldn't all go to the concession stand. So the owner had us go down the aisle with cases filled with cold bottles of Coca-Cola and sell it to the audience. I really felt stupid.

But the king of the part-time jobs was with Western Fresh Fruit Products. This was a company that made applesauce and juices. Part of the process included crushing the apples. This process caused the apple juice to drain into large wooden barrels. After enough barrels were accumulated, we loaded them into a railroad car which was shipped out to a sister plant in Colorado. There the barrels were emptied of the apple juice and then were shipped back to us for refilling.

Now, that doesn't sound like a very glamorous part-time job. *But* sometimes those barrels sat for quite some time before they were shipped back. And it was literally impossible to totally empty those barrels. As a result, when a carload of "empty" barrels arrived at the plant, we were delighted. While unloading the barrels, we very carefully drained each one of them of every last drop, until we accumulated about a quart of highly fermented apple cider. However, it was now no longer cider; it was a very powerful liquor. In fact, it was so powerful that we couldn't drink more than three drinks without getting totally stoned. One day out of curiosity we poured some in a saucer to see if it would burn. Sure enough, a faint blue flame glowed over the saucer until we blew it out. We liked it a lot because it was most certainly the cheapest, yet most potent liquor available. It's a wonder we didn't get jake leg from it.

Another thing we liked about that job was that they kept an inventory of long-necked Pilsner glasses. I'm sure they weren't extremely expensive, but they appeared to us to be "classy." So right before we clocked out, we stuck two or three of these glasses upside down inside our jeans with our coats hanging over them to conceal them. We then clocked out, walked to our cars and drove away. We kept ourselves and our friends supplied with a good supply of these glasses.

We finished up our freshman year and returned home for the summer. Tony and I worked as roughnecks in the oil fields as part of a four-man oil well drilling crew. It was somewhat dangerous work, but we had to save up money for the next school year. The crew was comprised of a "driller" who was in charge, and who operated the powerful motors that ran the drilling. Next in line was the derrick man, who usually worked on a small platform about 40 feet up in the derrick or, more commonly, "rig." Then came the lead tong man, or "lead man," who worked on the derrick floor with the back-up tong man, or "back-up" man. The back-up man was the low man on the totem pole, and part of his duty was to collect samples.

"Samples" were bits of rock obtained from the bottom of the hole the rig was drilling. The hole, about eight inches in diameter, was drilled by using a drill bit, a tool that was made up of three metal wheels of teeth made of very hard steel that rotated around as the powerful drilling motors turned the drill pipe. The drill bit was attached to two 30-foot sections of drill stem pipe, 5-1/2 inches in diameter, with a two-inch hole running down the center. Those two sections of pipe, therefore, were extremely heavy. As the drill bit turned, the teeth bit off small chips of rock. While the drilling was going on, a powerful pump was simultaneously pumping a liquid mixture down the inside of the drill pipe, out the center of the drill bit, catching the small chips of rock and carrying them up the annulus of the hole, or the space between the outside of the drill pipe and the walls of the hole. When the syrupy liquid, called "mud," came out of the top of the hole, there was a small canal that carried the mud to a big mud pit about 20 feet wide, 40 feet long and 10 feet deep, dug out by a caterpillar. In the mud pit the sediment of rock chips settled on the bottom of the hole, and the pump then sucked the mud at the top of the mud pit back down through the drill pipe to the bottom of the hole, where it would again pick up chips of rock, and the process would start all over again.

The size of the hole was 12-1/4 inches in diameter for the first few hundred feet down; this was lined with casing pipe generally 8-5/8 inches in diameter. This was done to protect the underground fresh water. Below the fresh water level the size of the hole was the 8 inches mentioned above.

One of the jobs of the back-up man was to periodically catch some of the mud coming out of the hole. He then used clear water from a hose to wash the chipped rocks, so that they were cleared of the mud elements. This sample was then placed in a bag and logged and identified. The identification included the depth of the hole at the time the sample was taken.

Getting these samples was the whole purpose of drilling the well. Later, a geologist would come out to the drilling site and study the samples. He ran chemical tests on the samples looking for evidence of hydrocarbons. He inspected the samples under powerful microscopes and compared all this data with the logs obtained by electrical and radioactive logs done by specialized well logging companies. The geologist studied them, determined the underground formation from which they came, smelled them for the odor of oil, and ultimately made the decision whether to continue drilling, or where to stop drilling in case oil was found, and finally, when to give up drilling and write off the well as a dry hole.

The driller usually had enough experience to know when a drill bit was worn out from grinding on the rock. When the bit needed to be changed, all of the pipe had to be pulled out of the hole to get to the bit. The depths of these holes were up to 5,000 feet. The process of pulling all of the pipe out of the hole was called "making a trip."

Here is how it was done. The driller manned the control panel to the powerful engines, which was located near the drilling floor so he could see every thing that was happening on the drilling floor and could direct the men. The derrick man was on his platform up in the rig. The lead and back-up man worked on the drilling floor. When everyone was in position, the driller stopped the circular rotating section of the drilling floor. The rig had a huge cable pulley, called an "elevator" that was attached to the top section of pipe called a "Kelly pipe." The Kelly pipe was a square pipe that was inserted in a square hole of the drilling floor. The actual drilling occurred when the driller started rotating the drilling floor. This caused the floor to turn the pipe which caused the bit at the bottom of the hole to turn. The trip was started when the driller engaged the thick cable to the elevators that were clamped around the Kelly pipe, and literally lifted the entire length of pipe in the hole up to near the top of the rig. It was then high enough so that the coupling, where the first section of

Kelly pipe was screwed into the next section of Kelly pipe, was waist high to the lead and back-up men on the drilling floor. Each of these men then slipped a large metal wedge called a "slip" around the pipe at the drilling floor. The driller then slowly lowered the pipe until the slips caught and held the pipe firmly. At this point the two men on the derrick floor each grabbed a tong, or large pipe wrench, that was hanging counterbalanced from a cable. The tong was so large that one man couldn't even begin to lift it off the floor. So it was counterbalanced to allow the worker to raise or lower it with little effort. It was also on a cable so that it could be swung out to the pipe and then back out of the way. It had to be large and strong enough to break loose the joint where the two sections of pipe were attached.

Once the slips were in place and the pipe firmly held in place, the lead man swung his tong into place, locking it on the top of the lower section of pipe. The back-up man then swung his tong into place, locking it on the bottom of the upper section of pipe. The driller then engaged the cables at the end of the tongs, and the tight joint was then cracked loose so the top pipe could be unscrewed. When the top joint was loosened, the bottom tong was removed, then the driller rotated the floor which unscrewed the top joint the rest of the way.

When the top section of pipe was completely unscrewed, the driller then raised the pipe a couple of inches above the lower pipe still firmly locked in the floor. The derrick hand then physically pushed the top of that section of pipe into a storage section up in the derrick stand designed for that purpose. The back-up man then pushed the bottom of that section of pipe out far enough from the derrick floor so that it would not be in the way. The driller then slowly lowered the pipe until it rested on the outermost storage part of the derrick floor. There was an old saying for the back-up man that if his toe was under the pipe when the driller lowered it, don't ask the driller to lift up the pipe, just pull your foot back, because that part of your foot has been cut off. That is how heavy the pipe was. After that section of pipe was lowered to the floor and the derrick hand had pushed it into its leaning position at the derrick platform, the derrick hand then released the elevators. The driller then lowered the elevators down to the drilling floor, and the lead and back-up man clamped them to the section of pipe sticking out of the floor. The driller then started pulling the pipe up to the derrick man. The two men on the floor pulled the slips out away from the hole, and the pipe then rose to the next section, and the process started all over again.

Finally all of the pipe was out of the hole and standing alongside the rig. The last section with the drill bit was pulled out and, using the tongs, the bit was unscrewed and a new bit screwed on. Then each section of pipe was reattached in reverse order, until all of the pipe was back down in the hole. This process was different, in that while the elevators were taken up to the derrick man's platform to clamp onto the next section of pipe, the lead man would be looping a chain loosely around the pipe end that stuck out of the drilling floor.

When the elevators clamped on to the next section of pipe and lifted it, the back-up man held it and guided it to a position above the section of pipe sticking out of the floor. The driller then gently lowered the top section into the bottom section. As soon as he did this, the lead man looped the chain from the bottom section to the top section, similar to the way you would snap a bull whip. The back-up man had to be ready for this because he had to cup his hands around the chain to prevent it from slipping down from the top section. The driller then engaged the motor pulling the chain while the lead man pulled on the other end of the chain, increasing the tension on it. This caused the chain to catch the pipe and turn it, screwing it into the lower section.

Many a finger was ripped off in this fashion. This step was repeated until all the pipe was back down the hole. Then another section of pipe was added, and the driller now had a fresh 30 feet of the square drill pipe sticking out of the derrick floor. The driller started the rotating drilling floor, and the drilling continued. After the trip was completed, we cleaned up our gear and relaxed until the next crew came on duty. It was hard, dirty work, but the pay was good, and we managed to save some money over the summer. It was also very dangerous work as the possibility of injury was very high, and occasionally men were killed on the job. When making the trip to change the bit, each of the four men had specific functions, and their timing had to be good or it slowed down the whole crew. Everyone also had to be very alert during the trip. When you lost focus of what you were doing, that is when you got hurt.

The derrick was rigged with a "Geronimo" line. This was a safety line for the derrick hand. Occasionally, oil or gas was discovered and caught fire unexpectedly while the derrick hand was up in the rig. This was his way of getting out of the rig in those circumstances. The Geronimo line was a long cable from the derrick man's level reaching out about 50 yards where it was anchored to the ground. An upside down "T"-shaped metal leg was attached to a wheel mechanism around the cable. To get out of the rig in a hurry, the derrick man straddled the upside down T with his legs, pushed off from the derrick, and the wheels gave him a safe descent to the ground. The wheels were also equipped with a brake mechanism so you could slow the wheels down as you neared the ground. The derrick man on my crew had never ridden the Geronimo down. He was actually afraid of it. I thought it was a lot of fun, and when things were slow I'd climb up in the derrick and ride it down, yelling "Geronimo!"

It was during this summer that I met my first true girlfriend, Dixie Rassette. Dixie came from north central Kansas and was a school teacher just out of college. She was just a little on the short side, and although slender, was not frail. One of the things I liked about Dixie was that she knew what she liked and was not bashful about going after it. Me, I was just learning to exercise my own free will after so many years in the seminary and the domination of my mom and older brothers. Dixie really liked me and made no bones about it. And when we were together, I really felt good just being with her. I had never felt like that before in my life. It wasn't a sexual thing; it just felt damn good.

However, my mom let it be known that she didn't care too much for Dixie because she wasn't Catholic. She was very cool toward Dixie during the rare times that Dixie was at our house. In Mom's mind, she thought Dixie was chasing me, calling me on the phone, etc., and she thought that was wrong. How I felt about Dixie never seemed to enter her mind. And I liked her a lot. It appeared to me that Mom wanted complete control over us kids and exerted all the influence over us she could muster.

One of the favorite night spots for us in Hoisington was the VFW Club. On weekends we all gathered there to drink and dance to the jukebox music. One of the weekends when Dixie came to town we had a great time partying at the VFW. As the evening grew on, Dixie wanted to get a little "fresh air," so we went outside. She wanted to walk around the block where there was a little more privacy. We looked up into the starry sky as we casually walked along, and then we stopped in the shadow of a huge tree next to the sidewalk. We stopped, embraced and kissed long and hard. It was really great being wanted by someone, especially by someone I liked. Dixie asked me to pick her up and carry her in my arms. She said it made her feel so secure just being carried by me. She wasn't heavy enough to really tax me, so I carried her like that for about a half a block. Then we stopped again and helped ourselves to more of that sweet kissin'. I really felt good being alone with her. Looking back, I felt a real bond with a girl for the first time in my life. After awhile we returned to the club and continued partying.

The summer gave way to fall, and it was time to go back to school at Hutch. By this time Tony and I had saved enough money so that we could buy a blue '51 Ford with overdrive. We rented a house on the west side of Hutchinson with two other students, Jim Mathews and Monte something. Monte didn't work out too well, so he soon moved out. Jim had been in the Army and had severely injured his knee. It constantly caused him severe pain. He was a good guy who didn't ask too much of you and tried to hold up his end. Tony and I both developed a strong friendship with him. We could see he was in pain almost all of the time; then he learned he had leukemia. Eventually he had to leave school and was admitted to the Veterans Administration hospital in Wichita, where shortly thereafter he died. It was a real loss to us, as we had also become friends with his family as well, including a very cute sister.

During the first few months of school, we sometimes came home to watch the high school football games. Hoisington was about 60 miles from Hutchinson, and we had to take county roads to get there. Most of Kansas is set up in square miles, so the county roads often went one direction for a couple of miles, then took a 90-degree turn and go for a couple of miles, forcing you to constantly slow down.

One Friday night, four of us decided at the last instant to go to Hoisington for the football game. But the problem was, it was due to start in about 45 minutes. We decided to make it anyhow. On our way out of town we picked up a pint of whiskey and headed for Hoisington. I was driving. The Ford had overdrive and I used it all the way. We passed the pint around periodically as we went, because we wanted to have a good jump on the evening by the time we got there. We were roarin' down the road, when all of a sudden I felt the steering wheel shudder for an instant, and then it felt like something hit underneath the car. But whatever it was stopped just as quickly as it started, and everything seemed okay, so we decided not to stop and check out the car.

We made that 60-mile trip in 45 minutes, and the bottle was empty when we got there. We got out of the car, and I checked to see what had happened to the car on the way. The left front wheel was turned so that I could get a good look at the tread. I almost fainted when I saw that there was a strip of tread, about 12 inches long and 2 inches wide, missing from the center of the tire. We must have thrown that during the high speed run to get to the game. Why the tire never blew out, I'll never know.

In a lot of respects Hoisington was an unusual town. Its population was about 5,000. Railroad tracks ran east-west right on the south edge of town. Just south and east of the tracks was a huge round house. I think it was the Union Pacific engine turnaround point. The round house is where the railroad engines turned around. They did so by driving onto this huge round rotating platform. After the engine was stopped, the platform then began turning until it had turned 180 degrees. The rails were lined up, and the engine was now headed back the opposite direction.

The roundhouse had not been in use for many years, and one summer the wheat harvest had been so good that the Bartlett Grain Elevator rented it to handle the overflow of wheat. Tony and I worked there, scooping wheat with shovels to help unload the wheat trucks. Later on, we also helped in the construction of another huge circular grain storage bin that can be seen all over Kansas, especially at Hutchinson. The circular frame was built on top of the foundation and left an area of about six inches between the inside and outside of the frame. Ribars, or metal rods, were placed in this space to increase the strength of the walls. As the concrete was poured, we jacked, or turned, a screw-like mechanism that gradually pulled the frame up. We poured more concrete, then screwed the frame higher, until we reached the height of about 100 feet. Some of the men couldn't stand that height and had to quit. But Tony and I took her all the way to the top, even though it got more dangerous the higher we got.

The area south of the tracks was called "Southtown." This is where all of the Negroes lived. I can't think of a single Negro family that lived north of the tracks. The streets there were gravel, the houses generally wood frame, and not well kept. Tony and I developed a friendship with one of the black kids from Southtown and frequently went to the swimming pool in Great Bend with him in our group. We didn't have anything against the Negroes, but were aware of the separation.

Southtown also had the "Big House," which was a multi-story whorehouse. As we got older and more daring, after a night of partying and the taverns were closed, we'd go down there in groups to get more beer. The air was always a little electric, because you never knew if one of the Negroes would get belligerent. We never, ever partook of the ladies of the night. Just one look at them and you could tell they were diseased and generally stoned. Besides that, they were ugly enough to make a strong man puke.

In Hutchinson, one of the favorite spots for the college kids was the Brown Wheel. It was a club where you could meet girls, dance to songs like Bobby Day's "Over and Over," and have some drinks.

One night Tony and I walked in, and right away we both noticed this very sharp chick. Without saying a word, we both knew we were going to put a move on her, because she looked like the best thing that bar had ever seen. I should tell you that all my life in any kind of a one-on-one contest with Tony, I usually managed to come out the winner. But not this time. Before I could blink my eyes, Tony was over in her booth, and the two were instantly attracted to each other. I never had a chance. I hated losing, but deep down I was very happy for Tony, as he really fell for Verlee, and I wasn't about to get in his way. If it had been anyone else but Tony, I would have. Tony eventually married her while I was in the Army.

Besides, I had a girlfriend, Dixie, even though she lived a long way away and I didn't get to see her that much. Occasionally, Dixie was able to come to Hutch, and she and I and Tony and Verlee went out to the Brown Wheel, or "Tan Spoke" as we tabbed it, and had a great time together. We danced a lot, and Dixie and I felt the need to go out to our car and get some "fresh air," a term we coined for kissing and romantic snuggling. We paid no attention to the sneering looks we got from the others when we came back in, because, frankly, we didn't give a damn. We liked the hell out of each other, and that was all that mattered to us.

We went swimming together with other couples in the Great Bend sand pits and did a lot of things together. I remember once we were returning from Great Bend after a movie with another couple, and Dixie and I were in the back seat. About a mile from Hoisington we began a long, sweet kiss, and our lips were locked all the way into town, across the railroad tracks and right down main street. We loved it, and the rest of the world could take a hike.

While Tony and I were going to Hutch, we had two younger sisters, Rosalie and Judy, who were either still in high school or a year or two out of high school. They had some classmates or friends, most prominent of whom were Mary Sue Anderson and Phyllis Neal. I wouldn't describe them as girls on the prowl, but our sisters thought it was a little bit odd that the only time they came over to visit them was when Tony and I came home from Juco for the week ends. Mary

Sue was really a nice girl. She had a great personality and enjoyed just being the average girl. Phyllis was a little pudgy and also came from a large family. She had a huge crush on our older brother Dave, but he was a little too old for her, so she didn't have a chance. When they came over, we inevitably put some 45 rpm records on and practiced dancing. While nothing serious ever developed out of these times, it did help Tony and me learn how to dance and mix with the girls.

When Tony and I came home from Hutch, the VFW was still our main spot. As time went on, a lot of my brothers and sisters wound up having a lot of good times there. I think it was there that my brother Max met his wife Opal. Max had also dropped out of the seminary, and Opal was in nursing school in Great Bend, 10 miles south. This was another time when two of we brothers stumbled across a real pearl, and I was blown away by Max. He really moved in on her, giving me no chance. Rumor has it that he told her the first night they met that he was going to marry her. And he eventually did. Anyway, Dixie and I were still pretty thick.

Back at Hutch without older brother Dave around to ride herd on us, Tony and I started to develop some bad habits. Our grades were okay, but we could have done a lot better. We just liked to party too much. And we didn't have much money, so we occasionally wrote hot checks at the grocery stores and bought beer. Then we had to beat the checks to the bank.

That's when disaster struck our family. It was in late fall of 1958 while we were at school that Dad fell out of a derrick and was seriously hurt. He was expected to be out of work for at least a year. The big problem was that there were still five kids living at home and in school. How was the family going to survive? Dave was a junior in petroleum engineering at Oklahoma University, and it was the kind of a degree that if you took a year out, you basically had to start all over again. Max was still in the seminary at the time, so he couldn't come home. I got a call from Mom to come home, drop out of school and support the family. There simply was no other solution.

So, home I came and started looking for work. There was an opening in Great Bend at Garvey Drilling, an oil well drilling company, for an inventory clerk. I applied for it and got the job. I was scheduled to go to work the following Monday. That night I got a call from the sheriff's department in Great Bend, wanting to know if I was going to be home the next day. I nervously said I would be. They wouldn't tell me what they wanted, so I had to wait until the next day.

When they came to the house, they placed me under arrest for writing a $10 hot check in Hutchinson at a grocery store. They transported me to Great Bend and put me in a cell. I thought my world had ended. I had known about the hot check and had given the money to Tony to take to the grocery store and pay for it. Instead, he had used it to buy beer and never told me about it. This was a major disaster. How was I going to explain to my boss at my new job why I failed to show up on the very first day I was supposed to go to work? I was miserable. As I sat there in that jail, I knew my whole life was over. I could never face my friends or family again. I was a convict. I made up my mind that if and when I got free, I was going to disappear and never return.

After I had been in jail about four hours, a deputy came to my cell, unlocked the door and ordered me to follow him. I was scared as hell. What was he going to do to me now? He had me sign some papers, and then he told me I was free to go. What? I asked why, suspecting all kinds of things. He told me that someone from my family had driven to Hutchinson, reached the manager of the store, paid for the hot check, and the manager graciously agreed to drop all the charges when he was told all the circumstances. I called home and told them I was released. I was very relieved when they arrived to take me home. That four hours in jail was probably the best thing that ever happened to me.

The following Monday morning I started to work at Garvey Drilling in Great Bend. I was officially an inventory clerk, posting to inventory records all the different sizes of drill pipe, fittings, bits, and oil well-related parts. We had a huge storage yard where they kept these items, and occasionally I would have to go out and do a physical inventory, counting each item. Because of my upbringing, the seminary, and the new responsibility of supporting the family, I was fairly conscientious in my work. After all, the whole family depended on me. I think I was making $450 a month. Even for those days that wasn't a lot, but at least the family wasn't starving.

Six weeks later my boss called me into his office, told me he liked my work, and said that the parent company, Petroleum, Inc., wanted to transfer me to Wichita to work as a production clerk. I told him my situation and said I would first have to work out some place to stay before giving him an answer. My dad's sister, Daisy Lancaster, lived in Wichita and said they could put me up for a small room and board charge. Dad let me use his own car, a '53 Chevy, a car that he was really proud of. So I accepted the promotion and moved to Wichita. After moving, each pay day I took a little money for myself and sent the rest home by mail. Believe me, Mom was really happy to have that money, and in no small measure it helped them through a fairly substantial family crisis.

But Wichita was lonely. I didn't know anyone. And bless her heart, Daisy could talk your arm off. About the only entertainment I had was to go to a small local bar and sip (yes, sip) a beer while watching TV. I didn't have enough money to afford drinking more than one or two draws. "Peter Gunn" was popular at that time, and I never missed it. There is nothing more lonesome than sitting by yourself in a small empty bar watching TV.

As the months wore on, I realized that I really needed to have my own place. I found a very small one-room apartment on Broadway, about five blocks north of where I worked. It had a small stove and refrigerator, and the rent was about what Daisy was charging, so I decided to move. After a few months there, I moved in with a couple of guys I ran across who had an apartment on East Kellogg. When one of these guys made a sexual advance on me, I got the hell out of there fast. I found another apartment the very next morning and was gone. It was on Broadway near Murdock Street.

Just as I had settled into a bit of a grove, my life changed again. It was around March of 1959 when I got my "Greetings" letter from the President of the United States. He wanted ME! However, since

I was the sole support of the family, the local draft board granted me a one-year deferment before having to serve in the Army.

As a production clerk, I kept a separate page on each well where the company was producing oil or gas; this page was lined so that each month I could record the total cost of the well, as well as the production in terms of dollars. With each new month's income and expense data, I graphed them by month and year. In this way management could look at this graph and visually see any trends that were developing on each well.

Another responsibility I had was to double-check the percentages of royalties for each well and apply them to the income to determine the amount of royalties to pay. Royalties were money paid by the producers to whoever had interests in the well. The producer generally paid the farmer or landowner a one/eighth royalty interest in the well production. However, the producer had to foot the entire bill for all of the drilling and producing costs *if* the well came in, or was able to produce sufficient oil to make the well a profitable venture. The producer usually had a seven/eighths interest. To lessen the financial burden to him of drilling the well, he then sought investors who purchased interests in the well. In many cases we had well over 50 royalty owners or investors. When contracts were submitted to us, my job was to double-check the addition of all the interests to make sure they totaled 100%. This entailed adding eight to ten decimal digits for up to 50 investors. Generally they were correct, but every now and then I found one row of decimals that didn't balance. I then took them into Roy Anderson, who got a bang out of this, because it made our company look good to all the outsiders. They had all missed it by the time the contract got to us, and we found it.

I was still going with Dixie, but since we now lived so far apart, the courtship waned. She did manage a trip to Wichita, and we rekindled the flames of affection. Her kisses were really sweet. Reminds me of an expression that my dad used from time to time. He'd say that was "as sweet as a woman's kiss and tender as a baby's breath." That was Dixie. I think it was in late fall of '59 that I saw

Dixie for the last time. I was in Hoisington for the weekend, and Tony loaned me his '51 Mercury so I could drive to Russell, pick her up and bring her back to Hoisington so we could all party again at the VFW club. It was on that date that she gave me a really nice gold cigarette lighter. It knocked me right off my feet.

We had a great time that night, but I had to make the 30-mile trip to take her back to Russell. Of course, on the way back we pulled off the road and smooched for a while. When we started to leave, I had problems with the car. As I pulled up to the county road back to Russell, the motor died, and I couldn't get it started. It had an automatic transmission, and they are very hard to push to get started. So here I was way out in the country, early in the morning with Dixie, and the car wouldn't run. I didn't think there was anything seriously wrong with the car, so I walked out on the county road and flagged down a man in a pickup. He was kind enough to get his pickup behind my car, pushed it out on the road, then get me going about 40 mph. The engine finally coughed and started running. We sped up and continued on to Russell, where we kissed good-bye before Dixie got out and hurried into the house. I think that is the last time I ever saw her. When I finally got home after dawn, I was as tired as a stray dog.

But back to Wichita. My apartment was right around the corner from the Murdock Lounge. Any place was better than being cooped up in an apartment, so I started spending evenings there. They had a shuffleboard, jukebox, etc., and I started meeting some new people. I developed a friendship with a couple of guys, and the three of us rented a three-bedroom apartment about a block from the lounge. These guys were a little older than me, were definitely straight, and we had a lot of good times together. We got so good at shuffleboard that when we walked in, we immediately challenged the winners of the two teams playing. If we won, the losers had to buy us a beer, and the challengers had to pay for the next game. Many were the nights that we enjoyed free beer and free shuffleboard all evening long.

On Sunday I went to mass a few blocks down the street on Broadway. I found out that there was a very active singles social club in the parish called the "Padilla" club. When I say active, I mean *active.* There were at least 100 members, and we religiously had a meeting once a month. We conducted about 30 minutes of business, covering things like dues, membership, activities, etc.; then we moved all of the chairs to the sides, had the tubs full of ice and beer, a phonograph, and danced up a storm. My two roommates and I formed a small three-man band. Bob nailed a round metal Schlitz tray to a mop handle and created some rhythm by tapping the mop handle on the floor and tapping the tray with a hammer handle. My other roommate played bongo on an upside-down bucket, and I played the trumpet, which was a toilet plunger. We wailed long into many a night.

I developed a helluva crush on a good-looking blond, who had what I thought was a really sweet personality. We happened to sit next to each other in a class out at Wichita University, so I got to know her. She was also a member of the Padilla club and occasionally came down to the Murdock Lounge. I made all the moves I could to get her attention, but, despite all my efforts, she was completely mesmerized by this totally worthless, arrogant jerk. To this day, I'll never figure out how some very sweet girls can be totally enraptured by some real losers. But then, I still remember what Dad told us boys. He said, "There is only one way to understand a woman … and it's a crying shame that no one has ever found it out." Boy, did he ever know what he was talking about!

The Padilla Club had so many members that we formed our own bowling league. I had never bowled much before, but did it anyhow, since there were a lot of girls and beer involved. Occasionally, we entered tournaments or bowling matches across town. I remember once we were all so drunk that we got confused and were bowling our balls while the rack was down. Once we reached that point, we knew it was time to shut it down. How we ever got away with that, I'll never know.

We also scheduled parties out at the local lake on weekends. Everyone was in their swim suits, and we took over a big section of the beach, swam and drank beer all afternoon and long into the evening. There was a pair of sisters in the club who were complete opposites. One was tall and brunette, and the other was an extremely small and frail dishwater blonde. She was so small that she had the lightest bowling ball she could find, and it still took an eternity for her ball to travel down the lane. We could almost drink a six-pack waiting for the ball to hit the pins. Both of these girls were after me, and when we were at the lake, the small one in her swimsuit inevitably finagled her way on to my lap, and I had the hardest time getting her off without hurting her feelings. She was almost throwing herself on me to the point that it was embarrassing and really turned me off.

For a while I ran with another friend named Murphy, who truly was Irish. We hit it off real well and partied hard together. One night, after a hefty amount of beer drinking, we felt especially daring. Anyone who was anyone knew about a whorehouse in the colored section of town. The smart ones also knew that it was pretty dangerous to go down there late at night after a lot of beer drinking. But Murphy was a pretty husky kid and I was no slouch, so we decided to pay a visit to this whorehouse.

We went to the liquor store next door, bought a pint of whiskey and headed for colored town. We found the whorehouse, got out of the car and were immediately greeted with loud noise emanating from the house. We looked at each other, shrugged our shoulders and headed on in. As soon as we got in the front door, it got deathly quiet. The front door opened into a large living room where a crap table had been set up, and a crap game was in progress. But it stopped the moment we walked in. There were about 15 of the meanest-looking Negroes we had ever seen, and they were glaring at us. The tension was so thick you could cut it. But fortunately, we came prepared. We pulled out our pint of whiskey, took the lid off, each of us took a swig, and then we handed it to the nearest Negro. This was the moment of truth. For a moment nothing happened. Then the Negro broke into a smile, took the bottle, took a swig, and passed it around. The tension immediately dissipated and the crap game continued.

We watched the game for awhile, when all of a sudden two Negroes started an argument over the game and began shouting at each other. Tension time again. Both men pulled out long butcher knives they had slid down the insides of their trousers, and we thought all hell was going to break loose. But the two worked it out peacefully, and soon they were back rolling the dice and yelling their heads off.

Murph and I wandered upstairs where the whores were. We weren't interested in doing business; we just wanted to look around. Some might snicker at that, but that is the honest truth. We walked into one bedroom, and there sat the ugliest, drunkest Negro woman I had ever seen. Not only was she ugly and drunk, but she actually had big scabs on her skin. Both of us almost lost it right there. I think that one sight completely sobered us up, and we decided to leave. We said good-bye to our "new" friends and left the pint with them as we left. We went straight home and crashed into bed.

In the fall of 1959, Judy came to Wichita to go to X-ray technician school. She was new in town and didn't know anyone, so I felt I should help her to meet some new friends. There was a Padilla Club function one night, and I had planned to take her to it. But first I stopped off at the Murdock Lounge for a beer or two. Then something came up and I stayed there a lot longer than I planned. By the time I went to get Judy, I had a pretty good glow on. As I was on my way, I passed a popular club where a lot of kids our age liked to gather. It was about the time that Bobby Darin's "Mack the Knife" was popular. The street in front of the club was a major boulevard, so there was an island separating the traffic. I was in Dad's car, his prize Chevy. I was traveling fairly fast in the far lane from the club so that it was on my left, and I had to look across the island to see it. I looked over to the club to see if I recognized any of my friends' cars, and then it happened.

All of a sudden there was a loud crash and I was hurled forward into the steering wheel and dash. Fortunately I wasn't knocked out, because I immediately got out of my car and very quickly saw that I had slammed into a parked car! How stupid of me! Not only did I damage the car I hit, but I knocked it forward into the car in front of it. The hood ornament of this car punched a neat clean hole in the trunk of the car in front of it.

I knew if I stayed on the scene I was a sure shot for a DWI. As people started coming up, I casually walked across the street, went into the club and got a cup of hot coffee. I needed to sober up fast. I drank it down as quickly as I could, then got some Dentyne chewing gum and started back to the scene.

The police were there when I arrived, and I told them I was the driver of the car. The officer asked me where I had been, and I told him I had gone into the club to call the police. I wore glasses then, and they had been knocked off. I told him that I couldn't see well without my glasses, and someone found them inside the car and gave them to me. The officer asked me if I was all right. I thought that was a little odd until I looked inside the car. My head had hit right at the center of the sun visor, bending it neatly. Both my knees had hit the lower part of the dash, slightly crunching in two round dents.

The officer asked me what happened, and I told him that as I was passing the club someone had called out my name. I turned to see who it was and why they called, and then the next thing I knew, the collision occurred. He must have bought my story because he didn't give me a single ticket. The wreckers came and removed my dad's car. It was completely totaled. Oh, boy, was he going to be mad at me! The collision also totaled out the car in front of me. I really must have been moving when I hit. Of course, who knows how fast I was going after quite a few beers? I guess I should have known right then that I had a drinking problem. At first, Dad was very upset over his car, but we had insurance and he was able to get a replacement.

By Christmas Dad was better and was able to go back to work. This meant that I could start keeping more of my pay check. I got a call from Mom, and Dave needed $30 to get membership in the Petroleum Club, a petroleum engineer club at Oklahoma University. He was now a senior and just didn't have the money, so I scraped it together and sent it to him. I think he still has a plaque acknowledging the membership. It obviously was pretty important to him, so I didn't mind it at all.

The following spring I got another "Greetings" letter from the President. This time I couldn't avoid it. I had to go. I turned in my resignation with the company, and they were disappointed that I had to go. I had developed a good relationship with the president, Paul Shivel, and we carried on a running debate over whether John Kennedy would win the election the following November. I was convinced he would, and Paul was on the other side. When JFK did get elected, I wrote Paul a friendly "I told you so" letter. I was surprised when he sent me a nice letter back.

I moved back to Great Bend, packed my suitcase, and on May 15, 1960, took the train to Kansas City to report for induction into the Army.

6

TWO-YEAR ARMY HITCH

(I'll Never Do It Again, but I'll Never Give Up the Memories, and Now I'm Really Proud of It)

I ARRIVED AT Union Station in Kansas City the afternoon of May 15, 1960. I was now 23. Apparently there were quite a few inductees, as there was a huge bus waiting for us, and we filled it up. We were taken to an Army facility where we were all given thorough physical examinations. They weren't trying to be nice to us; they just wanted to make sure they didn't induct someone with a real physical problem. That would become an even bigger problem for the Army after they were formally inducted. Yes, it included the embarrassing "coughing" routine. After they had culled out those with sufficiently serious physical deficits, there was a brief swearing-in ceremony, and we had to raise our hands and answer "I do." At that very instant we became the property of the U.S. Army, and they never, ever let us forget that. I was assigned a serial number of US 55694434 and told to drill that into my brain so I would never forget it. I guess it worked, because I still remember it.

We boarded a bus and were told we were going to Ft. Leonard Wood, Mo., a post in the south central Missouri area near Rolla. When we arrived, we were assigned a barracks, fed and bedded down for the evening. The next morning we were rudely awakened before 6 a.m. by a bellowing sergeant, yelling at us to get up, get dressed and get outside into formation. We then shuffled off to breakfast and returned to our barracks.

We were then taken to a supply section, where we were measured for our clothes and boots, were issued them, as well as ID tags, and returned to our barracks. There we changed into our new Army fatigues and boots. We were then marched to the barber shop for the traditional scalping, which I'm sure most of you have seen in movies or TV. After that, our training began in earnest. They made us "fall out," an expression for getting into formation in front of our barracks. They made us line up in four rows of ten to a row, an arm's length apart. The drill sergeant introduced himself to us. He told us that he was our "God" for the next eight weeks, and laid out his and the Army's rules and regulations and what we would be doing. Four of us were made squad leaders and placed in charge of our squad of 10.

One of the horrors of boot camp is "KP," short for Kitchen Police. If you were unfortunate enough to be assigned to KP, you had to get up at about 4 a.m., report to the mess hall and start peeling potatoes for the day's meals. You also had to help cook the meals, then clean up the mess hall; on top of that, you had to participate in most of the training of the day. If you drew KP, you did it for a week at a time. KP was also used as a form of punishment. If a recruit got into trouble or upset some of the cadre, they were promptly assigned to KP. I felt fortunate that I didn't draw a single day of KP while I was in boot camp.

At first, the bulk of the training was teaching us how to march. That is why they called our sergeant the "drill" sergeant. He drilled us and drilled us, for hours and hours. It really accomplished two major purposes. It helped getting us into better physical shape, and it gradually indoctrinated us into responding immediately to his commands without thinking. The Army didn't want men who were thinkers; they wanted machines that responded automatically to a command.

I'm not going to spend a lot of time going through all the training, as most people have a fairly good concept of it, either by having done it themselves or through the media over the years. But there are some notable highlights that I'll tell you about. Naturally we all had to learn how to shoot our rifles, the M14. The M14 had a 7.62 caliber slug, and the round was about three inches long. At one stage of training at the rifle range, the recruits stood inside a barrel sunk into the ground, so that the top of the barrel was at ground level.

This put us in the position of resting our elbow on the ground as we fired. We were in full uniform including helmets.

There was a tower located behind the row of barrels, and the sergeant in the tower was the command center for the firing line. Before any firing, he yelled through the PA system, "Ready on the right?", then, "Ready on the left?" If the firing line sergeants raised their hands, then he gave the "Commence firing" order. They were very, very cautious, because many of these recruits had never even held a weapon before.

One day a green recruit got confused and accidentally fired his weapon without the "Commence firing" order. Standing behind him was a big black master sergeant, who carried a baton. The master sergeant stepped up to the trainee and whacked him hard on his helmet with his baton. This totally startled the kid, who was already trembling. In a completely uncontrolled reaction, the kid jerked the rifle up over his head, and while it was pointed directly at the master sergeant's head, the kid accidentally pulled the trigger! There was a metallic click, and everyone froze in deathly silence. Then the master sergeant grabbed the rifle, checked it and found that there was a live round in the chamber, but for some reason the round hadn't fired. *It was a misfire!* That was the first time I had ever seen a black man turn almost completely white.

The Army was very touchy about what you called your rifle. If anyone *ever* called his rifle a "gun," they made him stand in the barracks in his shorts, holding his rifle for 30 minutes, telling everyone, "This is my weapon (pointing to the rifle), and this is my gun (pointing to his penis). This is for firing (the rifle), and this is for fun (the penis)." You only made that mistake once, and the smart ones never did. Watching one recruit do this was enough for me.

After about four or five weeks of boot camp, we all qualified for our first weekend pass. I think they wanted to allow us to blow off a little steam. And that is exactly what all of us did. Those who had girlfriends had them waiting just outside the main gate. As soon as they walked out of the gate, they took off together. Those of us who didn't have girlfriends took off for Rolla, the nearest town. It was

Saturday night and the bars and clubs were roaring. There were whores all over the place, and we had all just been paid for the first time. So everyone was dying for beer and some female companionship.

The biggest bar was a real zoo. There was no way that I was going to touch any of those "skanks." I was contented with just sitting at the bar, listening to Roy Orbison's "Only the Lonely" and "Pretty Woman," drinking beer, and watching what was happening. A lot of the recruits spent an entire month's pay on beer and whores on that one Saturday night. It got to the point that I would time some of the whores. I think the best time for taking a recruit out, taking care of him, and getting back inside for more business was a mere six minutes. It was a real den of iniquity, and I'm glad that I was only an observer. The next Monday morning there were quite a few recruits who stumbled out of the sack in bad shape.

There were two aspects of training that are worth relating. One was the 50 caliber machine gun night drill. The Army had built a 50-yard course that was covered with barb wire stretched in close intervals about 18 inches off the ground. They mounted 50 caliber machine guns and sprayed bullets about three feet off the ground, while we had to crawl on our backs with our weapons above us, under the barb wire fence until we had crawled the length of the course. As we were crawling, we could see the orange tracers of the machine gun fire, and we really hugged the ground. I don't know if it is true or not, but they said that one recruit years before had become hysterical, stood up frantically, and was cut in half by the machine guns.

The other exercise was a three-man assault on a designated point. This was designed as a 200-yard assault with very little cover. I was the leader of my group, and the objective was to direct one man on my right with hand signals to get up and run as fast as he could to his next point of cover. The instant he hit the deck, I was to then direct the other man on my left to do the same, then I was to follow. As soon as I hit my cover, I had to be directing the man on my right again. In this way we had to hop-scotch to our objective as quickly as possible.

I was fairly athletic and quick, and I must have drawn a couple of pretty good men for my trio. They timed each group to see how long it took. I was determined to move with lightning speed. I moved and signaled so fast that we never had all three men sitting in cover at the same time. We went down that course with the speed and quickness of a very combat-seasoned team. When we reached the end, the cadre were all excited, clapping their hands and yelling. "Now, that's the way to do it!" We must have broken the record. The reason this sticks out in my mind is that these cadre were not just military trainers. These were "lifers," men who actually had the experience of live combat in the Korean War. And for them to be that excited and smiling, I knew we must have done one hell of a job. They immediately wanted my name and wrote it down.

Soon boot camp ground to a close, and all of us received our new orders. I was ordered to get more training on the same base in BAAC, Basic Army Administration Course, or clerk typist school. This was a real blessing. I had the great education from the seminary, and now the Army was giving me intensive training in typing. I took full advantage of it.

There were 245 in our class, and among them were quite a few WACs. This was something new. In the Army with girls? It sure beat marching all day. Of course, we all competed for their attention, and, with odds of about 30 to one, not too many succeeded. I was one of those who didn't. At the end of each week we were given a comprehensive test over the material. This included typing speed, as well as English and other administrative skills. They posted the class standing after each week, and after about four weeks I was leading the class. This continued through the seventh week. We now had one week to go. Then I heard the rumor that whoever graduated at the head of their class was automatically assigned to Headquarters Company right there at Ft. Leonard Wood.

That was the last place I wanted to spend my tour of duty. Ft. Leonard Wood was called "Little Korea," because it was hot as hell in the summer and cold as the arctic in the winter. Besides, if the Army was going to take two years out of my life, I damn sure didn't want to spend it in the U.S. I wanted to go to overseas, preferably to Europe. So I completely blew off the whole last week, never cracked a book, and then purposely flunked the last week's test. Man, was I mad when I still won top honors for the whole eight weeks. I was really down in the mouth. Not only did I expect to miss going overseas, but on graduation day I had to stand up on the grandstand with the other top graduates and all the brass, while all the classes marched in parade in front of us. I had to stand at parade rest in the hot afternoon sun, while my classmates at least got to move around a little while marching. The brass commended us, gave us our new orders and we were dismissed.

I dreaded even opening the orders. Dismally I tore the envelope open. To my complete surprise I was ordered to report to Ft. Dix, New Jersey for two weeks of *Chaplain's Assistant school(?),* and then on to permanent duty in Augsburg, Germany. I literally fell off my bunk! I was going to Europe after all! Who cared what I was going to be doing there? I just wanted to get there! Then I realized that I must have been assigned a Chaplain's Assistant MOS because of my history in the seminary. Three years removed from the seminary, and it was still helping me out. The Good Lord sure worked in strange ways.

Two weeks later what seemed like thousands of us boarded a troop carrier in New York for the six-day Atlantic Ocean trip to Bremerhaven, Germany. Although there must have been at least 2,000 troops on that ship, most of us had never been on a ship that size before. It was okay for the first day or so. As time passed, I began to see some of the others bent over the rails, barfing their meals into the sea. But I felt fine. In fact, I was quite proud that by the third day I still had my appetite and even used some of the meal tickets that some of the sicker troops gave to me. The fact that I hadn't sat on the stool during those three days didn't bother me, as I thought it was simply constipation caused by the sea.

But the evening of the third day it happened. I was going up one of the stairwells to the upper deck, when a kid was coming down the stairwell. Just as we both hit the same landing, this kid suddenly upchucked all over the landing. The combination of the sight and the sickening smell hit me like a ton of bricks. I immediately started puking, and I know I would have made Mt. Vesuvius very proud. Up came three full days of food, all over the stairwell and down the steps. Men were trying to come up and down the stairwell, and as soon as they hit this spot, it started a chain reaction, and pretty soon there were six or seven men puking. I gingerly climbed my way out on the deck and seriously wondered if I would ever really survive. I gradually started feeling better, but I never used that stairwell again. And I really felt sorry for the poor souls who had to clean up that mess.

After six days the ship docked and I made my way to my post, on the Gablingen Kaserne in Headquarters Company in the 24th Infantry Division about five kilometers outside of Augsburg. This was to be my new home for the rest of my tour of duty, some 19 months or so. I reported to the company office, was assigned a barracks, took my duffle bag over and unpacked. We had about six men to our room, and each of us had a large metal locker and the standard Army cot. By now all of us had learned that you kept your locker locked at all times. It was an accepted fact that almost everyone was a thief. You simply had to operate on that basis for your own protection.

The next day I met my chaplain, Captain J.J. "Jarrin' Jack" Murphy. He was a native Irish priest and as gung-ho and hot-headed as they came. Our office was in a building where the only other occupants were the Protestant chaplain, the reenlistment office and the office for myself and the Protestant chaplain's assistant. There were storage rooms in the back, but they weren't used.

I settled into the normal routine of reveille at 6 a.m. when roll call was taken. If you were late, you were put on report, and this could haunt you when you applied for a pass. So most of us had our shirts out and unbuttoned, boots unlaced, and we looked like hell. It was generally dark, so the sergeant never really inspected us. After reveille we cleaned up and headed for the mess hall for breakfast and the usual SOS (shit on a shingle), sausage gravy on toast. Usually there was a jukebox blaring out the most recent popular tunes. After breakfast we had a period of drilling where we marched to keep those skills sharp. Occasionally, there was the mile run to help keep us in physical shape. Then we reported for duty at our office.

The Protestant chaplain's assistant, Jon R. "Jack" Stockwell, came over after I did, and while we officed together we got to be really good friends. Jack was from the Sacramento, California area and eventually brought his wife over. She was pregnant and had her baby shortly after she arrived. Jack was then allowed to move off base.

This was a very tragic friendship. I had received a knee injury requiring surgery at the military hospital in Augsburg. I worked this surgery to my advantage as much as I could. I knew that as soon as the surgeon released me, I would have to report back to my unit. During my recuperation, the routine was to get up about seven, make our beds (not bunks), have breakfast, return to our beds, and wait for the doctor's rounds. After his rounds, we essentially had the rest of the day free. We played a lot of pinochle, read a lot of books, got free coffee and cigarettes from the Red Cross cart that came along the hall, and watched free movies in the evenings. When you compare this routine with reveille at 6 a.m., obviously the hospital was by far the easiest duty. So when the weekly evaluations were made, I told the doctor that the knee still hurt like hell. He'd keep me in another week. I milked this as long as I could and squeezed out 63 days of easy duty.

While I was recuperating in the hospital, I was riding the elevator one day, when it stopped and two corpsmen wheeled in a cart on which there was a small bundle covered by a sheet. I asked them what they were doing, and they said they had the sad task of taking a little dead baby to the morgue. My heart hit the floor. Aw, man, anything but that. I mustered enough composure to ask them if they knew the name. They looked at the chart and read the name, "Stockwell." Then the rest of me hit the floor! Could that be Jack's baby?

As soon as the elevator stopped, I rushed out to the nearest pay phone and desperately tried to reach Jack or his wife. But I was too late. They had already packed in a flurry, and the Army had immediately flown them back to the U.S.; they were already en route. I was really disappointed that I didn't get a chance to express my condolences to either of them. I did write them, but that is not the same. Years later I was in California and called Jack and found out that he drove a Coca-Cola delivery truck. I few more years later I was out there again and called. His wife answered, and after the usual chit-chat I asked for Jack. She said, "Don, I guess you haven't heard. Jack got cancer about a year ago and died." I was stunned and could tell she was still hurting from his loss. Now she was a widow with kids to raise. Life just isn't fair sometimes, is it?

Shortly after arriving in Germany, I carried on correspondence with Dixie. It always gave me a warm feeling to get a letter from her. After a while she told me she had met another guy, and eventually they got to be serious. She finally wrote me and told me that he had proposed to her. I sensed that if I had aggressively pursued her, I probably could have changed her mind. But here I was across the Atlantic and all, and I didn't think I was ready for marriage yet. So I wrote her a last letter, wishing her the best of luck.

Before Jack's wife came over, we drank a lot of beer together at the Enlisted Men's Club in the evenings. They had that good German beer and it was cheap. This may sound sacrilegious, but in all fairness there just wasn't anything else to do. Occasionally someone who had seen Jack and me at church would come over and berate us for being "loose-moraled" and drinking. Our favorite reply was, "Yes, and we pick our nose and lust after sinful women, and we'd better see you in church on Sunday!" That usually shut them up.

Soon I met a very unusual fellow, Walter Bealer, from Atlanta, Georgia. He was truly intelligent and actually could hypnotize men there at the Club. I know, I have always been skeptical of such things, but I saw him do it on too many occasions. I've seen him many times put someone under, tell him that after Walter brought him out of his hypnotic state, when Walter touched his nose with his finger, that soldier would get up, go over to a wall, put his hand on the wall, and could not remove his hand from the wall. A few minutes after Walter had brought him out, he would touch his nose, and the soldier would do exactly as he was told. Then I watched as many as six soldiers try to pull that soldier's hand off the wall, and they couldn't do it. As skeptical as I was, he made me a believer.

Walter was really a fun guy. He was part of the great Southern aristocracy, spoke with impeccable grammar, and in that beautiful Southern drawl. He dearly loved his Georgia and couldn't wait until he got home. For that matter, all of us, from the day we arrived, started counting the days before we rotated back home. As your time got shorter, you became a "short-timer" and started using expressions like, "I'm so short I could sit on the edge of a piece of paper and my legs will dangle." Late one evening, a bunch of us were at a table in the cafeteria on the base eating bowls of chili. Walter was really short then. There was the ever present jukebox, playing all of the recent favorites like Faron Young's "Hello Walls," Leroy Van Dyke's "Walk On By," and Patsy Cline's "I Fall to Pieces." Walter was about half way through his chili, when someone played Ray Charles' "Georgia." When "Georgia" started playing, Walter had a spoonful of chili about halfway to his mouth. He literally froze, his thoughts and heart transferring instantly to his home in Georgia. His spoon fell out of his hand spilling chili all over the table, and he sat there in a teary-eyed trance till the song was over. He dearly loved his Georgia.

Jack and I really had a sweet arrangement. Since we both had to be on duty at the little chapel for services on Sunday, we were given a full day off during the week. We could sleep in, do anything we wanted. And when we were on duty, we had a very light load as a clerical assistant for the chaplains. We typed out a few forms, took care of our chaplain's appointment book, cleaned the offices, typed letters, and generally sat around and shot the breeze. Our chaplains had jeeps assigned to them, so we were responsible for the jeep and the little two-wheel trailer that went with it. When we went on maneuvers, we had to load up the jeep with the field altar tables, chalices, wine, hosts, etc. When on maneuvers out in the fields, the chaplains went to the soldiers and said mass where the soldiers were, giving them Holy Communion. I set up the altar, served the mass, and generally assisted Father Murphy.

Since I drove a jeep, I had to attend meetings on driving on the German highways, etc. One of the things that was hammered into us, was that under no circumstances were we to accidentally run over and kill one of the local citizen's chickens. It seems that the way the Germans looked at it, if you killed their chicken, you also deprived them of all the eggs and chickens that the dead chicken would have had. So, when one was killed by a U.S. soldier, the Army received a bill for $600. And the Army had to pay it.

The Army at that time had just introduced a new jeep. It was much lighter, wider, had a low center of gravity and, more importantly, it had four-wheel drive. The windshield could be lowered down toward the front and locked down. The four wheel drive proved to be a problem to me at a very critical time. We were on maneuvers, and part of the maneuvers included crossing a river about 40 yards wide. This was not your typical lazy, slowly meandering river. It had a wild rushing current, and you could tell right away that if you fell into it, it was *auf wiedersehn, adios,* and *sayonara*. They *might* find your body somewhere in the next country. To make matters worse, there was a steady drizzle, so the banks were very muddy.

The Corps of Engineers had constructed a pontoon ferry on the river and were ferrying vehicles across the river. My turn came, and I had no problem getting my jeep down the muddy side and out on the pontoon ferry. As we crossed, I could see that we really didn't have a lot of room on each side of the ferry. We reached the other side of the river, and the engineers anchored the ferry. They motioned for me to drive off and up the other bank. It was muddy and steep, and I knew it would take some expert driving to negotiate getting off the ferry and up the muddy bank. I thought I had the jeep in four-wheel drive and started off the ferry and up the muddy bank. However, as I got near the top it was evident that I wasn't in four-wheel drive. The rear wheels started spinning, and I couldn't make it. I braked the vehicle and slowly backed it down, got back on the ferry, and again tried to get it into four-wheel drive.

I thought I had it this time and tried again. But no, I had the same result, and I backed down a second time onto the ferry. This alone was quite an experience in itself. Finally, a mechanic hopped into the passenger seat, jiggled with the four-wheel gear and told me to try again. I did, and this time the jeep clawed its way up the bank and on to flat land. I thanked the mechanic as he hopped out, and it was only then that I realized how close I had come to a serious, possibly fatal accident.

About a year after I had arrived, we went on two-weeks, full scale, battle-simulated maneuvers at Graffenwehr. We were in full battle gear, jeep, trailer, tents, the whole works. We moved from one spot in the woods to another and slept in our tents at night. Father Murphy was my commander during the maneuvers, so I generally drove him wherever he directed. At night I bedded down in my little tent near our jeep and trailer. On one occasion, after I was in my sleeping bag, Jarrin' Jack slipped by my tent and whispered to get my attention. I answered, and he said, "Here, give me the bottles in the morning," and gave me a few bottles of that good old German beer. I really appreciated that.

The German bottles were unique in that they had reusable lids. The lids were held tight by strong wire springs mounted on opposite sides of the bottle. When you wanted to open the bottles, you pushed the wires one way on both sides and that released the lid. When you wanted to close the lid, you pushed it over the top of the bottle and pushed the wires the other way, sealing the bottle.

Toward the end of Graffenwehr's two weeks, we bivouacked the last few days in tents near some concrete block buildings. They served as our mess hall during the days, and movies with beer during the evenings. On the very first night there, we were watching this movie and drinking cans of beer, when someone tossed an empty beer can into the metal trash barrel right next to me. It made a loud noise during a very tense part of the movie and really upset one of the sergeants. He was dead certain that I had done it and didn't believe a word I said. Of course, the real perpetrator didn't step forward and take me off the hook. The sergeant reported it to the CO, who promptly ordered me not to drink any more beer the rest of the Graffenwehr stay. Damn.

Well, I had to drink something, so I decided to drink quart cartons of milk. I was drinking a carton of milk in the mess hall while my friends were drinking their usual cans of beer, when the CO walked in carrying a big stein of beer. I should tell you the CO was really one dumb, naive officer. I don't mean to be disrespectful, but he was just in some other world. He looked over at me, saw the carton, and you could tell he was convinced that I had beer in my carton instead of milk. His face told me that he was certain he had finally caught me disobeying a direct order. So he walked over to me and confidently ordered me to pour some of my "milk" into his stein. I told him, "But, sir, I really am drinking milk." He refused to believe me and ordered me again to pour away. So I did. Out came the milk into his beer. His face went a deep red, and he just turned around and walked out. We laughed about that for weeks.

Gradually, I developed a circle of friends from all parts of the country. There was George "The Hump" Hembt from New York state; he got his nickname because after he reached a certain level of drunkenness after a long night of drinking, he had a strange way of walking back to the barracks. He half-walked, half-stumbled bent over forward at the hips, so that he was staring right down at the ground. Frequently, we had to redirect the aim of his walk, as he would wander off course. Then there was Mac "The Mole" McClain. He got his nickname from working down in the armory way down in the basement. His job was to account for and oversee security for all of our weapons. Security of our weapons was obviously a very important concern. These two and I eventually inherited the dubious honors of being called the battle group boozers, because we could literally out-drink everyone on the base. There really wasn't much to do in the evenings, because they only allowed so many soldiers to have passes, and the rest generally didn't have much money. So we began spending many evenings at the Enlisted Men's Club on base, drinking beer and listening to jukebox records like the Drifters' "Save the Last Dance For Me." Five or six of us usually walked in together, and we each ordered a big stein. Jack Stockwell was usually always broke because he was either sending money home to his wife, or saving to bring her over. But Jack usually came along with us anyhow.

Those frosted German steins were huge; I think they held a full liter of beer. We really had to be on our toes after we were served. Jack had a partial removable dental plate with about three false teeth in it. If we let our guards down, the first thing he did was dip his partial plate very quickly in everyone's stein. Naturally, none of us would drink them then, so Jack now had five or six steins to drink the rest of the evening. We liked Jack a lot and knew his situation, so we only good-heartedly gave him hell for it.

One day the battle group had what they called a "field" day. It was supposed to be a morale booster, a day of beer drinking, outside games and a lot of interface between the enlisted men and officers. One of the events was an open wrestling match inside the motor pool building. A huge square mat was spread out on the floor, and anyone who felt tough enough could take on whoever was on the mat. When Mack, George and I arrived, a Spec 4 by the name of Parker was on the mat. I'd had a few beers by this time, and Parker really didn't look that imposing to me. We wrestled bare to the waist, so I could see he looked a bit barrel-chested, but beyond that, not that impressive. So I said I'd challenge him. Both Mac and George went bonkers. They pleaded with me not to do it. They told me Parker, who was about to rotate back to the U.S., had a reputation of being one of the baddest men on the Kaserne. But I'd had a few beers and was undaunted. I stepped on the mat, and the other soldiers gathered around, anticipating a slaughter.

Since I didn't know anything about Parker, I decided to adopt a defensive ploy. Parker stepped in, arms up ready for the attack. As soon as he got close enough, in a blur I grabbed his wrists with my hands. I clinched my wrists as tightly as I could around his wrists and refused to let go. Parker tried to get his hands free, but he couldn't. I could see a mixture of frustration and anger begin to cloud his eyes. Again and again he tried to wrest his hands free, but I doggedly hung on. By doing so, I had effectively taken his hands out of the match. He got more and more frustrated. Finally, he gave me the opportunity I was looking for. He threw his body sideways to try to get his hands free. I timed my move just right. When he was slightly off balance, I suddenly released my hands and went on the attack. I stepped right into him, chest on chest, got my arms around his neck and drove him backward into the floor, with me landing right on top of him. His shoulders slammed into the mat, and it was a clean pin. The match was over. I got up, casually brushed myself off and looked around for challengers. There were none, so I intimidatingly walked off the mat. As I took my fatigue top from Mack and George, they didn't have to say a word. Their wide-eyed look told me they had a completely new respect for me.

Germany was like living in a completely different world. The roads were used only by cars and trucks, no bicycles. Instead, and quite wisely, the Germans had built a narrow second road along the main roads just for the bicycles. And were there a lot of bicycles! The cars were primarily VW's or Mercedes Benzes. All the cabs were diesel-powered Mercedes. Since most of us had no cars, we used the cabs very frequently. The roads and streets meandered aimlessly in contrast to the square blocks and square miles of roads I was accustomed to back in Kansas. You could sense that the incongruity of it all was the result of literally centuries of time, and that the history of each road could probably be traced back to a point in time when it was a simple foot path. It felt strange being in a country where history stretched back well over a thousand years, as opposed to the few centuries in America. In just about every village I found entire sides of buildings painted with beautiful murals. I spent a considerable time just walking around places like Garmisch and Munich looking at and taking photos of these colorful murals.

Oktoberfest was a favorite time among the Germans. They set up huge beer tents, where you could get the biggest steins I have ever seen full of really powerful German beer. At one end was a stage about four feet off the floor and large enough for a complete orchestra. The orchestra played all the favorite German songs, and we all sang, soldiers and civilians alike, hooking our elbows together and swaying back at forth. The orchestras were very accomplished and professional. Although we were easily recognized as American soldiers, when I requested that they play "Stars and Stripes Forever," they played it with deep enthusiasm. Everyone was interested in just plain good fun, and there were no animosities at all during these celebrations.

However, in some of the people I sensed a love-hate relationship toward us. On the one hand, they seemed to hate us, because we came over the Atlantic and helped to crush them as a nation not much more than 15 years before in World War II. A mere 15 years before. There were still a lot of Germans around who had been in that war, and they had truly been a very proud nation. On the other hand, they had to face reality. They lost the war, and no matter how superior they might have felt, their country was now occupied with many U.S. military bases, and that provided a huge economic surge for their economy. That they liked. They loved having all of the U.S. soldiers spending their U.S. dollars in their country. You could see it in their eyes.

About a mile from our base was a little village called Gerstofen. As with every German village, it had its Gasthaus, or guest house (motel), where you could drink and eat into the wee hours of the morning, listening to the jukebox, and even spend the night in a bed with a mattress about 16 inches thick with what I presumed to be goose feathers. This was really going back in history. It was the favorite watering hole for me and my buddies. When we got hungry, we ordered food such as *wurstsalat,* or slices of German hard sausage and onions, doused with a weak vinegar. Mmmmm, it was great.

Although it would make some interesting reading, I won't spend a lot of time going into all of the nocturnal escapades that we engaged in, as that alone could fill volumes. I won't get into how we used many different ploys getting off and back on the base without passes, going over the barbed wired fences late at night, how I was able to go AWOL to Munich for a weekend and not get caught, how Mack, George and I could go down to Gerstofen and drink the whole evening for $5, or about some of the German girls, or *schatzies,* who were hunting husbands to take them back to the good old USA.

I had been hoping to go overseas so I could see other parts of the world. And now that I had made it to Europe, I wanted to see some of it. So during the summer of 1961, Mack, George and I took a week's leave to Paris. Paris. One of the cultural centers of the world. Our train pulled in, and we caught a cab to Pigalle. This was the section of town that we heard was the center of Paris' night life. We located some inexpensive rooms near Pigalle and then headed for the bars. We bar-hopped that night and weren't really impressed that much with the "can-can" girls and the overall night scene there. It just didn't measure up to what our expectations had been.

The next day we decided to see some of the sights. We started out with the Eiffel Tower. That was awesome. Over 1,000 feet high, and it was the highest point in Paris. From there, you could see all over the city. The Arc de Triomphe was another fabulous sight. It looked like it was solid granite, about 100 feet high, 20 feet thick, with the arc in the center and an eternal flame below. Circling the Arc was at least a 10-lane circular intersection. It appeared that all of the major streets started at the Arc and branched out into all directions, so that the Arc looked like the hub of a wheel of streets. Trying to navigate this circular flood of traffic was more thrilling than a New York City cab ride. It seemed like you had cars coming at you from all directions, trying to get to the inside or outside of the circular flow of traffic. Somehow we managed to get underneath the Arc on foot and took a closer look at the impressive monument. It was awesome.

The major promenade in Paris was the Avenue Des Champs-Elysees, which also led to the Arc. We walked down this very wide street, with trees growing in perfect symmetry along each side. There were numerous sidewalk cafes and bars, and it was very pleasant just sitting in the warm summer sun, watching this strange world. We found out that the next day or so there was the famous July 14th French celebration of Bastille Day, a day Paris citizens celebrated the storming of the Bastille prison, *built in 1383,* and marked the end of absolute royal power. That was over 200 years before America was even discovered! We were told to get there early, or we wouldn't get a good spot to watch. We did, and were glad we did. The French displayed all of their military might, their impressive cavalry, tank brigades, and thousands of briskly marching soldiers. They were in their dress uniforms and were very sharp-looking. The crowds along the street had gleams of pride in their eyes. Through the people you could feel the history. They were proud that they had thrown off the oppression of the monarchy and seized their own freedom, centuries before. And although they could easily tell we were American soldiers, they held no resentment to us. In fact, they were grateful, because we had helped to return their freedom to them less that 20 years before.

One of the thrills was to ride the "Metro," the underground mass transit railway system. This Kansas boy had never seen anything like this before. We could get anywhere we wanted to, and fast. We took the Metro to Notre Dame, the famous church with bells that were rung by Quasimodo, then the Louvre art center, and walked along the Seine. What struck me most about Notre Dame was the steps outside leading up to and into the church. They were worn very deeply from the stepping of the shoes climbing them. One look at them told me that they had to be centuries old, and that the number of people who had climbed them had to be countless.

One morning the three of us got up around noon with huge hangovers. We knew we needed some of "the hair of the dog that bit us," so we stopped at the first bar we came to, which happened to have the bar set up right on the sidewalk. We walked up to the bar, got our drinks, and turned to watch the French world go by. After a few minutes, a man walked down the sidewalk, and just as soon as he came abreast of us, he fell to the pavement and went into some kind of seizure. That really didn't help our stomachs at all. We weren't about to get involved, what with being foreigners, so we tried not to watch. We expected the bar owner to rush out and give the man some assistance. But he didn't. And neither did any of the other shopkeepers. Here this man was flat on his back in full seizure, and the people just walked right on by as if he didn't exist. That stunned us. Soon a police paddy wagon came by, stopped, and two police officers jumped out, picked the man up without a stretcher, tossed him in the paddy wagon and took off. We looked at each other in total amazement, then quickly had another drink.

When it was getting close to the time to return, George, Mack and I checked our return funds and found that we didn't have enough money to buy train tickets back. Oh, boy! We could just see ourselves being listed as AWOL and getting into all kinds of trouble. There was only one thing to do. One of us was going to have to wire home for funds. So then we got into a heated discussion over who was going to do the wiring. I finally gave in and wired home to my folks, saying we were stranded in Paris and needed money to get back to our base. We were told at the cable office that it would take 24 hours. We showed up the next morning hungry and almost completely broke. We waited nervously, wondering if the money was even going to come. Finally it arrived, almost $20. That was more than enough to get all three of us tickets and a bite to eat as well, so we headed back. We arrived back at the base on the last night of our leave, so we could be ready for duty the next morning. I was exhausted.

Reveille was at 6 a.m. The wake-up sergeant in our company was a Sgt. Schnack. Sgt. Schnack was a short, squat "lifer." A "lifer" was a derogatory description we used to describe a lifetime military man who lacked the brains or moxy to exist in civilian life and sought refuge in the military. Most of us in Headquarters Company either had college degrees or some college education. So we weren't stupid. And we openly ridiculed Sgt. Schnack because he had been in the Army for close to 18 years, and his rank was barely above ours. At 5:45 a.m. Sgt. Schnack came through the barracks, waking everyone up. He told me to get out of bed, but I told him I was on leave until 6 a.m. He told me to get up anyway and left. I decided to stay in bed for another 10 minutes. But before the 10 minutes was up, Sgt. Schnack came back, saw me still in bed, and told me he was going to put me on report for disobeying a direct order. That could have meant big trouble. He put it in his report, and I was called before the company commander. I pled my case, and the CO decided to give me an Article 15 (meaning it became a part of my military file) and restricted me to the base for a week. Big deal! I was so broke I wasn't going anywhere anyhow.

I settled back into my normal routine. I saw to it that the chapel was open on Saturday for confessions, and on Sunday got there ahead of time so I could set out enough wine and hosts for mass. I acted as usher, took up the collection, arranged for readers during mass, and sometimes served. After mass I had to take the collection over to the chaplain's office, count it, fill out a deposit, and turn it eventually over to the division chaplain. It was easy duty, since I got off a full day during the week.

I wanted to spend my Army career in Europe because of all of the history there. And although I had seen some of Europe, I still wanted to see a lot more. In late December of 1961, I got a call from a friend of mine, John Fitzpatrick in the Division Psychiatrist's office, saying he and Chuck Steiner, another Catholic chaplain's assistant in the 34th Infantry Division, wanted to take a two-week leave going all over Europe, and wanted to know if I wanted to come along. I jumped at the chance. My chaplain had left his 1959 Nash Ambassador with John while he was on duty with the 19th Infantry Division in Berlin.

So we all put in for leave and started making preparations. I borrowed some clothes from Jerry Poucher in C Company, had Sp5 Casillas arrange for some food from the mess hall, went to the company "banker," Bill Carruth, and borrowed $100. I'm not going to tell you the interest he charged. So I had about $120 cash, enough clothes and extra food to cut the meal costs.

We left on January 8, 1962, got on the Autobahn and headed straight west, bypassing Stuttgart. We crossed the border into France at Krehl. The border guards merely checked our ID cards and DA 31's (leaves), and waved us on without even looking into the station wagon. We drove through Strasbourg and started for Nancy. After we passed Nancy, we pulled into a little French village, St. Dizier, about 7:30 p.m. We decided to spend the night there and found rooms for about $1.25 apiece. We cleaned up and headed down for the little bar. We had a glass of wine for about eight cents, or 40 old francs. We went down the street to another bar and had some more wine, then continued on until we found a restaurant. I wasn't too hungry because I had eaten some salami sandwiches along the way from the food we brought with us. Still, my two buddies had filet mignon and I had a fromage (cheese) sandwich. We then headed back to our rooms and bedded down for the night.

The second day we were on the road by 8:30 a.m., and since we were only about 200 kilometers from Paris, we arrived there by noon. This is where the fun really began. The French drivers were absolutely reckless. It was a nightmare of "chicken." It seemed their objective was to see how close they could come to hitting you, without actually doing so. We headed for the USO to find some inexpensive hotels. To do so, we had to go around the Arc de Triomphe and along the Avenue Des Champs-Elyses to the USO office. We selected the hotel Villarret on the Rue de Acacias, where we found adequate rooms for about a $1 each. It was difficult finding parking because many European cities have blue parking zones where you are only allowed to park for one hour. Incidentally, this was the same hotel I had stayed at on my first Paris trip. We checked in, cleaned up and hit the streets right away.

Our first stop was Notre Dame. I wasn't too excited about it since I had seen it before, but I soon found out that I had missed the treasury of Notre Dame. It was only open at certain times, and we hit it just right. It was virtually a museum and contained old vestments, paintings, as well as chalices and ciboriums made of exquisite gold. They were hundreds of years old, and their value was inestimable. We spent a lot of time there, and it was around five when we left and found it was now raining. We ducked into this little café/bar right near Notre Dame, and had supper along with some good French wine.

We wanted to get into the Museum of Paris next, so we hopped the Metro and were there in 10 minutes. However, we were too late and found it was closed for the day. So we got back on the Metro and in short order were in Pigalle, the world-famous party spot. I quickly explained to Chuck and Fitz what was going on. We walked along the main street until a side street branched out. Lined up along both sides of the side street were the "ladies of the night," who were so old they looked like a Miss America contest, circa 1940. Ugh. Were they ever ugly!

We stopped and got some French hot dogs. They were made of a long, slender bun that was jammed down a long spike that heated the bun from the inside. Then they stuffed some hot mustard into the hole and shoved the hot wiener inside as well. Actually it made a pretty good hot dog. We then rode some bumper cars and finally landed at my favorite Paris bar, the Canada. We sat at the bar and warded off the women, drinking French beer till about 11:30, when we headed back to our hotel rooms and hit the sack.

On the third day we got up at about 8:30 and loaded up the car. I paid for the rooms with two cartons of cigarettes and got five francs to boot. We headed out of Paris towards Versailles where all the famous kings resided. You could spend a week there, and we didn't have that much time, so we drove around it, enchanted by the beautiful French architecture. We continued on our way, saying our daily rosary as we went. There were so many roads criss-crossing in Versailles that we got thoroughly lost. Finally we found the right road, taking us through old Orleans and Chateaureaux, where we entered the Army COMZ headquarters post. There we had some good American food for lunch, then continued on our way south through Limoges, finally stopping about 8:00 at a little French village called Brive. We wanted to get an early start the next day, so we hit the sack right after eating.

The next morning, our fourth day, we drove south, went through Toulouse and Tarbes, and arrived at Lourdes about one in the afternoon. It seemed unusual to us that we had sunny weather right up until we got there. As soon as we got there, it started raining. We stayed about 40 minutes, saw the religious attractions, got some Lourdes water, and continued on our way. We thought it was odd that as soon as we left Lourdes, the sun came back out.

We headed west toward Bayonne and Biaritz on the Atlantic coast. The country became quite hilly; I think they were the foothills of the Pyrenees mountains. We pulled into Biaritz, France about 8:00 and found a quaint hotel about four blocks from the ocean. The ocean air was refreshing. We walked around, looking the town over. We stopped at this café/bar establishment where they were watching television. We sat down, ordered drinks and watched television also. We couldn't understand it, but the realization struck us that their television was a poor copy of American television. The same was true with many things we saw, such as service stations and new buildings. We got the distinct impression that Europe was trying to copy America. This was followed by a deep sense of pride in our home country. It was evident that we were world leaders and other nations were imitating us. It really made us feel good.

A humorous incident happened while we were at that bar. The owner had a big white male poodle that was sleeping in a corner. The bar had an elevated section about five steps up. A man came in with a small black female poodle, took it up the steps and commanded it to stay at the top of the steps. While we were sipping our drinks, the male poodle got up and evidently wanted to check out the female. It got as far as the bottom step, when a sharp command from its owner sent it back to its corner. After awhile the male tried again, with the same result. After an even longer while, the male poodle tried a third time and actually got its paw on the bottom step, when its owner gave it the same sharp command. The poodle turned and looked forlornly at the owner, then sadly looked up at the cute female poodle, turned around, heisted his leg, *urinated on the steps,* and went over into its corner and went to sleep. I almost fell off my stool! If that male poodle had been human, I know exactly what it would have been saying.

On the fifth day, we got up and I used my battery-powered Norelco to shave. The electrical current in Europe is 220, so we had to bring along a transformer to reduce the current to 110 before we could recharge our shavers. We crossed the border into Spain a short distance south of Biarritz. I was amazed at how easy it was for us to go from one country to another. Less than 20 years before, World War II was being fought and all of Europe was dominated by Germany. Yet, here we were, going in and out of countries with very little scrutiny. All we had to do was show our DA 31s, and Fitz had to show his international driver's license, title to the car and insurance, and they waved us right on through.

So now we were in Spain, the third country on this leave. We drove along the coast to San Sebastian, stopping now and then to look at the ocean and take pictures. Once we arrived at San Sebastian, we turned inland to the east towards Pamplona. We wanted to take in a bull fight if we could, but unfortunately it was out of season, and we would have had to go quite a distance south to find one, so we discarded that idea. As soon as we left San Sebastian, the land started rising, and soon we were in hills, and then small mountains. The road became much more perilous. We finally reached the highest point, then started down, following a little stream that was flowing down out of the mountains. It was extremely scenic.

We wanted to reach Zaragosa to get some Spanish gas stamps at the air base there, so we drove right through Pamplona without stopping. If we didn't get to Zaragosa in time to buy those stamps, then we had to pay a horrendous 60 cents, or 75 pesetas, a liter. In Europe they sell gas by the liter, not by the gallon. We arrived at Zaragosa with plenty of time to spare. By now we had found the easiest way to find any American base in Europe. Rather than pour over maps and take endless wrong turns, all we did was pull over to the side of the street and park. Usually within a few minutes an American car came by, which was usually driven by an American stationed near there. They gave us directions we could easily follow, and bingo, we were on the base. And what a base this one was! It was the most modern military base I had ever seen, and realized that the Air Force really went first class. We bought our gas stamps, ate at the snack bar and continued on our way to Barcelona on Spain's east coast.

We didn't want to make it all the way there that day; we just wanted to get close. We wound up in a little Spanish town called Lerida. Lerida. Wow! Up to this point I generally was the one who suggested that we go out in the evenings for some beer or wine and had a bit more experience than my two buddies in that area. But on this night Chuck and Fitz couldn't get into our hotel, cleaned up, and back out on the street soon enough. Why? Because, as we were driving into Lerida, we all began to notice the vast number of very attractive young ladies. And these were not the Pigalle "ladies of the night." These were home-grown, normal and beautiful Spanish girls. The town was literally running over with them. And as we drove along the streets, we could tell that the local people didn't get to see too many sleek American cars, because everyone stopped what they were doing and stared at us. This was heaven!

We grabbed the first pasada we could find for about a buck apiece, changed clothes, and hit the streets. It was about 9:00. As we went out our hotel door, we stepped into a crowd of about a thousand people. They had designed the midtown district without streets. Instead of streets, there were very wide sidewalks with business establishments on both sides. We passed a bar and spotted a sizable party of very attractive girls inside. I call it a bar, but that doesn't adequately describe it. As we entered, we found on one side what we traditionally called a bar, serving beer, mixed drinks, etc. On the opposite side, however, there was a counter similar to what you would find in many drug stores in the USA; at his bar they served pastries, soda pop, etc.

We sat at the bar sipping our drinks and tried not to be too obvious in ogling the girls. It soon became apparent that we had a serious problem – the language barrier, even though it was obvious to all of us that we would have enjoyed each other's company. After a while they appeared to be leaving, so we decided to leave as well. (We weren't stupid). When we stepped outside, the most attractive of the girls approached us, and our hearts started fluttering. She began speaking in very broken English, and we were stunned. She had been studying English for only two months and had never had the chance to talk to anyone who actually spoke English. This was just the break we were looking for, so we started trying to communicate as best we could. We carried on for some time with our hopes rising. But, alas, we soon found out that Lerida was also a very traditional town, and one of the traditions was that everyone was home by 10:00 in the evenings. The girls soon left, and by 10:00 the streets we completely deserted. The contrast was amazing. At 9:00, hundreds and hundreds of people; at 10:00, not a soul in sight. What a disappointment. We had no choice now but to hit the sack ourselves.

The next morning, the sixth day, we got up really looking forward to this day. We were near Barcelona, a city on the east coast of Spain. Back on our post in Gablingen we had heard that Barcelona was *THE* party spot in all of Europe. I had already been to Garmisch, Munich, and Pigalle in Paris, so I knew this had to be something if it was superior to those spots. We wanted to eat first, and heard that there was a U.S. Navy store in Barcelona that had good food. We went to the port looking for it, but couldn't find it. However, we did find a U.S. Navy LST docked there. We decided to see if anyone was on board. We walked up the gang plank and whipped a salute on the officer, asking permission to come on board. He gave us an affirmative, and on board we went. He took us down to the board room, poured us some coffee, and we shot the breeze for a while. Eventually, some more officers came in, but none of them knew where the store was, so we left.

As soon as we left the ship, we bumped into a hustler, and he gave us directions to the store. He even gave us a map and showed us exactly how to get there. We were slightly suspicious about his motives and, sure enough, he wanted us to buy military gas stamps and then sell them to him at a nice profit for us. He would then sell them to the locals, making a nice profit for himself. We told him we would and left, but we never returned. We didn't want to get involved in anything illegal.

By the time we got to the store, it was closed. Two other soldiers showed up, also wanting to get into the store. We struck up a conversation with them and offered them a ride to their hotel. We had to stay somewhere, and this solved that problem for us. We got there about 4:00 and parked as close to the hotel as we could, about a block away. Fitz stayed with the car, while Chuck and I went in to register. That one-block walk was quite an event. It was like a war zone. There were at least 50 little girls, aged from three to nine, who were begging for a peseta from us. There were also at least 10 men, literally *begging* to shine our shoes. What really impressed us was that all of this was taking place right downtown. We checked in and returned to the car. When we arrived, Chuck was just finishing up getting his shoes shined.

Or so he thought. He took in the sights, not paying much attention, as the man worked on his shoes. In about two minutes the man had put on new half-soles, and demanded 105 pesetas, or roughly $2. That was enough for two nights at the hotel. Oh, well!

We had some souvenirs we wanted to get while we were there and set out doing that first. I promised to get a bottle of Quarentra-Treys for a waitress at the Enlisted Men's club and a rag doll for Stockwells' baby girl. Chuck and Fitz found what they wanted, and we returned them to our rooms. It was now time to eat, and we found a cafe nearby. We ordered steaks and made sure that the waitress understood that we wanted them well-done. The Spanish liked their meat rare, and if you didn't make this very clear to the waitress, you were served a steak that was so rare it was almost bleeding.

Well-fed, and pretty well ready for some serious partying, we left the café. Before we had left on this trip, I told both Chuck and Fitz that, while I wanted to see as much as I could of Europe, when we got to Barcelona, I wanted to do some very serious partying. They both said they had the same idea, and so off we went.

We started at the Pan Am bar and were talking to an American oil man, when I glanced up and saw a buddy from C/S Company back on our post. I knew there were quite a few soldiers from our post who partied down here, but didn't expect to run into one so soon. I went over, said, "Hi," and he told me there were more men from our post upstairs in the main part of the bar. So upstairs we went, and found no less than eight other soldiers I knew from my post. When one of them saw me, he jumped up and yelled, "Hey, girls, here's a live one!" Immediately I was besieged by at least five ladies of the night. If I could have made it to the buddy who yelled, I would have let him have it right there. Finally I sicked them on to Chuck and Fitz, who didn't want to have anything to do with them. I finally got over to my buddies, sat down, and right away was offered a marijuana joint.

I have always been apprehensive of doing anything but alcohol, and maybe a very rare "Bennie," or Benzedrine. I've always been afraid that if I took something like that, it would lead to something stronger, and pretty soon I could see myself hopelessly hooked on something powerful like cocaine. So I turned it down and stuck to plain old alcohol.

This place was really too wild for me, and I finally got tired of turning down one lady of the night after another. So I collected Crowley, Fitz and Chuck, and we found a nice quiet bar down some stairs below a restaurant, called the "Kit Kat." We ran into some more buddies from our division there. After a few drinks, two of my buddies wanted to take Fitz to the "Tequila" Bar for some tequila. By 11:00 Chuck was pretty high, so I helped him back to his room and got him settled down. I was worried about Fitz, so I headed for the Tequila Bar, too. I bumped into him as he was staggering out. God, was he drunk, and he had no idea where he was. It took me a while to get him to his room and into bed, but I got it done. I went back to the Kit Kat, had a few more drinks with my buddies, and hit the sack myself.

I woke up the next morning around 11:00. This was the seventh day of the leave, January 14, 1962. It was Sunday and the three of us wanted to go to mass. However, Chuck and Fitz were gone from their rooms. I looked around for a church but couldn't find one. I returned to the hotel, and by this time Chuck and Fitz had returned. They gave me directions to the church, and Fitz went back to his room to bed. He was really hung over. It must have been the first time that he was what I would call "smashed."

I made it to the Cathedral of Barcelona in time for the 12:30 mass. It had been built in the 15th century and had the Spanish motif. The floors were worn down from centuries of people shuffling across them. It reminded me of the steps to Notre Dame in Paris. There were many altars along the sides, with about six masses going at the same time. I found one that had just started and went to mass. When I returned to our hotel, Fitz said he felt well enough to hit the road again.

We hadn't gone very far when Fitz pulled over, got out and got rid of an orange he had eaten that morning. A little bit further, he stopped again and got rid of it again. Fitz just couldn't handle any more, so I took over driving while he crapped out on the back seat. After a couple of hours, I pulled over to get some gas, and by then Fitz had recovered enough to take over driving. We crossed the border into France just north of Figueras on the Mediterranean. We stopped to eat at a very small French village, and by this time we had all recovered enough so that we really were hungry. We decided to eat in grand style that night, regardless of cost. We gobbled up the appetizer, tore into the main course, then munched on the delicious fruits and vegetables. That was the most expensive meal of the trip, and we enjoyed it to the fullest. It cost us about $2 each.

We climbed lazily into the station wagon and got back on the road. I sat in the back seat, and the combination of the previous night's escapades and the fabulous meal had me dozing off in no time. About 11:30 they woke me up. They had pulled off the road, told me we were a few miles outside of Avignon, and that we were going to camp out that night. We got out our sleeping bags and air mattresses and bedded down.

About eight the next morning, the eighth day, we were up and rolling. Father Murphy wanted us to wire him on the 15th to let him know how we were doing. He was planning a leave as soon as we got back, and he needed to make sure the station wagon was back. We pulled into Marseilles, found a telegraph and told Father all was well. We told him to wire us in care of the USO in Rome if he needed anything, since we expected to be there the next day.

Leaving Marseilles, we followed the French Riviera east towards Rome. This was some of the most beautiful scenery I had ever seen in my life! Since it was mid-winter, the climate was too cold for swimming, so we didn't think we should waste our time on the beaches. There were many palm trees along the streets and roads, and we saw very many expensive, chauffeured limousines. This continued all along the French Riviera, through Toulon, Cannes and Nice, and across the border into Italy. Again, we were amazed at how the border guards just waved us on through. It sure made us proud to be Americans. We must have really demonstrated some awesome power during World War II.

Soon we came into Monaco. It was right on the sea, and very mountainous. The scene was right out of the movies. We couldn't pass up the world-famous Monte Carlo casino, so we drove down to it. Since it was way out of our league, all we wanted to do was take a look at it. As we slowly drove around Monte Carlo, we saw about a thousand guards and hundreds of fabulous automobiles. We could easily see that this was the world's greatest gambling spot.

We continued along the Riviera until we reached a small village called Verazze. We found a room at the pensione for about $1.30 each. After a few glasses of wine, we hit the sack a little early, since we hoped to reach Rome the next day.

The next morning, the ninth day of the leave, we ran into the worst driving conditions of the whole leave. The roads weren't in poor condition. It's just that we were either going up a long, steep climb or coming down a long stretch, having to slow down for one sharp curve after another. Since the road followed the edge of the Mediterranean Sea, we were treated to one breath-taking sight after another. First the sea, then the beautiful mountains. Our eyes just didn't deserve the prolonged and repeated fantastic scenery. We slowly made our way to Genova, went right through it and continued to Livorno. There was an American base there, Camp Barby, and we wanted to get some Italiana gas stamps. If we didn't, then we would be paying 100 lire a liter, or 400 lire a gallon, or 65 cents a gallon.

We reached Pisa and stopped to see the famous leaning tower. It was an awesome sight. We picked up a couple of swabbies whose carrier was anchored about a mile outside of Livorno, and they took us to Camp Darby. We got the gas stamps; then the five of us went over to the snack bar and got some good American food. We called them swabbies, and they called us shallow mud marines. Fair enough. They invited us out for a tour of the carrier. We really wanted to go, but we had to wait for a boat to take us out to it, and that would have really ruined our time table. So we had to decline the offer. They, in turn, offered to show us around a destroyer that was anchored about a hundred yards away. This we could do, and did. After that tour I was sure glad I was in the Army. Those poor sailors were so crammed for space, it reminded me of the troop ship.

We got back on the road about five and got as far south as Crossetto, where we decided to spend the night. I have to say that, so far, of all the countries we had been to, the one I liked most was Italy. The weather was sunny, the scenery was by far the most beautiful, and the Italians treated us like a million dollars. We ate, then stopped in this little bar for some good Italian wine. After a few glasses, I decided I wanted a Nikolaski. We had this drink frequently back in Germany. It's made by laying a slice of lemon over a shot glass of cognac. You place a teaspoon of coffee and a teaspoon of sugar on the lemon slice. Then you put the whole lemon slice in your mouth, chew it up, and wash it down with the cognac. They didn't serve that drink, but had the ingredients, so I made it myself for about 17 cents. After a couple of those I was really ready for bed.

The next morning, the tenth day, was **THE DAY**. Today we were to be in Rome, the headquarters of Catholicism and site of almost everything famous in our church. We made it by 10:00, coming in on the via Aurelia. We found the USO, picked up the wire from Murph, telling us he was expecting to go on leave on the 22nd. We wired back that we would be back on the 21st. This was the 17th.

I knew there were some SVDs from Techny going to college in Rome, so I looked up the SVD number and called them. I reached a Fr. Wiltgen, who told me there were about 10 or 15 men there from Techny. He invited us out the next day, but told me to call first so he could round up some of the USA SVDs to meet us. We then found a hotel, checked in, and this time we took a lot more care in cleaning up. Rome was to be the epitome of the leave, and we wanted to see it in grand style.

We then went downstairs to eat what was our first real Italian meal. The Italians are never in a hurry to eat. They take their time. The waiter gave us a menu in English so we knew what we were ordering. We started with the appetizers, and I had a bowl of vegetable soup. It was the best I'd ever had, thick, with lots of vegetables. The main course followed only after everyone was finished with the appetizer. Then came the fruits or dessert. It was superb food, a real Epicurean delight.

Now we were ready for some serious sight seeing. At the top of our list and right up the street within walking distance was St. Peter's. We got there very quickly and started exploring it. There isn't a language sufficiently developed to describe it fully. As we stood in the center of the church, there were countless famous statues, including what looked like tiny cherubic angels along the walls. From where we stood, the little angels' hands appeared to be the size of tiny doll hands. But when we walked over to them and placed our hands over the angels' hands, our hands only covered about half of each hand. Everything was perfectly proportionate, and that is why they appeared so small from a distance. We took our time and thought we had covered it pretty thoroughly, but found out later we had only scratched the surface. When we thought we had seen everything, we headed back for the car, as the rest of the sights required driving.

We drove aimlessly for a while; then Chuck suggested we make a dry run on the SVD house, so we could find it easily the next day. It took us some time to find it, but we did. Once there, we felt we ought to say hello, so we knocked on the door, and a diminutive pious brother ushered us into a waiting room. It wasn't long before there was a knock on the waiting room door, and in walked Dan Crowley. I couldn't believe it. He and I had been classmates for the six years I had been in the seminary, and I hadn't seen him in five years! We spent what little there was left of the afternoon bringing each other up to date, and made arrangements to pick up Dan and two of his companion "Fraters" the next morning to tour the city. God, what luck! Not only were we in Rome, but we were also going to have personal guides from some clerics who lived there. Wow!

The next morning, the 11th day, we woke with delirious expectations for the day. We skipped breakfast in a hurry to get over to Frater Crowley. They were waiting and were quite impressed with the late model American car. There were three clerics, Dan, Ed Gabe, who was to be ordained a priest the following March 17, and Jim Martin.

They took us first to the Circus Maximus, where most of the Christians were martyred. I have to be candid. It looked like an ordinary race track of some sort. It felt strange being in a place where 1,900 years ago the blood of Christian martyrs had been shed. I wondered how deep their faith must have been, and how brave they had to have been, wondering if I would have had that same courage.

From there we went to the Church of St. Alexi. Alexi was said to have come from a very wealthy Roman family, then left all his wealth to follow Christ's teaching. He remained a pauper by choice, and years later returned to live as a beggar under his own father's steps for 18 years without his family even knowing who he was. We stepped to a very old, thick door that was the center of interest, as there was a small keyhole in the middle of the door. When you peered out through the keyhole, you had a direct sight to St. Peter's.

The Vatican Museum was our next stop. We had missed it the day before because we didn't know it even existed. Thank God for our cleric guides. It was filled with the famous works of the world's greatest artists, including Michelangelo and Raphael. We passed through the famous Sistine Chapel and Michelangelo's famous paintings. Our clerics pointed out that, at that time in history, Raphael was actually recognized as the number one artist in the world, and Michelangelo, second. However, Michelangelo could turn out a complete figure in five days, whereas Raphael took a month. So Michelangelo was chosen.

The figures on the walls and ceilings, even after centuries of time, seemed so alive that I almost expected them to leap off the walls. We saw hundreds of priceless drapes, statues and mummies, until we completely lost the ability to even begin to comprehend the beauty and worth of the things we saw. To this day, I have not seen a museum that could even come close.

Then we went to St. Peter's, this time the right way, with clerics. As soon as we entered the main entrance, Frater Jim Martin pointed out that when you walked up the center of the church, you found little bronze plaques in the floor. These plaques were measurements of how far the largest churches and cathedrals of the world would reach from the back of St. Peter's, if they were placed *inside* St. Peter's. We read the plaques as we walked along and found the one for St.

Patrick's Cathedral in New York. It came about halfway inside St. Peter's. Our guides told us that the inside measurements from the entrance to the rear was 212 yards. That's more than two football fields! We all felt like a mere speck of dust in history.

Our clerics then ushered us to the treasury of the Basilica. This included too many priceless items to enumerate, but among them was a chalice made of pure platinum. We were then taken to the elevator to the Dome, something else we had missed. The Dome is 435 feet high. We got as high as 380 feet, where we could step out and gaze at all of Rome and its many historic edifices. The clerics pointed out the Ethiopian seminary that had been moved inside the Vatican when Mussolini was invading and conquering Ethiopia. When we stepped inside, we found that if we placed our mouths close to the walls and made a sound as quiet as a whisper, it traveled all the way around the dome, and we could hear it very clearly when it come back to us.

By then it was time to eat, and our guides had the perfect place for us. After all, a couple of them had been in Rome for a few years and knew the right places. We started our meal just before 1:00 with real Italian spaghetti and meatballs. This was washed down with some Chianti and allowed to settle. We were then served the main course, and finally, the dessert. By the time we left, we had consumed three bottles of Chianti and it was now 3:00. It had taken us two hours to eat.

The clerics suggested a short road tour outside Rome, and off we went. We saw various historical structures, roads, and came back into Rome on the famous Appian Way. This was the famous road that I had studied in the seminary when we had to translate the Latin *Julius Caesar.* I had expected it to be some wide, beautiful boulevard, but it was barely wider than a two-lane street and reminded me of a typical side street back home. We could tell it had carried centuries of travel. I knew this was the road that Roman emperors and Generals traveled many centuries before.

The catacombs were the next stop. We paid the small entrance fee and had to wait a short while for an English-speaking guide. As we started down, the guide explained to us that the tunnels, if laid in a row, would extend 10 miles. He showed us the little underground Chapel of the Popes, where some of the martyred popes were said to have been buried. Next came the Chapel of St. Cecilia. Cecilia was a very beautiful young virgin who refused to give up her faith. The Romans had attempted to suffocate her in one of the baths, but when they returned later to dispose of her body, they found her still alive. So they decided to behead her right there on the spot. They swung the sword three times, and *still* didn't get the job done. So they just left her there, and soon she died. Other Christians found her body, took it to the catacombs and buried it. In the year 1529 they opened her tomb *and found her body still completely intact!* It's unbelievable! And I understand that her body is still intact to this day. We finished the catacomb tour and returned to our car. It cast a pall over us to see first-hand the persecutions these early Christians had suffered and the strength of their faith. I couldn't help but wonder if my faith would have been that strong.

We continued around Rome, saw famous church after famous church, and then were shown the famous statue of Moses that Michelangelo had sculptured. When he had finished it, it was so lifelike that he commanded it to speak to him. When it didn't, he became so angry that he took his hammer and struck it on its knee. The blow chipped a piece off the knee, and it has been that way to this day. We saw another church that was famous because its ceiling was laid with the first gold that Columbus brought back from the new world. We toured the Coliseum, then the forum where all the famous speeches were given.

Right next to the forum was the Maritime prison, where the Romans kept and killed all of their enemies. St. Peter himself was said to have been kept there, and made a little fountain so that he could baptize the guards that he had converted to Christianity. It was a very small, two-room prison, on the same level as the entrance to the forum. Whenever a famous general entered Rome on a triumphal procession, his number one prisoner was killed in the Maritime prison at the precise instant that the general passed under the arch into the forum.

It was starting to get late, but our clerics had two more things that they wanted to show us. First was the "Church of the Bones," as our friends called it. And it was open only to clerics and their guests. What they wanted to show us was actually located below the church. They showed us four subterranean chapels with altars that were made out of the bones of *4,000 Capuchin monks!* We could actually see the real bones, and wondered how many of these pious monks were actually saints, looking down to us from heaven. This was unbelievable.

The last stop was the Fountain of Trevi. There was a legend that if you tossed a coin into it, you would at some later time return again and throw another coin into the fountain. I tossed my coin in, and my two buddies snickered. But who knows? By then it was so late that we had kept the clerics right through their supper. So we decided to treat them to a quick meal before getting them back. All we could find on short notice was some pizza and beer. The pizza was awful, but that beer sure was good. We hurried and got the clerics back just after 8:30, a little late for their evening vespers. We thanked them profoundly, as they had given us the tour of our lives. Literally. We got back to our hotel, had a few drinks at the bar and hit the sack, numbed by all that our human eyes has seen that day.

The next day was the 19th, our 12th day of leave. We told Murph we'd be back on the 21st, so we had some traveling to do. We backtracked to Livorno and Pisa, stopped at Camp Darby for lunch and some good old American food, and got on the autostrada (turnpike) to Prato, just outside Firenze. Then we took another autostrada through Bologna to Modena. There we left the autostrada and headed straight north. Our goal was to get to Verona, as that would put us close enough to Gablingen, so we could return in time the next day. We reached Verona, but the hotel prices were completely exorbitant, so we decided to go a little further. We were entering the Alps, so there weren't too many hotels. We found what amounted to a European truck stop, judging from the 20 or so trucks parked outside. European trucks were different than the ones we were accustomed to in America. They looked a lot bigger and usually had a second, and sometimes a third trailer.

We checked in, went downstairs to eat, then settled into the bar. A cute waitress flirted with us, and we with her, but that was all it was, a flirt. I wound up watching an entire movie on their TV and didn't understand a word that was said. We were all pretty tired, having traveled 450 miles, the most we had done on any day on the leave, so we hit the sack.

The next morning, the 20th and 13th day of the leave, we knew that, with a little luck, we could make it all the way back. When we first started, it looked like a bad driving day with clouds and drizzle, but as we drove along, the clouds disappeared and were replaced with beautiful sunshine. We were getting closer and closer to the heart of the Alps and intended to cross them at the Brenner pass. We went through Trent and Bolzano, then headed for the Italian-Austrian border. After exchanging our Italian money for Austrian Schillings, we crossed the border right at noon, again amazed at the ease with which we passed through the border guards. Our timing was just right. There was a lot of snow, and this slowed us down some, but we thoroughly enjoyed this part of the trip. Mile-high mountains were on both sides of us, taking our breaths away as we went along. One beautiful scene followed another as we headed for Innsbruck. This appeared to be a fascinating place to visit, maybe even to live, but unfortunately, we didn't have time right then to explore it. So on we went, without stopping. Soon we crossed back into Germany at Garmisch. We stopped there and had a big steak dinner. It was great. Fitz had been shaving on paying his fair share, so Chuck and I ganged up on him and made him pay for it. Fair is fair. In another two hours we were back in Augsburg. It was Saturday afternoon, and the post was almost deserted. We felt as though we had been completely around the world. We had driven 3,500 miles in 13 days, had been through seven countries, to the Atlantic coast, all along the Spanish, French and Italian Rivieras, saw the secrets of Rome, the beautiful Alps, and I could go on and on. The trip cost me $110. It was the trip of a lifetime.

It was late January, and I was due to rotate back to the States in May. Four months. I was becoming a real short-timer. Somehow the normal routine got to be less and less important. My thoughts started gradually gravitating to going home, seeing my parents, brothers and sisters, and what I was going to do with my life. I had read a book about the famous lawyer, Clarence Darrow, and that caught my interest. I started thinking a lot about becoming a lawyer after that, and from then on that was in the back of my mind.

I decided not to let anyone back home know when I was going to arrive back in the States. I wasn't too sure myself when it would be. The Army gave me a complete physical, because when they let me go they wanted proof that I was in top physical shape. This was part of the rotation process for everyone. They didn't want anyone to come back after their discharge and claim they had an injury that related back to their military service.

Soon, my time came. I said my good-byes to all my friends and packed my duffle bag with the things I wanted to bring back. When I went down to the Administration Office to get my orders, the Administration Captain called me in for a final chat. I'll never forget what he said, because he really knew what he was talking about. He said, "Hochanadel, I know all about you and your beer-drinking reputation. And before you left, I wanted to tell you that if you could ever get rid of your drinking, you're going to be all right." I felt a twinge of guilt, because deep down I knew he was right. I knew I had been drinking far too much, but just chalked it off to the boredom of military service. I thanked him, got my orders and left for Bremerhaven. I had some friends in the medics, and they gave me some pills to prevent sea sickness. Thank God for that.

The voyage back was a thousand times more pleasant than the one coming over. I can remember leaning on the rails at night, looking out over the sea, with the big moon hanging on the horizon. That is a very romantic and sentimental sight. The light from the moon descended to the horizon, then came in a beautiful line right up to the ship. It made me feel all warm inside, at peace, and happy to be alive.

When we docked in New York, I was in for another surprise. I felt they would just hand us our last pay, give us our discharge and then we were free, no longer property of Uncle Sam. Instead, we had to take everything out of our duffle bags and pass an inspection of everything we were bringing back into our country. This was a more thorough check than we had experienced while passing in and out of countries all over Europe. While I resented the intrusion, I was actually a little more proud of our country. I felt the U.S. was a lot more selective than the other countries as to who and what they let into their country. I finally passed inspection (they found nothing), got my discharge and final pay, and caught a cab to Grand Central Station. My military career was now officially over.

7

CHICAGO'S TWO YEARS

(The Elixir of Love, the Trauma of Tragedy, and the Beginning of Metamorphosis)

SO, HERE I was, a civilian at last. I was now 25, and a free man again. God, did it feel good! I browsed around Grand Central Station, just drinking in the sweet feeling of freedom and mulling over the last two years. A lot had happened on the home front. Tony had married Verlee right before I left. Rosalie had married Martin in November of 1960, Dave had married Lyla in February of 1961, and Max had married Opal about two months later. Rita and Teresa had married in 1952 and 1954 and were busy having kids.

Max had moved to Chicago, which was more or less on my way home, so I decided to visit him for a few days before going back to Kansas. I caught the next train to Chicago and settled in for a relaxing train ride. I had dinner in the diner, enjoying the nice silverware and cloth napkins. By this time I felt like a well-seasoned "world traveler," so the excitement I felt was well controlled. We pulled into Chicago about 2:30, and I headed for a phone booth to call Max. Opal answered the phone. I told her I was passing through on my way home and thought I'd visit them for a day or two. She was very delighted and gave me directions to their apartment, 4528 North Clarendon Avenue, on the near north side of Chicago.

I caught a cab and headed north on Lake Shore Drive. Lake Michigan provided beautiful scenery as we drove along. I arrived and found Max's apartment. Opal was thrilled, and had already called Max. Max was exuberant that I had decided to visit them and couldn't wait until he got off work. He worked for Cook County Welfare Department and was getting a Master's degree in Social and Industrial Relations at Loyola University night school. He arrived home shortly and just couldn't believe I was there. He was really happy to see me, and, to tell the truth, I was really happy to see some of my family.

They had a hide-a-bed, so I stayed a couple of days. Before I left, I bought them an LP album as a token of appreciation for being such gracious hosts. Then did I ever get a jolt. After I gave them the album, Max pulled an old receipt out of his wallet, handed it to me, and told me that we were now even. I looked at it, and it was a receipt for the $20 that he had wired to me in Paris! He was the one who had come up with the money and wired it. Wow! That was a year and a half earlier. Apparently everyone at home thought that I needed bail money to get out of jail in Paris, because Max tried to coax me into admitting to that, now that I was home. I suppose that would have made a good story, but it wasn't the truth, and I had a hard time convincing him of this; we had simply run out of money.

I caught a train to Great Bend, Kansas, where Mom and Dad now lived. Max had bought a small house for them, was making the monthly payments on the mortgage, and also maintained it. This was really a generous gesture by Max, because it gave Mom and Dad some real security for basically the first time in their lives. Dad found a job as a janitor at the First National Bank, so things kind of leveled out for him and Mom in their later years. Dad used to tell his friends that he was really "cleaning up," or "mopping up." He had a great sense of humor.

After a week or two, I realized that there really wasn't much opportunity in Kansas, it being a small state and all. Max was in Chicago, and that looked like the land of opportunity to me. So I called Max and asked him if I could stay with him if I moved to Chicago. He and his wife very kindly agreed to it, so I packed and headed north on the next train.

Here I was, back in the big city of Chicago, the Windy City. The first order of business was to find a job. I hit the want ads and saw some openings in companies located right downtown in the loop. Well, why not go all the way to the top? Max helped me figure out the bus schedule, since I didn't have a car, and the day after I arrived in Chicago I walked into the offices of Texaco, Inc. at 332 S. Michigan Avenue. I was interviewed by a Mike Begley, the credit manager, took some aptitude tests, passing them with flying colors, and was hired on the spot. Thanks again, seminary. I started work the very next day as a "credit clerk" in the credit department.

Within a couple of months I was promoted to "credit man" and assigned credit responsibility for a district, or geographical area in the upper Midwest. My job was to approve commercial lines of credit to farmers and businesses in that district. Each month we received a multi-carboned statement that included that month's purchases and payments, as well as an ending balance. I had to analyze each statement to determine if any invoices were past due and, if so, get them collected. Some of the statements were so active that they contained as many as 20 pages a month. If the remittances weren't correctly applied, the statement became hopelessly out of balance. To avoid that, we had to be very exact in our analysis. Occasionally, there would be a turnover in the office, and that's when we usually discovered many of the accounts were terribly out of balance. Gradually, I developed a reputation for analyzing some of the toughest statements, so I was often given the task of straightening out the most complicated accounts.

I met a lot of good people while I worked with Texaco. The longest-lasting friend was D.L. "Lee" Winger. He eventually got married and had a little boy, born deaf. This required that he and his wife learn sign language when the boy got older. John Frale was another. He was known as a tough credit man. If the account didn't meet his criteria, he absolutely would not approve credit. He indoctrinated his sales force effectively to his toughness. As a result, he usually had a very good collection percentage. The collection percentage was the percent of the total balance for each district that was in current status.

John also introduced us to the Wilkinson sword razor blades when they came out. Up to that time, each razor blade lasted only one shave, then you had to replace it. Most of us used the metal double-edged razors, where you turned the bottom of the handle and the caps of the blades would open. You then removed the old double-edged blade and replaced it with the new. This kind of razor is somewhat rare today. Anyhow, the English Wilkinson blade could be used for up to seven shaves. This totally revolutionized the razor blade industry.

Ken Smith was another credit man, in charge of the asphalt and petrochemical accounts. These were very large accounts in terms of dollar volume and required a very experienced credit man, which Ken was. He was about 40 and single. I learned later that he died of cancer. Jack Normand was an old credit war horse, a man in his 60s, who liked to have a few drinks with his lunch and smoked heavily. In those days you could smoke right at your desk, and many employees did so. One morning we were all called into the credit manager's office and informed that during the night Jack had suffered a ruptured aorta and had died. This was pretty sobering to all of us. One day he was there, and the next he was gone.

Mike Begley was a corporate climber, and his assistant was a Texan, Bob Smith. Mike was easy enough to get along with, except for one thing. After I had met my fiancé and became engaged, I wanted a week off for the honeymoon. I didn't have a full year in yet, so I didn't qualify for any vacation time. My only choice was to ask Mike if I could have a few days off without pay. But he wouldn't let me. So all we had was a weekend honeymoon. I never forgot that, and later on Texaco paid for that.

Texaco had a typist pool located on the next floor down. We had a dictation system whereby we could pick up our phone, dictate a letter to the typing pool, and usually within a day the typed letter was delivered to our desks for signature. Not a bad system. I could work pretty quickly, and many were the days I got mean looks from the typists when they delivered loads of finished letters to me. But what the hell, that was my job.

I generally rode the "L" to work, reading a newspaper on the way, usually the *Sun Times.* In those days, newspapers reported the news, the facts, what was happening everywhere. If you wanted an opinion, you went to the editorial section. Today, it seems the newspapers are trying to shape the public's opinion not only by their choice of what they report, but also by the slant in which they write the news items.

When I had first been drafted into the Army, I had a number of debts that were far too large for me to pay on my limited military salary. So when I was discharged, the first thing I wanted to do was to get all those old bills paid off. I bought a ledger book, listed each creditor, and then started sending each of them $10 or so each month. I was very religious about this. It was for this reason that I also decided that I would not engage in too many weekend "nocturnal escapades." I wanted to get those bills paid.

This monastic self-denial went on for about two months. Then I started to get a little bit itchy. I didn't want to put my **whole** social life on hold indefinitely. After all, all work and no play makes one dull. I was pondering this one Sunday during mass at Our Lady of the Lake Church, when I heard an announcement that the "Singles Club" was going to some event and were to meet on the steps of the church that evening. Well, I figured, what could be more harmless and inexpensive than going out with a church singles group?

So I decided to get out of the apartment and walked over to the church. There were maybe five or ten young people standing around on the steps. I started introducing myself, turned … and there she was. She was the most beautiful woman I had ever seen. Time seemed to stand still. She had a gentle, yet slightly insecure smile on her face. The group went out to wherever we were going, and all during the evening I felt strangely attracted to her. The evening ended (too soon for me), and I succeeded in getting her name before I went home. It was Joy Graves, and she lived about six blocks from Wrigley Field.

There was another Singles Club event scheduled the following weekend, and I constantly caught myself thinking of Joy and looking forward to seeing her again. Finally the weekend came, and I got there early, hoping against hope that Joy would show up. My heart skipped a beat when she did. I knew then that it was all over. She was the one for me. Cupid didn't shoot me with his little arrow. He impaled me with a thunderous lance of love right through the heart.

From that day on, I either saw her in person or called her. I was blissfully in love, and thought she was, too.

Labor Day weekend rolled around, and Max and Opal had left town for the holiday weekend. It was about six weeks after I had met Joy. This gave Joy and me some privacy at my apartment. I had a specific plan and definitely wanted privacy. We spent the afternoon there, just being together, listening to records or watching TV. Finally, I got up the nerve to ask her to marry me. My heart sank, as I was hoping for an immediate "yes." But I didn't get it. I persisted, and she finally said "yes." God, was I relieved, and very happy. Later, I realized that it was simply Joy's personality that prevented her from giving me a quick response, especially regarding something of this magnitude. Before going on, I can honestly tell you that Joy and I did not have sex that afternoon. In fact, we never had sex at all before we were married. And I'm embarrassed to say, it wasn't from the lack of effort on my part.

I guess I was somewhat of a traditionalist, because I felt it was appropriate for me to ask Joy's father, Ralph, for his permission to marry Joy. So I went over to her apartment with Joy and asked for his permission. I was expecting at least some kind of a questioning or lecture, but much to my amazement, I got neither. Nor did I get an answer. It was the same way with Joy's mother, Helen. As Christmas drew near, I wanted to take Joy down to Kansas to meet my family. Since we weren't married, I felt the honorable way to do it was to ask Helen for her permission. After all, this was her daughter. When I asked her, all I got was a dull stare and an unintelligible muttering.

That is when I started realizing that Joy's family was quite a bit different than my family. Although I didn't grasp it at the time, most of them had very severe emotional difficulties and were severely dysfunctional. Helen and Ralph had a very low emotional threshold. It seemed that when the emotional level raised even a small level, they simply tilted out. That's why I never got any answer from either Ralph or Helen. The mere asking of those two questions raised the emotional level above the level they could tolerate.

Eventually, it dawned on me that Joy's parents hadn't provided a strong structure and discipline for their children. She had a brother, Tim, who was about 17 at this time; a sister, Evelyn, who was about 13; and a younger brother, Charles, who was about 10. Ralph was in his 60s, and I thought he was quite a man to have fathered a son while in his 50s. Helen was in her early 50s, and quite a few years younger than her husband.

Once, while I was courting Joy, little Charlie broke his arm and had to wear a cast and a sling. They told me that the doctor was very emphatic that Charlie should keep the arm in the sling, or it would mend crooked. I was visiting one day when I noticed that Charlie was running around without the sling. It wasn't my place to say anything, and I didn't. But eventually Joy asked me to see if I couldn't get him to keep his arm in the sling. So I told Charlie to come over to me, and when he did, I took his arm and put it in the sling. Then I told him flatly to keep it in the sling. And he did. Until I left. Then off came the sling. He minded me, but not his own parents. Sad.

Another time, after Joy and I had come back from a date and were standing outside her apartment door, smooching up a storm, we heard Tim screaming at Helen at the top of his voice, calling her every name he could think of, in the filthiest of language. This was something I just could not tolerate. So I told Joy to give me her keys, unlocked the door, went in, got right in Tim's face, and told him that I had heard his screaming and cursing, and that no mother deserved that. I told him if I ever heard it again, I was going to kick the living shit out of him. He was totally stunned and should have been, because I was breathing fire when I said it. Although Helen really appreciated that, it didn't change things much. I really think that Joy, by virtue of being the first child, got the best, and last, of any real parenting from Helen and Ralph. And I don't think that was very much. Some people are just not cut out to be parents.

Ralph had an artificial leg. When he was younger, he lost it while trying to hop a train in Kansas City for a free ride. By trade, he was an elevator operator in one of the tall buildings downtown in the Loop. He was a member of a union and had done this for over 25 years. He dressed impeccably and had exquisite tastes, especially when it came to whiskey. He was originally from Kentucky, in the heart of bourbon country, and always had some fine bourbon on hand. We enjoyed many a fine drink together. He was also a connoisseur of good food, especially when it came to hams. He always had some delicious, sliced ham in the refrigerator, and it made for some great sandwiches.

Joy's whole family had a totally different way of life. They lived a block from the local supermarket, so they rarely bought food for more than a day. Since both the city bus and the subway transportation, or the "L" as they called it, was just a few blocks away, the family didn't own a car. This was a restriction on their social life, although they had relatives living in the Chicago area. If they wanted to visit someone, they had to take the city transportation or wait to be driven by a relative.

The neighborhood they lived in was primarily multi-unit apartment buildings. It was so congested that after work hours it was extremely difficult to find a place to park your car. One could easily spend 10 to 20 minutes looking for a single parallel space on one of the many one-way streets, and when you did, you had to walk a block or two to your destination.

Joy's parents were also paranoid about their living room window. The bottom of that window was about six feet above the sidewalk outside, so that outsiders, if they wanted to, could barely see into the apartment. To prevent that from happening, Ralph installed Venetian blinds and curtains that were almost always closed, especially in the evenings. I was told by Ralph's family that people would come by, see what you had in your apartment, such as a TV, get your phone number, call at different times to find out when you were not home, then break into the apartment and steal the TV, etc.

To make matters worse, they never rearranged the furniture, at least not in the living room. Joy told me that it had all stayed in the same position for as long as she could remember, and she was 23 then. As best I can remember, they only had a one-bedroom apartment with six people living in it. I think Evy slept on a hide-a-bed that was set up in the dining room, which, by the way, had no dining table. Joy slept on a half-bed in the living room. During the day they placed big square cushions on it, making it similar to a sofa. When people ate, they ate at a table in the kitchen.

Another strange thing I noticed was that Helen did little cooking. Everyone seemed to cook for themselves, and Helen never, ever ate with the family, at least when I was there. She always wanted to eat later, by herself in the kitchen. Helen rarely cooked supper, and when Ralph invited Joy and me over for Sunday dinner, he did all the cooking. It was really strange.

Joy's family weren't the only ones who were paranoid. I remember getting off the "L" after work one wintry day and walking home. The sidewalks were covered with ice that had melted after a snow and then re-frozen. I came upon this obese old lady who had a basket of groceries in each arm. She was struggling to keep from slipping and falling on the ice, and I was seriously worried about her falling and hurting herself. So, as I caught up with her, I turned to her and asked her if I could help carry her groceries for her. She looked at me with a look of total fear and yelled, "Get away from me! Get away from me!" I just shook my head and walked on home. What a way to live!

At any rate, after I proposed, it took both of us a few days to get over the jitters of such a momentous decision, and we gradually settled into a courtship routine. During lunch one day I went over to a jewelry store on State Street and bought a set of rings for $300, which was a lot of money at that time. I wanted to get my engagement ring on her finger as soon as I could.

I took Joy out the following weekend to one of the nicest dining places on the near north side of Chicago, the Ivanhoe. The Ivanhoe had an old English atmosphere and advertised an elevator ride down into the "castle dungeon." Joy and I got on this old wooden elevator, and it shook and creaked, so that we felt we were descending at least a hundred feet or so. The opposite door opened, and we entered into a very dimly lit, small room, and found in its center an old-fashioned round well, made of rocks. It even had an old tiny wooden roof over it, giving the whole room a very romantic atmosphere. At just the right moment, I took out the engagement ring, and Joy let me put it on her finger. We kissed lovingly, and I was on cloud nine. That is an evening I will never forget.

From then on, my life had changed dramatically. The metamorphosis had begun. Up to this point, I had been single, and all I had to worry about was myself. Now, a woman had entered into my life, and I had to start thinking in terms of the two of us, and maybe down the road, three or four of us. It was an entirely new feeling for me, one that I embraced willingly.

Joy and I were almost inseparable. One weekend we went to the Theater in the Round, where the funniest thing happened. At one point in the program, this nationally famous female vocalist was singing a very beautiful love song. The crowd was enraptured by it. The spotlight shone brightly through the darkness highlighting the singer. Part way into the song, a huge moth started flying around about four or five feet above the singer. Soon it caught the attention of the front rows, and then the whole crowd. Soon we were wondering if it was going to land on the singer or go away. But it didn't leave, it just kept flying. Then a quiet rustle of laughter moved through the crowd. I'm sure the singer noticed it, but being a true professional, she didn't let it phase her and bravely sang on, putting her whole heart into the song. Still, the moth wouldn't leave. The sight became more humorous as the song went on, until a wave of open laughter swept through the crowd. Finally, the singer stopped singing and demanded of the crowd, "Can anyone tell me what is so damn funny?" Someone in the front row pointed to the moth; the singer looked up, saw it, and then started laughing. She made a humorous quip and picked right up where she left off. She was a real pro.

Max and Opal were great people to live with. I can't even remember if they charged me rent. Opal was a great cook, but there was one thing she usually did that we still joke about today. After the meal was over, the three of us generally sat at the table and visited. As we did, Opal would keep nibbling on what was left of the entree, until eventually it was all gone. She was petite, but could she put the food away. Later in the evening, Max and I generally slipped over to the corner liquor store and got a quart of beer. After a while this almost became a nightly routine.

While living with Max, I may have said something to him that caused him to change his career. We were talking one evening and got on the subject of careers. I mentioned that eventually, sometime, I would like to be a lawyer, because when you looked around, anybody who was in a position of power, such as the U.S. congress, was a lawyer. I guess that got Max to thinking, and eventually he decided that he wanted to become a lawyer. So after he finished getting his master's degree (and I can still remember the mad rush one evening when he had about four of us madly typing his thesis to beat the deadline), he enrolled in law school at Tulsa University. The summer after Joy and I were married, he and Opal packed all their belongings into a two-wheeled trailer that Max had built from scratch, and headed for Tulsa.

Joy and I picked a wedding date of April 20 of the following year, 1993. I eventually bought a two-tone green 1957 Oldsmobile 98. It needed a new left front fender, and we had the tools, so I worked a couple of nights in a row replacing it. By this time Joy and I saw each other literally each day. But the wedding was drawing near, and this fender had to be fixed, so I told her I couldn't come over. She was really upset about that, but I told her the car had to be fixed. This was the first time that something had caused some friction between us, and she didn't like it. But it had to be done. As I was working on my car with Max, the door opened and in walked Joy. She said she was sorry for getting angry and brought me a sandwich to eat. I was really proud of her.

We made all the arrangements for the wedding. It was to be at Our Lady of the Lake church, right where I met Joy. Joy didn't have any close friends, so she asked me if I had a sister who could come up from Kansas and be the bridesmaid. My sister Judy was kind enough to oblige. I asked Tony to be my best man, and they all drove up together the day before the wedding. Mom came with them. Max persuaded a classmate of his, Father Ernest Brandewie, to celebrate the mass, which started at 10:00 on a Saturday. "Brandy" had been one of the top two singers back in the seminary at Techny and sang one of the most beautiful High Masses I'd ever heard. It was a very lovely ceremony, and the smile on Joy's face as we came down the aisle after the ceremony was the most beautiful and captivating I had ever seen before or since.

Ralph had rented the hall at the Sheraton Hotel near our area, and we held the reception there. One of our friends from the Singles Club was a photographer, and he took all the usual pictures, cutting the cake, kissing, etc. Tony made a good best man. My dad's brother, Del, and his wife, Isabel, were there from Los Angeles. As we were taking pictures and celebrating on the steps of the church, Del came up to me, put a silver dollar in my hand, and told me that as long as I held on to that, I would never be broke. I still have it today. And he was right, I've never been completely broke, although years later we would have to file bankruptcy.

After thanking our guests, Joy and I hurried to our apartments, changed clothes, and headed in my freshly waxed Olds 98 for Wisconsin for our honeymoon. Because that @#&$#^+% Mike Begley wouldn't let me off, it was going to be a very short honeymoon, just half a weekend. As I said before, I owed him (and Texaco) one, and would wait for the opportunity, which finally came many years later.

We spent Saturday night in southern Wisconsin, and discretion prevents elaboration of the events of that night and the next morning. We tried to make as much of a holiday as we could out of it, but there just wasn't enough time. The weather even worked against us. On Sunday, we encountered a late snowfall as we were driving around in Wisconsin. I'll never forget driving along with our windshield wipers on and wishing we had more time. But that's life.

Joy also worked downtown in the Loop, just a few blocks south of me, and ironically, for another oil company, Shell Oil Company. From time to time we got to have lunch together, and that was pleasant. Buckingham fountains were not too far away, and we often took sack lunches and ate them there in the warm summer sunshine. She worked there until she became pregnant to the point where she had to quit.

Joy and I now settled into married life. We moved into a one-bedroom apartment just off Pratt Avenue. It was on the fourth floor of a rather old, brick 12-story apartment building. The door to our apartment entered into a longer than usual hall, with the bedroom on the left. We had purchased a new double-sized bed from the Smythe Company, one of the more popular stores in Chicago. After the first few nights, we realized we needed a larger bed, so Smythe's was kind enough to exchange it for a queen-size bed, and we both were then able to get better sleep. The hall ended at the combination living room and dining room. We had the usual sofa, TV, and small dining table and chairs. The very small kitchen was off to the right. The whole apartment was Spartan, as it was our "starter" apartment.

As it is with most marriages, I suppose, after the wedding there was a period of adjustment by both of us. My feelings at this time are a bit difficult to describe. On the one hand, I loved Joy very much and wanted her to be very happy. But on the other hand, it was very frustrating for me. Joy tried to cook, but had never really been taught anything about cooking by her mother. So she tried to cook as best she could, and this was a source of stress to both her of us. I used to say that she was the only person I knew who could burn Jell-O.

But the greatest frustration of all for me usually developed on the weekends. This is when Joy was looking for entertainment, and she was looking directly at me to provide it. I didn't have a problem with that at all. But every single time I asked her what she would wanted to do, or where she wanted to go, *she didn't know!* So I went through an endless list of suggestions for entertainment, movies, plays, concerts, etc., and Joy had a very difficult time in deciding what she liked. It was almost like she had to have some ironclad guarantee that she would enjoy it before she would commit to going to it. There were times when I came up with something she enjoyed, but more times than not, if she didn't thoroughly enjoy it, then I heard about it from her later.

This was the real beginning of my metamorphosis. In a sense, I had to brush aside some of the things that I myself personally enjoyed, simply because Joy placed her own enjoyment on my shoulders. I suppose this is an adjustment that all newly married couples go through. It's now two people, not one. There has to be some give and take. But I think our situation went far beyond the norm. And I think it went back to Joy's lack of parenting, her lack of social development, and the paranoid circumstances in which she was raised. So, even though it was very difficult on me, I was starting to see that in a way, it wasn't her fault. She just had the misfortune of growing up with without good parenting. I am sure that I was not perfect myself during this time, but still, I spent a lot of time and frustration trying to make Joy happy. It was a real burden, and I started to realize that it might be better for Joy to be away from her family. They had a very negative effect on her, in the sense that the more that she was around her family, the more it reinforced the very attitudes that were causing me my greatest frustrations.

It got to the point that I eagerly volunteered to do the laundry. We had to go to a laundromat to get our clothes washed and dried. I looked forward to this, as this gave me a reason to get out of the apartment. I used a two-wheeled wire cart to take our clothes to the local laundromat around the corner. Because of the fear that someone would steal our clothes, it was necessary to stay with the clothes while the washing and drying was being done. It so happened that there was a neighborhood bar right next to the laundromat. I parked myself at the bar and drank beer while the clothes were being done. I usually milked about two hours out of this. It was a welcome relief that I actually looked forward to.

Discretion obviously prohibits me from discussing our sexual relationship at any time during our marriage. Suffice it to say that Joy never received any kind of guidance from her mother in this area, and she had some very deep-seated near negative concepts about sex that even frustrated me further. I suppose all married couples have a certain learning curve in this area. That's only natural. But in our case, it took a very, very long time before this natural perk of marriage actually became a perk. All of these things made my life fairly miserable for the first year or so.

Eventually Joy became pregnant. This was another huge change for both of us, a beautiful new feeling. It took me some time to fathom the concept that I was going to be a father and that the support of our family fell on my shoulders. The metamorphosis continues. Since I had been raised in an atmosphere where the father was the breadwinner in the family, I automatically accepted that role and really wasn't scared or intimidated about it. I really looked forward to it, and although Joy was a little scared initially, she also wanted to be a mother and relished the idea.

John F. Kennedy was President during this time, and on one occasion he came to Chicago. They announced that he would travel down Michigan Avenue in a big convertible so that the public could see him. I was outside our office with thousands of others when he came by, and I got to see him. He wasn't more than 40 feet away and looked to be a bit small, but handsome and healthy.

I'll never forget his assassination. We were all working in the office, when right after lunch word spread that Kennedy had been shot in Dallas. At first, we all thought it was a prank. No one in their right mind would do such a thing. He was such a great President. But someone had a radio in the office, and we gathered around it, getting periodic reports. It was true, he had been shot. But was he dead? We waited anxiously for more reports. We didn't care what our bosses thought. We were praying that he was alive. But then the fateful report came over the radio. John F. Kennedy was dead. We were all stunned and angry. Who would do such a terrible thing? Some of the ladies in the office cried. Some went home early to watch TV.

This was the President who said, *"Ich ben ein Berliner!"* and, "Ask not what your country could do for you, but what you could do for your country!" This was especially significant to me, because I had been all over Europe and realized what a great country we had, compared to all those in Europe. Our country was the essence of freedom, and light years ahead of the rest of the world. And Kennedy was our champion. What a waste of a great man!

In the years since his death, I have watched our country go in the opposite direction of his great policies. Gradually, our country has turned into a real mess, where the emphasis has been on what you can get out of your country for free. We have bred a dependency by the blacks and minorities on mother America. We have abandoned Kennedy's exhortation to ask what you can do for your country. To this day, I believe that Lyndon Johnson was the man behind the assassination. I believe he could see that he would never make the presidency through an open election, and the only way he would become president was to assassinate Kennedy.

In those years, presidential candidates usually spent a year or so campaigning, get themselves elected, then spent the next three years concentrating on running the country as a true leader. That's what made Kennedy so good. Today, it seems candidates never quit campaigning. After Clinton was elected, it seemed to me that every single thing he did was campaigning, starting with the day he was sworn into office. Just tell him where there was going to be a TV camera, and he'd show up. To me, he really made a joke of the presidency.

After the year's lease was up on our first apartment, we moved further north, close to Evanston, into a real nice apartment. It was the top floor of a house, with a separate entrance, in a neighborhood that was dotted with homes instead of the dirty and congested, multi-unit, tall brick high-rise apartments. On our first anniversary, April 20, 1964, Joy thawed out the portion of our wedding cake that we had frozen, put on her wedding dress, and we celebrated our anniversary in grand style, even though Joy was so pregnant she couldn't zip up her wedding dress. We were much happier by then. The thought of adding a baby to our lives gave us both a new purpose. Joy was almost seven months pregnant, and we were looking forward to our first child.

Neither Joy or I knew much about pregnancy and babies. Her mom was of very little use, and had been so for most of Joy's life. My mom was down in Kansas, so we didn't get any of the usual mother-daughter advice about things to watch out for, etc. We were on our own, flying blind. Toward the end of May, Joy was getting pretty big. The baby was due around July 1, so she started experiencing the discomforts that expectant mothers normally experience.

One Saturday night Joy was in bed and woke me up about 5:00 in the morning. She apparently felt she had lost continence briefly and had wetted in bed. She showed it to me, and, frankly, it didn't look like urine to me. We didn't know what to do. All this was new to us. Finally, she called her doctor about 6:00 that Sunday morning and tried to tell him as best she could what was going on. Her doctor diagnosed her condition over the phone as possible kidney infection and called in a prescription, telling Joy to stay in bed.

We got the prescription and she started taking it, but she still had a minor difficulty with continence. This continued until the following Thursday, June 3, 1964, when Joy started having severe pains. The doctor ordered her to the hospital, where she went into labor and gave birth to a baby boy, one month premature. He weighed five and a half pounds. The doctor assured us that he was fine, although he was having a little difficulty breathing. He expected that to clear up in a day or so.

Joy and I were on cloud nine. We felt a deep sense of fulfillment. We had picked the name, Michael Lawrence. Michael, because I really liked that name, and Lawrence, after my dad. When I finally got home that night, I proudly called home and told Mom we had a new son. I floated to bed that night, internally grinning from ear to ear. I was now a father and wondered what kind of son we would raise. Joy was very contented and had a truly angelic look of satisfaction on her face. She told me that she had always wanted to be a mother before she reached 25. She made it with 24 days to spare.

The next morning I called into the office and broke the news, telling them I wouldn't be at work because of the birth. I eagerly headed for the hospital and spent the day there with Joy. We were both hoping to get to hold Michael, but the doctor wouldn't let us, saying he had to be kept in the incubator in the premature baby ward, down the hall from Joy's semi-private room. We stood together and gazed at our son in the incubator along the wall on the right side of the nursery. Supper time came, and we ate.

It was about 7 p.m. when Joy and I started down the hall to see Michael again. When we got to the big viewing window, someone had pulled down the shade on the inside of the window. It was obvious that they didn't want anyone looking in. However, the shade didn't quite cover the whole window. On the right side of the shade there was a very narrow vertical slot, about a half-inch wide, through which we could look into the nursery. And, as luck would have it, that narrow slot was just enough for us both to look in and see Michael's incubator. Only now, there was a nurse intently watching Michael. Sickeningly, I started feeling that something serious was wrong. I should have moved Joy away from the window right then, but how was I to know what was going to happen?

As we watched, a doctor came in and assisted the nurse. They were both intently bent over the incubator, watching. Suddenly, the doctor threw open the incubator and frantically grabbed for Michael. By this time, I'd seen enough and shoved Joy away from the window, with my arm around her. Neither of us said anything. We just walked down the hall, and Joy got back into her bed. It was about 7:15. We were both silently hoping against hope, but deep down, we knew he was gone. A few minutes later the doctor came in, pulled the curtain around Joy's bed and told us that Michael didn't make it. He said his lungs just weren't developed well enough to allow him to breathe. He apologized profusely, but we were both too numb to absorb anything. He stayed with us a brief time, then asked me out into the hall. He said that it would help them understand how to treat premature babies if I would approve an autopsy. The very thought was very repugnant to me, and it really irritated me that he was asking me this, so soon after getting the shocking news. But I gave him my permission, thinking that maybe this might help someone else.

I was concerned with Joy and stayed with her as long as I could that night. She was teary-eyed the rest of the evening, and I felt completely helpless. I was really proud of the way she took it. She didn't go into screaming hysterics or threaten suicide, or anything radical like that. She bore the pain well. Going back to our apartment that night was torture. Not only did I feel like my heart had been ripped out, but now I had to also pick up the phone and call my mom. She got on the line, and I told her that Michael was gone, explaining what had happened and what the doctor had said. I hung up the phone and stared at the wall. The apartment had never felt so empty. Time seemed to stand still, and all I could faintly hear was the soft ticking of the clock on the wall. I couldn't eat, or even turn on the TV. I just sat there, hurting.

The phone rang, and my sister Rosalie was on the line. She was very distraught over Michael's death and just wanted to console me. I really appreciated that call, because I was about as low as I had ever been in my life. She told me that Mom was coming up the next day and would be with us. Although I don't remember doing it, I must have called Joy's parents and told them about everything.

I think Joy was released from the hospital the next day, and I brought her home. The apartment probably felt like a tomb to her. I know it did to me. Mom arrived, and I can't remember if she drove or took the train. It helped having her there, in view of the sad circumstances. I didn't realize it until some time later, but what happened to Joy the Saturday night before the birth was that her water had broken. The natural reaction was to be upset with the doctor, who should have told Joy to go to the hospital. We will never know if they could have delayed the birth long enough to save Michael. The other thing about this, and this really angered me, was that the doctor told us that Michael was fine. It would have been a lot easier on us if he had told us that the situation was critical, or at least serious. The shock wouldn't have been so great then.

I made the arrangements for a short funeral for Michael at a cemetery in Schiller Park. Because of the autopsy, we never got to see the remains. All we had was a tiny closed casket. We didn't even get a chance to take a picture of Michael. I stared at it long and hard during the ceremony, but I couldn't dwell on it too long, because I had to take care of Joy. She was taking it all very well, but still, I thought it was very important for me to be by her side if she needed me.

After the burial we returned to our apartment, and Mom headed back to Kansas. Before going, she encouraged me to get Joy out of our present atmosphere. I went back to work and had to face all of my friends at the office. They were all sincerely compassionate, but I really didn't like the attention that this tragedy brought me. I've always prided myself in being totally self-sufficient, and was uncomfortable with their expressions of true sorrow, even though I knew they were sincere and were just trying to be kind. It was a very tough time for Joy. Not only had she lost a baby, but then her breasts filled, and she had to wrap them tightly to cause them to dry up. I know that had to be a grim reminder.

For the next few weeks I did a lot of serious thinking about life in general, where I was, what I was doing, and where I was headed, how all this had affected Joy, and how to move on into the future. This tragedy seemed to be a catalyst, forcing me to step back and take a look at the big picture. If I continued where I was, working with Texaco, I felt that was really a dead end. I saw what had happened to Jack Normand, and how the individuality of those who worked for Texaco was gradually being drained from them. I considered the effects of Joy's family on both me and Joy. I could see that effect to be more negative than positive. Then there was the loss of Michael, and I started to thinking about how a change of scenery might be better for both Joy and me. I took a hard look at what I wanted to do for a career, and it became apparent that what I really wanted to do was to become a lawyer. I had been taking some night school courses at DePaul University, but getting a degree at night school would take an eternity. I knew if I wanted to get a degree, it had to be via full-time school.

I talked all these things over with Joy. I told her that I felt we needed a change of atmosphere, and that I wanted to get back into school. She didn't have any problems with me getting back into school. Max was now in law school at Tulsa University, and Tulsa was the oil capital of the world. That meant that it shouldn't be too difficult for me to find petroleum-related work there. I knew that because of my military service I could draw monthly GI Bill payments while I was in school. The more I thought about it, the more I leaned toward pulling up stakes and heading for Tulsa.

But there was one big problem. Joy was dead set against moving. She wanted to stay near her folks, but I felt that wasn't good for her.

I tried my darndest to persuade her that moving to Tulsa was the best thing for both of us. But she was adamant. The more I talked, the more she dug in. This went on for about a week or two, and eventually it became clear to me that she was not going to budge. I didn't realize it at the time, but what I was really doing was forcing Joy to choose between me and her own family. Even though her family had a lot of shortcomings, she still loved them, wanted only the best for them, and wanted to be near them. The mere thought of leaving them behind and striking out into the unknown with this country boy from Kansas had to cause her a lot of alarm. That left me with two choices. One, I could stay in Chicago, working at a dead end job, and not liking the relationship of Joy's family. Or I could get back into school and start working on a career that I wanted. So I made the decision to go to Tulsa and get back into school, with or without Joy. And that was the way I had to put it to Joy. I told her I was going to Tulsa to school, that I loved her very much and wanted her to come with me. For her, it was either come with me or stay in Chicago. It was a brutal ultimatum to give to someone you loved, but I felt it had to be done. I didn't want to lock myself into a career I didn't like.

When I told Joy my decision, she didn't talk to me for three solid days. I mean, not one word. I thought she was waiting me out to see if I would change my mind. But I didn't waver. I was committed. She must have finally realized this, as she finally agreed to come with me. In looking back, I really forced her, almost mercilessly, to give up the security of her family and cast her lot with me. And since she had been taught such tight dependence at home, this was a monumental step for her.

I resigned my position at Texaco, but Mike Begley persuaded me to take a "leave of absence," because that looked better on his record than a simple resignation. I rented a trailer, we packed all our belongings in it, and hit the road for Tulsa. I was looking forward to a bright new future with my wife at my side.

8

TULSA

(Tough Living, Another Dead Baby, and Finally Some Success)

WE PULLED INTO Tulsa during the mother of all heat waves. It had to be well over 110 degrees and seemed to stay there for the first full week we were there. Since we were renting the U-Haul trailer, we snatched up the first apartment we could find, rented it for 30 days, and unloaded. The apartment had no air conditioning, so it was like an oven, and the first night we got next to no sleep at all, and the sheets were wet with sweat. The next day I bought a box fan, and even with that blowing on us at night, it was miserable for both of us.

But at least we were in Tulsa, and I was looking forward to a fresh start. I was now 27, and happy to be back in school, working on a law degree. We didn't have much money. Joy had accumulated about $2,000 in savings before we were married, and I had a few shares of Texaco stock, but that was it. I would get GI payments while in school, but that wasn't enough for us to live on. I knew I'd have to get a part-time job. Joy found out that she qualified for unemployment benefits because of her work history with Shell Oil Company in Chicago. We didn't feel guilty about getting unemployment checks, because we were using them to better ourselves. We were poor college students and were starting over, almost from scratch.

I went by the registrar's office at Tulsa University and went over all the hours of credits I had from Techny and DePaul. They accepted enough to put me in the sophomore year in a degree in business administration. At that time we were allowed to use our freshman year in law school as our senior year in the business administration degree. This meant that I had to go to school full-time for two years, then switch over to a night school for the law school, and hopefully, find suitable full-time work. The tuition was $600 a semester, and this was a private school, not one of the state universities where tuition was less.

In those days students generally finished their undergraduate degrees in four years. When we enrolled in 15 hours, we did what it took to finish those 15 hours with passing grades. Our focus was on getting done. If anyone developed a problem, they usually took care of it during summer school. Taking more than four years was the exception. It seems in today's college environment that too many students take five years or more to get a four-year degree.

I found a rental house within walking distance from T.U. It was a small, square box of a house, set behind a home. I think our address was something like 404-1/2 E. Fourth. It was an older wood frame house, with an above-floor furnace and no air conditioning. Air conditioning in those days was a real luxury. We poor folk had to use a water cooler to cool the house down.

A water cooler was a huge metal box, about 30" x 30" x 30", anchored in one of the windows. Inside the box was a squirrel cage fan that blew air into the house. The sides of the water cooler contained porous meshes. Water was circulated down the top of the meshes, so that they were always wet. The squirrel fan sucked the air through the wet meshes and fanned the air into the house. The flow of air through the wet meshes cooled the air coming into the house and provided some relief from the heat. The only problem was that the air coming into the house was moist and dampened everything in the house. Still, that was preferable to the insufferable heat.

As fall of 1964 rolled around, I started school. I carried 15 hours each semester, made average grades and never dropped a course. I wasn't too concerned with making high grades, because my goal was law school, and they couldn't care less what your business administration grades were. What really impressed me about T.U. was that for the four semesters I took in the next two years, some 20 courses, I never had a teacher who held less than a doctorate degree.

As for the curriculum, the only gripe I had was that I had to take two successive, "new math" courses on the "set" theory. The teacher was a young Ph.D., and he told us all on the very first day that we would probably never see this material again after we graduated, but the school said it had to be taught, and he was only doing his job. It was a difficult two semesters, and I got passing grades, but it bothered me that I was having to spend my time and money on materials I would never use, even if I decided to stay in business administration.

Max and Opal had already moved to Tulsa, and Mark and Luanne had moved there as well, so we saw a lot of them. One of our favorite pastimes was to go over on Friday nights to Max's house, drink beer, eat pop corn, and watch the Friday horror movie, or "bloop-de-bloops" as we called it, on TV. That's where we saw the original "Little Shop of Horrors." We laughed at that movie until we thought we'd die.

Max was a business manager at a state hospital for retarded children. He took us on a tour once, and we saw some of the "freaks" of nature, the hydrocephalic babies and kids with enormous heads. You had to have a strong stomach to go on the tour. You really felt sorry for the kids. Still, each had his own unique personality. Mark worked at Ryder Truck Rentals, renting out trucks and trailers. I held down various part-time jobs, such as a posting clerk on weekends at a produce company, then an evening manager at a convenience store.

I finished one year at school, and the summer of 1965 came. It had been a miserable year for Joy. She had constant stomach problems, and her doctor diagnosed it as colitis, which I understood was a general name for a group of similar ailments affecting the stomach and intestines. She constantly had pain and gas in her stomach and had to be careful about what she ate. Combine that with not having really wanted to leave Chicago, and with her husband at school or working and having lost a baby, and wanting to have a baby, Joy really didn't have too much to be happy about. And she had at least one miscarriage during this time. But we survived.

We tried very hard to get pregnant again. Joy even started plotting her temperature to determine when she ovulated. When the temperature indicated ovulation, into the sack we hopped. It soon became work for both of us, with all of the enjoyment gone. It really had to be rough for Joy all during this time. Finally, we decided to forget trying to get pregnant and let things happen in their normal course. We were obviously straining too hard. Only then did sex start being fun again.

The fall of 1965 brought good news. Joy was pregnant! Boy, were we happy. This time we knew a little more about being pregnant, and we were around some family members who knew something about pregnancies, especially Opal since she was a nurse and had a few kids by this time. So we finally got a break. Joy could now contentedly sit and gestate, all the time looking forward to being a mother again. Winter passed, and the pregnancy went along fine. Joy started showing her pregnancy, and soon we could feel the baby kicking inside. What a glorious feeling. It made all the work worthwhile.

Then the specter of trouble reared its ugly head again. Joy started spotting, and we immediately went to the doctor, our hearts sinking. Joy wasn't quite six months pregnant. He put her in the hospital instantly and ordered complete bed rest, hoping to delay birth. I spent as much time as I could at her side, trying to keep her spirits high. But just like her first pregnancy, they couldn't stop her from going into labor, and she gave birth to a little girl, Marla Louise, on March 10, 1966. She weighed a pound and a half. But she was alive. She was three months premature. It helped our spirits to know that this hospital, St. John's, had a national reputation for taking care of premature babies. Even so, the doctor told us she had one chance in a hundred of surviving. He also warned us that, even if she survived, there was a good chance of brain damage, caused by the lack of oxygen to her brain. Her lungs simply weren't developed enough to get the oxygen to the brain. At least this time the doctor was honest with us.

So now the hoping and hard praying started. I let the folks know the situation, and we had a lot of support from Max and Opal, and from Mark and Luanne. Joy was released from the hospital and visited as often as she could. We only had one car, and Joy didn't know how to drive yet. I suppose that added to her sense of frustration in that, if she wanted to go anywhere, she had to walk or be driven. While this was going on, I had a job as a night poster at Utica Square

National Bank, which happened to be located right across the street from St. John's Hospital.

Gradually, my routine settled into going to school, then spending some time with Joy, then to the hospital to visit Marla, then across the street to work, then back to the hospital for another visit, then back home to Joy. The nuns had placed Marla's incubator right in front of the viewing window, so we could easily see her. It seems that as the days passed, I must have spent an eternity standing and watching Marla. I wanted so badly to smash through the glass, open the incubator and take her in my arms. But I couldn't. All I could do was to stand there, staring at her, silently loving her and telling her to keep fighting. I spoke to her a lot with my mind. I ached with a lot of pain and a lot of love. It hurt to see her lying there so tiny, occasionally stretching out her tiny arms and legs, and to see her body tremble with a sporadic shudder.

Pretty soon a week went by and our hopes increased. Then another week. Then into the third week. The doctor said that her odds had now increased to 50-50. Our hopes soared, and we prayed even harder. How Joy was able to maintain any kind of sanity through all of this was a miracle. Joy and I were sitting at home late in the evening, April 1, exactly 21 days after Marla was born. It was April Fool's Day. The phone rang. It was too late for it to be a friend or relative calling. Slowly, I got up and went to the phone. Somehow, I knew what was coming, and so did Joy. The phone felt like it weighed a ton when I picked it up. It was the hospital. Marla had caught an E-Coli infection, and it killed her. As I hung up, I looked over to Joy, and as gently as I could, told her the bad news. Again, she took it extremely well. She bottled up the hurt as we sat on the couch with me holding her. We just stared at the opposite wall a very long time.

Later I called home, and again broke the bad news. I called Max and Mark, then made arrangements for a short funeral service and burial at Calvary Cemetery. Mom drove down from Great Bend and gave us as much support as possible. This time we could see and touch Marla. The casket was about the size of a shoe box, and her head was about the size of a lemon. When I touched her, she seemed

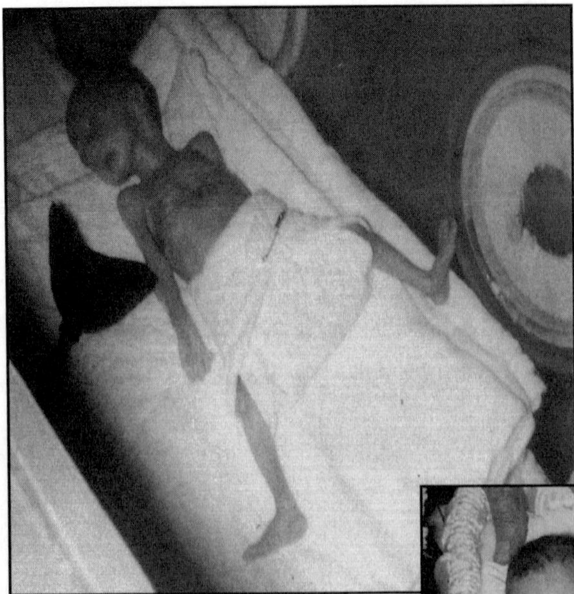

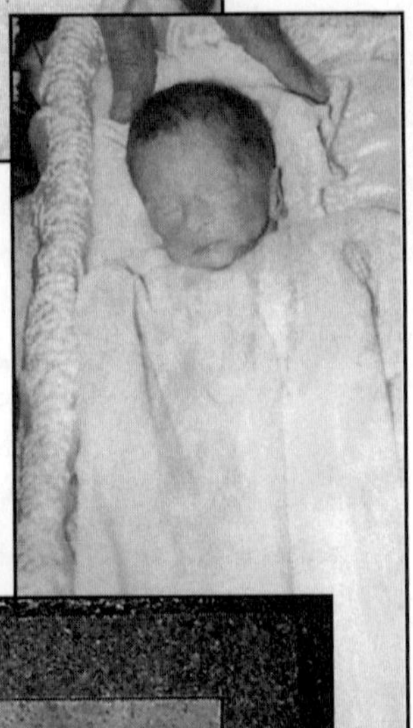

OUR DARLING ANGEL
MARLA LOUISE HOCHANADEL
MAR 10, 1966 – APR 1, 1966
SLEEPING IN GOD'S KEEPING

to be as cold as ice. She looked like a beautiful angelic statue. We drove out to the cemetery and had a short service at the grave. I remember being very concerned for Joy and trying to console her by putting my arm around her. But she shoved it away, saying she was okay. I felt hurt that Joy didn't want me to console her. This was what a husband was supposed to do. I guess I was surprised at how strong she was. Perhaps, in trying to make her feel better, I was trying to make myself feel better.

In looking back now, I realize that up to that point I had not been a source of very much happiness to Joy. I had known her less than four years. And in that time I had given her a son who died after one day, then I forced her away from her family and totally uprooted her life, taking her to Tulsa. Then I gave her a daughter who died after three weeks. We were college poor, without a dime to our name. We couldn't even afford a small gravestone. We were living in minimum existence housing with no air conditioning. Yet, somehow, Joy and I both survived this. Literally, the only thing we had going for us besides each other was that I was in college and determined to get a college education.

Perhaps it was a strong faith in God that helped me through all this. I really believed that God was all-powerful and that he orchestrated everything that happened, either directly or by simply standing by and letting them happen. In looking back, maybe God was doing some "cleansing" with me. I knew one thing for sure, that he was God and he had a unique plan for each of us. The only problem was, he never let us know in advance what it was. Maybe if he did, it would scare the hell out of us. Without being really vividly aware of it, I think this is when I started telling God, "Your will, not mine." Once I made that commitment, then it became a lot easier to accept what happened to me.

Somehow, life went on. I finished my two years of full-time school and started looking for a full-time job. I saw an ad in the paper where Texaco, Inc. was looking for help in their credit department right there in Tulsa. I called to make an appointment, gave them my name and told them that I had worked for Texaco in Chicago. My appointment was June 6, 1966, and I entered their modern, four-story office building. I met with the credit manager on the fourth floor and spent about 10 minutes visiting with him. He quietly asked me when I could start to work. I told him I could start the next morning. He said, "Fine, fill out these forms." I was a bit stunned and asked him if he wanted me to do any aptitude testing, etc. He said he didn't have to because he had talked to Mike Begley in Chicago, and Begley had given me a glowing recommendation. He hired me on the spot, based solely on that recommendation. God at work again?

So I went back to work with Texaco. I was now 29 and Joy 27. Finally, we had a decent income. In fact, I made enough so that within a few months Joy and I were able to buy our first house on the southeast side of Tulsa, at 7743 E. 28th Court. Our monthly house payments were a whopping $112, and we bought it for $15,250 from a foreigner by the name of Dadgoo. It was a three-bedroom, half-brick, ranch style home, with a one-car garage and fenced-in back yard. And, it was air conditioned. What a relief! We had what to us was a modern kitchen, with a counter separating it from the dining room, and a large living room. We were now living in tall cotton.

A few months later, Joy started having medical problems. She had a gynecologist who had the worst bedside manners in the world. Joy frequently came back from his appointments more confused and upset than when she went in to see him. One day she came home, was very upset, and said the doctor told her she had to have an operation. She apparently had an ovarian cyst. So surgery was scheduled, I took her to the hospital and waited in the waiting room. Before going in, the doctor asked me if I would like to see the cyst, and I said, "Sure."

She wasn't in surgery too long, and pretty soon the doctor came out and had the cyst in a jar. It was about the size of a baseball and looked like a big chicken gizzard. He also told me that before they scheduled surgery, they ran a pregnancy test and it came up negative. But once they had made the incision, and had Joy open, they could see from the size of her uterus that she was pregnant. The doctor said that if they had known she was pregnant, they would have delayed the surgery. He told me that more than likely the surgery would cause her to miscarry, and that's what happened the next day or so. When is this string of bad luck ever going to end? God?

By this time Joy was totally fed up with hospitals. As far as she was concerned, she never wanted to see one again. And who could blame her? But a few months later, she had to have oral surgery, and the doctor preferred to do it in the hospital. And he wanted to keep her in the hospital at least one night. But Joy wouldn't hear of it. She didn't want to spend another night in the hospital the rest of her life. She made him do it at his office. So, after the surgery and some recovery time, I had to carry Joy, heavily sedated, out to the car, drive her home, and then stay with her until she recovered. After all the horrible memories, I could easily see how she had such an aversion to hospitals.

It was about this time that Joy wanted to learn how to drive. So I took on the task of trying to teach her how to drive. I would never, ever recommend that any husband try to teach his wife how to drive. Joy was 27 and had never driven in her life. I took her out to big parking lots and let her get behind the wheel and gradually got her more and more experience. I was trying to prepare her for the driving part of the exam. I knew they would take points off if she didn't stay in her lane. So when I was teaching her, I hammered and hammered that into her head. I could write pages about this. She flunked her first driving test, and we had to go back to more training. She went back the second time, and this time she passed. By this time, Max had graduated from law school and was now an assistant prosecutor under S.M. "Buddy" Fallis. Of course, Max had called the highway patrol office and put in a "kind word" for Joy. So now Joy could drive by herself, and now I was really worried. But this gave her a little more freedom, and for that I was happy.

Even with the new job and house, a very important ingredient was still missing from our lives. We still wanted children. Max agreed to do the legal work for us. So we went down to Associated Catholic Charities, got all the adoption forms, took them home and started filling them out. When we were done, we weren't really sure that we wanted to adopt a baby. Although Joy could still get pregnant, it was sadly obvious that she had a hard time carrying a baby full-term. And now she only had one ovary, so we felt this further reduced our chances of getting pregnant. Perhaps the strongest consideration was whether either of us could go through losing another baby. So we decided to take the pressure off ourselves and do the adoption.

We turned in the papers in November of 1966 and were told that it would take from six months to a year. Not too long after that they told us that we were approved, and then we really did some serious soul searching. Did we really want someone else's baby? Then we started realizing the huge difference between adopting a child and having your own. Once you were pregnant, there was no turning back. But with an adoption, you could always change your mind. Yet, there was really never any doubt. We wanted a baby, and if it took an adoption to get one, then let's get on with it. So we just waited, expectantly, but still a bit apprehensively.

In the fall of 1966 I finally started in law school. I had dreamed of this for many, many, years, and I was in overdrive when the school year started. Tulsa U law school was on the trimester system, which allowed us to pick up eight hours of credit per trimester. We took three a year, so we could get 24 hours a year. I took no chances. This was a new ball game for me, so I studied hard.

The exams were strictly essay tests for all courses. You had to both know the law and how to pick out the issues in a factual situation. They also allowed you to type your tests if you wanted. I felt it was worth at least a half grade point if the teacher could just read your writing, so I decided to type mine. I knew how to type (thank you, Army), so I bought a portable electric Smith Corona typewriter. Exams came, the grades were posted, and lo and behold, I made the Dean's Honor Roll. I was on cloud nine. That solidified my determination to get my law degree, because I knew I could do it.

I think it was after the first of the year that the Student Bar Association held its annual Christmas party. It was held in one of the upper conference or ball rooms of one of the downtown hotels. There were wet bars set up where you could get beer and mixed drinks. A few professors were also there. Students were sitting at tables, and were having a good time. It was the first one for me, so I tried to be as inconspicuous as I could.

All of a sudden, there was a loud commotion, and a fight erupted between two students. They looked like they were going to kill each other. Then suddenly they stopped. It had been a mock fight, put on by two students in front of the evidence professor. It seems they had to present both sides of a criminal case in class with the professor as the judge. But since the judge witnessed it, he couldn't be the judge, and the whole thing went for naught.

As it got later in the evening and all the professors had left, everyone was feeling the effects of the drinking, including myself. I was talking with some students, when in walked a really good-looking young lady. There was a separate area in the room for dancing, and she went to that area, set up some music and started an erotic dance. Then it dawned on me that she was a stripper. Now I was certainly no prude by any stretch of the imagination, but somehow, this just didn't seem right. She danced and started peeling off clothes. The more she peeled, the more upset I got, especially since the D.A. was cracking down on strippers going too far. Besides, we were aspiring young law students, and we of all people should be learning deep respect for the law.

The students were really whooping it up the further the stripper went. She kept dancing and peeling, until she was completely nude. I couldn't believe it! And then she started doing high leg kicks at the crowd. I was infuriated. If the police walked in, we'd probably all be arrested, and I could see the headlines in the newspapers. The next day I sent a typed letter to Dean Petersen, the head of the law school, with a copy to the president of the Student Bar Association, and strongly voiced my objection to what had happened. I didn't care that I was a lowly freshman; this should never have been permitted to happen.

A few days later, I was working at my desk when the president of the SBA came into our office and asked if he could talk with me privately. We went down the hall, and I could see that he was very nervous. He was very apologetic about the whole thing, admitted that they had made a mistake, and literally begged me not to do anything further. Since all I wanted to do was voice my objection, I told him that, and he was really relieved.

The next day I got a message that Professor Kirkpatrick wanted to see me. He taught criminal law, a course that I was going to take the next trimester, so I hadn't had him as a professor yet. He retired as a colonel from the military and had a reputation of being a very tough man. After I entered his office, he motioned me to sit down. I had no idea what he wanted. He then held up my letter to Dean Petersen and said that the Dean had passed the letter on to him and had told him to "hold my hand." He told me those were the Dean's exact words. I started sweating, thinking I might have marked myself with all the teachers for the rest of my law school career. Oh, boy! But then he said, "That's what the Dean told me to tell you. But here is what I am going to tell you. If something like this ever happens again at this school, not only will the perpetrators be completely expelled from school, but so will the officers of the SBA." He then thanked me, shook my hand, and said that was all. Whew!

The second semester came and passed. I had let up a little on my studying, but I think I may have still barely made the 3.0 grade point honor roll or slightly below it. The third trimester started, and four of my eight hours were criminal law. It was one of the easiest courses because all of the students liked it and had visions of being the next Perry Mason.

I had joined the Delta Theta Phi legal fraternity soon after starting law school. I should point out that I was never very high on fraternities or sororities at the undergraduate levels, as I felt they tended generally to be a snobbish group of spoiled brats who were riding through school on their parents' finances. I had a lot more respect for those who put themselves through school. They were the producers. Delta Theta Phi didn't have a huge membership, but it was a group of fairly likable guys. I was surprised when I was elected the Dean, or the equivalent of the president. We didn't have a long list of activities, and about the only big function was the Dean having to represent our "senate," named the "Gavin" senate at the national convention in Los Angeles, all expenses paid. That was hard duty, but someone had to do it.

Toward the end of the third trimester, the school scheduled its annual awards banquet, and I really didn't plan on attending. By this time I had learned that quite a few of the male students were married and their wives were working full-time, so their husbands could concentrate on school full-time. So, while I had to work full-time during the day, they had the luxury of spending that time studying. It was just not possible for me to compete for class honors or to get on the prestigious law review editorial staff. I just physically didn't have the time. As a result, by this time I was contented with just getting passing grades, yet still learning the material well enough so that I could pass the two-day state bar exam. Passing that was what gave you your license, and that single document was what we were all after anyway.

Somehow I got an invitation for me and my wife to attend the awards banquet. What the hell, it was a free dinner, so Joy and I went. After the dinner, Dean Petersen approached the dais, made a short speech, then started announcing the awards. I sat there, a bit aggravated, because those who were getting the awards really owed it to their wives. Eventually they came to the freshman class awards. I thought, fat chance. The Dean announced the winner of the outstanding first year day student, then went on to the Faculty Award for the Outstanding First Year Evening Law Student. And he called my name. I almost fell out of my chair! I walked to the dais, the Dean shook my hand and handed me the plaque that went with it. This really floored me, because I knew that there had to be other students with better grades. I couldn't help but think that the episode with the SBA stripper had a lot to do with it.

The final exams for the third trimester came and went. The teachers allowed us to give them stamped post cards addressed to us with the course on the back. When they gave us our final grades, they wrote them on the post card, and sent them to us. In this way we found out our grades sooner and didn't have to go down to the law school to find them out. I was working one day when Joy called to tell me that I had received a grade card in the mail. I asked what course, and she told me criminal law. I felt I had made at least a B, and even had hopes for an A, because the material wasn't that difficult.

I asked her what the grade was, and she asked me what an "F" meant. At first, I thought she was pulling a prank on me. But soon, I realized that she wasn't kidding, I had made an F. I was stunned, shocked, numbed, and even angry. Angry, because I had been going to school for three years, and Joy wasn't even interested enough in my school to know the grading system. This was the first F I had received in my life. Outstanding First Year Evening Law Student? Huh! I had just flunked half my hours for the trimester. I was deeply depressed the rest of the day, and went home from work with a very heavy heart. Sure enough, it was an F.

It just didn't make sense to me. Surely, there had to be a mistake. I set up an appointment with Professor Kirkpatrick to see if an error had been made and, if not, to see if I could talk him into a higher grade. He quietly went over the score I had made and the scores of the other students and showed me how he calculated the curve. I had missed a D by a single point out of a possible 120 points. Professor Kirkpatrick pointed out that the class was loaded with seniors and that had really pushed the curve up. I tried my best to talk him out of that point, but he wouldn't budge. He was really tough, and he was probably trying to teach me a lesson. And I got it.

Fortunately, the school had a policy where you could try to improve your grade by taking the next final exam in that course, without having to take the course over or pay tuition. So I waited until the next final in criminal law, took the exam, got an A, and wound up with an official grade of C. Thank God.

It was May 1, 1967, while Joy and I were sitting at home during the evening, watching TV. Probably "Secret Agent Man," or something like that. The phone rang. It was Associated Catholic Charities, and they wanted to know if we were still interested in adopting a baby. I thought they were just updating their files, as we thought the adoption might take a year, and barely six months had passed. I asked Joy, and she said yes, so I told them we were still interested. They said, good, because it was born yesterday. I went rigid with shock. I looked over at Joy and told her that they said our baby was born yesterday. They wanted to know if we could go over to Oklahoma City in two weeks to pick him up. I told them we could, and they said they'd follow everything up with a letter. When I hung up, it was very quiet, all except for the TV. I walked over to Joy and sat down beside her. We were both filled with blissful amazement. Our own baby son. We were stunned, and yet filled with very nervous anticipation. This had caught us completely by surprise. And neither one of us had ever taken full-time care of a baby. Were we prepared?

After the initial shock, we made all the preparations for Richard Wade Hochanadel to come home. We bought a bassinet, crib, a dozen or so bottles and nipples, baby clothes, plenty of diapers, and a new washer and dryer for the dirty diapers. Our nervousness increased as the day came closer for us to pick up Richard. We took the Interstate to Oklahoma City and found the office of Associated Catholic Charities. We met the monsignor, who went over the final forms, had us sign them, and then gave us the address and directions to the convent where we were to pick up Richard.

My nerves were already rattled as we started to the convent. We were about halfway there when steam started pouring out from under the hood. Oh, no. The car just barely made it to a service station, and by now I was almost a basket case. I explained to the station operator the situation, and he went right to work. It turned out to be a blown heater hose and only took about 10 minutes before we were on our way again.

We found the convent, a non-pretentious, multi-storied tan brick building, and we went in the entrance. A sister greeted us, and we told her who we were and why we were there. She asked to see identification from each of us and copies of the papers we had signed at the ACC office. Then she asked us to wait a few minutes, and left. A few minutes later, the door opened, and she returned. However, she now held a bundled-up little baby with her. She approached Joy and handed the baby to her. It was our son, Richard. He was asleep and was the most beautiful thing I had ever seen. So soft, so peaceful.

Neither Joy nor I expected the feelings that followed. My happiness zoomed, but along with it, a sense of humility, and even a twinge of guilt. We had agreed to pay all the medical bills, so in a way I felt as though I were "buying a baby," and I felt a little guilty about that. Then I felt a lot of compassion for the mother, who had carried the baby for nine months, gave it life, and then had the courage to give him up to strangers. She must have really loved the baby very much to do this. Somehow I felt that the mother knew she either didn't have what it took to be a mother, or she had a domestic situation that prevented her from keeping him. We felt she gave the baby up out of love for it, hopefully to some willing parents who would give him a good home. We wish to this day that we knew who and where she was, so that we could go to her and thank her. She has or had to be a tremendous person.

Joy carried Richard to the car, and I helped her into her seat. We found the Interstate and started back. Joy got a little tired of holding the baby, so she laid him down on the seat between us. He slept all the way home. We took him in the house and put him in his bassinet. Although he was still asleep, we just stayed by his side and watched him. Nothing mattered so much to us in the world. There aren't adequate words to express our feelings.

Soon we eased into the role of being parents. I was now 30 and Joy was about to turn 28, but we never really gave much thought to our calendar ages. We dealt in everything in how we felt, and despite our adversities, we still felt young. We did the usual diaper changes, feeding, burping and rocking Richard to sleep. It truly was a labor of love. Now Joy and I felt a deep sense of completeness. No one will ever know how good we felt.

Richard's coming put a different spin on our lives. There were now three of us, and when we went anywhere we had to make allowances for him. About this time I was starting to get some faint negative rumblings from upper Texaco management over being in law school. I could sense it, because some of these people barely had a bachelor's degree, and the specter of having a lawyer working for them created a bit of insecurity on their part. So I decided to lay out of school a trimester for that reason and be able to spend more time at home with Richard and Joy. That eased off the pressure at work and gave me more time with my family.

Richard was as easy a baby to raise as you could want. He slept most of the night right off the bat. We kept him in the bassinet next to our bed at first. Then, as he got bigger, we moved him into his own bedroom. We had decided long ago that the baby was going to adjust to the house, not the house to the baby. So when it came time for him to go to bed, Joy rocked him to sleep, put him in his crib in his room and shut the door. From that moment on, we didn't turn down the TV, whisper or go out of our way to be quiet. We did everything exactly the way we normally did it.

There are two baby incidents that vividly stand out in my mind about Richard. The first occurred one Saturday morning when Richard must have been about eight months old. I had a huge hangover from the night before. Joy had Richard laying on a clean diaper on the living room floor, and he was very constipated. He needed to poop so bad that his face was in contortions from the discomfort. But we had no suppositories. So I got dressed, hurried out to the nearest drugstore, and came back with the suppositories. To make matters worse, Joy wanted me to do the dirty work. So I knelt down and tried to stick the suppository up his rectum. But it simply was too tight. And I could see why. A hard turd was lodged right at his anal opening, so that everything was as tight as a drum. I realized that to get the suppository in I would first have to push the turd back in a little bit. I took my index finger, placed it on the turd and pushed it in gently, then harder, and then it started moving back in.

At this point I thought my next step was to insert the suppositories. But I soon got an unexpected surprise. As soon as I removed my finger, this must have given Richard's system enough power to let the turd come out on its own. As I looked down in total bewilderment, a long brown turd, at least a foot long and round and straight as a broom handle, came easing out. I thought it would never stop.

I looked at Richard's face, and you have never seen a more blissful look of relief in your life. He was grinning from ear to ear. Joy and I laughed till our sides hurt.

The second episode happened about the time that Richard had learned to pull himself up and stand in his crib. Once he reached that point, then, like any other normal baby, he would hop up and down on the springs, while holding on to the side of the crib. Well, we put him to bed in the normal manner, pinning the dry diapers on before putting him down. In those days we used huge safety pins to fasten the diapers, not the easy disposable tape diapers that mothers have today.

The next morning Joy and I could hear Richard jumping up and down in his crib, and since it was Saturday, Joy asked me to take care of him. I went down the short hall to his room and opened his door. As soon as I opened the door, I was almost knocked over by the pungent odor of fresh poop. And then I looked at Richard. I couldn't believe my eyes. As I was choking on the odor, it soon dawned on me what had happened. We must have not pinned the diapers tight enough the night before. It was obvious that during the night Richard had taken his usual pee, but then he must have also taken a poop as well.

When he woke up, he naturally pulled himself up on the side of the crib and started his usual bouncing up and down. This caused the heavy, wet diapers to eventually slide down his legs. Richard must have looked down and saw a "new toy" in his diaper. And did he ever play with it. It was in his hair, all over his face, on the sides and ends of the crib and all over the bed clothes, even in his mouth. My only regret is that I didn't take pictures of him. What a sight! After that, we made certain we had those diapers pinned on tight.

I returned to night law school for the second trimester and resumed my march toward the law degree. After the first of the new year, or in early 1968, rumors started to fly at work that the regional credit office would be dismantled and each of us credit supervisors would be relocated to the districts they were handling. I had Little Rock, which covered the whole state of Arkansas. But this created a big problem, because Little Rock had no law school. If I took the transfer there, that meant giving up any chance of getting the law degree. This bothered me for some time. We also had the Oklahoma City district, but that was handled by another man. Well, we'd just have to wait and see. I had one big thing going for me, though. My district, Little Rock, had taken national honors in credit and collections, and there was a letter of commendation in my personnel file from *THE MAN,* the general credit manager in Texaco national headquarters in New York.

Texaco was able to totally dominate the lives of some of their employees, something that rubbed me the wrong way. I attended a retirement celebration of an assistant district manager in charge of operations. At one point in the speeches, his wife was allowed to address us. She said that after all these years, Texaco had been first in her husband's life. But now, she said, she came first and was looking forward to a long and happy retirement. I thought to myself that this was very sad. Here she had to wait all these 40 or so years before her husband put her first. And now, when his health was bad and he probably couldn't really do or enjoy much, she finally had her husband back. I vowed I would never let anything like that interfere with my family. It would always come first.

After I finished the second trimester, this gave me 32 hours of law school, and I had then completed the requirements for the bachelor's degree in business administration. The following June, 1968, I graduated with that degree from Tulsa University. One down, one to go.

Max, Mark and I did a fair share of beer drinking during these times, and sometimes they got way out of hand. There is one harrowing experience that is worth relating. It was a Sunday afternoon, and we were all gathered at Mark's house for a barbeque chicken cook-out. Gery was visiting at the time and had just bought a brand new red MG convertible. It was a small two-seat convertible, and pretty as could be. After quite a few beers, we decided to take Gery over to see the house that Joy and I bought. We decided to take Gery's car, so he could show it to us.

However, it only had two seats. Well, that really wasn't a big problem. Two of us decided to sit on the trunk, with our legs dangling inside the back of the seats. It seemed safe enough, because we could stick one of our hands between our legs and hold on to the car as we went. This, of course, left our other hand free to hold a can of beer. So off we went, with me sitting on the trunk behind the front passenger. We directed Gery to the Skelly By-Pass, an expressway to my house. As we started down Skelly, Gery decided to show us how fast his car would go, and before long we were doing 115 mph! The wind was blasting me in the face, and I was hanging on for dear life.

Finally, we got off Skelly and came down the frontage street toward my house. Gery had to turn left to go down my street. However, now he wanted to show everyone how well his car cornered. So he sped up to about 50 mph and then suddenly jerked the car into the left turn. Well, the car made it fine. But I didn't. The next thing I knew, I was getting up in the gutter of the street, next to the curb. By this time, the other three were wondering where in the hell I was. They spotted me and backed up to me. I stood up shakily and showed them that I still had my beer and hadn't spilled a drop. The only problem was, I had a long gash on my middle finger, from just about the tip down to the second knuckle, and then across that knuckle. And I was bleeding all over the place. If I had been sober, it probably would have killed me.

So I had to go to the hospital. Since Gery was new to Tulsa, Max convinced him to let him drive, since he knew exactly how to get there. But this time, because of my injury I got to sit in the passenger seat. Max had also had quite a bit to drink. In fact, as we pulled into the emergency area of the hospital, he completely misjudged the curb in the covered area, rammed into it so hard that it bent Gery's fly wheel and cost $600 to fix it.

They took me into the emergency room and started cleaning up my gash. I had apparently slid my open gash along the gutter, where there were pieces of glass, dirt, sand, grease and all the things you find in a gutter. The doctors and nurses had to clean out under the flap of skin all of these foreign matters before they could stitch me up. They had to, or the chances of infection were very high. So they spent a very long time picking all of this out. After about an hour and a half they were done, and they gave me 16 stitches, some prescriptions to prevent infection, and sent me on my way. We headed for the nearest drugstore, but before I would let the pharmacist fill the prescription, I had to have his assurance that the medications would not interfere with our beer drinking.

When we finally got back to Mark's house, all our wives were really mad at us, especially Joy when she saw the huge bandage on my finger. We never told her what actually happened until much later. I think that is the maddest I have ever seen Joy, and she had every right to be. What a crazy thing we did! I should have realized it then, but this was an early warning of a serious drinking problem I had. I didn't drink just one.

May of 1968 brought a big surprise to Joy and me. She missed her period. Was she pregnant? By this time there had been so many false signals, no one could say. So all we could do was wait. She missed the next period as well. Then her tummy started to show it. Soon it became undeniable that she was, in fact, pregnant. By this time we were naturally apprehensive. Were we going to have to go through another death? Thank God we had Richard, in case there was another dead baby. There wasn't much we could do, except wait and let Mother Nature take her course.

Joy and I were visiting my folks in Great Bend, Kansas, on one of the summer holidays, when I got a call from Ron Booker, who was then my credit manager. He said he had to ask me directly whether I would take a transfer to Little Rock if I was transferred there. I told him I wouldn't take the transfer. This put the ball back in his court. He had to either send me to Oklahoma City, or face losing me and having a vacancy to fill. For all I knew, when I got back to Tulsa, I might not even have a job. Fortunately, however, he persuaded another credit supervisor to take the Little Rock district, and I accepted a transfer to Oklahoma City.

So, next stop, Oklahoma City.

9

OKLAHOMA CITY

(Family Grows, Pass Bar Exam, Start of Alcoholism, and the Dumbest Mistake of My Life)

As I TOYED with the sub-title for this chapter, I mulled over many different selections. After much deliberation, I felt (and painfully so) that this sub-title most honestly represented my six years in Oklahoma City. I say "painfully," because I made some great strides during these years (with Joy's help), and it's a shame that a growing drinking problem marred those accomplishments. I wish I could have left out the *"start of alcoholism"* part, since that would mean that I would have probably experienced even greater successes down the road. Nevertheless, I promised to be honest.

This was the summer of 1968, so I was 31 and Joy was 29. Richard was a little over a year old, and Joy was pregnant again. We sold our house in Tulsa relatively easily and netted enough so that we could buy an even better home in Oklahoma City. It was a two-car garage ranch style, with three bedrooms and a fireplace. It was much more modern than our last house, with a patio and was completely fenced. In fact, we bought it from a Texaco supervisor who was being transferred to Tulsa. Ironic, isn't it?

I learned I could transfer the 40 hours of Tulsa University law school credits and now needed just two more years of night school to get the degree of Juris Doctor, or "doctor of law." However, it meant that I had to go to school in the evenings from 6:00 to 9:00 every Monday through Thursday. It would be quite a load for me, especially after working all day at Texaco. It also meant that Joy was alone a great deal of time with Richard.

I settled in at the district office with the title of Credit Supervisor. My office was at the same location as the sales and operations office. Sales was responsible for finding dealers for all of Texaco's service stations in the district, and operations was in charge of delivering the fuel and oil to the stations. We were getting more and more into tires, batteries and accessories, so a new station operator had to have a fair amount of capital to start his business. The sales reps brought me the financial information on the prospective dealers, and I then did a financial analysis and verification of bank balances, etc. If they were solid, I approved them. If not, tough.

It's odd that during these months I don't recall being extremely anxious or worried over Joy's pregnancy. You'd think that, with our two previous babies' deaths, we would live in constant, excruciating anxiety. Perhaps having Richard, and that, combined with both the job and school, was probably why I don't recall really being that worried. Joy had to be a nightmare for her doctors, because they kept changing the due dates for the baby. Christmas came, and Joy was getting bigger. That much I did know.

As soon as I arrived at my new office, I noticed a quaint idiosyncrasy. The district manager, C.F. "Buddy" Gardenhire had a habit of chewing on an unlit cigar. He never smoked it, but just liked having one in his mouth. The odd thing was that there were about six other employees who did the same thing! Talk about brown-nosing! It fell right in line with Texaco's basic theory of not wanting thinkers. They wanted people who followed policy to the letter. I think ultimately that my own individuality and pragmatic approach to situations was a factor in my eventual departure from Texaco.

January came. It was a Saturday morning, so we were sleeping late. As we started to get up, Joy said she didn't feel quite right. We deliberated a few minutes about whether we should go to the hospital. Finally, to be on the safe side, we decided to head for the hospital. Joy called her doctor and told him we were on our way. We pulled into the Emergency Room entrance, and the nurses put Joy in a wheelchair and took her to the delivery room floor. I parked the car and went upstairs to the nurse's station. As I was standing there, they rolled Joy by on the way to the delivery room. I still didn't know anything, and felt they would let me know if and when anything developed.

As I was standing by the nurse's station, her phone rang, and someone was giving the nurse some blood types. I overheard the blood type and asked the nurse if she had been talking about Mrs. Hochanadel. She said she was, so I had to tell her that the blood type she had just repeated was not Joy Hochanadel's. She looked at me oddly and asked how I knew. I told her I was her husband, and I was sure that blood type was not hers. She got very nervous and immediately called the lab. A couple of minutes later the phone rang, and they gave her some new results. It seemed the lab had mistakenly switched the blood samples on my wife and another patient. She was white as a sheet when she told me this and thanked me profusely for speaking up when I did.

A few minutes later a doctor came out of the delivery room, looking for Mr. Hochanadel. I identified myself, and before I could say anything, he stuck his hand out and said, "Congratulations. You have a new son, and both he and your wife are doing just fine." I was shocked into total numbness. We hadn't been at the hospital more than 45 minutes. In fact, I was just in the process of trying to find out if this was a false alarm or what. I was completely unprepared for this. It was just too quick. The emotional relief was greater than the deflation of a dirigible. I could feel a huge burden suddenly just evaporate from my shoulders. I was allowed to see Joy, and she had our new baby in her arms. It was the most beautiful sight in the world. Joy had a look that rivaled that of the Madonna. You could see that, now, finally, she felt fulfilled as a woman. She was serenely proud.

We named him Donald Lawrence Charles Hochanadel after me and my dad. We might have trounced on tradition by naming the second son "Junior." However, this was the first natural son to survive, and so we named him that anyway. He was born January 11, 1969, and we were now a "big" family of four. The metamorphosis continued, as now there were four people who depended exclusively on me.

Maybe this is a good time to talk about kids in general. Today,

I look around and see many families with only one or two children, or maybe one boy and one girl, the so-called "perfect" family. I have always felt sorry for these people. I call these families "pot luck" families. What happens if the one boy or one girl gets killed, or worse, turns out to be a terrible person? What a horrible, lonely, and miserable way to spend your later years ... alone and living with the hurt of having no children, or with the depressing disappointment of knowing your child was worthless. That is pot luck on the hugest of scales. But not me. I'd rather go through the hell of raising kids and spend my later years ... happy, watching my kids grow and having their own families.

I can't begin to tell you the number of people I know who are very wealthy, with lavish homes, luxurious cars, exquisite furniture and lots of money, but whose only child is totally worthless, or who is no more than a fading, painful memory to them. I suppose I'm echoing the feelings of my father and mother when it comes to kids, but I really believe kids are the future of society. As we raise our kids, so goes our society in the generations ahead.

My father wrote an essay on the subject of having children in 1952, a fact that I didn't find out about until long after his death. I was given a copy of it, but just filed it away for many years until just recently. I was looking for something when I ran across it and sat down and read it again. His feelings reached out and absorbed me. Only then did I start to comprehend how great a man this simple, poor human being was. On the following two pages is his essay exactly as the way it was written.

I still get goose pimples every time I read it.

(No) More Than One To a Customer

By Lawrence Charles Hochanadel (1952)

It was during World War II that the greatest thrill I ever experienced became known to me. It was during the times that I would see great crowds of people waiting in line just to be able to buy a pair of nylons, or when I would see people crowding every way, just to buy a scarce item, marked "only one to a customer." It was then that I saw how insane people could become over some insignificant piece of rag or a new tire, and all the time not to be fighting for something greater than everything else in the world — LIFE; and by life, I mean children.

I had begun to think that maybe God might decide to allow "one to a customer." I just wondered how many of the people would be in line, fighting to the front, to receive a life to raise into a man or a woman. I just wondered and wondered.

Then the thrill came to me that the King of all creation in all of His supreme power and glory had looked down from His throne in heaven, and of all the millions of His people, He had chosen us, of all these people, and had selected us, not once, but 12 times, to have another of His infant children, that only one divine person, God, could breathe life into.

Then it was that the thought entered my mind that maybe God was particular who it was, that He let only certain people have His babies. That maybe He knew everyone was not fit to be parents of His loved ones.

So the people who saw to it in their own way that they didn't have children were only following out the plan God knew they would; but this was not the plan of God, as he said to multiply. He never did say to wait till after your first million, or how many to have. God didn't care who you were or how poor you were. But He will remember, above all, how many you didn't have, when you could have — that is the thing that scares me, the same as it scared me each time we had a new baby in our home.

I want to thank God for giving me the strength to accept all of my children without ever thinking of not having any one of them. But God did see that we were able to take care of them because I could never have done it myself.

It was when I found out we were going to have our first baby that I got scared. I didn't seem to know anything about having babies. I was afraid things might not all be all right. Maybe the baby would be crippled or deformed. Maybe my wife might die during childbirth. I was really worried.

Then I started to think, and I must confess I had the sneaky feeling I was taking advantage of God. I went to praying to the mother of God. Each night I knelt down on my knees and asked the Blessed Virgin Mary to watch over and protect my wife, to take care of her, and not let anything happen to her, because she was going to have another baby. Then, for 12 consecutive times, I asked her for the same favor. I would ask her to look out for the new baby, to let it be born pure of heart and soul, and mind and body, with a love of God and all that is pure and holy.

Twelve times this request was granted. So after all this happened to me in my life, I don't have much courage to ask for riches and power. The power of God has been shown to me too often for me to want to be able to try and take it away from someone else.

This all brings me back to the things I was talking about in the beginning. Maybe there are some things in this life that there are more than "one to a customer." There was in our case. And, instead of waiting in line, it still is a long wait. Two hours to wait in line for a pair of nylons was tough sometimes, but as beautiful as they were, it was worth it.

So imagine how much greater the happiness to wait nine months for your baby. But, believe me, it would be worth it, life, itself, by you, from God.

Finis
Lawrence C. Hochanadel
Daddy of one dozen children 50/50, 6 boys – 6 girls

So now Joy had two kids to take care of while her husband was either at work or at school. But, together, we managed. I was getting used to my usual six-pack of beer every Friday night and gradually started looking forward to it. I don't recall doing too many things socially with Joy on the weekends. She had a cousin, Annette, whose husband, Norman, was with the Air Force at Del City, on the other side of Oklahoma City. We went to a local lake with them a time or two, and I played poker maybe once a month with her husband and his friends. Joy wasn't too happy with that, and I eventually dropped it.

School and work wore on into 1969. Fewer and fewer courses remained to be taken before I could graduate. Soon, Christmas of 1969 approached. Joy had always been a very difficult person to please with a present. I tried hard to get her the things I thought she liked. However, most of the time she took them back or exchanged them, or got the cash. I always struck out on things like clothes, jewelry or perfumes.

This year Joy let me know that she wanted a "unique, personal" gift. I thought and thought and looked throughout the stores for something I thought she would really like and keep. Finally, I had an idea. While I was at work or at law school, poor Joy had to take care of the kids, and I wasn't around much for support, except for weekends. So I drafted a short personal note to her, took it down to an engraving firm, had them inscribe it on a six-inch by eight-inch gold plaque. It went like this:

A TOKEN OF APPRECIATION

In these days of growing demands on our time, attention and thoughts, there is a tendency to take for granted our finest luxury — an understanding wife and untiring mother. That we have in you, sweetheart. We may not always show our gratitude, but the boys and I are aware of the chores you do ... wash the clothes ... do the dishes ... cook the meals ... dress the kids ... change baby's diapers ... get up and give the baby his 5 a.m. bottle ... vacuum the carpets ... wash the windows ... pick up

the toys ... dust the furniture ... food shopping ... make the beds ... fold the diapers ... take kids to the doctor ... write all the family letters ... trim the hedges ... rake the leaves ... mop the floors ... arrange for babysitters, etc., and you get all this done with a baby tugging at your knees, whining to be held — and with an incessant little boy constantly bugging you for something, and a husband who is always preoccupied with his job, law school, his fraternity, the newspaper or some football game on TV, and never has time to simply sit and pass the time of day with you. To say we appreciate it is not enough, honey. So we are giving this plaque to you, my sweet wife, and the boys' caring mother, with our best love and the pledge that in the years ahead we will better appreciate you ... our most precious asset.

Don, Richard and Don, Jr.
Christmas 1969

I thought I really had her this year. After all, this took some planning, some soul-searching, and putting my true feelings and love for Joy in writing. I thought it would be something she would cherish for many years, knowing that all of her efforts were noticed and appreciated. I watched with hopeful anticipation as she unwrapped it, took a short look at it, shrugged her shoulders and set it aside. She didn't like it. My heart sank. I guess I may have been naive, or even stupid, thinking she would like it, but I really had been burned out on getting her something I thought she liked, only to find out she took it back. This difficulty haunts me to this day, even though ever so often I get lucky.

By this time Joy was about five months pregnant. Things went smoothly with this pregnancy, and on April 10, 1970, Kurt Bradford Hochanadel was born and was healthy. There were now five in our family, and I really was the provider now.

In August of 1970, my mom came down and stayed with the kids so Joy and I could go to Las Vegas. That was quite an event for us. Since we had been married, we had never really taken a true vacation or even had a decent honeymoon for just the two of us. So we really anticipated having a great time alone together. We made reservations a couple of weeks in advance to see the King, Elvis. The last available show was the midnight show on a Wednesday.

Joy was terrified of flying, so I had to do a lot of talking to get her to go. She hung onto me almost the whole flight, and even the slightest turbulence caused her a wave of anxiety. We arrived in one piece, got to our hotel and started having fun. We did all the usual gambling, but had to watch our money since we didn't have a lot to spend. One night Joy loosened up a bit and had a little too much to drink. I managed to get her up to her room, and she fell into the bed. She was so tipsy that she asked me to make the room stop spinning. I laughed as I sat on the bed with her until she dropped off to sleep. I covered her up and headed back downstairs for more fun.

The highlight of the trip for me was to see Elvis. I couldn't wait. Unfortunately, it was the midnight show, and I started drinking well before it started. We had to get in line at a certain time so we could get the best seats. When we moved up in the line so that it was our turn to be seated, I gave the maitre d' a $20 tip. He marched us right down in front and sat us at a table of eight. The end of the table was right next to the stage, so we really had some class seats. We ate, then had some more drinks. The pre-show acts came and went as did many more drinks. Finally, Elvis came on, and he put on a fantastic performance. He was the epitome of showmanship. He was truly the King, and no one will ever touch him. His arrangement of "Suspicious Minds" was sensational. My only regret was that by the time Elvis came on, I was so drunk I could hardly see straight. I've kicked myself about that ever since. Overall, it was a great vacation for us.

It wasn't long after that that I started to realize that I had a real drinking problem. I could not go a weekend without having at least a six-pack every Friday evening, and many Sunday afternoons were spent drinking beer. I even attended a few Alcohol Anonymous meetings, but somehow it disgusted me to see these other people debasing themselves by publicly saying that they were alcoholics, that they couldn't control it, and that they would stop. At the next meeting the same people confessed of drinking and made the same public self-effacement. A few days later, as I was coming out of a liquor store, one of the AA members was on her way in. She didn't seem to recognize me, so I wondered just how much AA really helped. Then I just quit going.

It seemed that the closer I got to finishing law school, the more static I was getting from my Texaco supervisor in Houston, Pat Richardson. He was always negative when we spoke, and I knew he was trying to get me to quit. I think with my getting the law degree, he felt I posed a threat to him. But he just didn't have anything concrete to use to fire me. In fact, during this time I wrote and assembled a 90-page Credit and Collections Manual for all the sales reps in the district. It was the first one in Texaco's history and was really useful to the sales reps when they were out in the field and had a credit question.

It was while working with Texaco that I got a real taste of how deeply radical some of the black people had become over the race issue. We had a black warehouseman who was the friendliest, most likable person you ever met. He always had the widest, brightest smile on his face. To me, he was a ray of sunshine. We held an all-district party one night at a motel for all employees and their spouses. When this black man walked in with his wife, my face lit up and I hailed him, "Hello, Sunshine!" Very shortly, some of the other men took me aside and away from him and his wife. They explained to me that his wife was very active in the NAACP, and she was livid over what I called him. My God! He was my friend, and I was just saying hello as a friend. I certainly wasn't trying to assert a superior posture. Give me a break!

Nonetheless, Richardson and I both knew that I was using Texaco to work my way through law school. Late in the fall of 1970 he came up to Oklahoma City and wanted me to meet him in his motel room. I just knew he was going to fire me. We met, and his demeanor and flow made it clear to me that he wanted me to quit. He literally was trying to brow-beat me. But I wasn't ready to quit yet. I was at the tail end of law school, and I didn't want to contend with looking for a job at this time. So, despite his pressure, I stayed on.

Mom and Dad's 40th wedding anniversary was October 29, 1970. We all decided to give them a huge surprise anniversary celebration. Our sister, Teresa, lived in La Crosse, about 35 miles or so from Great Bend. She had a big two-story house, and we all agreed to meet there the day before. We had arranged for the priest to say a mass and planned on them walking into the church and unexpectedly finding all of their kids and grandkids there. However, Father felt this might be too severe a jolt on them, so he told them in advance. We had a beautiful private Saturday mass, and Mom and Dad repeated their marriage vows. All of the effort was worth it, as they were beaming with pride.

That night we held a big party at Teresa's house. Teresa and her husband, Arlon, had 10 kids, so they didn't have too big a budget. Someone had bought a five-pound length of bologna, and they made this into a sandwich spread. It tasted terrible, but when you're hungry anything tastes good. Mom and Dad were there, along with all 12 of their kids and their spouses and kids. It was a huge crowd. We were all really heavy drinkers in those days, and the beer flowed freely.

I had bought a battery-operated tape recorder for law school and brought it along. Throughout the evening, we did interviews with everyone, including Mom and Dad. Many of us were extremely drunk, and some things on that tape were so gross that later I wanted it destroyed. My older brothers kid me about that to this day. I was really drunk, and for some reason went outside. The temperatures were at or below freezing that night, and for some crazy reason I insisted on sleeping in our station wagon. Everyone thought that I had completely lost my bearings and was lost, and so they all scattered out looking for me. When they found me, I stubbornly refused to leave the car. Crazy. I really feel ashamed of that to this day. I had completely forgotten about my kids and left their care up to Joy. Kids were lying on the floors upstairs like sardines. I heard the next day that many of them were passing gas, and the upstairs really stunk by morning. This whole affair is a bad memory to me and serves as a constant reminder of how alcohol can totally ruin your life and the good things in life.

I graduated from Oklahoma City University Law School on December 18, 1970. The next and final hurdle was to pass the State Bar Exam, which was scheduled in February in Norman, Oklahoma, at Oklahoma University. Our class kicked in $50 each, and we hired practicing attorneys to deliver a four-hour session each Sunday afternoon on his area of expertise. We had a secretary in the classroom with a tape recorder, and she then typed each complete session, and we all got a typed copy of the session. This was the perfect preparation for the bar exam. In fact, it was so good that I felt I learned as much in these sessions as I did taking the whole course in school. I actually felt that going to all those classes and taking all those courses for all those years was almost a waste of time.

The bar exam itself was a two-day affair, so I decided to spend the night in Norman. All of the exams were essay exams, so I took my typewriter and typed my answers. Again, I felt it gave me an edge if the examiner could at least read it. At the end of the first day, I crossed off those subjects that they covered on the first day. That narrowed the subjects that we were going to be tested on the next day. I grabbed a quick meal, picked up a pint of whiskey and headed for my room. I drank whiskey and crammed until midnight, consuming the whole pint. The whiskey was my "sleeping pill."

The next morning I felt fine, dug right in on the rest of the exam questions, and when I was finished, I felt I had done a good job. But you never know. So the long wait for the results was a little worrisome. When they printed the list of successful applicants in the paper, it included my name. A couple of weeks later we were sworn in before the Supreme Court at the State Capitol in Oklahoma City. I had made it. I was now licensed to practice law. My dream had come true. All those long years of poverty I had put both Joy and me through should now be at an end. All those years of giving up my weekday evenings and forcing Joy to take care of the kids were now finally over. Now we could begin real, normal living.

But then I made the dumbest mistake of my life. What I should have been doing was looking for an attorney or two that I could associate with and should have been saving money to start my practice. I simply wasn't wise enough to see that. Sure, I rationalized that I had a wife and three kids, so I couldn't take the $500 a month legal jobs that a lot of the other married students could, whose wives had put them through school and now were going to keep working so their husbands could build their practice. Simply put, I lacked the guts to depend on myself, to hang the shingle out, and start my practice. Sure, it would have been tough for a few years, but in the long run, I would fulfill my professional dream and reap the financial rewards as well.

My position at Texaco was now critically tenuous, and I was actively looking for a new job. About this time one of the sales reps brought me a $66,000 term tire order from a company called Public Leasing Corporation. The term order meant that they paid it off on extended terms after delivery, one-third in 30-day increments, or 30-60-90, as we called it. Public Leasing was a public over-the-counter truck and trailer leasing corporation based in Oklahoma City. The real money behind the company was Bill Kerr, one of the sons of the famous Oklahoma Senator, Robert S. Kerr. They were having some financial problems and were looking for their first general credit manager.

I didn't have the authority for the $66,000 order. But Pat Richardson in Houston did. So I assembled all of the supporting credit information and sent the file off to Richardson, recommending approval. I made sure that the information I had was accurate and followed company procedures so they couldn't later blame me. Richardson received the file and approved the order. It was probably the largest tire order in the district's history.

During the next two weeks I met with Gerald Buckner, the president of Public Leasing, and we worked out my coming aboard as their first general credit manager. My job as the company's first general credit manager was to establish some control over what customers we leased trucks and trailers to. The company had been burned in the past by customers who rented a full rig, paid for a while, then we never heard from them again. They were running all over the country, wearing out our equipment and making a fortune without paying us a dime. I had to stop the financial bleeding.

The controller was Dave Patrick, a soft-talking, unemotional, untrustworthy individual. I learned very quickly to be extremely cautious with him, and with Buckner. These two had their own agendas, and they were truckers. That meant that if they didn't like the way you were doing things, they eliminated you in a flash. Buckner, especially. I soon realized I was window dressing, as far as Buckner was concerned. If I turned down a deal that was a bad credit risk and Buckner liked the deal, he approved it anyway. He had the authority, but his judgment was poor from a financial standpoint.

The first $22,000 payment to Texaco for the tire order approached, and I was concerned that Patrick would fudge on its payment. I made sure he wrote the check, and that Rusty Seamands, the Texaco sales rep, picked it up. I called him later and suggested that he convert it to a cashier's check as soon as possible. He went to our bank after 2 p.m. when all banking was the next day's business, and convinced the bank to issue a cashier's check. However, later that same afternoon, sure as hell, Patrick put a "Stop Payment" on the Public Leasing check. When the cashier's check came through, our bank refused to honor their own cashier's check! I'd never heard of such a thing. Texaco wound up suing the bank over it, and lost. That one really surprised me.

Buckner threw wild bashes frequently and was always trying to get his secretary to sleep with him. He didn't care who knew either. On one occasion he had Patrick cut a big check, took it to the bank, cashed it, had our two contract pilots fly him and a bunch of friends to Dallas, where they rented an entire floor of a large hotel and held a wild orgy, complete with high-class prostitutes. All of this made for an unpleasant and insecure place to work. Yet, I had a family to support, so I had no choice but to continue work, while I kept an eye out for another job.

The Oklahoma City branch had the highest activity, so the first thing I did was to hire a credit manager there. I had met a fellow, Jim Tipton, who managed a small loan office near my house, where I made small loans from time to time. I knew he wasn't happy there, so I offered him the job, and he took it.

We had under contract a tough, hard-nosed ex-FBI agent, who was "on call." We brought him in when the going got really hairy. An example of this was when we had a large account out in Los Angeles who was causing us a lot of grief. He was terribly delinquent on his account, jimmied with the mileage equipment, and was very demanding in every area. Buckner sent me, Patrick, and our ex-FBI "collector" out to L.A. to straighten him out.

We met at the branch office and learned that one of our tractors leased to this account was in our garage for servicing. We had our mechanics drop the rear axle off the tractor so it couldn't be driven. Soon we got an angry call from the customer, and he ordered us over to his office. We walked in, and our "collector" immediately sat down on the edge of this guy's desk with his .45 automatic visibly sticking out of his back pocket. He then told the customer that he had heard there were some problems, and they were going to stop right now. The customer looked at the gun, then at us, and from that day forward we had no more problems with him.

Patrick liked to chase women, so that night we went out on the town. As we went from bar to bar, he eventually located a bar that had a show featuring an entirely nude couple. By now it was pretty late and we were both feeling no pain. The show started, and sure enough, both the male and female dancers were totally nude. As they danced to "My Sweet Lord," they had frequent physical contact with each other's critical parts. This act was not your typical "T & A" redneck stripper act. They were professional dancers and had some impressive, smooth moves. But to this day, I will never know how the male dancer could remain completely flaccid throughout the entire performance. And every time I hear that song, I can't help but think back to that performance.

During these years many of us kids visited Mom and Dad on holidays, bringing our families. Mom's house wasn't big enough to handle all of us. It had only one bedroom upstairs for Mom and Dad, and the basement had a second bedroom, a small den, wash room, and toilet and shower. The den had a hide-a-bed that provided more sleeping. Mark and his wife, Luanne, generally stayed at her folks' house, and Gery and his wife, Joyce, stayed at her parents' house. So, when we all descended on the old homestead, there was a huge crowd of kids and grand kids.

Usually at these gatherings, the beer flowed freely. There was a single large tree out in the right front of Mom's yard that we nicknamed the "beer" tree. It had a picnic table, and we brought along lots of lawn chairs and coolers, so we could hunker down into some serious beer drinking. I remember arriving at Mom's house once, and Dave, Gery and some other brothers were sitting under the beer tree, drinking beer. They kidded me about not bringing any beer. I told them I'd be happy to spring for a six-pack. They laughed at me in mock derision. A six-pack! They informed me in no uncertain terms that they were buying in full case quantities.

In looking back, there is no question that these weren't really visits, in the true sense of the word. These were no more than plain and simple beer busts. We all drank far too much, and many of us had to be full-blown alcoholics even at that early time. It's a wonder that we didn't get killed while in a drunken stupor. I could never drink "a few"; I had to drink until I was totally drunk and could sleep with no difficulty at all.

Mom pushed heavily for having annual family reunions. One of the first ones was held out on a small farm about six miles south of Hoisington, that my oldest sister, Rita, and her husband had bought. It had an old house on it that had been vacant for years. It had one bathroom in it, but it didn't work. They told us that it would be fixed in time for the reunion. The yard was mowed, and we started arriving, some of us bringing pop-up RV trailers, and others with tents. The reunion I remember the most was in 1971, around the fourth of July. I had just bought a brand new gun-metal gray Dodge Charger, that was my very first brand new car. Boy, it was powerful, and I was really proud to bring it to the reunion, I had also brought with me a huge fireworks display that turned out to be a real treat for the kids. Martin, Rosalie's husband, had arranged for an enormous charcoal grill on which we intended to grill an entire pig overnight. We fired up the grill and started cooking the pig, which would take all night to cook completely.

The beer flowed freely again, and most of us got stone-drunk that night. To make matters worse, the toilet had not been fixed, so if anyone who had to go, they had to rough it out in the trees. That really upset my wife and the other women. Nevertheless, we had plenty of beer, and that was the main thing. I remember passing out on someone's lawn chair and crushing it in the process. One of my brothers, also drunk, poured water over me, waking me up. I came awake, roaring out of the chair, took him to the ground and was just about to start pounding the hell out of him when I came to my senses.

Another sad thing about these drinking bouts was that getting the kids ready for bed was the exclusive responsibility of my wife. She had to take care of that by herself. She drank very little, and in looking back, these drinking bouts must have been very little fun for her. Her husband, none other than me, was usually completely drunk by the time the kids were to go down for the night. I had to assemble the pop-up RV before she could put them down. I must not have snapped down the side covers well, because during the night one of our baby sons, while sleeping, fell out of the side of the RV to the ground. It's a wonder he wasn't killed. And I'm sure it was no fun for Joy to have to sleep with a drunk, passed-out husband.

During the middle of the night I was awakened by a lot of screaming about a fire. In a drunken stupor I could see that the charcoal grill itself had caught on fire, and Martin with the help of a few others was furiously trying to put out the fire. It looked like they had it under control, so I rolled over and went back to sleep. The next morning I got up with a big hangover, and the reunion started in earnest. The pig was a disaster. It was fully cooked, but it tasted terrible and even smelled sour. Very few of us got past one bite and had to scrounge up something else to eat for lunch.

After lunch we decided to have a softball game in the farm field next to the house. It was a very rough field, but we still set up the bases and had a game. I remember Dad coming up to bat. This was pure heaven for me. I remembered with a lot of nostalgia the days back in Olmitz, when Dad played in baseball games behind our house, and it really felt good to see him play. To me, this was the highlight of the reunion. Even though he was 63 at the time, he still managed to get a hit and run the bases. I thought that was remarkable for someone his age and was even concerned that he might hurt himself, or have a heart attack.

Max came to the reunion with a brand new station wagon. I think it still had the dealer tag on it. Sometime during the day, he and Dave decided to go down to a farm pond nearby with their sons and do some skinny dippin'. I wasn't interested, mainly because my kids just weren't that old, so I stayed at the farm. As they were coming back, Max came over a hill on the narrow country road just when another car was coming from the other direction. Both drivers were caught completely off guard and almost hit head on. Fortunately, they just sideswiped each other, and the left side of Max's wagon was smashed from the front all the way to the rear. Thankfully, no one was injured. Max, however, almost fainted when Gery, who was a police officer at the time, had just seconds before the collision made Max's two sons get their heads and arms back inside the car. If he had not made them do so, they probably would have been decapitated.

In thinking about all of the years that all of us Hochanadels drank so much beer so often, it is a real wonder that we have not had someone killed, or even injured, because of drinking. The times that I drove while completely drunk were much too numerous to count, and my brothers were the same way. When we die and go to heaven, I'm sure that our guardian angels are really going to want to settle the score with us.

Eventually Public Leasing went into Chapter 11 bankruptcy, and things really got scary. This was during the early fall of 1971. I never knew from one day to the next whether they would lay me off that day, or whether my pay check would clear. It was extremely stressful, so I started looking in earnest for a new job. An ad in the paper for a general manager of a warehousing company caught my eye. It looked like it had the salary potential, but I didn't know squat about warehousing. Still, I applied anyway.

Soon, an appointment was set up with a fellow by the name of

Len DiJacomo out of Dallas. He logged a full day of interviews, and that night called and wanted five of us the next day to undergo some aptitude testing, including the Wunderlich test. We showed up, and I sailed through the tests with ease. Len's assistant was so impressed, he asked me if I had the answers before I came in. Apparently, I had the highest scores they had ever seen. And why shouldn't they be, with the great seminary education and the college and law degree? They offered me the job that same day, subject to the approval of the regional vice-president.

The company was the D.H. Overmeier out of New York, and it was a national warehouse company with branch offices in 45 cities. I caught a flight to Dallas for a pre-New York meeting with DiJacomo, then flew on to New York to meet Dave Douthit, the V.P. By this time in my life, I had seen all of the country, west coast, Chicago, New Orleans, and, of course, Europe. But New York is a world all by itself. The cab rides are far more exciting than any ride at an amusement park. The cabbies could cruise through spaces where, if they had another coat of paint, they'd never make it. They were really pros. The garbage collectors were on strike, so garbage was literally piling up in the streets, so that the whole city stunk.

A mere cup of coffee cost a fortune. The best part of the whole trip was the delicious steak I had brought up to my room around 10 o'clock. There's nothing like a good bottle of wine and a great steak in the privacy of your hotel room.

The native New Yorker has a real superior attitude problem. They could spot a "foreigner" very easily and treat them with open scorn. I got the impression that if anyone was from any area west of New York City, they considered them stupid country bumpkins. That was fine with me, because as long as they thought they were the center of the universe, I felt they would have no interest in coming out where we lived and contaminate our great living conditions.

A week later I met Len at the warehouse office. I met an elderly gentleman, Curtis Roberston, who had just sold his 40-year-old, 250,000-square-foot public warehouse company to Overmeier. Overmeier had 240,000 square feet of its own 30-foot clear ceiling space as well. Of that, 80,000 square feet had been leased out to Southwest Warehouse Company, yet another public warehouse company that Overmeier had just purchased. My job was to take these two companies and meld them with Overmeier's own space into a single operation. Len spent a whopping three days with me, showing me the business, then shook hands and headed for Dallas.

Talk about biting off a big chunk! Here I was, general manager over 120 employees, mostly teamsters, with almost 500,000 square feet of industrial warehouse space, and I didn't know a damn thing about the business. It was a real baptism of fire. I started with a real bang. I noticed that I had three men doing manual labor in the warehouse who were all over 70 years old! I just couldn't see how men that old could do a full eight hours of manual labor, so I called all three of them into my office at the same time, and told them I hoped they enjoyed their retirement. Thankfully, none of them had a heart attack. I didn't feel too ruthless, since each of them had a full pension from the teamsters. Although it wasn't my primary intention, I think this set the tone with the teamsters, because they knew right up front that I could make the tough decisions.

I then hired an assistant manager to help me with the operations while I worked with Chris Richardson in the office. Mr. Robertson had agreed to stay on for four months to help in the transition, and his secretary, Ruth Bergin, decided to retire. Ruth was the wife of the warehouse manager, John Bergin. It was a tight-knit little group. For my secretary, I hired a young woman named Gloria, who was a former barmaid. I could sense that she was a hard worker and wanted out of that rat race. And she turned out to be nearly perfect for the job. She worked her tail off, couldn't stand doing nothing, and was always looking for more to do. The assistant manager didn't work out, though. He just rubbed the men the wrong way, so I knew I had to make a change. It's hard admitting you made a mistake, but it's worse letting it fester. I invited him out one Sunday for a cup of coffee, asked him for his keys and told him good-bye. There's really no easy way to do those things.

With all the changes, service went to pot in about two months.

Proctor and Gamble showed up one day and fully had the intention of moving out. They were about 30% of our revenue and a huge drawing card for new business, so I knew that somehow I had to talk them out of it. I determined who was the boss of the two and got him to come back to my office. I explained to him the changes, the commitments we were making, and how much it would disrupt their business. He had some real moxy and bought my pitch. His associate, on the other hand, was a real, dyed-in-the-wool dork. They left, and we all set about getting our service levels and paperwork flow in order.

It was right in the middle of all this, just after the first of the year in 1972, that I got a call from home. Dad had a heart attack and was in the hospital. He was just 64 years old. Mom said he was doing fine and that I shouldn't worry. Still, when Friday rolled around, I headed to Great Bend to see him. I visited him Saturday and Sunday, and he was up and around. He really looked like the same old Dad. Just before we started back to Oklahoma City, I made one more visit to him. He was sitting on his bed, and I was sitting across the room from him. While he was talking, suddenly he started crying. It wasn't a soft cry. He actually broke down and sobbed. It caught me completely off guard. I had no idea what brought it on. Inside, I felt compelled to go over and put my arms around him and hug him. But I wasn't sure how he would take that, so I didn't move. I was frozen into inactivity. He managed to get control of himself, and we continued visiting. I will never forget that moment, watching Dad with tears streaming down his face. I would give anything to have that moment over again, so I could go over, put my arms around him and just hold him tightly. I will always regret not having done so and will live with that regret all my life.

We returned to Oklahoma City, and I returned to work. About a week later, on January 17, 1972, I got another call from home. They told me that the doctors had just told Dad he was released to go home. Dad had a wonderful talent of making everyone around him smile and had gone out into the hall to the nurses' station to thank all the nurses for helping him. It was then that he was struck with another heart attack, and this one was massive. He never recovered and was dead within an hour. As soon as I heard the news, I immediately and vividly recalled the last time I saw him. I grimly recalled his tears and how I stupidly didn't go over and hug him. It hurt, badly. That is an ache that I will take with me to the grave.

At his funeral his six sons were the pall bearers. We all considered it an honor that we would have killed for. Although Dad was just a simple janitor at the First National Bank, the bank placed an ad in the paper announcing that, in honor of Lawrence Hochanadel, the bank would be closed the day of his funeral. We all thought that was a sincere class act by the bank and was a memorial to how much the bank appreciated him.

When I returned to Oklahoma City, I still had my hands full at work. I called on my old friend, Jim Tipton, again, who I knew was not happy at Public Leasing. We went over what I was trying to accomplish, the mess I had, and he agreed to come aboard as my assistant. We gradually got better control of the operation, and our service came around. I had a very simple method of management. I placed Jim in charge of the operations, and Chris in charge of the office. Although we had over a hundred employees, I told them that, as far as I was concerned, I only had two employees, them. I gave them all the responsibility and the authority to go with it. If anything happened, I simply went to them. If something good happened, I praised them, and if something bad happened, I asked them how, why, what, and what they needed to correct it. It worked beautifully, and soon we had one of the smoothest running branches of the whole Overmeier system.

Public warehousing is different from private warehousing in that in public warehousing we owned none of the products we stored. Commercial companies who didn't want the investment and personnel headaches of staffing their own warehouse simply sent us their products. We provided the crews, fork lifts, racks, pallets, etc., to unload, store, fill their orders and ship them. In a way, we were like a bank, where products were deposited with us instead of cash. In return, we were paid handing and storage fees.

We had many nationally known customers: Johnson Wax,

Borden's, Ralston Purina, and many of the cigarette accounts. We were really sensitive about the cigarette accounts, because this product was a criminal target. If a railroad car of cigarette products was spotted at our warehouse the evening before we opened and was broken into, the first call was to the ATF, then the police. And it happened. And they got caught. Because of its sensitive nature, the cigarette companies conducted blind inventories. They simply walked in out of the blue completely unannounced, identified themselves and told us to shut down all shipping immediately. They then conducted their own physical inventory, checked the bills of lading, orders on hand, and checked the balances against their records. These reps generally set up two days for these inventories, based on their experiences in other such public warehouses. But it was common for them to finish with us in half a day and find everything in perfect balance. They liked to schedule us, because that gave them a day and a half to just goof off. I don't think we ever lost as much as a pack of cigarettes.

Soon after I had reached 30, nature had started taking its toll on my hair, and I began balding. I was too young to be bald, so I succumbed to the temptation of getting a wig. When I came to work the first day with the wig, I got a ton of good-natured ribbing from my crew. But what the hell! Gradually, they got used to it. The biggest problem with the wig was that about every three days I had to put new double-sided tape inside it so that it stuck to my scalp. This constant changing got to be a real pain in the neck.

It was during the fall of 1973 that I started to notice that Joy was having a difficult time coping with everything. She had a husband who was regularly drinking heavily, she had lost her first two babies, been uprooted from the dependency bred into her from her parents, she now had three sons to care for, and her husband had been out of night school a little over a year. She seemed to have a difficult time focusing or being organized. I remember a short visit by my mom on the way to visit some relatives in Shawnee, Oklahoma. When Mom came in, she told Joy that she could only stay about an hour for lunch, and then she would have to be on her way. Joy, who was supposed to make the sandwiches for lunch, started to visit with

Mom and totally forgot that she was on a tight schedule. Finally, we had to tell her that Mom was waiting on the lunches. She then had to hurry to throw them together. There were many similar incidents like this that I should have picked up on as the harbinger of a more serious problem.

Joy had a good deal of anxiety during these times. I recall an incident as we were driving out to Colorado on vacation when Joy suddenly had what I felt was an anxiety attack. She was very nervous and anxious to the point that she was almost consumed with paranoia. I literally had to pull the car over to the side of the road, get out, go around to her side of the car, help her out, and stand holding her for about 20 minutes. As I held her, I could feel her heart beating at an unbelievable rate. Finally, she calmed down enough for us to continue. The kids all took this in, and I often wondered what went through their minds as they watched.

Except for Joy's tension, we had a good time on that vacation. I remember pulling that pop-up RV trailer all the way up Pike's Peak, along the narrow road with no rail to prevent you from driving off the edge and plunging thousands of feet down the side of the mountain. It was beautiful to see the quilt clouds blow over the top of the ridges, like fluffs of cotton. We stopped at a trout stream and helped the kids catch trout.

In the fall of 1973 Overmeier held a national sales meeting with all its branch managers at the Playboy Club Resort in Great Neck, New York. Although my branch was a very profitable branch, company-wide a cash flow problem developed. We had a new capable president, and I think they wanted to reassure us that everything was okay. They were going to present awards for the best branches, and some of my friends from the other branches felt I was a shoo-in for our district. By this time I had reduced the personnel from well over a hundred to about 85, all on the same level of income.

On the arrival day, we checked in and started gathering for drinks. There weren't any meetings scheduled that day, so we simply partied. Eventually the partying turned into a poker game in one of the rooms, and I must have drank and played poker until at least three in the morning. I was really out of it, and my roommate wasn't in his bed when I crashed. I don't know how late he stayed up.

The next morning the meeting opened with introductory comments from our president. He said there had been a lot of changes over the previous year and started enumerating them. Finally, he said there had been a big change out in Oklahoma City. Don Hochanadel now had hair on his head, and he asked me to stand up so everyone could see it. The problem was, I was still sleeping in my room. I didn't get down to the meetings until ten, and my buddies told me all about it. I was too hung over to worry about it. Besides, I had one of the top districts in the company. What were they going to do, fire me? No way. I was exonerated in a way when the very next morning the president himself overslept and missed the start of the meetings. Oh, well! This probably cost me the top award, though, as they gave it to Ellington out of Phoenix.

After I had returned from New York, I went back to work as usual. One day I walked in, and I noticed that all of my employees were looking at me oddly. I couldn't figure out what was going on. I thought that maybe I had cut my face shaving, so I went into the bathroom to check it out. I looked in the mirror, and no, I wasn't bleeding. Then I looked up to my head. Then I understood. I had forgotten to put my wig on before I came to work. I sheepishly hurried out the back door, went home, got my wig and returned. Jim and Chris didn't rub it in too hard, but it wasn't long after that, that I decided the wig had to go. People were just going to have to either like or dislike me in my natural state. Besides, wigs were a form or being phony.

Our main office and warehouse were located on South May Avenue just across from the race track. Behind us was an area called "Mulligan's Flats," an old decrepit neighborhood made up of weedy fields and some very old wood frame houses. A young pup wandered by the warehouse one day, and Wayne Bergin sort of adopted it, feeding it some Ralston Purina dog food from the warehouse. Joy and I had no pets yet, and the boys were getting older, so we decided to take him home with us. Since we knew where he came from, we named him "Mulligan." He was white, with semi-long, white hair, and was about half the size of a shepherd dog. The kids took to him like a duck to water.

Unfortunately, the company's cash flow problem worsened. We learned that the president was working day and night to try to sell the company. Damn! My two years of worry-free employment looked like they were going up in flames. What was going to happen now? Would the new owner bring in new people? Would I have a job? The pay checks came out of New York, so I had no control over the cash and didn't know if any of our pay checks would clear. That old gut-wrenching job insecurity returned like an old, ominous enemy. On November 23, 1973, I got a call from New York. The company had just filed Chapter 11 bankruptcy. I was to immediately inform all employees of this, because each of them were now creditors of the company for the eight days of pay that the company owed all of us. They also instructed me to try and get them to keep working. Fat chance!

I called all the office personnel together and gave them the news, and then did the same with the warehouse crew. They were really upset. These were rough teamsters men, and in the previous year I had gradually phased in an eight-day holdback on their pay checks. Before Overmeier bought the company, they only had a three-day holdback. They knew right away that they stood to lose eight days of pay. It didn't make any difference to them that I was losing eight days as well. Nor did they care that I had nothing to do with the home office declaring bankruptcy. All they knew was that I was the company's representative, and I was there. So their anger at what the New York office had done was directed at me.

I tried my best to convince them that the only way all of us would have a job was to keep on working and getting our customer orders out the door. If we didn't, then we would certainly lose them all. But they didn't buy it. I told them I would see what I could do with New York, and scheduled another meeting with them the next morning. I returned to my office and tried to quell the natural concerns of all my employees. Word came back from the warehouse that

I was a marked man, that the men were going to carry chains to the meeting, and if I went out into the warehouse, I'd get a fork lift shoved up my ass. Bull shit! I walked right out into the warehouse as openly as I could, to let the men know I would not be intimidated. No one messed with me (thank God), and I returned to the office.

I thought about the situation for some time, then placed a call to Curtis Robertson. I knew he was on a long-term pay-out with Overmeier, and that placed him in the same boat as we were. He was now nothing more than a secured creditor, and any chance he had of getting his money depended on us staying in business. He agreed to come down the next day to the meeting, since many of these men had worked for him for most of their lives. I also called Pinkerton and arranged for a personal bodyguard for the entire next day. He was waiting outside my rear entrance when I arrived and stayed an arm's length from me the whole day.

Robertson arrived, and the men gathered in the lunch room for the meeting. Some of them did have chains. Robertson was beautiful. He told the men exactly the same thing that I told them, and gradually they started to listen. Finally, they agreed to continue working, as long as I had assurance from New York that they would be paid for the work they would be doing. I verified it with New York, and the next day we started shipping. I think as the days passed and the men saw that I was not abandoning ship, they felt better and actually tried to do a good job.

But the next crisis soon hit. I knew it would take a huge miracle for our accounts to stay with us. No reasonable company could run the risk of having millions of dollars of their products in the possession of a company that had just filed bankruptcy. The phone started ringing off the wall. One customer after another insisted on moving. I couldn't blame them. But I also couldn't possibly physically ship them out all at once. So I put my foot down, told them all that I understood they had to move, but it had to be in a very controlled fashion, one at a time. I did not want to run the risk of anyone making a claim against me later that I lost, or, worse, "took" some of their products.

So the mass exodus started. We needed revenue for me to pay everyone, so I insisted that each customer pay direct to me storage and handling charges in advance before I touched their products. It was hard-nosed business, but they really didn't have any choice. I told them to blame Overmeier in New York, not me. One by one, I let each of them move out, but had very good records to back up the inventories and shipments.

Richard was now six and in the first grade; Don Jr. was just turning four; and Kurt would be three in April. The family was growing up. The stress I was under didn't help my drinking any. It became considerably easier to drink beer a little more frequently. I was leaving no stone unturned in my search for a new job, while I tried to keep things together at the warehouse.

January 1974 passed, then March and April, and finally the start of summer. Richard had started to develop into a tall, left-handed kid. We joined a T-ball team, and I could tell right away that Richard was a natural athlete. He took a vicious swing at the ball and could run well, even though his feet were a bit big. In one game he drove the ball well over the outfielder's head so far he could have crawled around the bases. But they had a safety rule that the batter couldn't throw the bat after he hit, and the umpire ruled that he threw his bat, ruling him out. Boy, Richard was upset, and so was I. No matter the ruling, they couldn't take from my memory the blast that he hit. It was awesome.

By this time, mid-summer of 1974, most of the accounts in the warehouse had moved out. I hadn't been successful in locating another job. We were just barely generating enough revenue through repairing pallets to feed the few of us that were left. Jim Tipton had naturally left and teamed up with Charles Cook, who owned some commercial space, and started a new public warehouse company — which is what I should have done, and probably would have, if I hadn't had my hands full with the mass exodus. Jim managed to land some of the accounts that left me, and his business eventually prospered.

Things were looking pretty bleak, when I got a call from a gentleman with the executive recruiting division of Peat-Marwick-Mitchell in Dallas. He wanted to know if I was happy where I was, and would I consider making a change. Talk about timing! I tried to act as coy as I could, and told him I would consider making a change, but only under the right circumstances. He made an appointment to fly up from Dallas and met me at the office. He gathered the usual information about me and left.

The following week he wanted to know how I felt about Little Rock, Arkansas. Of course, I had nothing but good things to say about it, so he arranged for my wife and I to fly over to Little Rock to meet the owner of Central/Terminal Distribution Centers and Poteet Truck Lines. They were looking for a new president for these companies. We flew over, and were taken out to dinner by Henry Nichols, the owner, and his wife. They had reserved a separate room in one of the nicer places and had the whole management staff from these companies there as well. I spent the whole evening answering the bombardment of questions I got from everyone. Finally, around 11, I made a comment about it being late and almost magically everyone agreed with me, and we returned to our hotel.

The next morning Henry showed me his business and offered me the job, agreeing to pay for the move, and a company car as well. La dee da! As if we had any choice. We returned to Oklahoma City, happy to be starting a new job with better pay and benefits. The Lord was really looking after us. When he was ready for me to have the next job, he sent it my way. Actually, I was quite proud to have been "found" by a professional head-hunting firm. So ended our living in Oklahoma City. Six years, and a helluva lot had happened.

10

LITTLE ROCK

(Good Paying but Stressful Job, then Extended Unemployment)

ARKANSAS IS ONE of the most beautiful, natural states in United States. Joy and I had visited the Bella Vista area in the northwest corner of the state while we were living in Oklahoma City. It was one of those promotional weekends, where they provided you free accommodations for the entire weekend, if you let them attempt to sell you a lot. It was a natural retirement area, with lots of golf courses, hospitals, trout streams and clean air. We had the kids with us, and they got a bang out of the trout fishing.

There is a stretch of Highway 7 just south of the Missouri-Arkansas border which was so scenic it was ranked nationally in the top 10 most scenic routes in the U.S. I had traveled to Conway, Arkansas while in the Army at Fort Leonard Wood, when a married draftee asked me to spend a weekend leave with him. I had never been to Arkansas before, so I went along. That Highway 7 wound up and down, around and back so much it was like a 50-mile roller coaster ride.

We got there late Friday night with ample time to party. I wound up partying so hard and drinking some local home brew, that I actually got sick. As we were driving down the road, I had to stick my head out the window and puked up my guts. I was really bent out of shape. The next morning I woke up with the biggest hangover I had ever had and was very embarrassed as well. I felt a little out of place that afternoon, sitting in the living room while my friend's horny wife was sitting on his lap and almost trying to do him right there. That was my first taste of Arkansas.

Joy and I traveled to Little Rock for the usual house hunting weekend. Henry had a friend in the real estate business, and she showed us a few houses before we settled on a house located near the top of a steep cul de sac, 3314 Rocky Court. The street was correctly named, because lawns were almost non-existent, especially in the back yards. In fact, our back yard and that of the house behind us was divided by a very small, dry brook that only had any kind of water in it when it rained heavily. We bought the house and relocated.

By this time I was 37, Joy 35, Richard seven, Donald five and Kurt four. We managed to get Donald in the kindergarten at the Catholic School, but there was a waiting list for Richard's grade, the second grade. So Richard had to go to the local public school. What an experience that was! They were busing Negro children from the poorer neighborhoods to this predominantly white school. In fact, his teacher was Negro. We tried to be good Catholics and were trying to teach our kids that all people, including Negroes, were created equal. Still, it didn't take two weeks before Richard, purely through his own experiences in the second grade, had formed a strong bias against the Negroes. At supper he told us stories about how the Negro kids were very unruly in class, would not mind the teacher, disrupted the class, and even stole money from her purse. He told us that at recess the Negro kids formed gangs and caused trouble for the white kids. One day he came home with a puncture wound in his arm where another kid had actually stabbed him with a pencil. And these were just second-graders!

During the first grade in Oklahoma City, Richard had displayed some academic slowness, and his grades were poor. With this kind of atmosphere in school, Joy and I were fearful that the entire second grade would be a total waste of time for Richard. We thought of holding him back a year, but he was already so tall we were concerned with the long-term emotional effects on him. In other words, if we held him back a year, he would be at least a foot taller than everyone, and we didn't want him to feel like a "dumb big kid."

We decided to have him undergo psychological testing to see exactly where he was. They tested him for four hours, and the net result was that Richard had a super awareness of everything around him and had above-average peripheral vision. This resulted in reducing his attention span dramatically. He could be looking directly at his teacher, but out of the corner of his eye see a bird land somewhere, and then he would turn and look at it, losing concentration. After consultation with the psychologist, we concluded that the best thing to do was to leave him in his class and give him a private tutor after school. We found him a tutor, and for the entire school year, three days a week, we hauled him there for the tutoring. I am convinced that the only way he learned enough to make it through the second grade was because of the tutor.

One of the major accounts we had in the warehouse was the Mars company, who sold candy bars such as Milky Way, Snickers, etc. Occasionally there were damaged boxes that Mars wanted us to destroy. Well, I just couldn't see throwing away all of that good candy, so we had a steady supply of candy. We had so much of it that I let Richard take full boxes to his class, since so many Negro kids were very poor. This must have impressed the teacher quite a bit, because one day Richard brought home a whole stack of "Thank You" colorings and notes from each kid. It really was a pleasant gesture, and I still have those notes to this day.

In late summer of 1975 I let Richard play little league tackle football. There was only one coach, so I became his assistant. This was my first experience with just how radical some parents could be with their kids. If they weren't succeeding, I could hear their dads yelling threats of punishment from the side lines. We finally had our first game, and received the kick-off. Richard was one of the up men, and the ball came to him. I yelled at him to just run for the goal line. He was taller than most of the kids, so the defenders took swipes at him but couldn't tackle him. He went all the way for the touchdown. His teammates all ran down and patted him on his back, cheering. He loved it. And for the next two games he begged to carry the ball every time. It took two full games before we got that out of his system.

But getting back to the rabid parents. After about three games of listening to the dads screaming and yelling at their kids and threatening them with punishment if the kid didn't play up to the parent's expectations, I had enough. I called time out, walked over to the sideline and called all the parents together while the kids were out on the field. I quietly told them that they were ruining their kids' concentration and morale. Then I told them that if I heard any more screaming or yelling by them, I would immediately bench their kid and he would not play any more in that game. Then I returned to the field, and we continued the game with the kids now starting to have a lot more fun. After the game, the officials came over to me and thanked me for getting it stopped.

After the first year we were allowed to enroll all three kids in the Catholic school, Kurt in kindergarten, Don in the first grade, and Richard in the third grade. This was the fourth different school for Richard, something that was starting to bother me. Since this was a parochial school, it was a lot stricter, and I think the kids were starting to get a much better education.

As the kids grew older, they started to make a much greater demand on my time. We used to play "Octopus" in the living room. I'd lay down on the floor, spread-eagled, and then tried to snatch the kids as they circled near me, pulling them to me so I could tickle them. They would wait until I was occupied with one of the kids, and then they all would pile on me. Once I got Donald to laughing so much from my tickling that while he was on top of and looking down on my face, he puked right on my face. I shot off the floor, washed myself off quickly, and then we all laughed some more. From then on, I was much more careful where the kids were when I tickled them.

Our subdivision had its own private, fenced-in swimming pool. The kids were at the age where swimming was a lot of fun for them, so we spent a lot of time there. I wanted them to learn to swim as soon as they were old enough, because I felt it might save their lives on down the road. The kids loved it when I did a "preacher's seat" or a "cannon ball," because I was a pretty big guy and created some huge waves. They loved to be swamped by the waves. But their biggest bang was when I did the famous "butt dive," the one I perfected back in the seminary. The kids frequently begged me to do that dive, and when I agreed, they went to their friends and told them it was coming. We really had a lot of good times there at the pool.

Mulligan came with us to Little Rock. Since our yard wasn't fenced, we tried to keep him in the house. But it wasn't long before we gave up on that and let him run free. We were at the pool one day when Mulligan got cornered by a huge ferocious dog, and a fight ensued. The huge dog had Mulligan on the ground, with its fangs bared, ready for the kill, when its owner called him off. Mulligan shot out from under him and blazed a torrid path back to our house. When we returned to our house, we found him still under our car in the driveway. He was smart enough to know that the other dog was too big to reach him there.

You know, sometimes you just can't believe how stupid some people are. At the top of the next cul de sac over lived a woman who had some kind of AKC registered female that she wanted to breed with a similarly registered dog. But for some reason, when her dog came in heat, she put it on a chain and hooked the chain on a clothesline outside in her unfenced yard. I suppose she didn't know that when a female dog is in heat, every male dog for miles around picks up the scent and comes a runnin'. And Mulligan was no slouch. The owner caught Mulligan with her dog, chased him off, then called our house, mad as hell. Joy took the call, but we didn't get too excited about it, because she was the one that was dumb enough to put her dog outside.

This woman was very happy when she learned her dog was going to have puppies. She was really looking forward to a beautiful litter of AKC registered puppies. Finally, they were born. Then our phone rang again. Every single one of the puppies looked exactly like Mulligan. I laughed till I thought I'd die.

We went out of town for a weekend once, probably to visit Mom in Kansas. Unfortunately, we didn't know that we forgot to put Mulligan out of the house. We got back around 6 p.m. with the sun still up. I unlocked the front door and started to enter the house, when Mulligan shot past me. He took about 10 quick steps and then took about a 20-minute leak. Can you imagine that? He had held himself for two full days and didn't relieve himself in the house. How's that for house training!

Across the street and a few houses down the hill was a family by the name of Gillenwater. They had a couple of boys about the same ages as our sons, and they all played together. From time to time they would get into typical kids' squabbles, and before long we learned that these kids had really bad tempers if they didn't get their way. One of their kids got so mad once that he went into the house to get his BB gun. When I found out about it after I got home, I went down to their house, got right in the face of their dad, and told him that if I ever saw his kids outside with a BB gun, I was going to take the gun away from them, bring it back to his house and wrap it around his head. He didn't like to hear this, but I was really mad, and he didn't want to take me on. Needless to say, those guns never appeared again. I could never understand parents who allowed their sons to have BB guns in a residential area. To me, that was running the risk of a kid having an eye put out. It just wasn't worth it.

Another favorite pastime of the kids was catching small lizards that seemed to be everywhere. They were lightning quick, but the boys still were able to catch them. We also enjoyed taking the boys down the hill to a very small, almost dry stream that ran along the swimming pool. We'd hike a mile or so along it, looking for lizards or garter snakes. Richard had a sharp eye for snakes, and he reacted very quickly when he spotted one. We were going through the woods once, when suddenly he pounced on something. By the time I reached him, he was holding this four-foot-long shiny black snake. I almost filled my pants right then. But it turned out to be a harmless king snake. He kept it for a while, then turned it loose when I told him it was used to being free and might die in captivity.

There really was an abundance of small wildlife where we lived. The kids frequently came home with baby rabbits that they had caught. This led to a plea for full-grown rabbits, so we bought a big rabbit cage and put it behind the house. From time to time the kids would let these rabbits run free in the back yard. They had to be very careful, though, because Mulligan's natural instincts kicked in, and eventually I think he killed one before the kids could get to him. On one occasion Donald had chased a baby rabbit down a small hole that was dug in the very corner under the porch. Naturally, he stuck his arm and hand into the hole, felt something furry, and pulled it out by its leg. When he got it out, though, it wasn't a baby rabbit. It was a big rat that promptly bit Donald on his finger. Donald dropped it at once, and came into the house for medical attention. He was okay, and I plugged the hole so we wouldn't have that problem anymore.

Richard seemed to be really attracted to animals and nature. Little did I know that he would become an excellent bow hunter and fisherman. In fact, Donald and Kurt would eventually also excel in those areas. Richard wanted a gerbil, so we got him one with a cage, etc., and he spent a lot of time playing with it in his room. Fate, however, was not to be kind to the gerbil. I came home one day, and Joy told me that Donald and Kurt had been playing with the gerbil and had accidentally killed it. They had been playing catch with it and bounced it off the ceiling. I think Donald was six and Kurt was four at the time, and they really didn't know the gerbil was that frail. Either that, or they really didn't 'fess up to what they really did. But I still felt they had to be punished because they were playing with the gerbil without permission. For punishment I made them give Richard the silver dollars I had given each of them a year or two earlier. Then we went out and bought Richard another gerbil.

This seems like a simple enough incident, but I think it was the first evidence of perhaps a natural inclination of most dads. I am going to come right out and say that I probably had already started favoring Richard. I don't know if it was the result of his being the first and oldest son, or whether it was because he was adopted after having lost two babies. By now, Joy and I had told Richard he had been adopted. We were told that it was best that an adopted child find out about his adoption from the adoptive parents, rather than from some other source. We wanted Richard to know that he was special, that we picked him out specially. Our other kids had come from inside their mom, and we in a sense had to take what we got. He seemed to handle it very well. But in looking back now, I can see that for whatever reason, I did start to favor Richard. With that being said, I'm not going to beat myself to death over it. Who said we had to be perfect parents? As long as I know I was trying to be fair, I can live with that. Who was it that said that the only problem with being a parent, was that it was strictly on-the-job training?

These were some golden years for me with the kids. They were older and no longer babies. They could talk, were developing their own personalities, and we could do a lot of things together. And as far as I'm concerned, there is nothing more beautiful than the uninhibited, true smile of a kid. Those are priceless and make all the trouble worth it.

I recall a time when we had been on a trip to Silver Dollar City, I believe, when one of those golden moments occurred. We had been driving for many hours and were about two hours from home when I pulled over to get some gas. Richard and Kurt were asleep, but Donald was awake. I quietly asked him if he wanted to come in the station to get something, and he came in with me. He picked out some cupcakes, or something similar. We left the station, got back on the road, and as we were traveling along, Joy turned around and saw Donald munching on the sweets. She made a casual comment to me along the lines that he was going after the sweets like a little pig. Donald didn't slow a beat, and after a short pause we heard the words "Oink, Oink" come from the rear. Joy and I laughed hard over that one. Donald really nailed that one.

It's kind of odd, but I don't remember too much about drinking during our two years in Little Rock. I'm sure I drank, but I must have slacked off quite a bit from the Tulsa and Oklahoma City days. Maybe it was the new job and the fact that the kids were getting older and demanded much more of my time. I just don't know.

A few years before this, Dave and Gery started a tradition that grew from year to year. It started with those two going on a fishing trip to one of the lakes in south central Missouri. On the first trip they roughed it, pitching tents, the whole bit. Dave had a small boat with a trolling motor, and I understand they had a lot of fun, except for the threat of copperheads. Then they persuaded Mark to join them. A year or so later, they started to put pressure on me to join them for this week of fishing and fun with brothers. While we were living in Little Rock, I finally broke down and told them I'd come. They sent me all the directions, dates, etc.

As the time drew closer, I started to get a strong objection from Joy. She didn't want to be left home alone with the kids for four days. She said it wasn't fair her having to watch the kids while I was having all that fun. That part of it is true, but the other part was that she was really dependent on me. I was her security. And after all those years of night school, I suppose I did owe her more time with me simply being around. I agree that men need to be the cornerstone of the family, the anchor that the rest of the family can always depend on. It simply was the order of things. When it came the day for me to leave, Joy was really upset. So, here I was, right in the middle. She absolutely didn't want me to go. At the last moment I caved in to Joy and decided not to go.

The problem with that was that I had no way of reaching Dave, Mark and Gery to tell them I wouldn't be coming. Later, I found out that they had even gone to the trouble of nailing paper plates to trees along the route to help me find them. They waited for me at the cabin all evening, and when I didn't show up, they started worrying that I had been in an accident. Finally, about 11 that night one of them called me to find out where I was. I caught so much hell from my brothers over this incident that I made up my mind I was never going to commit to anything and then not do it. They still razz me today about that, and I probably will have to live with that until the day I die.

Although I had the fancy title of president of two companies, Central/Terminal Distribution Center and Poteet Truck Lines, this job was never really much fun. When I arrived, a fellow by the name of Phillip Webb was trying to act as interim manager. Phil actually worked for S.R. Nichols, the elderly father of Henry Nichols, my boss. S.R. Nichols owned Southern Compress, a cotton compress and warehouse, and was the one who had made all the money. He was truly a Southern gentleman. I could sense that Phil was happy to see me arrive, so he could get back to working for S.R. He obviously knew a lot more about that business and felt a bit out of place in the warehouse business.

I never really liked Henry for a lot of reasons. It wasn't too long until I realized that he was simply a spoiled brat, riding on his dad's coat tails. He didn't have a college degree, because I was told he couldn't emotionally stand taking a final exam. So he edited what college courses he took and received no official credit. He drove a Jaguar and had a "personal secretary" named Shelby Baker, who had a fine figure. Many of us felt there was more than a mere business relationship there. Shelby was very possessive of Henry, and she obviously had her hooks into him big-time. If anyone crossed her, she had a direct line to Henry, and she seemed to have an inordinate amount of control over him. Henry was married and had two small sons, so I could never figure out how his wife allowed this apparently "close" relationship to continue. She seemed like a very personable woman, but maybe the big house with the pool and the money helped her look the other way.

Henry, Shelby and another operations-type fellow, Chad Kumpfe, officed near downtown, whereas my office was in the warehouse in an industrial section of town. I don't think I could have stood it if we were all in the same building. I didn't like Chad Kumpfe either; I felt he was a simple con artist and just another sycophant of Henry's.

The operation at Central/Terminal was very unusual. We had about 35 warehousemen and drivers, and every single one was black. It would have been literally impossible for me to have hired a white man. He wouldn't have been able to take the pressure. This also presented some interesting management opportunities. In 1974 and 1975 the country was suffering the effects of the Mid-East oil embargo. This was a severe blow to many companies in the U.S. Cash became scarce. Money managers started looking at their balance sheets to see where their assets were. They pounced on the "inventory" assets and started thinking of ways of converting inventories into dollars. This focused their attention on their inventories stored in our warehouse and in warehouse companies across the nations. They started reducing inventories drastically, and without a good turnover in our warehouse, it hit our profits hard.

So I had two management battles to wage: reduce costs and try to maintain sales. I took a hard look at Poteet to see if we could expand their hauling authority. It had only a very limited intra-state authority, and I soon discovered that the cost of expanding that authority was prohibitive. In the current freight scheme of things, the whole trucking operation was marginal at best. So, after trying unsuccessfully to sell or lease out its authority, I decided to shut it down and dispose of the equipment. This was a positive move and freed me to focus more on the warehouse.

The warehouse, however, was not as easy. Little Rock is not really that big a city, even though it is the biggest city in Arkansas. In fact, 50% of the population of the entire state was rural, meaning that 50% of the population lived either on farms or in towns under 5,000. Compared to the states around it, it was a commercial midget. We had no true attraction to entice businesses to set up a multi-state warehouse system with us. The states around us were far more capable from both a geographical and transportation standpoint. I tried to develop new business, but without much success.

Focusing internally and trying to hold down costs was a very interesting venture. Every time I came up with a new, more cost-efficient method of handling merchandise and took it to the warehouse crew for implementation, I got very little cooperation. What I was proposing was very sound, and I tried to present it to the men in a professional manner. Then it dawned on me that the ancestors of all these blacks had been slaves. And they still had a lot of that "slave" mentality. So I called them together again, and this time I presented it to them in the same manner that a plantation owner would have presented it to his slaves. This they understood, and they easily accepted and followed my directions.

By now I had learned that there were two groups of people in Arkansas, the rich and the poor. And the rich made damn sure that they stayed rich, and kept the poor, poor. Little Rock was a very cliquish town, where the locals gave you a cold shoulder right from the start. That was another thing that bothered me about living there.

I never could suck up to someone just to be accepted. In fact, I had never, ever worried about being "accepted." If people didn't like me the way I was, well, that was just too bad. I certainly wasn't going to put on a false front for anyone.

During 1975 the company more or less maintained the status quo. In light of those financial times, that was a success story all by itself. Nevertheless, Henry was pushing hard for higher profits. We had regular upper management meetings at his house, and the meetings included a business professor from the University of Arkansas at Fayetteville. We were all asked to write up a lengthy report on our industries and an analysis of the market, etc. This professor raved about how professional my report was and actually said it was one of the best he had seen in years. But that still didn't increase profits. At Henry's urging, I hired an assistant who was to work almost exclusively in sales. Henry had been contacted by a Mike Conan, who talked a great talk. He seemed to have an inside track on a couple of large distribution accounts, and Henry hoped he could bring us new business. So we hired him.

About this same time, during the fall of 1975, Henry started talking about selling the company. At first he skirted around it, then finally he called me down to his office one day and said that he had made the decision to sell it. He wanted to know if I was interested in it. I told him I would consider it under the right circumstances. So he put together a complete proposal and presented it to me. I reviewed it, and it was very one-sided. While it didn't require any cash from me (which I didn't have anyway), Henry retained such a tight security interest in everything that the whole proposal simply meant that I was buying a job for 20 years.

If we were wild about Little Rock, maybe we would have viewed it differently. But we just weren't that crazy about Arkansas. It was a very backward state, and there was a lot of poverty. Finally, the purchase would have tied me to Henry for the next 20 years, and I just didn't like him. So I turned it down. Henry grimly told me that he intended to sell it, and any new owner he located might want my job. I told him I was aware of that.

Meanwhile, I was becoming more and more dissatisfied with Mike Conan. He wasn't bringing in any new business, and by now I had enough experience with him to know that he was totally phony. Henry had found him, and now I wanted to fire him. I wrestled with this for about a week and then decided that I needed to meet with Henry and simply tell him I wanted to terminate him. I scheduled a meeting with Henry at his office, and we met. Before I could tell him why I was there, he told me that he had just sold the company. This didn't surprise me much, but when he told me he had sold it to Mike Conan, that really caught me off guard. It took all the grit I had to keep from busting out laughing. Here I was ready to fire him, and Henry had just sold him his company. Good God! Henry gave me some severance pay and turned the company over to Mike. Then a year later, after Mike had run the company into the ground, Henry had to step back in and take his company back. Oh, well!

By this time Dave, Max and Mark and their families all lived in Johnson County, Kansas. Dave, a petroleum engineer, was moving up the corporate ladder of Panhandle Eastern Pipeline Company. Max was a National Labor Relations Board attorney and was wanting to move out to the west coast. Mark was in the marketing department of Kennworth, a top of the line truck manufacturer. He had just been promoted to general manager of Kennworth's company-owned truck dealership in Omaha.

Johnson County is the southwest quadrant of the Kansas City metropolitan area. It's on the Kansas side of the Missouri/Kansas border and has been the most progressive, well-managed, cleanest and safest suburban area of Kansas City. I had made a number of trips there, spending time with all three brothers. The job market was very poor in Little Rock, so I was invited up to Johnson County by these three to stay to look for work.

Spring of 1976 came, and I had now been out of a job many months, with little or no prospects. Money was almost gone. We were going nowhere fast. There were a lot of factors to consider. Obviously, Little Rock was a dead end. Not only were there few jobs for my level of management, I just didn't like the state. There were many more job opportunities in the Kansas City area, very good schools in the Shawnee Mission School District, and (here we go, again) I had an older brother, Dave, who lived there. Richard had been in four different schools in the past four years, and I felt we needed to land in a permanent place so he could have some stability.

So, in the final analysis, the choice was really an easy one. We decided to move to Kansas City and put the house up for sale. We were now many months past due on the mortgage, but found a buyer who paid us enough to pay off the mortgage and left us enough to pay for the move to Overland Park. I made a trip to Overland Park and soon found a suitable rental house at 7914 West 92nd Terrace. It wasn't very fancy, but I was hoping we wouldn't be in it too long.

We rented a U-Haul truck, packed everything we had in it and started on our way. I drove the truck, and Joy followed in our 1973 wood grain and yellow Ford station wagon. Joy was a fearful driver and absolutely hated expressways, so I was worried about her. But we had to go, so off we went. I was really pleasantly surprised that Joy was able to follow the truck on those winding, up-and-down Arkansas highways as we headed north. We spent one night on the road. I backed the truck up to a tree, making it impossible for anyone to even open the doors; then we settled into the motel.

The next morning we continued the trip, came up on Highway 71 on the Missouri side, headed west on I-435, got lost, but eventually made it to Dave's house. We pulled up outside, said our hello's and thus started our roots in Overland Park.

11

OVERLAND PARK, KANSAS, 1976-1979

(Beginning of Roots, More Struggles, and then the Bottom)

IT WAS EARLY June of 1976 when we pulled up at Dave's house. I was now 39, Joy was almost 37, Richard nine, Don Jr. seven, and Kurt six. We spent the night at Dave's house and the next morning drove the truck over to our rental house. We managed to get the truck unloaded and returned it to U-Haul. Our new home wasn't anything special, simply adequate. I set up a desk in the basement and set about finding employment. This was the highest priority, since we were very low on money. In fact, I eventually had to borrow $300 from Mom. I chose her because she had just recovered $5,000 from an airline for an injury she sustained when flying out to Seattle to visit Max.

We enrolled our kids in Valley View School, about four blocks from our house. Richard was in the fourth grade; Donald, the second; and Kurt, the first. It was the fifth different school for Richard, and we had made up our minds that Overland Park was going to be our permanent home. For the sake of the kids, there would be no more transfers. Dave's wife, Lyla, razzed us a little about where we set up home. Seems it was in the Nallwood Junior High district, whereas her kids, four boys and a daughter, were going to Hillcrest Junior High, an arch rival of Nallwood in all little league sports. And their kids were heavily involved in them.

I wanted my kids exposed to all the sports they wanted to play. Tony and I had been decent athletes and had always regretted that we lived out on the farm where we never got the chance to play sports before high school. So this was important to me. Little league baseball was played in the "3 & 2 Baseball Club." The league had already started its season, but we went out to the complex one night to see if we could get our kids on a team. This was quite a well-developed complex. It had nine well-maintained diamonds, completely fenced, including bleachers for both the home and away teams. Every diamond was lighted, allowing games to be played up to midnight if necessary. There were two concession stands and a league office, where the manager on duty stayed while they played the games. During the evening's games I looked up John Toal, who was the manager of the Nallwood fourth grade team, hopefully to get Richard on his team. Unfortunately, his kids had played together for a couple of years, and his team was already set. Nevertheless, he could see that Richard was a tall kid, and I knew he had a good arm, so I thought Richard had a good chance the following year. The best we could do this year was to join the "summer camp" the league sponsored for the very young and those who had never played before. In all honesty, I think the boys weren't too interested in this, but I knew they had to start learning somewhere.

Before long, I stumbled into an opening with a company called Centropolis Warehouse, near the I-70 and I-435 junction on the Missouri side, not far from Royals Park and Arrowhead Stadium. Larry Derricott, the existing general manager, had accepted a job with a company in Louisville, Kentucky, but had agreed to find a replacement before he left. We interviewed and he filled me in on the position. I then met with Dave Padgett, one of the three stockholders of the company, and who was also a senior vice-president with Yellow Freight Systems, a very large national trucking company. They offered me the job for something like $18,000 a year and a company car. Did I really have any choice? Hell, no. I snatched it right up and started to work right away.

The other two stockholders were really works of art. Price Williford, about 60, was the most foul-mouthed, negative man I had ever met. Fortunately, he stayed away and didn't bother me. His cousin, "Skip" Sleyster, was the third partner. Price and Skip were each millionaires, partners in many ventures, and jointly owned an endless list of property along the Highway 40 corridor that ran parallel with I -70. Despite all that, they constantly fought each other, both verbally and physically. Skip ran a combination junk yard and salvage operation. Although he owned a decent home somewhere, he usually slept at the filthy office of Centropolis Crusher on the other side of I-435, or later on, in the upstairs portion of a combination car shop, junk yard and metal storage yard. He would also screw anything that walked and shave without shaving cream. Oddly enough, he was extremely well connected politically and wielded some behind the scenes political power.

Skip managed Centropolis Crusher, a crushed stone operation that made various sizes of crushed stone for commercial use, and a limestone powder that many industrial companies in the area purchased. It was even more unique in that they had sunk a shaft 1100 feet down to a formation of very high calcium carbonate limestone. This separated Centropolis from all of the other limestone mining companies in the Kansas City area. Kansas City is unique, in that on the surface throughout the metropolitan area are many limestone mining operations which had been mining the limestone for years. These other operations, however, simply mined into the side of a cliff, perhaps 50 to 100 below the surface. It was a much lower grade limestone, but satisfactory for most asphalt and road construction companies.

This surface mining industry had been going on in Kansas City for 50 or more years. The formation was thick enough so that the miners blasted out the limestone, leaving 25-foot-diameter pillars approximately 35 to 40 feet apart. The pillars held up the superstructure, preventing the roof from falling. Eventually, someone got the bright idea of using all of this vacant space for storage. It had many natural attractions – year around temperatures of 65 degrees, very little maintenance, minimal fire danger, because rock doesn't burn, and other advantages. They were also weatherproof, immune to heavy snow, rain or even tornados. There were literally hundreds of acres of this storage space all over Kansas City.

Then someone got the bright idea of turning it into freezer space, with a temperature of 10 degrees below zero. After the geological studies showed it could be done, then they installed huge compressors, and acres of rooms were gradually frozen until they reached the 10 degrees below zero temperature. Once they reached it, then the cost of keeping it that low was much lower than above-ground freezer space. After all, solid rock doesn't change temperature very easily. Then they built railroad spurs into these underground warehouses so they could receive and ship frozen products on a regular basis. It became so developed that Kansas City became known as the leader in the nation for frozen food storage and distribution.

Centropolis Warehouse also had its freezer space, a single four-acre room, served by both rail and tractor trailers, or "reefers" as they called them in the industry. We also had an eight-acre temperature and humidity-controlled room and a two-acre storage room. We also could double our space by developing even farther back into the cave. Mining had ended in our cave many years before, so we didn't have the constant dust that some others had.

I really stepped into a mess when I took the job. They had just started the entire warehouse and crusher project a few years before. They had arranged interim financing for the construction of the warehouse interior and the 1100-foot-deep shaft through Continental Mortgage Investors (CMI) in Florida. Diversified Mortgage Investors (DMI) had committed to the long-term financing after the projects were completed. The problems started when CMI ran out of funds before the projects were finished. This forced the stockholders to put substantial funds into the projects to finish them. To make matters much worse, CMI went into bankruptcy, so we were now under control of the bankruptcy court.

All of this led to a suit filed against CMI and DMI for $55,000,000 by the stockholders for failure to fully fund the construction. CMI and DMI responded with a counterclaim of $8,000,000 against the stockholders based on their personal guarantees of the loans. This litigation was well in progress when I came aboard and naturally impacted the longevity of my position with the warehouse company. It wasn't the best of circumstances to work in, but again, did I really have a choice? I had to start somewhere, and I had a family of five to support, three of which were now in school.

So I started working on the things that had to be done. I made personal contact with all the major customers, informing them of the change of management and answering any questions, so that we didn't lose their business. Within six weeks, Skip and Dave promoted me to president of Centropolis Warehouse, and also appointed me a vice-president of Centropolis Crusher. In the latter capacity I was to provide financial advice and coordinate the litigation with CMI and DMI. Our lead counsel was Bob Oberlander of Linde, Thompson, a very big firm in Kansas City. Paul Cowan was his chief associate on the case.

As to operation of the warehouse, although frozen foods were new to me, they were similar to what I had been doing. You established your rates by knowing all your costs, then charge your customers a storage rate to cover them and provide a reasonable profit. It worked the same with the handling charges. We charged our customers so much to unload their rail cars of products, place them in storage, then fill and ship their orders. We were unionized through the Operating Engineers, something I would remedy later on down the road.

During my tenure with the company, I attended a frozen foods convention in San Francisco, where I met many large accounts in our industry and attempted to sell them into giving me their business. These conventions were a combination of work and pleasure, so I got to see a lot of the sights of this beautiful city. Most people know all of the tourist attractions, so I won't spend time going over them. One thing that really stood out was that on almost every block in the downtown section of town was a store that sold every type of sex article imaginable. I had heard that this city was the center of gay rights, and those stores certainly confirmed that reputation. I knew few people at the convention, so it was a lonely trip.

During my tenure at Centropolis, I also attended a frozen food convention in New Orleans. This was a horse of another color. I did what I could to scare up some business and saw a lot of the New Orleans sights. My largest account, a private label firm out of Tulsa,

Oklahoma was attending the same convention, and we had plans for me to take them out to dinner. That is one dinner I will never forget. The owner brought his wife, his sales staff and others along so that there were at least 12 in our group. I didn't have any credit cards, so I set the meal up at my hotel, which featured one of the top restaurants in town.

I really splurged on that meal. We had a sculptured ice statue as our centerpiece and individual gifts for the ladies. Everyone selected the most delicious (and expensive) appetizers and wines. Then we moved on to the delectable entrees. By the time the meal was over, I had spent over $800 and simply charged it to my room. Thank God the hotel let me pay my bill by company check, or I would never have been able to pay for it. Any way to get the job done.

Somehow Dave and I were appointed co-administrators of the family reunion for 1976. Since the family was growing in leaps and bounds, we thought it would be great if we could schedule it at an area where there would be activities for kids of all ages. We located Allendale, a camp about 35 miles southwest of Overland Park. It had two levels of rooms similar to a motel that provided adequate room to handle our group. There were five huge ponds, four of which were for fishing and the fifth for fishing, swimming and boating. The staff prepared one main buffet meal Saturday and Sunday, so that cut down on the cooking, etc. The only negative was that there was no air conditioning, and that made it difficult for those of us who were spoiled by cool homes. So what if we lost a little sleep?

We rented the whole complex for the entire weekend. Arrivals were on Friday, Saturday was for visiting and activities, and Sunday was the departure day. I really had a lot of fun getting ready for this. I had commemorative trophies made for the fishing contest, one for the largest, most and smallest, for different age groups. The kids and dads loved the contest and really got after the fish. Richard won the biggest fish for his age group, and I got a lot of boos over that.

Another big event was the parents vs. kids softball game. As the time drew near for the game, everyone went to get their mitts, bats and balls. I had bought a green pair of sweat pants, a white knit shirt and baseball cleats. Somewhere I found an Oakland Athletics baseball cap, so I brought it along. To add a little excitement, I brought along a long black curly wig. This all added up to a long-haired Oakland baseball player. My brothers and sisters saw me walk along the rooms on the upper floor, down the steps, and then toward the group. Many of them stared at me for a long time, trying to figure out who I was. Finally, when I got close enough, they recognized me and busted out laughing. They really got a bang out of that and had to take pictures. Their laughter and smiles really lit me up. I've always enjoyed putting smiles on people's faces, because it is hard to be sad when you are laughing.

The game started and the kids were really determined to win. Some of the kids were now in high school and very good athletes. On the parents' side, we had to allow the wives and spouses to bat and play, so we had a number of women who had never really participated in any sporting activities. But the object was fun, and fun we had. There was one scary moment for me when the parents were at bat. Dave was at the plate. There were so many kids that the outfield was really stacked. Among the left fielders was my son, Donald, a mere seven years old. But he was so far out in left field that I didn't think I had to worry about him getting hit by a long fly ball.

Boy, was I wrong! Dave put on a good show at the plate, as most of us did; then he swung mightily and drove the ball toward left field. He was so confident that he didn't really start running. He stood there and admired his long blast. I looked out into left field, and there was Donald, trying to zero in on the ball. From where I was he looked about an inch tall. I had visions of the ball coming down on his head and driving him into the ground. I watched in horror as he doggedly tried to follow the ball. Finally, it came down way out on the horizon, and the force of the ball knocked him down. I was already on my way out to him when he got up and held the ball in his mitt. He had actually caught it! Dave was so stunned he just fell flat on his back. I have never seen a better catch. I think the kids won the game, but none of us really cared, as we all had a great time. That was one of the best reunions we ever had.

By the fall of 1976, I was looking for a house to buy. It was going to take a minor miracle, because we had very little money. I finally located a house at 9237 Lowell, actually right around the corner from where we were living. A family by the name of Dwork were trying to sell the house, which was a split-level with three bedrooms on the upper level, with the kitchen, dining and living rooms. The lower level consisted of a large paneled den with a fireplace, a huge washroom, and a spacious two-car garage. It also had a patio and fenced-in yard.

When I showed the house to Joy, her first reaction was negative, saying that there was no way that she could keep such a big house clean. Over the years I had started to realize that Joy's first reaction to virtually everything was usually negative. This put me in the position of either never attempting any forward movement, or just going ahead and doing it, despite Joy's negative reaction. I felt she should have really liked it, because it had a modern kitchen, dishwasher and ample cupboard space. It was far nicer than what we were living in at the time.

I sensed the sellers were in a tight bind to sell, so I hammered down the price. By the time the dust settled, we were able to buy the house and move into it for about $750. I even got the seller to pay a portion of the closing costs, and I assumed his loan. It was a sweet deal, and years later we would be glad we did. God was really good to us.

The kids were enrolled in Valley View Elementary School, about five blocks away on 95th Street. Richard was in the fourth grade, Donald the second, and Kurt the first. The hardest adjustment had to be made by Richard, since this was his fifth different school. He was unlucky in that he drew a first-year teacher who simply was not cut out for teaching. In fact, after that school year he quit teaching and went into selling insurance. Things culminated when Richard got into a fight with a kid who would turn out to be a long-time friend and sports teammate, Todd Norman. I got called to the school and was disturbed that the principal accepted everything the teacher claimed and never gave any weight to Richard's side. It was obvious that he was going to back up the teacher, no matter what. I had no choice but to chalk it all up to experience. But the three-day suspension had a positive effect on Richard, and he never had a serious disciplinary problem after that.

With the end of summer came YMCA little league football. Richard was the only one who could play tackle football, because that was the earliest they offered. Donald and Kurt had to play flag football. I was for sports for the kids for many reasons. It taught them to compete and be on the same level as everyone else. We lived in an area where some of the parents had a great deal of money, and their kids wore the best clothes, had the best toys, etc. We had very little money. So, to me, sports was the great equalizer. When a kid stepped out on the field, he had to leave his parents and their money on the sidelines, and was judged solely on what he himself did.

When you looked at my three kids, they were a strange lot. Richard was tall and slender; Don, Jr. was average height, wiry, and quick as a cat; Kurt was big-boned, stocky and very strong. Richard played tackle football for a few years, then gave it up after the eighth grade. I tried not to put pressure on him to continue, since by that time it was obvious he was cut out for baseball and basketball. The only problem with little league sports was that the coaching is most often done by volunteer parents, and sometimes their experience was poor. Still, it was better than nothing.

Football season gave way to basketball, or the Great American Basketball League. I tried to avoid coaching my kids for many reasons. I really didn't feel qualified, didn't want to put pressure on my kids, etc. But I did coach Richard in his first basketball season. I picked a bunch of kids from his football team who looked like aggressive athletes and started working them. They seeded teams in leagues according to their practice games. Most of our kids had never played before, but they had a lot of hustle.

In our first game, our kids totally dominated the other team and didn't allow them a point in the first half. We started the second half, now at the other end of the court. The other team had the ball and put up a shot. It missed, and Richard got the rebound. Without thinking, he quickly put up a shot, and in it went. The only problem was that it was the wrong basket. He had scored two points for the other team. I guess it had a twinge of mercy, because it saved the team from a shut-out. The final score was 26 to 2. We still laugh about that today.

We had a kid, Billy Goodnow, on our team, and it was obvious that he was the worst basketball player on the team, and maybe in the league. I learned later that he had a neurological problem of some sort that required medication. We had rules that ensured all the kids got playing time. About two-thirds into the season, Billy had never taken a shot, and I was still trying to get him to quit guarding his man when we had the ball.

During a game late in the season, the officials called a technical on the other team, so I had to pick someone to shoot the free throw. I decided it was time for Billy to take a shot. When I told Billy to shoot it, all of my players, including Richard, moaned and looked at me like I was crazy. But what the hell, he paid his money. He deserved some fun, too. So he stepped up to the line, and in a weird, unorthodox shooting motion, shot the ball toward the backboard, jumping up as he did. The ball bounced around the rim and finally FELL IN! He made the shot! Unfortunately, he stepped over the line when he came down, and the basket was waved off. But you could tell he didn't care. He had made his first basket in a real game, and that made his whole season. No one would ever take that away from him. At the end of the season, his mother wrote me one of the tenderest letters I had ever received. That basket had been a big highlight in that kid's life, and she wanted me to know it. That letter made all the work worth it.

As 1977 came, two major influences began to be more and more evident. One was my drinking. By now I was drinking every night. I generally stopped off at the liquor store on my way home and bought at least one, sometimes two 16-oz. six-packs of Coors and a half-pint of whiskey. In Kansas, the beer served in bars and sold at grocery stores was 3.2% beer, whereas liquor store beer was far more potent. I had to have the powerful stuff to get the glow I was addicted to, then finish with some shots of straight whiskey.

The second influence was Joy. After a few months, the school routine set in, and gradually Joy's ability to cope became less and less. Her meals were more in the nature of just getting something on the table so she could relax, knowing she had made supper. The meals were not very tasty, but the kids and I got used to it. I dubbed them the "paper plate specials," because she served them on paper plates to avoid having to do the dishes. She dealt with everything with one thought in mind – how much trouble was it for her? I know now that she was not consciously trying to shirk her responsibilities. Her tank was just empty. I didn't realize this as it was happening, but she was losing ground as time went by. I was either too drunk or occupied with work to realize what was happening to her.

Joy didn't have many friends, other than family, such as Dave and Lyla and other relatives. For some reason during these times, it was just hard for her to make friends. This seems strange in that Joy had a personality that was completely the opposite of offensive. When mixing with others, she was more on the quiet side, and never, ever had a bad thing to say about anyone, no matter who they were. That was and always has been a hallmark of her personality. Her lack of friends was another major reason why I wanted our kids in as many sports as possible. This would put her in direct contact with a lot of other mothers at the games, and, hopefully, she would find some new friends, and her life would be happier. Unfortunately, however, she had very little interest in sports. To her it was boring and, yes, too much trouble. This potential avenue of friends was simply a dead end.

With the spring of 1977, Richard and Donald played baseball at 3 & 2. Richard was in the fifth grade level of league play, and Donald in the third. Since I had coached Richard, I felt I should also coach my other kids as well, so I signed up as an assistant coach on Donald's team. Terry Nielson was the head coach, and Rod Truog, Jerry Howser and I were the assistants. Terry was truly one of the rarest of men who ever walked the earth. He was mentally sharp, had a great sense of humor and, above all, he loved kids. He was in it for the kids, not for himself, his ego, or to further his own son. As a result, the kids were loose, had fun, and we wound up winning the league title. Each kid got a trophy, a league champion patch for their league nylon jacket. Donald was a bit on the small side compared to a lot of the other kids and usually played second base or outfield. I can recall a lot of good plays and hits he made, but what stood out about Donald was that he never backed down from a situation. He never got intimidated at the plate and made some great plays in the field.

Kurt was in soccer. He was to soccer what a Sherman tank was to battlefield maneuvers. Soccer was a fast-growing sport at the time. Many mothers wanted to interest their kids in soccer to divert their interest away from tackle football. They didn't want little Johnny to get hurt. This was funny, because as soon as most of the kids reached the tackle football age, they threw away their soccer shoes and wanted to play football. The players wore socks that came to their knees and inserted plastic shin guards inside them to protect their shins. Kurt and an opposing player went after a ball once, and both kicked at the same time with all they had. There was a terrific impact as shin met shin. Kurt got up and I could tell he wanted to cry, but he held back the tears. The other kid didn't get up. Kurt had literally shattered his shin guard, and although the kid wasn't seriously hurt, they carried him, crying, off the field. After that, everyone got out of Kurt's way. Keep in mind, these were mere second-graders-to-be, perhaps late seven or early eight-year-olds.

Near our house at the intersection of 95th and Metcalf was a pond called Glenwood Manor. It was nice to take the kids fishing there, walking distance from our house. A little creek ran north from it, and I must admit that it was a kid's dream to explore. Unfortunately, Overland Park had quite a few of these small creeks, some cemented into drainage ditches, and others simply naturals. We had some big rains, and there had been a kid or two killed while playing in these ditches and streams during rains. So I laid down an ironclad rule that my kids absolutely could not play in that creek. Naively, I believed they obeyed.

One evening Donald didn't come home for supper. I went out

looking for him everywhere I knew, drove up and down the streets shouting his name, but had no luck. I went over to Glenwood Manor and looked for him there. No luck! Richard and Kurt said they had no idea where he was. I was at wit's end as darkness fell. With darkness, we had no choice but to call the police. We were now starting to fear the worse, although we never said it. The police came, took a report from us and an 8" x 10" school photo. They then started the search. Soon friends like Ernie Rohr started showing up in front of our house. A CB club heard about it, came by the house and sent their members out looking for Donald, staying in contact via CB.

Ten o'clock rolled around, and still no sign of Donald. All three TV channels showed Donald's picture on the news and asked if anyone had seen this child. I told the police my kids liked to go over to Glenwood Manor and fish. Pretty soon a police helicopter hovered over the pond with a bright spotlight piercing the waters and the shrubs around it. By now, I was getting desperate. I spent most of my time out front, hoping he would somehow show up. It was a long vigil. Around 11, I looked down the street and saw a kid down at the corner. The sight drew me down there, and as I got closer, it looked like Donald. Finally I got close enough to see that it was him! I ran down, hugged him and made sure he was all right. I choked back the tears as I happily walked him back to our house and told the police that he had been found.

I thought there would be a lot of smiles and the police would leave, also relieved that it was not a kidnaping. But I was completely caught off guard when the police politely insisted that Joy and I both go outside while they talked to Donald. I thought they were just going to ask him everything that happened to him. But as more time passed, I started to realize that they were interested solely in his welfare and wanted to make sure he was safe at home. Apparently they wanted to explore whether or not he was the victim of child abuse. When they let us back in the house, it was my turn, and I gave Donald an "appropriate" tongue lashing. Donald later told us that he had tried to sneak in the back sliding doors, but they had been locked.

By the summer of 1978 all three of the boys were heavily into almost all of the little league sports ... basketball, baseball, football and soccer. We hauled them to all the practices, and I tried to watch all the practices I could. I felt it was important that my kids knew I supported them, and there were many other dads watching as well, so it was a chance to meet and shoot the breeze.

Terry Nielson turned into a terrible tragedy. He was in his early 30s and developed cancer. This man had the greatest positive attitude of anyone I'd ever met. He made practice and games pure fun. There was no pressure, and he could make a kid feel like a million dollars. After I heard about the cancer, I went down to his house to see him. He and his wife, Doris, were separated at the time. His mom was with him, and it was awkward. You never know how to feel in this situation; you just let them know you care. He told me that he had been asked by the hospital to head up a morale group for the cancer patients. This was another indication of his great attitude. We were pretty good friends by this time, and he voiced the only complaint I ever heard from him. He told me that his wife was really pressuring him for money, which he didn't have. He said that here he was, fighting for his life, and she was after money. I could tell it really saddened him.

But the cancer moved fast. In a little more than a month he had to be admitted to the VA hospital. I went up to visit a couple of times, but they weren't much of a visit. He was really loaded with medications and almost in a coma. I took his hand, and he slowly turned his head to me and said, "Hi, Don." Then he drifted off into sleep. I sat there for quite awhile, hoping I was some solace to him. I glanced at the sheets, and his testicles were swollen as large as grapefruits. Not much later he died, and I was really proud to be asked to be one of the pall bearers. As I stood by the grave, I wondered why it had to be the real pearls who were taken from us. Why always the good guys? I didn't know him that long, but I guess I had learned to love him in that short a time, as much as a man can learn to love another man.

I can relate endless stories about little league sports, because I became really involved, even to the extent of being a board member of the YMCA Football Leagues. To put this in perspective, we had close to a hundred teams covering all grade levels through the ninth grade. After that, they went to high school. Overall, the sports were good, and a lot of kids got to learn the sports. But there was always a great deal of politics that were sad. Things like dads coaching to make sure their kid got the choice position.

I'll just relate one example. When Donald started tackle football in the fourth grade, his coach, Jim Knight, noticed his quickness, agility and competitive spirit, and worked him into being the quarterback. They lost one game that season and were co-champions. The next year in the fifth grade, another fellow joined the coaching staff who had been back-up quarterback to Ron Vanderkelen at Wisconsin the year they went to the Rose Bowl. His son was a tall natural athlete. Gradually, this assistant coach got the coach to consider his kid for quarterback. Donald remained quarterback all year, and the team lost just two games.

When the sixth grade rolled around, Donald was still quarterback. But when Jim Knight worked with the defense, the assistant started putting his son in at quarterback. By the midway point of the seventh grade, the assistant's son was installed as quarterback. Don't misunderstand me. The kid, Mike Brandt, had a golden arm and could really throw the ball. And he was about as good a kid as anyone could want. What irked me was the way his dad worked him into the position by becoming an assistant coach. Then came the famous Nallwood Junior High clique – Brandt, Whitworth, Ogg and Dean. Donald was relegated to purely a blocking back for the rest of the year. He took it well. By the ninth grade Donald was a defensive end and made the League All-Star team at that position. To put the finishing touches on the story, when these kids reached their senior years in high school, Brandt had an injury that took him out for the whole season, and none of the other three kids in the clique were even playing football.

By late summer of 1978, Joy's emotional problems worsened. The parish had a "Casino Night" scheduled on a Saturday night, and Joy wanted to go. When we arrived, Joy started getting very nervous, and after about an hour wanted to go home. I was surprised, but took her home. That's when things really got bad. She had what I thought were severe anxiety attacks. About every half-hour she begged me to hold her. I'd hold her for about 15 minutes, then she would be okay for about 30 minutes. The kids tried not to be conspicuous, but I could see they knew something was seriously wrong. I hated them having to see Joy in this situation, but there was just nothing I could do about it. They were having to witness their mother going to pieces right in front of them. Oh, how I hated them having to witness it. It was that way the rest of the evening. I had hoped she would be better the next day, but she was worse. It continued all day Saturday and Sunday, and Monday morning we went to Johnson County Mental Health on Lamar and 63rd. Dr. Ericson was her psychiatrist, and he gently spent sufficient time with her and me to know she needed to be hospitalized. He asked her to voluntarily admit herself to the mental hospital at the Rainbow Unit, near Kansas University Medical Center.

I took her there, handed the papers to the receptionist and waited. After a few hours, the nurse in charge finally came out to see me, told me that they had heavily sedated Joy, and that there was nothing I could do the rest of the day. I felt completely helpless. I returned home because the kids had to have someone there. The next day I returned and wanted to see Joy. They took their sweet time before letting me see her for just a few minutes. She looked horrible. She was almost in a trance. She recognized me, but her reaction was very minimal.

In the hall the nurse explained that they had her heavily sedated to establish a starting point. She said that they would start cutting back on the medication very gradually, when they felt Joy was capable of coping with more. Until then, they said, she would be like she was for quite awhile.

This really put a load on me. In addition to work, I had to visit her as much as I could and also take care of the kids. Richard was 12, Donald 10, and Kurt nine. Fortunately, they could dress themselves, get their breakfast and get off to school. Dave and Lyla helped out a lot. Visiting time was very limited at the hospital, so I was able to keep up with the laundry, making supper, etc.

A week went by, and there wasn't a lot of improvement. Then another week went by, and there was a little improvement. Then the doctor allowed us to visit Joy as a family. This, again, was awkward. I hated the kids seeing her almost zombie-like, but she was their mother, and maybe it would do her some good. She showed no reaction, probably due to the drugs. Then they let us take her outside into the little fenced-in park. A few more weeks went by, and then they allowed her home for one day on the weekend, then for an overnight stay at home. Finally, for the whole weekend.

When they at last let her come home, she had been in the hospital for six weeks. I was glad to have her home, even though she couldn't do much, and we all had to be careful not to create any excessive tension to upset her. It was hard on all of us because we felt so helpless. I felt so bad for the boys, for them to have to see their mother this way, but what could I do? She had a strict regimen of medication and regular outpatient care at the psychologist, first alone, then with me and her. After a couple of months of this, we quit going because we didn't think he was doing any good.

In the fall of 1978, the litigation at the warehouse started to produce results. I had managed to keep the warehouse operation going, and it was a viable entity. The CMI and DMI boys were tough to deal with, but we worked out a mutual agreement whereby the owners would allow a peaceful foreclosure on the property, and in return they would relinquish any right to the property and be released from their personal guarantees. It was really a sweet deal for the stockholders, since they could retain their personal wealth, and write off the $200,00 or $300,000 as a loss.

So the property was sold on the country courthouse steps for something over $9,000,000. DMI became the new owners and brought a fellow by the name of Reeder in to take over. He was a real shark, and it was easy to see he had done this many times before. He grabbed all the accounts receivable and told all the accounts payable that they were just out of luck.

I knew that my days were numbered. They kept me long enough to train somebody new. They hired an Iranian book keeper who had taken an American name, Tony Shaw. They made sure he knew that he worked for them, and not for me. They wanted me to concentrate on sales, so they sent me to Chicago to call on all the large businesses there. I knew before I went that it was a waste of time. They were expecting me to double the business overnight. Even though I took Joy with me, it was miserable. Our flight arrived around midnight, and the wind chill was 50 below zero. We had to pay double price to get a cab to get us to our hotel, finally getting there around two in the morning, hungry and not able to get anything to eat. While I called on accounts, Joy walked around Merchandise Mart or caught the "L" to see her folks. It was a completely useless, wasted trip.

Richard was in the sixth grade; Donald, the fourth; and Kurt in the third. It was basketball season, and all three were playing. Richard was a tall kid, so he started playing at center. He was also left-handed, so that made him a bit unusual. I recall one game when we got a glimmer of his true athletic ability. Hank Norman was the coach, and his son Todd was a superb guard. It started as a typical little league game, but it turned out to be a very exciting one. It went right down to the wire. We were behind by two points, with just one second remaining. We had the ball out of bounds about three-quarters away from our basket.

Hank called a time-out and set up a play where the ball was to go to Richard since he was the tallest player. Our only chance, and it was very slim, was for the other team to foul him when he tried to catch the ball. He would then go to the free throw line, and if he made the first one, he got to shoot a second one. If he made it, then the game was tied and we could win it in overtime. The ball was thrown in, and Richard went high in the air to catch it. Sure enough, they fouled him, just as time expired. Not many of us expected Richard to make both of them, so we started gathering our things together to leave. Richard and the officials were the only ones on the court. They handed him the ball, and he bounced it a few times, came set, and lofted the ball in the air and into the hoop. Well, it wasn't over yet, so we sat back down. The air was thick with tension. Both teams on the bench were standing and hanging in suspense. The official handed Richard the ball. He bounced it again, then calmly put up the shot. The ball seemed to be in slow motion as it arched in the air and swished through the net. The score was tied, and his teammates swarmed him. We eventually lost the game in overtime when Richard fouled out, but this episode was the first of many where Richard came through under severe pressure.

About this time I decided we needed a basketball hoop so the kids could play basketball in our driveway. Skip at the crusher gave me a 20-foot-length of five-inch pipe, and I bought a backboard at the local sporting goods store. We dug a deep, wide hole, dropped the pipe in, poured in concrete with rocks, straightened it with a bubble level, tied it down, and let the concrete set. Then we attached the backboard so that the rim was exactly the correct height, and the boys had a hoop. That was one of the most important things I did for the kids. They spent hours and hours out there playing, right up to the day we sold the house.

Eventually, Reeder decided he knew enough about the business, and I was given my walking papers. Hello again to my old nemesis, unemployment. I drew weekly unemployment checks and went through the drill of looking for a new job. But you know what? There aren't that many general manager jobs laying around, waiting for someone to take them. And, of course, I had my good old friend, booze.

Little league baseball started, and all three boys were playing. During the summer, since our complex was completely lighted, we had games that started at nine o'clock in the evening. That meant two hours of game, then the ride home, putting the time around 11:30 by the time we got home. They did not permit drinking at the complex, so naturally, when there was a nine o'clock game, I generally had a pretty good glow on to carry me until I got home.

On July 6, 1979, Joy gave birth to our fourth son, Michael Dale. I had always loved the name "Michael," and even though we had named our first son Michael Lawrence, he was not living. I suppose some might question our judgment in having another child at our age – I was 42 and Joy was 40 – but we just took life as it came. Joy had used birth control pills for some time after Kurt was born, but her doctor told her that prolonged use of them was medically dangerous. Frankly, this is an area I didn't concern myself with, because to me it was a "woman's" thing.

On the subject of sex, I am sure that sex was not much fun for Joy while I was drinking. I was usually very drunk, and I'm sure she more or less tolerated it, rather than experience blissful fulfillment. Joy never really had what I would consider a normal attitude about sex anyway. I am certain she was a virgin when we married, and, as a result of having to hear her parents having sex at night, I felt she had a basic aversion to sex. I think initially she felt it was something "dirty," and I spent many, many years trying to teach her that sex was one of the rewards of marriage. There's a lot more I could say on this subject, but it would not be fair to Joy, so I'll just leave it at that.

In late July of that year, we got a call from Colorado. Tony was critically ill in the hospital and might not live. I had to be with him as quickly as I could get there and caught the very next plane. I was told that Mom and Dave were also flying in, as was Tony's oldest son, Lance, who was in Omaha in a football camp at the University of Nebraska. When I landed in Denver, it was almost eerie that all four of us met up in Stapleton Airport within 30 minutes of each other. We headed straight for the hospital.

I was not prepared for what greeted us when we got there. Poor Verlee was obviously shook up over what was happening, but was holding up very well. She filled us in on Tony's condition as best she knew it; then we asked to see Tony. I wanted to be next to him as soon as possible. They told us we could see him, but warned us that Tony was heavily sedated and might not even recognize us.

When I first saw Tony, I didn't recognize him at all. What I saw was a huge bloated man lying on his back and breathing very heavily. Tony's stomach had swollen up about twice the size of a fully pregnant woman. We approached the bed, and I tried to get Tony's attention. He was almost completely comatose, but he was lucid enough only to recognize us briefly, then drifted off again. I sat next to his bed feeling completely helpless. God, I didn't want to lose Tony.

I found out later that he had swollen so big that it was impossible for him to sit on the toilet stool. He simply bent over as much as he could and tried to hit the stool. His wife or his kids would have to clean him up when he was finished. Poor Verlee told us how stubbornly Tony had refused to go to a doctor or the hospital. Finally, when he started having the DTs and scaring the daylights out of his kids, she called an ambulance. That was the only way she could get him to go. I knew from experience that Tony was an extremely stubborn person and appreciated how hard it must have been on Verlee.

After awhile, I went out into the hall with the others. I knew that Verlee was terribly worried, so I decided not to press her for more information. Instead, I went to the nurse's station, identified myself and asked about Tony's condition. The head nurse was kind enough to pull the chart and look it over. She then told me that the first thing they did was draw blood and then ran an extensive series of tests. She said that Tony's blood test results, meaning the levels of iron, potassium, etc., were way out of line across the board. And so many of them were so far out of line that their first objective was to just to try to get them back in line. Then they would try to tackle his problem. I thanked her and went back to our group. Since we were virtually helpless, we left for the evening, except for Verlee who wanted to stay.

The next day we arrived at the hospital early, hoping to be there when the doctor arrived for his rounds. We planned well, because we got to talk to him. He was polite and caring, but not optimistic. He confirmed what the nurses had said about his blood test results, went over what he was doing for Tony, and told us to be patient. That was hard to do when your brother was in critical condition. It didn't help matters when I found out that the ward where they placed him was the ward for the terminally ill cancer patients.

That afternoon I was able to spend a few minutes alone with Tony. I felt closer to him than at any other time in my life. He was now much more lucid and wanted to tell me about his drinking. It was as though he just had to get it off his chest. He told me that each morning he had a beer or two before leaving for the high school where he taught. He said he drank a beer on the way to school as well. After morning classes he returned to his car and drank a beer on the way home for lunch. During lunch he had a beer or two and maybe a shot of vodka. On his way back to school he drank another beer. At the end of classes he returned home, drinking a beer on the way. Once home, he drank beer until about eight, then switched to the hard liquor, until he drank himself to sleep. After he told me all this, he seemed much more at peace. And my love for him swelled even more.

By the next day it was obvious that his condition was somewhat stable, with a gradual improvement in his blood tests. It was now obvious that he was going to be in the hospital for a very long time. Dave raised the question as to when we should return home. I told him that as long as Tony was in the condition he was in, I just could not leave him. I don't know if he and Mom left or stayed longer. I know I stayed at least another day or so, until the blood tests returned a lot closer to normal. We now knew that his kidneys and liver were functioning, at least enough to keep him alive. This was a huge step forward. Now he had at least a fighting chance. Finally, the doctor said he thought Tony would survive this episode, but that his liver was in such bad shape that if Tony ever drank again, it would kill him. He gave Tony about five years to live. What a shame. He was just 41 years old.

I returned home, stunned and shocked by what had happened. I stayed in phone contact daily until Tony was better, and finally, he was released from the hospital. Now we could all relax and pray that Tony would prove the doctor wrong, and that he would never drink again. The whole gross, morbid affair scared me into quitting drinking. I never had another drop ... for a whole month. Big deal! Then I picked up right where I had left off. I rationalized that I could always quit drinking long before I reached the condition that Tony did.

Unfortunately, by the fall of that year my drinking really took control of me. I was now buying two full six-packs of liquor store beer **and** a half-pint of whiskey each night. I'd come in through the garage, so I could sneak one six-pack into the laundry room and hide the cans all over the place. I put the whiskey inside my trousers and sneaked it under some clothes in my dresser drawers. So, as far as Joy knew, all I was drinking was one six-pack a night. Boy, was she wrong! I managed to drink all I had every night. As the evening wore on, I even sneaked the empty cans out to the trash in the garage, to throw her off.

Each morning I'd get out of bed, hung over, with diarrhea until noon, and swearing that I would not drink that night. I hated myself for being weak. I was disgusted with myself for having broken each day every promise not to drink that day. I started hating it when there were nine o'clock 3 & 2 baseball games, because it interfered with my drinking. So I slammed down a lot of beer before I went.

One evening, about seven, I started backing out of my driveway to go out to the damn ball park. We lived on Lowell, which was a through street and carried a lot of traffic. I didn't see a car coming up the street and backed out into the street. Fortunately, the woman in the car saw me and swerved, but I still clipped her rear fender. Oh, no. I could just see a DUI, and I didn't need that. There wasn't much damage, and I was able to talk her into just sending me the bill, and I would pay it. I told her I had a kid out at a ball park and I needed to pick him up. She bought it, and I was off the hook.

I knew then that I really had a problem. I was as low as I could be. Alcohol had me in its clutches and was now running my life. I felt totally lost and knew that something had to happen, or I was a goner. It began to dawn on me that my days had been shrinking. They were becoming shorter and shorter. I started measuring them in terms of hours before I could start drinking and found that I slowly started drinking sooner and sooner each day. This meant I became totally drunk sooner each day. So my days were shrinking.

12

OVERLAND PARK, KANSAS, 1979-1982

(Sobriety, Bankruptcy, Employment, Unemployment, and More Kids)

IT WAS DECEMBER 5, 1979, a typical evening at home. Richard was 12 and in the seventh grade at Nallwood Junior High. Donald was 10 and in the fifth grade, while Kurt was nine, and in the fourth grade. It was around 10 o'clock, and I was well into my second six-pack of beer. I'd also had a few shots of whiskey. I had a full glow on and was feeling no pain. Michael, our baby, was sleeping in the bassinet upstairs in our room. All of us except the baby were down in the den watching TV. Something came up and I started into a mild tirade at Joy. I was the type of person who could tolerate a lot, but occasionally, when I reached a certain point, I let it all out.

This was one of those times. I really started unloading on Joy about everything under the sun, the poor housekeeping, undone laundry, poor meals, you name it. When I was early in the tirade, all three sons – Richard, Donald, and Kurt – got up in unison and started upstairs to bed. No one said a word to them, and none of them said a word to each other. They just got up together and went upstairs. It was apparently obvious to them that they had heard this record many, many times before and didn't want to hear it again.

After they left, I was stunned into silence. I hadn't even considered what effect I was having on the kids. Joy was the one who was always wrong, and I was the "pillar of strength" in the family. I was the good parent, and Joy was the inadequate parent. The more I thought about it, the more horrified I became that I might be subconsciously teaching these kids to also be heavy drinkers. I knew that children of divorced parents generally got divorced themselves. A rush of realization swept over me that I, the mighty one, might be marking my own kids for life, dooming them to a hell of drinking and unemployment, thereby ruining their lives, too.

Then I really got scared. It was one thing for me to ruin my life through drinking. It was a completely different thing for me to ruin four or five other lives, too. This I couldn't bear. I knew that alcohol had captured my life, and since I was the only one being hurt, that was okay. Nevertheless, when those three kids silently got up in unison and went upstairs to bed, I knew that I was also ruining their lives. That was an unbearable thought. I just couldn't stand that.

I knew that something had to be done, and right away. Fortunately, I was out of a job and had been so for at least seven or eight months, so I had a very flexible schedule. The next morning I didn't tell Joy anything. I just went over to the church and asked to see Fr. Wicke. I really liked him as a priest. He was an older priest with pure white hair. His sermons were laced with experience. I broke down and cried in front of him, told him about my drinking problem and that I knew it was time to solve it. He counseled me and suggested Alcohol Anonymous. I knew that was where I was headed anyhow, but before I left, I got control of myself and knelt down and asked him to bless me. He did, and I walked out of the church and got into my car.

I sat there for a few minutes, building up courage to go to AA. I had done a little scouting and had found out that there was a rear entrance. Thank God. I just couldn't stand the thought of anyone seeing me go in the front door on 80th Street, a somewhat busy commercial street. There was a gravel parking lot located in the back, and it took me a few minutes to find it. From the car I scouted the area. There was an old set of wooden steps that I was sure led up to AA. When it looked like no one was nearby, I eased out of the car, and as inconspicuously as possible, casually walked up the steps. At the top landing I entered the door as quickly as I could, then stood there gathering myself.

On my right were two small restrooms and a very small meeting room for about 10 people. Next to this was a much larger room that appeared to be a meeting room for as many as 50 to 60 people. I walked the length of that room and entered the front room. This room fronted the street, had five or six sofas, easy chairs and coffee tables. To the right side of this room was another smaller, private room for about 10 to 12 people. There was a lot of cigarette smoke, and I could see a commercial coffee pot.

I tried to look as casual as I could, but I guess my newness showed too much. One of the six or seven men came over to me, stuck his hand out, and said, "Hi, I'm Frank." I told him my first name, and he asked me to sit and join them. We sat in a corner, and I know he knew that this was the very first time I was there. He also had the perception to know that inside I was desperate. He eased a lot of my initial nervousness and started talking about his drinking problem and the difficulties that it created. Frank told me about the peace he had reached by being sober, and many other things. He explained generally how AA worked and told me there was a noon meeting that he'd like me to attend. I didn't commit myself, but hell, I didn't have a job to go to, so it wasn't like I was missing out on anything important if I went. I decided to give it a shot.

This was December 6, 1979, and turned out to probably be the most important day of my life, although I didn't know it at the time. As noon approached, people from all walks of life started filing into the large meeting room. Tables were set up in a square so that everyone sat on the outside, with no one on the inside. In this fashion everyone could see everyone else. I took a chair with my cup of coffee and lit up a cigarette. Soon someone said, "Let's start this meeting with a moment of silence. Then he led everyone in the "Serenity" prayer that goes like this:

"God, grant me the serenity to accept the things I cannot change, the courage to change the things I can, and the wisdom to know the difference."

I'd heard this prayer before, but didn't know that it was used this much in AA. In fact, it may have originated in AA. I just don't know.

The meeting leader then asked if anyone had a special problem or subject that they wanted to be discussed at that meeting. I don't think anyone spoke up. He then asked if there were any people there for the first time. I meekly raised my hand. He thanked me for coming and said he hoped I would come back. He then started telling me about his drinking days and the things that led up to his joining AA. He then passed it on to the next person, and those who had something to say did so. Each of them started out by saying, "My name is so and so (generally their first name), and I am an alcoholic." Some didn't want to talk and "passed." As it turned out, these good people basically held the meeting for me. I could feel them reaching out, wanting to help me. They worked around the table, and I opted to "pass." I wasn't quite ready to state openly that I was an alcoholic. Toward the end of the meeting, they passed around a small basket, and those who wanted to put a dollar or so in it to pay for the rent, coffee, etc. At the end of the meeting we all stood up, grasped our hands and said the "Our Father." That was the official end of the meeting.

As the members were milling about, quite a few of them came up to me and were sincerely interested in me. They urged me to come to the 6 p.m. meeting. During the meeting I heard many different horror stories from the members, each one telling openly and in detail how low they had sunk before the "Higher Power" finally gave them refuge. The "Higher Power" was the name AA gave to God, so that a fixed religious belief was not necessary in order to overcome alcoholism. These people were a lot different from the AA people in Oklahoma City. Many of these people had been able to stop drinking, some for a month, some for a few months, some for a year or two, and some for many, many years. I started to feel as though I might have a chance and saw a very faint glimmer of hope.

I went home about 3:00 or so with the determination that I would come back for the 6:00 meeting. I knew that if I didn't, then I might give into drinking again that night, and I was now determined to hopefully forever whip the drinking problem. Whether I told Joy about going to AA that night or not, I can't remember. All I vaguely remember is that I went to that meeting, and there were a lot more people at this meeting. Many appeared to be quite at peace, as though they had found their refuge in life and were happy. These were the ones who had many years of sobriety. There were others who were new just like me and were downright miserable. They were hanging on to their sobriety by their bare fingernails. I could see that they were on the verge of collapsing under the pressure to drink. There was a saying that circulated through these early meetings that if you wanted to remain sober, you had to go to 90 meetings in 90 days. That seemed like an enormous task, but there was another saying that also circulated even more, that you lived your life *one day at a time.* That became the ironclad motto of your life, if you wanted to stay sober.

I don't know how many meetings I went to, before I finally said, "Hi, I'm Don, and I'm an alcoholic." But I finally did, and it really wasn't that big a deal. These people already knew it, so they weren't surprised to hear me say it. On the contrary, they were very happy for me, because they knew that admitting it to yourself was the first step toward sobriety. Eventually I told Joy I was going to AA. I honestly don't remember her reaction. But I do know that when I told her the extent of my drinking, the two six-packs plus whiskey each day, she was stunned. She couldn't believe that I had been drinking that much.

Since I was out of work, I spent my time either looking for a job or at the AA hall. AA was my "country club." At all times there were generally five to 10 people there, even when there were no meetings going on. We'd drink coffee, share our experiences and give each other support. The club hired a fellow AA member to be in charge of the club during the day, answering the phone, selling books, etc. Someone had devised a card game called "Spite and Malice." Many members played this game literally for hours at a time. In a way, it was good therapy for them. I played quite a bit of it during my first 90 days, and even thereafter.

After I had been there for a couple of weeks and had attended about 10 of the big meetings, the ones at 6 p.m., I had voiced my worries and concerns about being out of work and how badly I needed a job. I must have brought this up a number of times, because after a meeting one night, a member by the name of Shep handed me a copy of the "Twenty-Four Hour" book with an inscription on the inside cover to the effect that, "Judge a man's worth not by what he has, but by what he is." I thanked him for it and still have it today. It is a small book that has on each page a short meditation and prayer for each calendar day of the year. The idea was to read your 24-hour book the first thing every morning to get your day started off right.

Alcohol Anonymous really helped me a lot. As I sat and listened to many of the members, both old and new, I started seeing the insidiousness of the disease and the absolute certainty that if I continued drinking, eventually it would kill me. It was terminal. They likened alcoholism to an elevator going down. You could get off at any floor by stopping drinking. But if you continued to drink, you would ride the elevator all the way to the basement, which was death. I also learned that generally alcoholics didn't quit drinking until they had reached their personal bottom. To one, that bottom might be a divorce because of drinking. To another, it might be a succession of DUI's. And to yet another, loss of health or a job.

I also learned that it was a disease and not a character defect. To those who are not closely exposed to it, that may seem like a cop-out. But it isn't. I knew from my own personal experience that despite a lot of qualities and talents that I had, I still literally had no control over alcohol. Seeing Tony the way he was should have convinced me to stop drinking forever. But I had lost control. I know that I would be dead and buried today if the Good Lord hadn't guided me to AA and granted me the gift of sobriety. That's right, a gift. I feel I have been given a second chance for a clean life. It shocked me to learn that for every alcoholic that stopped drinking, there were nine out there who were still drinking.

Soon we started covering the "12 Steps of AA." The First Step was, *"We admitted we were powerless over alcohol – that our lives had become unmanageable."* Well, that one was easy for me. I had already learned I was powerless, and there was no question that my life was certainly unmanageable. Here I was, 42, married with four kids, broke, in and out of work, on welfare and food stamps. I even had to fill out a form so my kids could get free lunches at school because I didn't have the money. I can only guess how they must have felt about that, because I know they knew about it.

The Second Step was, *"Came to believe that a Power greater than ourselves could restore us to sanity."* Although I had been raised a strict Catholic, I think this is when I really reached my deepest belief in a God and his power. As meeting after meeting went by and this step and theme was repeated and discussed, I began to realize that my God was my strength against drinking. I knew that trying to quit drinking by myself had been an utter failure. Time after time I had tried, but never succeeded. I was no match. I needed someone a lot stronger than me to lean on for support. It was God, the same one that I had learned about since a mere child. He was beckoning me to him, trying to tell me that He was my savior, my solution. I just needed to rely on him.

The natural sequence of the Second Step was the Third Step, *"Made a decision to turn our will and our lives over to the care of God as we understood him."* This proved to be the most powerful, dynamic and peaceful revelation in my life. This step alone has become the granite cornerstone of my life. It would be the basis for everything I did and would provide me the strength to get through everything I came across in my life. I now understood what the word "refuge" meant. It was like the calm, still waters of a secluded port in the midst of a hurricane of a life. He was the answer to literally every problem, to every crisis, and the cause of everything positive.

I soon realized that God was totally running the show. And what a sweet relief that was! Now, when I went to sleep at night and laid my head down on the pillow, I simply said to God, "It's time for me to sleep now. I'm going to turn all my problems over to you for now, and I'll work on them again in the morning." Then I would go to sleep. They had a saying in AA that no one ever died from lack of sleep. Ever since the eighth grade I had difficulty sleeping. There was the snoring in the seminary, then during college, then the Army, so I had a long history of having a very hard time of sleeping. And I still had a hard time sleeping, but gradually it got better. At least to the point that I could live with it.

Each morning after I woke up, the first thing I did was read my 24-hour book. Then I told myself that the single, most important thing I wanted to get done that day was not to take a drink. If I could get that done, then the day was a huge success. It didn't matter if I lost my job or my wife or children died, still, the most important thing was not to take a drink. This kept me focused and minimized what would otherwise be major crises. Don't misunderstand me. I loved my wife and family, but I certainly was no good to them dead. So I had to survive. That was priority number one.

I learned to start giving my problems to God. Without being flippant, I simply said, "Here, Lord, this is just too much for me. Would you carry this problem for a while?" Gradually, I learned that this is what God wanted. He wanted me to come to him for help. He wanted me to believe in him and depend on him. After all, he was GOD. And what were Gods for, anyway? We had an expression for it – "Let go, and let God." I'd always had a slumbering faith in God, but AA woke it up and helped me to start living it. It was as though I was starting my life over, only I was now 42 and married, with four kids. It was time to move forward.

There are a total of 12 steps in AA, the last of which is a commitment to helping other drinking alcoholics back to sobriety. I learned about all the other steps through the endless meetings I attended over the years. And over the years I did try to help drinking alcoholics back to sobriety and continue to do so to this day. But for me, my sobriety was won in Step Three. For me that was all it took. I just learned to turn everything over to God, and then my life became very easy. I remembered the words of the Lord, telling us about the lilies of the field, and how they don't worry about anything, and yet the Lord takes care of them.

But that realization didn't free me from my responsibilities. I remember Shep saying that the Good Lord is going to feed us, but he is not going to bring it to the nest. We have to leave the nest to go and find it. In other words, although God was most certainly going to solve all our problems, we still had to do all we could with the talents he gave us to try to solve them. We still had to find a job, work hard, love and feed our families.

Nor was this newfound sobriety and living faith in God Nirvana. It didn't mean that there would never be difficulties or crises in our lives. It was more of a panacea. If we followed the AA program and avoided drinking, then we became more impervious to the tribulations that all families face, the need for money, a home, a car that works, clothes or serious sickness. It was the medicine that let us experience those trials without going entirely to pieces and jumping back into the bottle. It was the lighthouse that guided us safely through whatever storm had struck.

And Lord knows, I had my share of trials right at that time. I was out of work, drawing unemployment and welfare, and frankly, desperate. All I could do was to start tackling these problems. I did everything I knew to do to find a job. I made personal calls and sent out endless numbers of resumés throughout the Kansas City area, as well as all over the country. And I prayed. Hard. Unfortunately, I was "over-qualified." With 250 hours of college credits, a bachelor's and law degree and upper management experience, there just weren't too many openings. I even worked through employment agencies, but that proved fruitless.

By the time I finally had made it into AA, I had already been out of a job for at least seven months. We were broke, drawing unemployment and food stamps. We couldn't even afford the $1.15 lunches for the kids at school and had to sign up for free lunches. Michael was a mere baby. Christmas was coming, and it was sure going to be a lean one for us. Our credit was so bad that we didn't have credit cards.

But there was one bright moment during all of this. My brother, Mark, lived in Omaha and was aware of our situation. Mark always had a generous heart, and I guess he just couldn't stand the thought of us having a bad Christmas. A few days before Christmas, he showed up at our house with his arms loaded with presents for everyone. And there were more than one for each of us. He meant to be our Santa Claus that year, and he was. Then he went back out to his car and came back in with a huge turkey with all the fixin's. He was going to make certain that we had a good Christmas. We felt a little bad when we saw the turkey, because they had just been put on sale, and I had just bought two big turkeys. We could barely get his into the refrigerator with ours. We still laugh about that today. Bless him!

Eventually, I found work with a firm called Gateway International, a large public warehouse in Olathe. The money wasn't the greatest, but it sure beat unemployment. At this point, as long as I was feeding the family and getting the kids through school, I felt that was progress. Especially if I could stay sober. Again, I was the general manager and had a crew of about 20 men. My assistant, Dave Murphy, a mid-30 single fellow, was as fine a person as you could want. His father was deaf, and he had learned sign language at the Kansas School for the Deaf there in Olathe, so Dave could also use sign language. He coached little league football and Babe Ruth baseball, so we had a lot in common.

By this time I was the proud owner of a beat-up old French Renault. It was old and had a few dings and dents, but I got some satisfaction over it being different. Joy was still driving the old yellow Ford station wagon that was going downhill quick. The window had been let down so often that the bottom of the storage compartment had rusted out, as well as the floor behind the driver. Old, used cars seemed to be the scourge of our lives. Nevertheless, they got us to where we were going.

I had never got caught up in the rut of keeping up with the Joneses. Long before Shep had made the inscription about the value of what a man was, I tried to live and teach my kids that what was important was what you were, not what you had. Sure, I wanted nice cars and other things, but material things were not that high on my priority list. That might seem odd, because Johnson County was loaded with over-achievers. These people had money, had $300,000 homes, nice cars, and their kids had anything they wanted. I'm sure many of them earned it, but there were a great many of them who inherited it. Or maybe I was just dumb. Who knows? More importantly, who cares? Happiness was the most prized possession to me.

I had been out of work for so long that our debts were insurmountable. In addition to having many medical bills as a result of not having health insurance, I became aware of a possible liability arising out of the underground warehouse company. It seems the food broker in Tulsa was now claiming shortages amounting to thousands of dollars (he was just jerking the chain of the new owners). Another possible liability I saw was from some of the creditors. When Reeder took over, he grabbed all of the accounts receivable and told the accounts payable to collect their money from the previous owners. Since these amounts exceeded $100,000, I could see some creditors coming after me. Although their chances of succeeding in a claim against me were very slim, I didn't want to put up with the hassle. So Joy and I had no choice but to file bankruptcy in July of 1980. It was a huge blow to our pride, but it was the practical thing to do.

As time went by, my sobriety grew, and I grew. My life was centered mostly in our kids. That was really all we had, kids. On November 25, 1980, Kyle was born. As I write this, I realize now that he was conceived when I was broke, out of a job, getting unemployment checks, drawing food stamps, and Joy was on mental health medication. My mom was in town when we brought him home from the hospital, so I took a chance and called up the *Overland Park Sun* newspapers and told them about Kyle being my mom's 66th grandchild. They came out to the house, did a long interview of her and took countless photos of her and the baby. Sure enough, in the next issue they spent almost a full page on her and Kyle, complete with pictures. We were really proud.

As time relentlessly passed, we kept going forward. I really don't know how we managed, but somehow we did. Perhaps the near poverty level of our existence had some adverse effect on our kids. I don't know. I know I was worried about it and tried to offset it by stressing how important it was to be good persons. As time goes by, it would be the final arbiter of whether the effort was successful. I guess if you wanted to point to one thing that was our strong point, it had to be that no matter where we were, we were always looking to the future. We knew we had to keep going, and as long as we kept trying, things would be okay. Giving up just was not an option.

Donald started showing strong aggressiveness in his personality. It was perhaps even before this time that he got a *Sun* newspaper route and managed to buy his own ghetto blaster. He was really proud of it and I of him. I suppose it is natural that the first child gets the most attention, no matter how much we parents try to be fair. I think our situation was compounded by the fact that we had lost two babies and Richard was adopted. Despite all that, I tried to be equal and fair with all of our kids. I think some of my brothers, as well as sons Donald and Kurt, will agree that I probably failed miserably in this regard. But at least I saw the tendency and tried to fight it. Donald and Kurt will always have my deepest apologies for not being more successful.

I will always regret one incident that I wish I could take back and live over. I was dead wrong and made a mistake that Donald suffered greatly for. The wall at the end of the hall way upstairs was lined with 12-inch square mirrors from the floor to the ceiling. One day, one of the kids had thrown a ball or something and broke one of them. I took out the broken pieces, located a replacement and put it in place. I then lectured the kids about being careful with them.

The next day, when I came home from work, the first thing I noticed was that another one of those mirrors was broken. I don't know why, but it made me mad as hell. Donald and Kurt saw it coming and headed into hiding. I found Donald, and to this day don't know why I just assumed that he was the one who broke it . I'll never know why. I do know that I gave him one of the hardest spankings he ever had, *and he wasn't the one who broke it!* It was someone else. This had to give him all the reason it in the world to hate my guts. I have been sorry for this ever since I found out I spanked the wrong kid. And it will pain me probably to the day I die. Here I was, trying to teach these kids fairness, and I demonstrated the exact opposite.

When we moved up from Arkansas, both Donald and Kurt suffered from allergies. Joy had to take Kurt in weekly and Donald every other week for allergy shots. They hated those shots, and it became more and difficult to get them to go. That didn't bother me as much as the steady cost the doctors charged. It was just bleeding us to death. After a few years of this, I finally had enough and said, "No more." We just quit taking them. And you know what? It didn't affect them one bit. They simply grew out of them, especially Kurt. He had asthma, and during ragweed seasons it really hit him hard. A couple of times I had to take him to the emergency room in the mornings because he just couldn't breathe. They'd give him a couple of shots, keep him for an hour or so and send him home. He'd be down for about a day, and then he'd be okay. Eventually the doctors prescribed a medicated puffer for him to use when he was wheezing, and that cleared up his bronchial tubes.

In the fall of 1980, Richard began the seventh grade, Donald the fifth, and Kurt the fourth. With the job at Gateway we eked out a meager living for the next two years or so. We still lived from pay day to pay day, but I remained sober. And that was the most important thing. As the kids got older, their world started to expand. Thankfully, there were a lot of kids in the neighborhood, so they spent a lot of time with them. They got into their share of trouble and fights, but fortunately there was never anything serious.

During the summer of 1981, we had all three sons playing little league baseball, each with 16 game schedules. There were times when I had sons paying on different diamonds at the same time. Little league baseball in Johnson County was a mixed bag. The facilities were great, nine diamonds, all with lights. When school let out, they played well after 11 o'clock. Mostly dads did the coaching, and there were the usual "Bad News Bears" incidents where fathers were trying to make super-stars out of their boys. And some coaches were on ego trips. Still, the overall benefits were good … but just barely.

In the fall of 1980, Richard, now in the eighth grade, made the school basketball team. I was both proud and happy. Happy, because we didn't have the luxurious things that many of the other families did, and this I felt helped Richard's self-respect. Not that it was low, but at this adolescent age peer pressure can be a real tiger. He could walk down the halls, knowing that he was part of something.

It's odd that I really don't recall any major events in the 1981 and 1982 period. You'd think that with being sober my memory would be much better. At any rate, by the fall of 1981, Richard was in the ninth grade, Donald in the seventh, and Kurt in the sixth. The kids were growing up. Richard was the starting center on the school's ninth grade basketball team. I'm going to tell you about one kid, only as an example of how bad coaching can ruin a good athlete.

The starting guard on Richard's team was an exceptional basketball player. He came from a basketball family and had played the game for many years. In the ninth grade, the teacher/coach was so mesmerized with this kid that he built the entire offense around him. As a result, he was the shooter. The rest of the players were to look to him to shoot. Well, this kid averaged about 27 points a game. That's quite a few points for a junior high guard. But if he was the only one shooting, *and was taught that,* then it is not so surprising.

The problem was that the other teams knew it and let him get his 27 points, but our team didn't get much more than that. So we lost the first five games and went into our sixth game against our nemesis, Indian Creek. They were unbeaten, with a 5 and 0 record. Then a surprising thing happened. Very early in this game, our guard picked up three quick fouls and had to sit on the bench. Richard was our center and had a hot hand that day. He was throwing in shots from all over the floor, off balance, falling down, you name it. It was one of those days when he could have just tossed it over his shoulder, and it would have gone in. He took 10 shots from the field and made every one of them. He also made seven of eight free throws, and we won the game. Our coach finally found out that he had more than one player.

But, getting back to the guard, he went on to high school the next year and was placed on the junior varsity team. Unfortunately, the coaches there didn't give him too much playing time, so he went from being the team leader one year to spending a lot of time on the bench the next year. After that year, he transferred to another school in hopes of playing. But he was an "outsider" there, didn't get as much playing time as he wanted, and in his senior year didn't play at all. He was a kid with great talent, but was sent down the path of ruin by his junior high coach.

During the summer of 1982, I asked Bill MacDonald, the high school baseball coach, to come out to one of Richard's games and take a look at him. Richard was now about six feet, five inches tall, with size 15 shoes. There weren't too many left-handed pitchers, so he made a rather imposing figure to the other teams. MacDonald looked at him, but didn't say much.

Also during that summer, Gateway decided to sell their building, so I was out of a job. Again. But thank God, I wasn't drinking. And that was the main thing. I was getting to be an old-timer, with almost three years of sobriety. As for work, surprisingly, I was out for just a month or so. A developer by the name of Aubrey Lloyd had about a million square feet of commercial warehouse space and sought me out to start up a new public warehouse company. His concept was to lease his space to the public warehouse company, which would keep growing and fill up the vacant space he had. I literally started the company from scratch. I was the only employee. I did everything, made sales calls, answered the phone, did all the typing, ran the forklift, everything. The pay wasn't that great, but again, I was feeding my family, and I wasn't drinking.

13

OVERLAND PARK, KANSAS, 1982-1986

(Concentrated Kid Raisin', More Financial Struggles, and Start of Drake Investigations)

I DON'T KNOW why, but as I get closer to the present, it is becoming increasingly more difficult to write. Perhaps it's because our kids are getting older, and I know that someday they will read this. Maybe I am afraid I will offend them, either with something that I include in the book, or by something that I left out about them. Nevertheless, since I am committed to a true autobiography, I'll plunge forward.

One thing is now crystallizing in my mind. As I look both backward and forward while I write, it is clear to me that the most important thing in my life was, and is, raising good kids. In my human frailty, I may not have always done or said the right things, but I think all my kids know that they are uniquely special to me. Sure, they were and are a lot of work and worry while raising them, but I cannot think of anything more valuable than kids.

I decided to make a chapter break here because our oldest was starting in high school. Mighty high school, with all its size, with the vast impact that it would have on kids. Where many would pour the foundation for the rest of their lives. Where some would fall into traps of chasing the wrong ideals. Where kids would be exposed to the explosion of new experiences, new pressures, and their independence from their families would take them a dramatic step forward, be it for good or bad. I saw a lot of both among the kids I got to know.

At the end of summer in 1982, I was now 45, Joy 43, Richard 15, Donald 13, Kurt 12, Michael three, and Kyle almost one. Richard was a sophomore in high school, Donald was in the eighth grade at Nallwood Junior High, and Kurt was in the seventh grade, also at

Nallwood. So we had kids spread all over the place. Little league baseball was over, and all three older boys had played. What a scramble! At about this time I ran across a poem that I felt really summed up my feelings about little league baseball. I have seen parents trying to re-live their frustrated athletic dreams through their sons, or get so angry that huge arguments happened with the umpires or other coaches. The most astonishing thing to me was that the parents at these times completely forgot about their son on the field and what he was thinking as these tantrums were happening right in front of him. Anyway, the poem goes like this:

JUST A LITTLE BOY

He stands at the plate with heart pounding fast.
The bases are loaded; the die has been cast.
Mom and Dad cannot help him, he stands all alone.
A hit at this moment would send the team home.
The ball meets the plate; he swings and he misses.
There's a groan from the crowd, with some boos and some hisses.
A thoughtless voice cries: "Strike out the bum."
Tears fill his eyes, the game's no longer fun.
So open your heart and give him a break,
For it's moments like this, a man you can make.
Keep this in mind when you hear someone forget.
He's just a boy, and not a man yet.

That almost brings tears to my eyes. I have never found out who wrote that so they could get their just credit. When it comes to kids, you somehow have to get inside their heads and hearts and try to find out what they are thinking and feeling. If you are lucky enough to be able to do that, then you can lead them up through the years to manhood without major problems.

Shawnee Mission South was Richard's high school. It was one of five high schools in the Shawnee Mission School District in Overland Park. These five high schools practically dominated the whole state in just about every category. They were all in affluent Johnson County. The parents were very, very wealthy to the extent that some kids actually drove Porsches to school. Wyandotte County, mainly Kansas City, Kansas, was just to the north of Johnson County, and was highly populated with low-income and minority families. To the east was Jackson County, mainly Kansas City, Missouri, also populated with minority and low-income families. These three counties make up the bulk of metropolitan Kansas City. Overland Park is the largest suburban city in Johnson County. We had the best of everything, fire departments, police, controlled commercial growth, streets, shopping and, of course, the schools. You rarely saw a dog running loose, because Animal Control was very tight, and the fine was stiff if your dog got loose. People could walk the streets without fear.

As school started in the fall of 1982, Richard made the junior varsity basketball team. By now he was about six foot-six and had size 15 shoes. He was also left-handed, which was a plus. He made the junior varsity team as a sophomore, and then in mid-season was moved up to varsity. He didn't get much playing time, but did get into some games when they were blow-outs. It was easy to see that basketball was Richard's favorite sport. When the team made it all the way to the state championship game, he actually got to play some when we were hopelessly behind. Overall, it was a great year for Richard. Maybe too great! Spring of '83 eased into the picture, and this created a real dilemma for me. Richard had just finished a very successful basketball year. He had received a fair share of print in the local *Sun* newspaper, a twice-weekly Johnson County paper, and was riding the crest of popularity. I could tell that he really didn't want to go out for baseball. However, I could also see that he really had a good left arm and might be that rare one who made it to the majors. I know, dads shouldn't make their kids play sports that they didn't want to play, and that was my rule, too. Still, I felt Richard was just too young to appreciate the talent that I thought he had. I recall vividly the day that baseball try-outs were being held. I took his baseball mitt and cleats to meet him in front of the gym. He was hoping to go home, but I convinced him he should continue with baseball. He made it obvious that he really didn't want to, but he went anyway. Some might say that I shouldn't have exerted this pressure on Richard, that I should have let him quit baseball. Still, I don't think I was wrong, and I think despite the end result, I took the correct action. He had a decent season and started to develop a split-fingered fast ball that really moved.

Back to the fall of '82, Donald had also made the eighth grade basketball team at Nallwood. This was really the team to make, because it was the only true school sport at the junior high level, and the gymnasiums were generally packed with students and parents. They had the usual cheerleaders, and the drill team performed at halftime. Donald wasn't a starter, but was usually the first man to come off the bench. By now, his quickness, agility and speed were starting to show. He could take two steps and be at full speed. I went to every game of both boys.

Very tight finances caught up with us in the spring of 1983. We had to put the house up for sale. Actually, our timing was good, because interest rates were low when I bought the house and were a lot higher when I sold it. We netted around $10,000, and that carried us for some time. I knew we had all these boys who were going to attend Shawnee Mission South, so I rented a house right off 103rd Street, a few blocks north of Shawnee Mission South. I had to fudge a bit on the ages of my two youngest sons, because some owners shied away from families with small kids, thinking they would tear up their property. We could actually walk out into our front yard and see the high school over the trees that lined Indian Creek. I thought our boys would enjoy the walk to school. Boy, was I wrong! That was beneath their dignity. They either wanted to drive or be driven. Unfortunately, we were limited to two beat-up old cars, one for me to use to go to work, and the other for Joy to cart the kids back and forth.

My brother Mark had been injured some years earlier in a truck accident and had hired a plaintiff's attorney, Bill Pickett, to represent him. A plaintiff's attorney is generally an attorney who concentrates his practice on attempting to recover for injured people, as opposed to defense attorneys, who defend the parties that plaintiff's attorneys sue. Mark's case had gone to trial sometime earlier in Wyandotte County, and he won a jury verdict of $985,000, which was the highest amount ever awarded in that County at that time. I was out of work ... again. And again, I was scratching for survival.

My brother Mark called me and told me about Pickett and wanted to know if I had ever considered doing any investigative work. I had never done any real investigating as such, but was open to anything. He said he'd pass this on to Pickett. A few days later, I got a call from Pickett, and he wanted to meet with me to explore the possibility of doing investigative work with him. We met, and I learned that he had quite a number of personal injury cases, mostly involving auto accidents, and needed someone to go out and get the facts, pictures of the scene, take taped statements, etc. I was willing to try anything, so I told him I'd give it a shot. We agreed on a rate of $25 per hour plus expenses, and he gave me a case to get me started.

I located an old Negro woman who witnessed the accident in which his client was injured, took a written statement, drew a diagram of the street scene, wrote a report, and turned it in to Pickett with my invoice. He went over it on the spot and wrote me a check while I waited. He liked the work, so he gave me some more cases. So began my career as a private investigator. I found that I enjoyed the work quite a bit. It was challenging to try to locate witnesses, to take clear, thorough statements, and basically, get the facts. I knew that in any case, the facts usually controlled the outcome of each case. So I concentrated on getting all I could, good or bad. If the facts were bad, that was every bit as important as the good facts, because it helped in the evaluation of a case and also influenced the strategy.

My new business needed a name. By now I needed a business card, a letterhead, etc. I recalled that Perry Mason had a top-notch private investigator, Paul Drake, so I named my business "Drake Investigations." Really original, huh? Pickett usually wanted a ton of pictures of the scene and all the vehicles to show the full extent of their damages and the force of impact. Sometimes I took as many as 75 to 100 pictures, had them printed in 8" x 10" sizes, and identified on the back as to the case, distance from impact, etc.

At first, I worked out of the basement in my house. As the business grew, I was away more and more, so that Joy frequently had to answer the phone. Since her mind was usually on housecleaning and things of that nature, as was that of every red-blooded housewife, calls from my clients generally caught her somewhat by surprise. This resulted in incomplete or incorrect message-taking and was therefore a detriment to my business. I remedied this by renting a small office in a building at 95th and Antioch for $100 a month. I lived a mere 10 minutes away, so it was very convenient. I moved my desk from home, added two chairs, and that was it. In my business I didn't have many visitors. A secretarial service answered my phone when I was out. I bought a portable Smith Corona electric typewriter and typed all my own reports and correspondence. Thank you, U.S. Army Clerk Typist School. Early on. I bought a Minolta 35 mm camera and a hand-held tape recorder.

I obtained my Kansas private investigator's license by filling out umpteen forms, giving my life history, and driving over to Topeka to take a written exam. It seemed to me the state wanted more information from me for the PI license than they wanted for the law degree. I was impressed. The KBI made a background check on me, and everything was in order. I paid my $200 and was given my license. That made me completely legal.

Soon, I started developing a very good reputation as an investigator. Pickett started relying on me exclusively, and other law firms heard of me through dealing with Pickett. Then I started getting calls from these law firms to do work for them. They needed an investigator who had a nose for getting the facts, while having a general understanding of the legal significance of the facts. By this time I had put on a little weight, had become more bald, and what hair I had left was greying. By nature I have always been jovial and personable to others, so it was easy for strangers to open up and talk to me. Add to that a touch of willingness to take scary risks, and I usually got all the shreds of facts and evidence.

In my business, pictures were worth a thousand words. To get these pictures, I had to occasionally walk in without permission and start taking them. My attitude was that I was going to take pictures until someone stopped me. Since they could rudely interrupt and ask me to depart the premises at any time, I needed a camera that shot photos both with and without flash in rapid succession. For this I purchased a 35 mm Minolta Maxxum 7000 with a 28-70 zoom lens. This gave me automatic focus on both near and zoom objects. I just needed enough light for the camera to pick up contrast. Then I added the Minolta Maxxum 1800 AF flash attachment with a lithium battery. That gave me the ability to shoot quick, successive, focused flash shots without waiting for the batteries to recharge. The final attachment was the Minolta Databack 70, which allowed me to have the date or time right on the negative. This was important, since the dates the pictures were taken could be of substantial legal significance. I still have that camera today, and I estimate that I have taken around 35,000 pictures with it. What is surprising is that the whole unit cost less than $1,000.

All during this time I was able to stay sober. I went to many, many AA meetings and even did some "12th Step" work. "Twelfth Step" work was the willingness to answer the call if an alcoholic was in trouble and needed help. If you became aware of a member who had slipped, or of an alcoholic who needed just someone to help him, then you had to be willing to do what you could. In a way, it was paying back for your gift of sobriety. It was about this time that a man who joined AA shortly after me, and had been dry for a few years, had a slip. His absence was noted, and pretty soon we were all aware of it. Apparently he really sank deep into the bottle.

His wife, a member of Alanon, called me, desperate for help. Alanon is a parallel club to AA for family members of alcoholics. Unless you are exposed to the disease, you probably wouldn't know that alcoholism is a family disease. "Family," from the standpoint that the whole family has to be a little bit insane to put up with and live with the spouse or family member who is the alcoholic.

I called another member, and we met and went straight to our friend's home. His wife let us in, and we went down to the den where he was. The scene that greeted us stunned even me, an alcoholic who had hidden booze all over the house. We found at least a 100 empty beer cans lined up against the wall and two or three *gallon* bottles of vodka. He was sitting on what looked like an Army cot, and his wife told us that he drank until he passed out; then he went to sleep on the cot. When he woke up, he started drinking again and watched TV until he passed out again. The only time he left the room was when he had to go to the bathroom. And he ate very little. Like naive amateurs, we tried to reason with him, to get him to admit himself into an alcohol treatment center. But he would have none of that. I learned first-hand that it is nearly impossible to reason with someone completely drunk. But still, you try.

So we went upstairs and talked to his wife. I told her that it seemed the only way she was going to get him to a hospital or treatment center was for her to have him declared legally incapacitated, have herself appointed guardian, and then she could sign him in. Apparently our friend heard us talking and came upstairs. He wanted to know what we were talking to his wife about and began to get very angry. Finally, he ordered us out of the house. We had no choice but to leave, very disappointed that we had failed to accomplish anything. However, that evening I got a call from my co-worker, who said he had received a call from this poor alcoholic's wife, and her husband finally agreed to go to the treatment center peacefully. I'm sad that I couldn't leave to help take our friend in, but at least he landed in treatment. And you know what? This friend came out of treatment, and I think has been dry to this day. Thank God for that. But the really sad statistic about alcoholism is that for every one that is dry and not drinking, there are 10 out there drinking and destroying their lives, as well as hurting the lives of those near and dear to them. Truly tragic.

During these years in the mid to late '80s my time was mostly taken up with simple survival, seeing to it that not only the material needs of the kids were met, but also the emotional. We never had much money, so when the other school kids went on lavish spring break trips, our kids for the most part couldn't. We had little or no true vacations. The closest thing to vacations were the family reunions, which I know were really not that exciting for my kids. See, most of my mom's kids inherited a very judgmental "gift." We knew what *everyone* should do and were not bashful about voicing our opinions. Then when they didn't do what we thought, we tried to make them feel guilty about it. We became very good at trying to put people on guilt trips. Thank God, eventually most of us began to realize that and made determined efforts to fight this negative inherited impulse. I don't think I have completely conquered that dragon, but I think I've got it whittled down to where it is manageable. That became just another negative legacy I didn't want to pass on to my kids.

Having said that, we still had our fun times. Dad passed on to us kids a lively sense of humor and a positive attitude, so we told a lot of jokes. We managed to have good times at Christmas and Thanksgiving, as well as birthdays. I always tried to come up with something special for each kid's birthday that was a big surprise to them and really made them glow. I didn't care if I had to spend our last few dollars, whichever kid it was would have a good birthday. Most of the times I think each kid had a good birthday. And despite the lack of funds, we still managed. I tried to teach my kids that the perfect gift was the one you chose by looking at the person for whom you were getting the gift and figuring out what he would really appreciate, and then get that gift. I didn't like the idea of asking what they wanted, because to me that was like ordering a gift.

As I look back, there were a few gifts that I got the kids that I would classify as huge successes. At one point Donald had an interest in playing the guitar and was trying to learn on a real piece of junk. I scraped a couple of hundred dollars together and went down to a major music store on Broadway in Kansas City, Missouri. I bought him a fine quality acoustical guitar, complete with case. He really glowed when he got it, and that made me glow. Donald really started practicing and eventually taught himself how to play. Years later, I found out that occasionally he went down to the Westport area with Johnny Chuang, a friend of his, and played along the streets of this tourist and party area. God, what balls!

Then there was the time that Kurt had a birthday, and I know he wasn't expecting much. Still, I again scraped the bucks together and got him an expensive (for us) music system, complete with two huge speakers, dual tape, turn table and equalizer. As I recall, he had just started college, and I knew from my college days that this would get a lot of use. Again, he glowed, and I glowed.

In the fall of '83 Donald was in the ninth grade at Nallwood Junior High. Junior high school at that time was the seventh, eighth, and ninth grades. High School was the 10th, 11th, and 12th grades. All summer long Donald had practiced hard at basketball. He played with Richard and Kurt out in our driveway well after dark. Since Richard was six-five and two years older, and Donald was only about five-ten, Donald was at a distinct disadvantage. But he still played hard, and gradually his quickness and agility helped him to the point where he was competitive. What was most surprising was Kurt. He was a brick wall on fireplug legs. But he was also a decent athlete and got to where he could drop in the long shots. And when he was under the basket, he took up a lot of room.

I mention this because I found out later that Donald was intent on *starting* on the ninth grade school team. However, when try-outs came, Donald got shafted. A friend of mine, Jim Knight, was coaching the eighth grade at school, so he watched the try-outs for both the eighth and ninth grade teams. And he had coached Donald on the school team the previous year. He told me Donald was a shoo-in to make it. However, when the names were posted, Donald's was not among them. I smelled a raw deal and scheduled a meeting with the principal. I was not about to let Donald be trashed this way. This was a very big blow to any kid's ego, to have played on the school team one year, then get cut the next. And all his classmates were aware of it. I knew that I had to cushion that blow to Donald's ego by going to war with the school.

I met with Mr. Brown and asked him what criteria the school used in determining which kids made the team. He treated me with a cavalier attitude, along the lines of, "Who are you to be questioning us?" But I was adamant. Grudgingly, he told me that they used a combination of basketball skills, grades and "conduct." I knew his skills were more than adequate and that his grades were also adequate, so I asked him to explain how he went about evaluating conduct. He told me that the administration passed a sheet around to all the present *and former* teachers, and asked them to rate each player's conduct on a scale of one to five. The administration then weighted each kid, and that information was passed on to the coaches. To this day, I am sure that the principal had his hands directly in on who was going to make the team and just didn't like Donald. Add to that the fact that I was not one of those parents who actively participated in the PTA and who brown-nosed the administration. I wanted my kids to achieve things on their own, without my politicking for them. I asked Mr. Brown to send me a copy of the evaluations, and he promptly told me that he didn't have them, and if he did, he still wouldn't give them to me. So, in other words, if a teacher way back in the seventh grade didn't like a kid, then two years later she could still get back at him by giving him a poor conduct mark. What was frustrating was that Donald didn't get a bad rating. The others just got a little better rating. So it was obvious that the school placed most of their emphasis on the conduct evaluation.

Well, I learned a long time ago that everyone has a boss. So I promptly fired a letter off to the superintendent of all the schools, telling him about what happened and asking for his assistance. They gave me the usual runaround and lip service, so I didn't get much done. But I did create enough hell so that at the end of that school year Mr. Brown retired. See, I knew what was going on at the school. The administration got their promotions and pay raises by having no "problems" and having students attain high grades. In other words, they simply tolerated sports. This really set me off, because I know that God gives each kid different talents. I have always felt that it was the role of the school to develop those talents, whatever they were. Some kids have great athletic talents, but not strong enough academic skills to focus on college purely for the academic achievement. I feel the schools should provide an atmosphere for them to develop both the academic as well as the athletic skills. Unfortunately, the 30,000 Shawnee Mission School District was ravaged by politics.

Although I didn't get Donald on the team, I think I accomplished what was most important to me, that Donald knew he had a dad who would not tolerate anyone screwing around with his kids. I hope that was some consolation to him for enduring the disappointment of not making the team.

Meanwhile, Richard, as a junior became the starting center on Shawnee Mission South's high school team. To us at the time, this was really the big-time. The stands were jammed at his games, the school band was blasting out loud music, the cheerleaders were going wild, and at halftime the drill team performed. He had been the only sophomore on the previous year's team who made it to the state championship game. Coach Sexton asked me if I would help put out a program to pass out at the home games. I'd been to a full season of high school games the year before and had seen what some other high schools had done. I put together a 16-page printed program that included photos of the teams, schedules and rosters of all the various teams, as well as the cheerleaders, drill team and wrestlers. It was a very respectable program, and I was really proud of it.

As a junior, Richard had a great year. At one point I think he led the league in free-throw percentage.

This was the year that Danny Manning was a transfer senior at Lawrence, a huge rival of SM South. He was 6'11" and one of the top seniors in the nation. We played them twice, first at home. We had some good players, but Manning was just too much for us, and they won. The next time we played them, it was in Lawrence, and I think they were undefeated. The Lawrence fans were screaming. Coach Sexton had decided to use a box and one defense, with Richard being the one. He was simply to try and stay with Manning no matter where he went, while the other four players set up in a four player box zone.

Prior to this, Richard had started complaining about his ankle, saying it hurt right on the top. The pain wasn't so severe that he couldn't play. It was just a nagging pain. I started taking him to doctors, beginning with a podiatrist. His diagnosis was that Richard needed surgery on both ankles. That didn't make too much sense to me, so I took him in to see Dr. Dale Darnell, an orthopedic surgeon who had coached in YMCA football and was one of the doctors for the Kansas City Chiefs. He took some X-rays and didn't come up with anything concrete. So Richard just lived with it.

Back to the game at Lawrence, Richard's team was going through their usual warm-ups, when suddenly his ankle gave out completely. I sat in the stands and watched with a sickening feeling as the assistant coach helped him into the locker room. A few minutes later, he came out and hid ice wrapped around his ankle. I could see the complete disappointment on his face. He liked a challenge, and he was assigned to defend one of the best players in the nation. But at the last minute, that opportunity was snatched from him. When I picked him up back at school after the game, he was really down.

We had a follow-up appointment with Dr. Darnell about a week later. I had made some investigative trips to the medical library and the University of Kansas Medical Center for some lawyers, so I decided to do some investigating on my own on tarsal navicular stress fractures. I located a study in some medical journal that was right on target. It had the results of treatment on some 19 athletes, the tests they used, casts, surgery, etc. At our next appointment I had this medical study with me and gave a copy to Dr. Darnell. He glanced at it, noticed that many of the doctors had taken tomograms to discover the fractures, and then told me that to be safe, he was sending Richard down the hall for a tomogram. When it was finished, we returned to his office, and, sure enough, it revealed a clean, complete fracture of the tarsal navicular. Dr. Darnell had no choice but to put it in a non-weight-bearing cast for six weeks. I was happy we found the problem, but disappointed because it meant Richard was going to miss his junior year of baseball.

I guess this time might have been a bittersweet time for Richard, though. We didn't have the money yet for him to have a car. Joy had to take him to and from school in our junky old yellow station wagon. Richard was so embarrassed that he had Joy drop him off in the sophomore parking lot, which was on the west side of the football field, which was on the west side of the main school. This way he could walk around the field and into school. He didn't want to be dropped off in front of the school, where his friends could, one, see that he didn't have his own car, and, two, see the bucket of bolts in which he rode to school.

In the fall of '84 all the kids started a new school year. Richard was now a mighty senior, even though he still didn't have a car. Donald was a sophomore and heavily into football. Kurt was in the ninth grade and also heavily into football. Michael started kindergarten at Nall Hills elementary school, a block from our house. He had a great teacher, Mrs. Dozier, but in looking back, we may have started him in school too soon. He had just turned five (July 6), so he was young for his age. But he did okay, and the year for him was uneventful.

Donald made the sophomore A team in football, and his aggressiveness helped him to progress well. One thing stood out about Donald. He had real mental toughness. He wanted to play football, bad. He pumped the weights and pushed himself beyond limits. He contorted himself so hard in bench-pressing that one of the PE teachers told me he was afraid Donald was going to seriously wrench his back trying to do too much bench-pressing. It wasn't until October of '84 that I was finally in a position to get Richard a car. I had felt really bad for a long time about Joy having to drop him off in the sophomore parking lot, even when he started the senior year. I'm sure there were some families that were worse off than us, but I really wanted our kids to have self-respect. Anyhow, I came into about $750. I must have just finished a big investigation or something, but it was a window of opportunity. I didn't expect to get him much more than a bucket of bolts for that little money, but started searching the paper. I ran across an ad on a 1972 Pontiac GTO. The price was in the ball park, considering that I might be able to negotiate some. The owner was home that evening, so Richard and I went over to take a look at it. I didn't know a GTO from a John Deere, but when we got there, I knew it would do just fine for Richard's first car. I asked all the standard questions and asked if we could take it for a spin. She said okay, so I drove it first to get a feel for how solid it was, then pulled over into a shopping center lighted parking lot. We popped the hood, and the engine seemed to be okay. Then I let Richard drive it. I didn't realize it at the time, but that car was made to order for a high school kid. It had a 455 cc engine and was Pontiac's answer to the popular Ford Mustang. It could flat get up and go. I asked Richard if he wanted the car, and he looked at me like I was crazy. I could see from his drooling that I had asked a stupid question. We took it back to the lady, I negotiated her down to our funds, and we took the car home. Richard was now on cloud nine. He took it to school the very next day, and after school promptly got a speeding ticket right in front of the school. Oh, well!

Richard couldn't wait until football season was over so that he could start playing basketball. He was coming off a great junior year, his ankle had healed well, and everyone had great expectations. He had played on summer teams, and all summer long went down to the outside court by the police station in Overland Park, where the very best players in the Kansas City area played. You got on a team of five, played the winning team, and then kept playing until you lost. This outdoor court was one of those mentioned in Al McGuire's book as a court where you had the best competition in the area. Al McGuire took his Marquette college team to the national championship, so he was recognized as an authority. Usually there were many former college and pro players who showed up because they simply loved the sport. So the competition was tough.

Basketball practices started, and everyone was looking for big things out of the team and Richard. I got my first inkling of trouble during warm-ups before the first game. Richard was casually tossing the ball up, expecting everything to go in. I got the impression that he felt all he had to do was show up for the game, and he was going to kick ass. As the game started, our team looked completely unprepared. The intensity of the other team was far higher than ours. Soon we were behind and trying to catch up. But the other team didn't waver. They had Richard defended well, and finally in the fourth quarter Coach Sexton had to pull Richard out. We lost the game, and Richard scored a mere two points. What a disaster! There was a lot of sad soul-searching after that game, for sure.

The dads in the stands critiqued the game, and it was obvious that Sexton was trying to have Richard take outside shots only. He didn't want Richard driving to the basket or playing the post under the basket. I thought this was a big mistake, because Richard had developed a reputation as a "garbage" man. In fact, at the previous basketball banquet the graduating seniors had presented Richard with a white trash can with the words "Trash Man" written on it. A "garbage" man is a player who scores a lot of points off missed shots by teammates.

The other thing I noticed, and I could be wrong about this, is that Richard may have had a classic case of "big head." He knew he was good and was grossly over-confident. This lowered his intensity level to the point that he wasn't prepared. And this I laid right at the feet of Paul Sexton, the coach. He had over 20 years of coaching, so I think he should have spotted that very early on during pre-season practices. He should have corrected that long before the first game. To me, this got right back to the attitude of the administration toward sports. They really never cared that much if the teams won. They were more afraid of a scene that could cause embarrassment to them. Again, their career was most important, far above that of developing good athletes.

Needless to say, it was a dismal season. There were some moments to cheer, though, such as the time that Richard stole the ball and drove the length of the court and slam-dunked it. The crowd roared. We did manage to salvage some self-respect in the last two games. The first one was against a good Rockhurst team. Rockhurst was an all-boy Catholic high school, and they always fielded a pumped-up team. Sitting in the stands, I could tell that Richard had all he could handle, sitting outside taking long shots. For the first time that season, he started faking shots and drove viciously to the basket for an easy lay-up. He simply took over the game and completely dominated it. It felt good to win.

But the last game of the regular season was the sweetest. We had a home game against West, who were undefeated in regular season with an 11-0 record. They had two 6'8" players, Pat Denny and a Matt something, both of whom were being recruited for college teams. If they beat us, they had a perfect league record. Again, Richard's intensity level was out of sight. And again, he wasn't going to sit outside taking long shots. I could tell Richard was taking this game personally. He was a demon under the basket and drove slashing to the hoop. He had the team in the lead when West made an adjustment where the defenders started collapsing on Richard when he got the ball. When that happened, Richard dumped the ball off to the point guard, Kyle Meade, who was hot from outside. When it was over, we had won, had ruined West's perfect season, and both Richard and Meade had over 20 points. That was a good game. At least we ended the season on a high note.

As '85 came over the horizon, Drake Investigations was growing in both billing and reputation. By now I was charging $45 an hour portal to portal. There was only one other private investigator firm that got more, $50. That was Clarence Kelly's, the former police chief of Kansas City and head of the FBI. My clock started running the moment I went out my door and didn't stop until I came back in my door. Not one single client ever complained about my rates or my bill, and I personally delivered the bill and my report along with photos, etc. I waited while they wrote me a check.

Well, I have to take that back. One lawyer did complain about the number of pictures I took. This is interesting enough to relate here. One Sunday afternoon I got a call from a lawyer from South Dakota. His father had a stroke and was in intensive care at St. Luke's hospital. While he was in the ICU waiting room, they brought in a 20-year-old kid who had just been in a motorcycle accident on a small country highway about 60 miles south of Kansas City. This lawyer said that while he had been jogging, he met and got my name from Bob Kingsland, a lawyer who formerly worked for Bill Pickett.

He wanted me to get right on the case, get statements and meet him at St. Luke's the next afternoon with my camera. I went to my office and got on the phone. Within 45 minutes I had the driver of the car on the phone and took a complete taped statement from her. This was critical, because generally if people talk to their insurance companies, they are told emphatically not to give anybody any statements. I got to her before she got to her insurance company. We met at St. Luke's, and I talked the hospital into letting me in ICU to take pictures. This poor kid was really in bad shape. He had casts on everywhere, and the left side of his throat was ripped open and was exposed so you could see the jugular vein pulse with his heartbeat. I took at least a full roll of film, then took off for the accident scene.

On my way, I picked up a copy of the police report so I could pin point the point of impact. It was the same old story with motorcycle accidents. It was a sweet old lady who was looking for cars before she turned left off the highway. Not seeing any cars, she turned left, right into the motorcycle that hit her right behind the right front wheel. The handlebar for the motorcycle almost took his throat completely out. I found the actual point of impact, took pictures of the gouge marks, and then pictures from all angles at 20-foot intervals up to 300 feet from the impact point. Then I located the motorcycle at a body shop, had it moved into the garage of the kid's parents, taking voluminous pictures of it before, during and after we moved it.

Then the last thing I needed to do was get photos of the sweet old lady's car. I finally located the farm, went to the door and found both her and her husband home. They had to be in their 70s. I mentioned something about insurance, and that I needed to take pictures of the car. They were uncertain as to whether they should, but I kept talking and finally got the husband to go along with it. They had the car in the garage under lock and key. The husband unlocked the doors and swung them open. But the garage was too small for me to get good pictures. I mentioned this to the husband and asked if there was any way we could move the car out of the garage. He said it rolled, so together we rolled it out into the sun. I quickly shot two full rolls of film from all angles and distances, then helped him push the car back in. Then, as quickly and casually as I could, I hit the road.

When I turned in my report, the South Dakota lawyer was upset that I had over 200 color 8" x 10" photos. At $3 a pop, that ran into some money. However, when that lawyer made his claim and filed suit, using Kingsland's firm as local counsel, they discovered during litigation that the sweet old lady's retired husband had been a railroader who believed in being covered by plenty of insurance. Everyone's jaws dropped when we learned he carried $1,000,000 in liability insurance. Now suddenly I was a hero, and the photos I took were used to impeach that sweet old lady, and the case was settled for around $750.000!

The other case was a simple case of locating a defendant so we could serve him with the lawsuit summons. This defendant was no one to mess with. I eventually found out that he was supposed to be a "collector" for organized crime in the area, that he was a karate nut and could kill you in seconds with his bare hands. He had used our client's head as a punching bag with his fists and had shattered his cheekbones to the extent that one more blow would have killed him. Some fellow made the mistake of catching him in bed with this fellow's wife. It made our defendant so mad, he torched this fellow's car. Another rumor was that this defendant, in trying to collect from another guy, caught him coming out of a Winchell's Donut shop, made him urinate on the donuts, and then made him eat them.

This is the only time in my private investigating career that I gave serious thought to carrying a weapon. I had learned as a general rule that if you carried a weapon, then you might have to use it. And if you did, then someone might use one on you. Or someone took your weapon away from you and used it on you. So I never carried a weapon.

Anyhow, Pickett wanted this defendant found in the worst way. He had been an employee of a car dealership when the assault happened, and the dealership lawyers refused to pay anything because they knew that without having served this "karate kid," we couldn't touch them. So I cautiously set out trying to find him. Somewhere I had learned that he had a wife in the area who, to escape him after they had checked into a motel, told him she was going out to the car to get a pack of cigarettes. She did, but she also got in the car and headed completely out of state. She was scared to death of him, too. I tracked down the wife through a brother who had a small business in town, and he let it slip that this defendant was back east somewhere. I coaxed him into telling me that he knew this because the defendant made collect phone calls to his wife at her brother's business. Finally, I got him to look up that number on one of his bills.

I traced that phone number to a pay phone inside a federal prison in New York. The defendant was being hidden by the feds in this prison. I met with Pickett and gave him the name, address and phone number of the prison. He was ecstatic and ordered his bookkeeper to write me a $500 bonus check on the spot. He then quickly prepared the necessary papers for an out-of-state summons and served the defendant, finally, in prison. Later I was told that the feds came running over to Pickett's office wanting to know how he found out where this defendant was. Of course, Pickett protected me, and the car dealership coughed up $40,000 in a lightning settlement. But, enough about private investigating.

Winter of '85 grudgingly gave way to the warmth of spring. Spring meant baseball, and both Richard and Donald went out for baseball. Richard was now more fully developed, and at six foot seven he was an imposing figure on the mound. Donald made the sophomore team, but gave up on the sport after that one year because he wanted to spend his time weight-lifting. Richard really came into his own that spring. His split-fingered fast ball was vicious. And he had ice in his veins. I recall a game at Blackbob Park in Olathe, when we were playing a team from Olathe High School. It was the bottom of the last inning and we were ahead by one run. The home team had loaded the bases, and there were no outs. That's when the coach brought in Richard to pitch.

Up to this point the home team was hooping and hollering, pounding on the dug-out, trying to unsettle our team. But when Richard walked up on the mound, suddenly it got real quiet. The

Olathe players got up and got close to the fence to get a good look at what was going to happen. They must have heard about Richard, because this alone gave him a lot of respect. He faced the first batter and struck him out. We began to breathe a little better. Olathe sent up a pinch hitter. Richard struck him out, too. They sent in another pinch hitter. But Richard blew three strikes past him, and the ball game was over. The interesting thing was that Richard never got that excited over it. His teammates came rushing out of the dug-out, but it looked like it was no big deal to him. That was not the only time he did that, either.

Richard had a great baseball season in his senior year. His ball moved all over the place, and he got a lion's share of strikeouts. He had two two-hit shut-outs back to back, the first 2-0 against a tough Blue Springs team, then the next another 2-0 shut-out against Olathe, when he out-pitched Skip Wiley, who went on to college and then minor league ball. The way he was throwing, I thought he had a good chance for a scholarship. SM South's team made it to state and won the state championship, the last one that they have won. There was a lot of talent on that team. There were at least five kids that were drafted by the pros or played in the minor leagues.

But probably the greatest thrill was the American Legion tournament in Bartlesville, Oklahoma, late in the summer. Bartlesville used to have a minor league team, so they had a big, beautiful park. Baseball was really big down there. This was the 35th straight year that they had this tournament, and you had to be good just to be invited. The eight teams came from all over the Midwest. There was a team from Omaha, who came down in style. They actually owned a huge luxury bus that some millionaire donated to the team. It had exquisite paintings on the sides and had to cost at least $150,000. Omaha also had a big right-hander who had a legitimate 95 mph fast ball. And he was just 18. The park was crawling with college and pro scouts from all over the country. It was a high school senior's baseball dream.

Our team was picked to start off the tournament on the morning of the first day. Our opponent was a highly rated Enid, Oklahoma team. Richard was picked to start for us. Fortunately, John Shore, whose son played on our team, set up his video camera and taped the whole game. Later he gave me a copy. We were the home team, so Richard took the mound. In the first inning he may have walked one, but he struck out three. He did the same in the second inning. Somewhere in here we picked up two runs and took the lead. After three innings he had nine strike-outs. We went into the fourth inning, and some kid got lucky and tagged Richard for a solo home run. Still, Richard struck out the side; he now had 12 strike-outs in four innings. We went into the fifth, and Richard was a little wobbly, but again, he struck out the side. By now the other team was so frustrated that they were missing the ball by from six to 12 inches. He now had 15 strike-outs.

We went into the sixth inning, and the other team started to bunt to shake up Richard. But our catcher, Jeff Ingram, was quick and accurate with his throws, and we got through the sixth with no damage done. Finally, we took the field for the last time, and the score was now three to one in our favor. Richard struck out the first batter; then the next batter got a hit into right field. Richard struck out the next batter, and then gave up a walk. Now the other team had two men on and the tying run on base. Our coach went out to the mound to see if Richard was tired. He stayed in, and the next batter worked the count to a full count, three balls and two strikes. The tension was really getting thick. Richard came set, rared back and blazed a fast ball toward the plate. The batter was waiting for it and took a mighty swing. But he missed the ball by six inches, and the game was over. We had won.

As the teams were congratulating each other, the public announcer came on and told the crowd that Richard had 19 strike-outs, a new record for the tournament. There's no way to describe how proud a dad feels at a time like this. I knew that years before when I saw Richard throw and felt he had a lot of potential, I had been right. After the team meeting, the players were released by the coach, and I got to shake Richard's hand, as did quite a few of our parents. It was truly a pitching gem. Thank God we got it on tape.

I walked out into the parking lot with Richard, as the team was getting ready to go back to their motel. Richard needed to get his arm soaked in ice water, as is customary for pitchers. As we were standing at the trunk of our car, a man walked up and wanted to talk to Richard. He was the coach of Oklahoma City University baseball and told Richard he'd like to have him pitch for him. We were caught a little by surprise, but the coach persisted and delivered quite a sales pitch. I looked over and there were a couple of other men who looked like they were waiting. I told Richard to go on and soak his arm. Then another coach from Barton County Community College approached me and expressed a high interest in Richard. Then another coach came up and made his pitch. They were literally stacked up three deep wanting to get Richard. What a deal!

Our team lost the next two games, and we were out of the tournament. I got to watch the big right-hander from Omaha pitch. There was no mistaking it. He had a legitimate 95 mph fast ball, and there were scouts all over the stadium clocking him. He pitched in two games, and I think they eventually won the tournament. But when it came awards time, the tournament committee selected Richard as the outstanding pitcher of the whole tournament. That big right-hander from Omaha was Greg Olson, who eventually became the ace relief pitcher of the Baltimore Orioles, and then the Kansas City Royals, making millions.

As I look back, I now realize that many of the memories a dad has about his kids are mostly those about his oldest kid. I guess the reason for it is that the oldest kid is the first kid to go through all the new experiences a family has with their kids. He's the first to go to school, the first into sports, the first into junior high, the first into high school, the first into college, and generally the first to be married and the first to have your grandchild. Maybe that is why it is not such a big deal when your next child or children grow up and go through those same stages. You've been through it with your oldest kid as a parent, so a lot of the glamor or trepidation is gone with each succeeding kid. That might be considered as a downside for the younger kids, but like most things it also has its upside. On the one hand, a dad is more protective of the oldest child and less protective of the younger ones. That means the younger ones are cut a lot more slack and have a lot less interference from their parents. Sure, each new stage is a new stage for each kid and is important for the kid. Still, having seen his older brother or sister go through it takes some of the fear or magnitude of it away.

The summer of '85 was bittersweet for me. There were a tremendous amount of things going on, all at the same time. Although I was near the top of my profession in the area, I was still not quite making ends meet. Bill Picket, within the space of 12 months, had settled four cases, on which I had expertly done the complete investigation from top to bottom, for over *four million dollars!* I started realizing that I was on the wrong end of the stick. So I started thinking about getting my license to practice law. This meant filling out all the papers, getting the appropriate character reference letters, and then somehow studying for the exam to be given the following February. I had been away from law for 15 years, so I had to almost start over. To make matters worse, you also had to take a multi-state multiple choice test that took one of the two days, and was *purposely* designed to fool you.

At the same time, we had to address the question of where Richard was going to college. Richard had met his first real girlfriend and was never home in the evenings. There were so many coaches soliciting him, that at times I would be responding to a long distance call from a coach, get a call-waiting beep, put the coach on hold, and it was another coach calling long distance. Then there were the house visits from coaches, some of whom were real crooks.

Coach John Davis, the only football coach in SM South's history, announced he was retiring after the '85-'86 season, so now the school approved a booster club. Coach Davis refused to allow one while he was coach. I heard that he felt that a booster club could only cause him grief, and he didn't want to fuss with any parents. Bill Tigreen, the athletic director, and Charlie Nichols backed him up completely on this issue. Again, they didn't want anything that could tarnish their precious image. At any rate, I had been so involved that I was elected the first president of the club. Now I had that added responsibility during that summer, too.

Additionally, Donald was now the oldest son in high school, and since I had produced the basketball program for Richard in his chief sport, I felt I should do the same for Donald in his sport. Again, I did the whole thing by myself, starting early in the summer. I got the printing bids, estimated the number we'd need for each home game, sold all the advertising, hounded the advertisers for their ads and their money, personally took pictures of each player as soon as practice started, had them developed and printed, and finally worked closely with the printer so that we had a high quality program. To crown it all off, I had sold enough advertising to allow us to simply give them away at the gates. I really wanted Donald to know that his efforts were being supported.

In addition to all of this, I still had the other kids to take care of: Donald, going into his sophomore year of high school; Kurt, going into the ninth grade; and Michael into the first grade. So I really had my hands full that summer. After a lot of deliberation, Richard decided to go to Labette Community College, where my brother Gery was president. I tried to help Richard as much as possible with this decision without making it for him. That was very difficult for me to do. Richard had developed a very laid-back personality and could really mask his true feelings, causing me to actually guess sometimes as to what his true feelings were. I don't know. Maybe he just didn't want to offend anyone, especially me.

The end of the '85 summer drew to a close and everyone was getting ready for school. By this time I was really disturbed that Richard was out every evening with his new girlfriend and other friends. I felt this girl simply wanted Richard more as a trophy than anything else. She came from a wealthy family, and it was important for her to have the best. And Richard was a tall, handsome, popular athlete. I wasn't very possessive, was I? Ha! Finally, the day before Richard's departure for college arrived. I had hinted to him the last few days that I wanted him to spend at least the last evening at home. I really wanted him to, and felt he owed it to Joy and me, especially since he had spent very few evenings at home the whole summer.

So we finished dinner, and time started dragging by. Richard wasn't home. And I started stewing. And the later it got, the more I stewed. Finally, when it was well past 10, I knew that Richard wasn't going to be home early that evening. Then I completely lost my cool. I picked up his double bed, hauled it out through the garage and pitched it into the front yard. Then I went back inside, got all of his clothes and pitched them out on top of his bed. I felt that, by God, if he loved his friends that much that he could go live with them and let them take care of him. I was really hurt. It never occurred to me that he probably had a lot of people to say good-bye to, especially since he was going down to Parsons, a very small town. And Parsons was no thriving metropolis, so he probably felt like he was leaving for the monastery. None of that ever entered my mind. I went to bed, and some friends of his came by that night and got his clothes. To this day, I don't know where he slept. I'm embarrassed by what I did and hope that time healed any hurt that I caused Richard.

The next day Richard showed up around noon at my office with Steve Grant, one of his friends. I could tell he didn't want to go to Parsons with me angry at him. I asked Steve to wait outside, and then I told Richard that I was really offended. We talked it all out, and he left for Parsons. I'm happy we had the chance to clear the air before he left. There is a lot to the old saying that you shouldn't let the sun set on your anger. I did, and I can certify that I was miserable. I guess the old saying is true, that the biggest problem with being a parent is that it is strictly on-the-job training.

The '85 fall school year started, and I was struggling with finances, again. A local grocery store near my office allowed regular customers to cash checks for cash. I had traded there for years and they knew me. As the need for cash increased, I started writing checks for cash and then worked like the dickens to beat the check to the bank. Many times I didn't make it and had to go over with cash to pick up my hot check. I was on a treadmill, because I had to buy food for the family.

Gradually, I increased the amount of the checks up to $250 each. Then when I found out that the store went along with this, I progressed to the point where I would write a check first thing in the morning for $250, and then wrote a similar one for the same amount in the evening. The next day I deposited the $500 cash in my bank near our house. I depended on the float of two, three and four days. As my outside income came in, every now and then I'd get caught up, but gradually it got worse. I was chained to this treadmill. Joy knew nothing about this whole arrangement, because I had learned a long time ago that she tended to be emotional about finances. And I was deeply worried that if she ever knew the full extent of how poor our finances were, she would go into depression and wind up back in the mental ward. So this was a burden I carried solely by myself.

Then the roof caved in. I got a letter from my bank, and they were on to me. They told me they were closing my account and would not honor any more checks. This was a major, major crisis. I didn't have the funds to cover the checks I had written, and I estimated them to total over $2,000. As I sat one evening in my small office, totally distraught, I was desperate. I needed help instantly. I had no other choice but to call Mark in Omaha, and after a few preliminary comments, I broke down, and sobbing, told him the jam I was in. Mark immediately understood the gravity of my situation, and bless him, he said he would loan me $2,500. I think he had to go down to the bank and borrow the money, but within a few days it arrived at my office, and I quickly covered all the checks I had out. That lifted a tremendous burden from my shoulders. I hadn't realized how great the pressure of writing those checks was. And all Mark said was, pay it back when you can. He set no time limit. Is that a brother, or what?

The finances were so bad that all I could send Richard was $30 a week. Thirty bucks. To last a full week, away from home, in a dinky dorm, and on weekends the school cafeteria was closed most of the time. It must have been a huge strain on Richard. I wish I could have sent more, but that was all I could do.

It was about this time that I had done a great injustice to Kurt. Good ole, good-natured Kurt. He started his work career by cleaning out the grease pit of a barbeque restaurant. This was really a dirty, filthy job. To get the job done, he was literally covered from head to toe in black soot and grease. He never complained, but after a couple of weeks of this, he quit, much to my relief. One of his next jobs was a sacker at Pak-N-Sav, a grocery store near our house. The wages were low, but over a period of time he started saving money. We opened a savings account at Metcalf State Bank for him, and I had to be on the signature card as well. Kurt banked as much as he could, until he got up to $600. Unfortunately, our finances were bad from time to time, so I "borrowed" from his account, then put it back. Finally, I really hit a low spot financially. As much as I hated it, I had no choice but to take his money and use it for the family survival. Kurt took the news good-naturedly. Deep down he has always had a big heart when it comes to the family, and he was a prince this time. Many kids would have really fought it, but not Kurt. Unfortunately, it was a couple of years until I was in a position to pay him back, but thank God, I did.

Michael started the first grade and we ran into problems right away. He simply had to be the first one done with everything. He didn't care how sloppy it was. His sole objective was to be the first one done. I remember sitting down with him and explaining over and over again that neatness came first. The teacher, Mrs. Pansing, constantly made him write papers over because they were just too illegible. Joy and I monitored his homework, and we constantly made him do papers over. Still, he never would slow down.

This went on for about two-thirds of the school year. Finally, I got a call from his teacher, and she said that his work was just totally unacceptable. This teacher had well over 20 years of teaching experience, so I relied fairly heavily on her input. I told her I would be in her classroom right after school and we would address the problem. I showed up, and she showed me Michael's papers. They were terrible. They were sloppy, illegible, and you could easily see he was just doing them as quickly as possible. It was now time to solve this problem. Something had to be done. So I told her to keep Michael after school the next day, and we would all then sit down and solve the problem.

The next day I walked in and the teacher was waiting with Michael. I was going to step right in and tell Michael that he just wasn't doing well enough, etc. But before I could get a word out of my mouth, Mrs. Pansing said to Michael words to this effect: "Michael, your work is simply not satisfactory. Therefore, until it becomes satisfactory, I am going to take away from you the privilege of playing with the toys as soon as you finish your work." I was stunned. Dumbfounded. In a sudden rush of perception, I now knew exactly what was going on. All year long Mrs. Pansing had been letting her kids play with the toys as soon as they finished their work. Michael, a first grader, knew right away what was fun – playing with the toys. He was no dummy. Finish the work as fast as you can, and then *PLAY! And that had not dawned on Mrs. Pansing for over six months!* Wow! And she with 20-some years teaching experience. I then asserted myself and told Mrs. Pansing that we now had a lot of *unlearning* to do. I told her to continue the positive motivation, but only reward neat and legible work. She agreed, and the rest of the school year we worked on unlearning what Mrs. Pansing had unwittingly taught Michael. Such a deal!

The bar exam was coming up in February of '86. I started cramming all I could. I assembled the usual bar reviews and started studying both at my small office and at the law library at the County Courthouse. I was very concerned with the multi-state one-day exam. It was a multiple-choice exam, but each question had a verbose narration of facts, and the answers were specifically designed to fool you. It was more of a reading and comprehension test than a bar exam, because it rewarded the speed readers. For most of us, we barely had time to read the question, let alone know the answer. It was tough.

A month or two later we were notified of the results. A score of 161 was required to pass. I scored a 158. We had the ability to ask for a re-check of our exam, which I did, but it didn't change anything. All that time and hard work down the drain. But this time I was more determined. I was allowed to take the exam again the next time it was offered, which was in July of '86. So I made plans to do just that.

Professional Baseball held their winter draft after the first of the year, and the California Angels drafted Richard. I was really happy for Richard, and very proud. I thought back to when he wanted to quit baseball, and I pushed him into it. That risk of pushing him proved to be worth it. When his girlfriend, Jean, heard about it, she promptly drove down to Parsons, a two-and-a-half-hour trip, and spent the weekend "sleeping on the floor," according to Richard. That really bothered me. I guess I'm old-fashioned, as we were brought up a lot differently. To me, Jean was just going down there to stake her claim to Richard. He was her property, and she wanted to make sure of that. I realize now that I didn't give Richard enough credit. I should have known that these things have a way of working out.

But I was concerned with the sexual connotations of such a visit and felt I should go down and have a heart-to-heart talk with Richard over his relationship. I drove down, and we went out to lunch. Richard paid me all the respect he should have, but I could sense he was surprised I was getting so worked up over this. Again, I know now that I didn't give him enough credit. He knew what was going on, and sure enough, he came home at the end of the school year a little early, went out to a party and found out that Jean had just been to the same party, etc., etc. So that was the end of Jean. I had let myself get all worked up over nothing. Again, on-the-job training.

When the next bar exam came up in July, this time I was better prepared. I still had a dickens of a time with the multi-state and thought I had done worse on it than the year before. So I braced myself for more bad news. But the results finally came in the mail, *and I passed! Wow!* I couldn't believe it! Here I was, 49 years old, and competing with the young kids right out of law school, and I still passed. I guess there is something to persistence. The swearing in ceremony was set for September 30, 1986. God, did I look forward to that.

14

OVERLAND PARK, KANSAS, 1986-1990

(Start of Law Practice, More Kid Raisin', More Trouble with Schools, Kyle Has Brain Tumor, More Sports, Things Look Rosy)

WHO IN THEIR right mind would start a law practice at the ancient age of 49? Most people by this time are well entrenched in their careers, blissfully looking forward to their golden years after retirement, starting to enjoy grandchildren, living in homes that are almost paid for, driving attractive, new, safe cars, and frankly, living a relatively stress-free life. But Joy and I, on the other hand, were still in the middle of raising five sons, ages 19, 17, 16, 7 and 6. We were living in a rented house, drove two beat-up old cars, had zilch for credit, had no credit cards, didn't have a single dime set aside for retirement, had no health insurance, couldn't pay our many bills, and had no savings.

All I had was blind faith that things would eventually get better and a dogged determination to go forward. Why? Well, I felt I had something that many people didn't have and that most people would give their last dime to have. I had a family. And a good family. Sure, we all had our imperfections, but we stood together and stayed together and stepped into the future together. I think our kids always knew I would do all I could for them. I wasn't happy about the limited finances we had, but I was doing the best I could, and I think the kids knew it. I knew that deep down each of my kids would do anything for their brothers, and that made it all worth while.

So I started practicing law. Law is a practice. It didn't take me long to realize that I was going up against lawyers my age who had been practicing for over 20 years, and were light years ahead of me as an attorney. I also knew I didn't have that same 20 years to sharpen my skills. I had no choice but to plunge into each new case, knowing that I would make some stupid mistakes, but also knowing that with each case I gained valuable experience. I also knew that because of my age and business experience, I should be a fast learner, and I was. There weren't too many errors that I made that I repeated. As I look back, I have to be amazed at the judges who patiently tolerated such rookie mistakes from someone my age.

Still, I did have one thing going for me. I had balls. When I was approached by a broker down the hall to represent him and a co-broker in a real estate case, I agreed to take the case on a one-third contingency fee basis. My clients felt that they had been cheated out of a half-million-dollar commission. After looking at the facts and the written agreements, I agreed with them. So it didn't bother me at all to file suit against one of the most prominent firms in the Kansas City area, along with three other defendants, over a multi-million-dollar real estate deal. The prominent firm promptly hired a former governor for their attorney, and the other three defendants hired the cream of the crop in Johnson County. I was up against the biggest guns in Johnson County, and I hadn't been practicing law six months yet. Oh, well! I knew I needed some heavy duty help, so I canvased the area for a lawyer knowledgeable in real estate and brought him aboard for a portion of the contingent fee.

Contingent fees. What are they? They are a system of fees where the lawyer agrees to work for a percent of the recovery, rather than being paid an hourly rate. The advantage to the client is that he gets his claim legally resolved and owes no fees, until and unless there is a recovery. Generally, contingent fees are one-third, but can go higher, depending on the difficulty of the case and the time commitment by the attorney. Some people might be offended by how "high" that rate is. But, on the other hand, there are many common, ordinary citizens who could never afford an attorney at even $5 per hour. They could have a legitimate claim, but have no money to pay an attorney's hourly rate. Without contingent fees, they'd lose their claim. The public might take exception with the ethics code that binds the attorneys to charge a reasonable fee, i.e., whatever the going rate is.

The logic is that if a lawyer radically lowers his rates, then he is either trying to buy business, or the client is not going to get the lawyer's best efforts.

And what about the times when a lawyer takes a case that appears to be a solid claim, literally spends months working on it, takes it to an expensive trial, only to have an unpredictable jury return a verdict for the other side? The lawyer gets nothing and frequently winds up eating his cash expenses as well. Contingency fees give even the poorest of our citizens the ability to have an attorney represent them. Without them, only the rich could afford lawyers and would run rampant over the average public.

Getting back to my first big case, we spent two full weeks taking depositions of all the defendants and chief witnesses. Then the defendants took our clients' depositions for a week. Since this was my largest case, I let the experienced Missouri lawyer carry the ball. The defendants finally filed a motion for summary judgement, asking the judge to dismiss the case because, as they claimed, there wasn't a dispute as to the material facts, and when you applied the undisputed facts to the law, their clients were without fault. Their motion and supporting brief was almost 400 pages long and contained around 120 indexed facts. These facts were statements taken under oath, so the defense attorneys had to have done a lot of research.

We went to work and responded with our answer, 450 pages long, and with 150 indexed facts. I literally spent three weeks on this answer. A hearing was set for the oral arguments, and again, I let my co-counsel do the oral arguments. All we needed was just one disputed material fact, and the judge should have denied the motion. Unfortunately, the prominent company had retained the former governor for their attorney. Governors carry a lot of weight with district court judges. The governor appoints the judges to fill the vacancies on the Court of Appeals and the Supreme Court of the state as they occur, as well as each county's district judges. That meant the former governor still had a lot of political pull with the district judges. We were very concerned with this political pull more than anything else. We knew there were many disputed material facts, but were worried about a possible political decision. Our fears were well-founded. When the judge's decision was received, he ruled against us and dismissed the case. We couldn't believe it.

Our only avenue was to appeal the decision to the Court of Appeals. I had never appealed a case before, but I jumped right in and went to work. We wrote the appropriate briefs, following the detailed procedure, and waited for the oral arguments. The day of the oral arguments came, and we showed up early, because on some cases the lawyers waive oral arguments, and you had to be ready in case your case was called early. As we were sitting behind the railing waiting on our case to be called, the three judges took their morning break right before our case. By the time the break was over, the good former governor appeared, and when the three appeals judges came in the side door, they all said "Hi,———" to the former governor. Then I realized that this same governor had personally appointed many of the appeals judges. My heart sank. Right then I knew we were dead.

Nevertheless, when it came time for our case, we had 15 minutes to present our arguments. I took 10 and saved five to respond to the other side, who had 15 minutes also. I thought I responded to the judges' questions well and naively felt good about how it went. This feeling was buttressed when one of the opposing counsel came up to me and congratulated me on my arguments, then took me aside and told me that I should have been the one who presented the oral arguments at the district court summary judgment level. I know a lot of that was just good courtesy, but it still gave my confidence a big boost.

Then came the interminable wait for the appeals decision. It came, and we lost. That's when I learned just how important a role political pull was to the judges. Who you were had a lot of bearing on the decision. I'm not saying that there was anything illegal or unethical done anywhere in this case. But I really wasn't too surprised when that district judge was appointed to the Court of Appeals a short time later. *C'est la vie.*

In the fall of '86 Donald was in his senior year in high school. He was, to quote one of his coaches, "a consummate leader." He was selected the offensive co-captain of the team along with the defensive co-captain, Bumper Landreth. Donald only weighed around 170 to 175 pounds, but he was a hitter. On offense he could block like a bulldozer, had excellent quickness, above-average speed and good hands. And he worked hard at the game and had tremendous mental toughness.

Kurt was a junior and was built completely different than Donald. Kurt was around 5'11" and weighed a hefty 260. He had always been an offensive lineman and was very smart. He literally knew what each player's job was on every play. He once told me that many times coming out of the huddle, the other linemen asked him which way they were supposed to block, etc. Kurt had short, stubby legs about the size of fire hydrants. This gave him a very low center of gravity, so he was nearly impossible to knock down. In his last two years of high school, his man never got to the quarterback. It was fun having two sons on the varsity team.

Michael was now in the second grade at Nall Hills and drew another "winner" of a teacher in the famous Shawnee Mission School District, Sandy Mallard. This one was an organization freak. Each student had to have a spiral notebook and started each day with writing the date and then that day's agenda. If the teacher had anything she wanted to convey to the parents, she then wrote a short note below this. Every evening Michael had to show this to us, and one of us had to sign our names to indicate that we had read it. I know her motives were good, and she wanted to get the parents involved. But after a few months of this, it started to get old quick, especially when the teacher started assigning us things to do. By December, Michael was beginning to get so tired of it he started to get stubborn about doing work over. Then he started losing interest in school in general, and we started getting notes from Mrs. Mallard that he was getting stubborn about doing work over, etc. It was obvious that he was losing heart.

It was now apparent to me that Mrs. Mallard was trying to teach a high school level of organization to her kids, despite the fact that they were only in the second grade. By February we were getting daily notes from Mrs. Mallard about Michael's forgetting this, or not turning in this, or on and on. I'd had enough, so I wrote her a long note, telling her that she was the teacher, that it was her responsibility to teach the kids, to find their "hot button," and to quit depending on the parents to do her teaching. She didn't flinch and didn't change a thing the rest of the year. But it did help me, because it reduced a lot of the stress on Joy, because now we didn't get too excited about her notes. I still have that notebook and chuckle when I review it. After these last two years, we decided it was time for Michael to go to Catholic school.

Richard had developed a back injury that impacted on his ability to pitch. I took him to every specialist I could find in the Kansas City area, but we never ever found out what the problem was. The California Angel scouts came up to Kansas City, Kansas Junior College and watched him throw 30 pitches in the dug-out, and one of the Yankee scouts told me he had two things that couldn't be taught – he was left-handed and six foot seven. Still, the Angels drafted him again. This was the spring of '87.

Kyle was just finishing up his kindergarten at Nall Hills. This meant that at long last all our kids were in full-time school. This gave Joy much more latitude in her day, and I was happy to see that. She could now plan her day and chart her chores. But what was very important to me was that she was home in case the school called because the kids were sick, etc. And I think this meant a lot to the lids. They always knew someone was home if they needed them. I really believe that part of the serious problem that society has today are too many single-parent families. The kid doesn't have the support that he gets from a two-parent family. And the reason there are too many single-parent families is that marriage is no longer the lifetime commitment that it was when I was growing up. As usual, the kids are the ones who suffer the most.

During baseball season in the spring of '87 an incident occurred at one of the high school games. Back in my little league years when I was an area director, I had fixed it so a couple of brothers could play football free. Their mother was raising them alone, and they didn't have any money for the fee, nor money to buy equipment. I got the league to waive the fee, and we found them equipment. Those kids and their mother were really grateful. At any rate, the high school baseball coach apparently struck the oldest kid in the dug-out during a game. His mother came to me, furious over it. I told them I would represent them in a civil action, but that if she wanted anything done on the assault charge, she would have to go down to the police station and fill out a complaint. She did, and the municipal case was set for trial. I went out and took photos of the dug-out where it happened, took three taped statements of eye witnesses, one of them an adult whose son was on the team. That man had a lot of courage. Most parents wouldn't want involved for fear of hurting their son's chances of playing. But not this dad. He was principled and stood up for them.

I turned all this evidence over to the city prosecutor, so that he could make his case. Mind you, this was the same coach who coached my oldest son, and I really didn't have any grudge against him. I just didn't think coaches should lose control and hit kids. The trial was held, and once again I ran into the old political nemesis. About 100 parents showed up in support of the coach, most of them with kids on the team, all trying to advance their son's stature with the coach. The judge wanted to see the two attorneys in chambers, and I don't know to this day what went on back there. But the prosecutor only put on *one* of the witnesses I provided him and rested his case. The coach was put on the stand and gave a cock 'n bull story about what happened. The judge in giving his ruling said that he didn't believe the coach's story at all, but found there just wasn't enough "anger" to form the "intention" of hitting the kid and found the coach not guilty. Oh, well, so much for justice.

The reason I mention this is that during the summer I got a visit from the football coach, Fred Merrell, who told me that all his coaches felt that because of my involvement with the baseball coach, they didn't want me to be president of the booster club. It was obvious that I was now an enemy of the administration, and have no doubt that the principal, Charlie Nichols, was behind this. By this time I was pretty well fed up with the administration and thankful that I only had one son left, and this was his senior year. So I stepped aside, but didn't tell Kurt anything about this.

Donald graduated from high school the spring of '87 and decided to play football at Hutchinson Community College, Hutchinson, Kansas. Ironic, isn't it, in that he went to the same college his dad attended. There is where we really learned about college football. Most of the players were black, and Donald had to stay in the dormitory. I traveled to a couple of his games in his freshman year, even though he played very little. He got a scholarship for the tuition and a student loan for his room and board. We had purchased a little Toyota Celica for him to drive, and that car ran, and ran, and ran. It lasted him all the way through all of his college.

In the fall of '87 Kurt was now a senior at South. It had all the possibility of a fantastic football season for the school, because there were over 30 seniors out for the team, and the line on both the offensive and defensive sides averaged about 240 pounds. Terry Mohajir was a strong and experienced tailback, and Garrett was a decent quarterback who could throw the ball. But it was going to be a tragic football year.

The best coach on the team, according to Kurt, was the offensive line coach, Kirk Miller. Very early in the season the team learned that he had a brain tumor and surgery was required immediately. This really cast a spell on the team. Nonetheless, they opened the season with a big win over traditional rival West in overtime. We next played the traditional powerhouse, Lawrence, on our field. That was to be the pivotal game of the season. If we could win it, then the rest of the teams weren't very strong, and we had a good chance of going all the way to state.

It was a tough game. Late in the fourth quarter Lawrence was ahead 12-7. However, we had the ball and were driving steadily down the field. With about two minutes left we were on Lawrence's four-yard line with a third and three situation. Coach Merrell called a time-out, and Garret came over to discuss this very important play. We all expected a power play over the left side behind Kurt, who was knocking defenders all over the field. Garrett took the snap, faked to Mohajir and threw a flat pass clear across the field. It was a difficult pass and dropped harmlessly to the ground. The fans were stunned. Why was the coach calling such a stupid play when our line was dominating?

Coach Merrell called another time-out and discussed the next play with Garret. The whole game was riding on this next play. It was fourth down. We all felt, again, that it would be a power play. Hopefully the coach learned something from the last play. Garret took the snap, again faked to Mohajir, and then *threw the exact same flat pass to the back!* And, again, it fell harmlessly to the ground. Lawrence then got the ball and ran out the clock. If ever there was a time when one or two plays ruined an entire season, this was it. Kurt told me later that the entire team moaned when Garret called those two plays in the huddle and begged him to check off and run the ball. But he had no choice. He had to run the play the coach called. It's really a crying shame when the players have a better grasp of the game than the coaches. And Merrell had over 25 years coaching.

This episode caused the players to lose confidence in the coaching staff. It was obvious that they were thinking, why bust your butt if the coaches were going to blow the games with dumb play-calling. Morale sank, and then the coaches started blaming the seniors. Then they started playing the juniors, and that made the situation even worse. The team started losing games they should have won easily.

Probably the supreme poor judgment call by the coaching staff came when we were in the three-game sub-state series to determine who went to state. Kirk Miller had died in the hospital during the first half. One of the parents happened to walk into the dressing room during halftime, and players were sitting around and crying. Apparently, in order to fire up the players, *the coaches told the players at halftime that Kirk had just died!* Can you imagine that? Most of these kids had never been exposed to death, and here the coaches were trying to fire them up ... with death! The players went out in the second half and played the worst they had played all year. Naturally, we lost.

The final touch to this disastrous season came at the last game. We arrived at Wyandotte for the game, and just inside the fence entrance stood both the principal and the athletic director with very grim looks on their faces. I couldn't figure out why they were so grim. The game started and we all noticed that Garret, our starting quarterback, wasn't even suited up for the game. Soon word spread that he had been suspended for some disciplinary reason. Well. Okay, if he did something wrong, then perhaps this punishment was appropriate, even though I disagree with punishing a whole team for the actions of one, especially at the last game. There are other methods just as effective. Kurt went both ways that game, had something like 13 tackles, but we still lost.

When Kurt got home that evening, he said he was glad that the season was over. We all felt the same way. He told us that the coaches wouldn't tell the players where Garret was and why he wasn't at the game. Player after player asked the coaches, but no one would tell the players the truth. Why, you might ask? Well, image was the most important thing to the administration of the school. They were literally afraid of some kind of ugly scene if the players were told the truth. They were afraid that all of the seniors might refuse to play, and there would be an image-smearing scene. Now I understood why the principal and athletic director were at the game. They wanted to stop anything before it happened. They really didn't give a damn about the players, just their precious image.

It was that night that I told Kurt about Merrell coming over to my office and telling me to resign from the booster club. Kurt couldn't believe it, and it infuriated him. From that day forward, he totally avoided Merrell at school. When Kurt passed him in school, he wouldn't even acknowledge him. A date was set for the seniors to take pictures and turn in money for the senior banquet. Kurt refused both, despite some of the coaches urging him to have his picture taken and to come to the banquet. He still refused, and I supported him. When they sent him his letter certificate, Kurt ripped it up and threw it in the trash. Merrell and the principal had turned him off so much that Kurt wouldn't even go out for wrestling that year, and gave up football completely. That was a real shame because there were some pretty good schools interested in Kurt, and he had the size. He could have made any college team.

This whole episode is indicative of the mentality of the Shawnee Mission School District administration at that time. It was ultra-political and image-conscious. The kids weren't really that important. The careers of the administration were what they were concerned with above all else. The superintendent, Raj Chopra, of Mid-east heritage, had completely mesmerized the female-dominated board of directors with his natural charm and charisma. And he was truly blessed with charisma. The directors were blinded by that and couldn't see that his first interest was in himself and that he was really a political animal.

Case in point. Every time his contract came up for renewal, Chopra usually had applied for positions in different districts and was usually in the final cuts. He used this as leverage to get not only his contract renewed, but had it sweetened, too. It was so bad that on one occasion he actually quit and took another position in another district. Cleveland, I think. He had been working there for a few months, and the Shawnee Mission District had been conducting a search for his replacement, when Chopra decided he had made a mistake. He didn't like it where he was. *The Shawnee Mission School District hired him back!* They said he was still the best candidate available! And don't you know it, when Chopra was finished with the Shawnee Mission District, he moved on after a year or two. Anyone in management knows you don't hire back people who have left you for what they thought was a better position. When they do that, they have decided you are number two in their eyes, and you don't let them come back. But they did, and he used them again.

I'll cover just one more example of how farcical the Shawnee Mission School District was, and then I'll move on. In the fall of Donald's junior year he took a course in German. His teacher was Mary Alice Daniels. Keep in mind that Donald's focus was on football. When he got home from school, he was dead tired, and I noticed he wasn't hitting the books too hard. The progress reports came out, and he was getting a failing grade in German. I asked him about it, and he told me that he really didn't know how to study for it because the teacher wasn't following the book. Okay.

I called Mrs. Daniels to see what we could do to get Donald's grades up. I told her I thought at least 50% of the problem was that Donald wasn't putting the effort into it. She quickly agreed. Then I related to her that Donald said she wasn't following the book, and he never knew what to study. She said: "That's right, I don't follow the book. If it were up to me, I'd throw the book out of the course." I was stunned and asked her: "Do you mean to say that you refuse to use the school book that the school district says you are to use?" She said that was true, and if I didn't like it, I should feel free to take it up with the administration. Now I was really flabbergasted. How arrogant!

But I restrained myself and felt rather than rock the boat on this one, I'd simply get Donald transferred to the other German teacher, one that Kurt had, and who was a decent teacher. I called Charlie Nichols, the principal, and politely asked what I needed to do to effect the transfer. He said that was against his policy, and he wouldn't do it. So I wrote him a long letter and reiterated my request. I hit a brick wall. He still refused. So all we could do was let Donald take his "F," hoping that he learned a lesson from this. I thought that was the end of it, but it wasn't.

After the second semester started, Donald came home one night and told me more as an afterthought that 29 students had started that semester in that German class. He asked if I wanted to know how many were in the class at the end of the semester. I asked him how many, and he said: "Seven." Wow. She turned off 22 of 29 students. What a terrible job of teaching! The thought of those 22 students who were turned off on a subject at an entry level was too much for me to stand still. It disturbed me even further when he told me she had another German class of about the same size for the second semester.

So I fired a letter to good old Raj Chopra and related all of this to him. I got a call from his assistant a few days later, and he said he was going out to South and would discuss the matter with "Charlie."

A few more days later he called me and said that "Charlie" had agreed that it was necessary to discipline Mrs. Daniels. Well, maybe we're getting somewhere. I felt they would take care of the problem, and I had done my civic duty.

In January of '87 Donald told me that Mrs. Daniels had been back in German class, had started out with about 30 students, and had run off around 75% of the students. This really was beyond comprehension. Well, I felt that you keep going up the ladder until you get to someone who can solve the problem. I decided to write a comprehensive letter *to the home address of each board member.* Maybe they didn't know what was going on and this would alert them to problems they didn't know existed. In the meantime, I had done a little research on Mrs. Daniels and heard that she had been teaching at East, had some problems there and sued the school district on some basis of discrimination. The district apparently settled the suit with her and transferred her to South.

A few days later I got a letter from Ruth Roudabush, the board chairman, saying this was an "administrative matter," and she was turning it over to the administration for handling. Talk about taking the ostrich approach. The whole board stuck their heads in the sand and hoped the problem would go away. I knew then that they simply would not take any action, and they didn't. And Mrs. Daniels taught until she was ready to retire. How rotten!

The fall of '87 was rough. Richard had been having problems with his back and decided to walk on at Kansas University to try to pitch. He worked up to fifth in the pitching rotation, but eventually had to give up the sport completely. So he continued in school at KU, rooming with a couple of other players, one of whom was Steve Renko, son of the major league pitcher, Steve Renko, Sr. Roommates come and go, and Richard invited me over one evening to meet their roommate, "Sam." He'd asked me over many times, and I hadn't accepted. But this time I decided to be "one of the boys." I arrived at his apartment, and out walks this good-looking young *woman!* Sam was a girl! Her full name was Samantha. I didn't quite know how to take this, but they each had their own private bedrooms, and they needed someone to share the rent. I hope that was all they shared.

Donald accepted a football scholarship at Hutchinson Community College and was working hard to land a starting position. There was a lot of talent in front of him, but he never let up. I was able to get out to see a few of his games, even though he didn't get to play much. We enrolled both Michael and Kyle in Holy Cross Catholic School. Lord knows, we had all we could take of the Shawnee Mission School District. So Michael had to adjust to new friends and new rules. And Kyle also had to adjust to new classmates and was in the first grade. He was a little over-shy, cried a lot, but had a heart of gold.

I was still trying to build my law practice, but as a solo practitioner it was very slow, and we just weren't making it. A lawyer I had done some private investigating work for, David Shaver, had been after me for many months to join his firm in downtown Kansas City. I had kept putting put him off because I didn't want the long drive to and from his office. My home was about 10 minutes from where I worked, and I couldn't see commuting 30 to 45 minutes one way each day. Finally, I had no choice, and we worked out an agreeable compensation package, and on March 7, 1988, I officially started as his employee. I remember that date very vividly because of what happened the following month. I could have started sooner if I wanted to, but delayed it to that date. Had I started on or before March 1, then my family would have had excellent medical coverage, effective April 1, 1988. But how did I know what was in the future?

In late March Kyle had been having headaches and seemed to be getting clumsy. I thought he had some flu bug and was just going through a growing spurt. Joy took him to the family doctor, but he couldn't find anything wrong with him. Still the headaches persisted. Finally, one night I saw Kyle walking along the hallway, banging the side of his head with the base of his palm. I asked him what he was doing, and he told me he was trying to knock his eyes back from being cross-eyed, the way they did that day at school.

Inside I cringed, even though I tried to stay calm outside. I now felt we might have a serious problem. Kyle appeared okay, so I waited until the next day and called the family doctor. I told him what had happened, and he said we needed to go to a specialist to see if there was anything seriously wrong. He set us up with an appointment with the Children's Mercy Specialty Center at College and Roe. It was for that Friday, at about 4:00. Joy took him in. I fought the Friday traffic, turned off 103rd Street and immediately saw that Joy's station wagon wasn't in our driveway. She wasn't back yet, and it was close to 6:00. I knew right then and there that we had a problem, a big problem.

I hurried over to the Specialty Center and reached the doctor's office as quickly as I could. They took me right into the office of the neurologic pediatrician, Dr. Dehkarharghani, and he told me that he was glad I had come. As gently as he could, yet quite seriously, he said, "Your son has a brain tumor." Just like that. He showed me the MRI's that he had just received and pointed to the tumor. There it was, like a big hurricane in the center of a weather map. He estimated it to be the size of a golf ball. Joy was out in the waiting room with Kyle, so I went out and brought her into the doctor's office. She took the news well. Then I told the doctor that I would like to break the news to Kyle. He was playing with some toys in the waiting room, and I sat him down away from the other patients and told him as simply as I could what he had. He was just seven, so I don't think it was that big an impact on him. Then Joy stayed with him as I went back into the doctor to address a course of action.

Dr. DK, as we all came to call him, told me that the greatest cause for concern was possible brain damage from the swelling of the tumor. The swelling put pressure on the brain tissue, and that pressure was what caused the damage. He said it would have to be surgically removed and recommended immediate hospitalization at Children's Mercy Hospital, by far the most advanced children's hospital in the area. I told him we would go right away. We headed home, and since Joy had Michael to take care of, we decided that I would take Kyle to the hospital. I packed a few things and off we went.

The admitting department seemed like they were taking forever, I was under a lot of pressure because I wanted Kyle admitted in a flash, so they could start him on steroids to try and shrink the tumor. Finally we got to his room, and they set up an extra bed for a parent to spend the night as well. The male nurse who was assigned to Kyle was fabulous. He really had a way with kids. Every so often he came in, shined a small light in Kyle's eyes to see how they reacted. This was how they could determine if the swelling was increasing. Fortunately, it wasn't.

I then had to make the calls to all the usual people. I remember calling Don in Hutchinson, and that was when I finally broke down. It was so hard for me to tell him that Kyle had a tumor. I cried and just couldn't help it. It was April 8. If I had started work with Shaver just seven days sooner, we would have had full medical coverage. But who can predict the future? It was just another bad break, and I knew the bill would be horrendous. Besides, my world had come to an abrupt and complete standstill. It was as if time were frozen, and the only item I could visualize was Kyle. Nothing else mattered. Not work, money, feelings, nothing. Kyle put our lives on hold. The weekend passed without incident, and Monday, the day of his surgery came.

Kyle was scheduled for surgery first thing Monday morning, but it wasn't until noon that they actually started. A lot of my relatives were there to give support, and Donald drove home from Hutchinson. Dave and Lyla were there. Needless to say, I was really stressed out. No matter how much you hope, you just can't keep completely out of your mind the thought that you might lose your son. You fought it, but it was there. Time slowly dragged on, and we got periodic reports from the nurses, but nothing of substance.

Finally, around 5:00 Dr. Hornig, the neurosurgeon who did the surgery, came out directly from the operating room. God, he was haggard. You could tell that he was totally drained and completely exhausted. I could tell that he had been under a tremendous strain from the operation. He told us that it was an astrocytoma tumor at the back of the brain right above the neck. He said they cut out the soft bone at the base of the skull and didn't replace it because it really didn't provide any protection, even if they did replace it. He thought they got all of it, but as any doctor would caution, he said they would have to take periodic MRIs to see if there was any growth. He answered all of our questions very patiently, despite his exhausted condition. I felt then that he had saved Kyle's life.

Well, we could all breathe a little easier. At least he had survived the operation. Dr. Hornig said that they had to keep him in recovery to make sure he stabilized before taking him to pediatric ICU. Kurt took Michael home, and the other supportive relatives left. Joy decided to wait with me until Kyle came out of recovery. Needless to say, we were pretty relieved, although we knew Kyle had a long way to go, and we still didn't know if Kyle would have any long-term residual effects from the tumor and operation.

Time dragged on, and they still didn't take Kyle out of recovery. They said he would be in there about an hour, but two hours later they still had him, and one of the nurses said they were having a problem with his temperature. Finally, about 8:30 they told us they were taking him up to pediatric ICU and we finally got to see him. Our hearts were twisted in a knot when we saw our little child on that gurney. He was so small and fragile. His head was covered with a bandage, and he was heavily sedated, so we didn't know if he recognized us. After letting us embrace him for a minute or two, they took him up to pediatric ICU. After they left, we both felt we could relax and started putting our family back together. Joy decided to go on home because she had the other kids to take care of, and I planned on spending the night. She left, and I felt safe enough to go down to the cafeteria to get something to eat. I sat there and ate, realizing that I was still in a daze over this terrible turn of events. But I soon knew that I had to do all I could to get Kyle back to health.

Now in a lot more relaxed condition, I went up to the pediatric ICU to visit Kyle and see how he was doing. They only allowed one close family member into ICU at a time, and we had to scrub our hands with disinfectant soap and put on a gown before we went in. As I stepped into this huge room, I was stunned by the sight. There must have been at least 10 to 15 little children and babies that were literally one breath away from death. The intensity of all the nurses was both overwhelming and controlled. They all knew that lives of little children were in their hands, and they were determined to keep death out of that room. It was medical war, and they were the warriors, with the spoils being the lives of the children.

The room was much like an emergency room in that the only privacy between beds was a curtain you pulled out from the wall. There was one or two small rooms in the corners where it was necessary to isolate the sick child. I located Kyle quickly, and the same male nurse who took care of him the night he was admitted was exclusively assigned to him. He knew me by then and acknowledged me briefly as he went about his care of Kyle. I could feel a sense of grim urgency about him as he intensely went about his nursing duties. I could also see the worried look on his face. God, he didn't want to lose Kyle.

I asked him what the problem was. He said that removal of the tumor had thrown Kyle's body "thermostat" out of kilter. He said that his "thermostat" was telling his body that his temperature was normal when, in fact, it was hovering around 106 degrees. He said he was very worried that hyperthermia might cause permanent brain damage. He showed me the full body-length cold pad that they had Kyle lying on, and only had him covered with a thin sheet. He was lying on his right side so he wouldn't be lying on the incision. There were tubes and machines all over the place. Kyle had an IV in his wrist and had tubes and wires connected all over his body. They ran to a myriad of machines both on wheels by the bed and on the walls that were giving digital read-outs of things like temperature, pulse, blood pressure, and Lord knows what else.

When I saw all of this and heard what the nurse had said, then I knew that the real battle had just begun. And I was totally helpless. Well, not quite. What I'm about to tell you is absolutely true. It is not embellished nor dramatized. It is exactly what happened. When my kids were very young and had played long and hard, so that they were over tired and couldn't sleep, I would sit on the edge of their bed and put the palm of my hand on their forehead with my thumb just above the eyelids. Perhaps it was the warmth from my hand, or just knowing that they couldn't move around, but after about 10 minutes, they usually were relaxed enough to go to sleep.

So I asked the nurse if it was all right if I placed my right hand on his forehead, and he said it was okay. Then I placed my left hand on his left shoulder and just stood there, holding him. It was all I knew to do. As I was standing there, the resident surgeon appeared and huddled with the nurse. I could tell that the nurse had been so concerned that he felt he needed to alert the doctor. Still, all I could do was stand there and hold Kyle, willing as hard as I could that his temperature would drop.

All of the machines were set to give new digital read-outs every 10 minutes. Ten minutes after I had started holding Kyle, new readings appeared. The temperature had dropped some, and the other readings had receded a little towards normal. Well, there was no way now that I was going to budge. I stayed right there. After another 10 minutes new readings appeared. The temperature had dropped some more, and the other readings were getting closer to normal. Now a team of horses couldn't have pulled me away from the bed. I stayed right there. The minutes ticked eternally by. Finally, the new read-outs appeared. *Everything was normal!* The nurse was visibly shaken. He couldn't believe it! Then a frown crossed his face. I asked him what the problem was. He said it wasn't supposed to go down that fast. Now he was worried that the temperature and vital signs would continue to drop. So the battle still wasn't over. I doggedly stayed standing there, holding Kyle. Finally after another 10 minutes went by, the new readings came out, and they remained normal. Kyle was out of danger and had stabilized. Only then was the nurse visibly relieved.

I can't say what really happened that night. Maybe it was God working a miracle, or just listening to my prayers. Maybe Kyle would have returned to normal by himself. I'll never know, and I'll never care. All I know is that he was over that hump and closer to returning to normal health. I know that the nurse had a look of disbelief in his eyes and looked at me as though I had some kind of supernatural power. Maybe there is some healing power of a parent's physical touching. I don't know.

Finally satisfied that Kyle had stabilized, I went down to our room and dropped into bed. I was exhausted. I took me awhile, but I eventually got a couple of hours of sleep. When I woke up early the next morning, I hurriedly showered and went up to see Kyle. He was still doing well. And so was I. At least until Dr. Hornig came by and asked me to step into the hall. I had a million questions, but before I could start he told me as gently as possible that initial tests showed that the tumor was malignant. My world stopped dead in its tracks ... again. He said he would have a doctor from the oncology department come by and fill me in on the various treatments. Great!

Outside the pediatric ICU room is a waiting room exclusively for the use of near relatives. It wasn't open to the public. We got to know many of the close relatives of the other children in the ICU. Right next to Kyle was a little 11-year-old girl with severe scoliosis, on whom they had performed an innovative new operation to save her life. This little girl was in critical condition in the ICU for the entire time that Kyle was in the hospital, six weeks. I don't know if she ever left, whether she lived or died.

On the weekend before Kyle's operation there was a cute little two-year-old boy whose parents gave him rides in a tiny wagon out in the hall. They told us that he had a hole in his heart, and the surgeons were going to repair it the same day that Kyle had his operation. The day after Kyle's operation I noticed the parents were in the ICU waiting room and were very sad. Without prying, I heard from one of the nurses that when the surgeons opened up the little boy's chest, they found the hole to be much larger than expected, and somehow a tiny bit of air had worked its way into the heart. It then traveled to the brain and essentially destroyed the brain. The poor kid was brain dead and died. I know I had my own grief, but what a terrible blow they had been struck.

Eventually they brought Kyle down from the ICU to his room. Kyle gradually started to coming around, but never talked or made any noises. Then Dr. Hornig told us that as a precaution he wanted to put a shunt into his head and insert it into a ventricle so that if there were a build-up of pressure this would allow it to be relieved, thereby preventing any brain damage from swelling. The brain has two ventricles, one on each side, and they are simply small holding tanks of brain fluids. He did the operation and brought Kyle back down to his room. The shunt had a small tube attached that ran from his head to the side of his bed, and then to a plastic bag that hung from his bed. It had to be lower than the bed to allow easy flow. From time to time I gently picked up the bag and held it in my hand. It was the strangest of feelings, holding a bag of your son's brain fluid in your hand.

Those days were dark days for me. Joy and I gradually shifted into a routine where I would work until about five in the afternoon, then go to the hospital, about 20 blocks away, where I would stay with Kyle until he went to sleep. Then I came home. Joy would take Michael to school, then go to the hospital and stay with Kyle until late afternoon. This was a source of great admiration for me. Joy was a timid driver. She still hates to drive, even ride, on freeways. The speed seems to give her anxiety flashes. To get from our home to the hospital, Joy had to travel along main streets through the roughest areas of Kansas City to get to the hospital. When I say rough, I mean really rough, with very high crime rates. But she rose to the moment, got lost occasionally, but always found her way.

Within the first few days of the operation, I got permission to take pictures of Kyle while he was in the ICU. I shot a full 36 photo roll of film of him in the bed from all angles with all the machines hooked up. I printed Mom and each of my brothers and sisters a full set of those pictures and asked them to pray hard for Kyle. I told them that the doctors said it was malignant. I found out later that a lot of their kids took the photos to school and had whole schools praying for Kyle. Even Holy Cross had a special school mass for Kyle, and all of the kids signed this huge 4' x 10' banner with get-well wishes. We hung it up on the wall in Kyle's room.

Kyle started coming around more and more. But he wouldn't talk, even though he was awake. Dr. Hornig explained that he was mute, or couldn't talk. He wasn't sure how long this would last. He explained that this type and location of tumor affected Kyle's physical coordination. And since, in order to talk, the brain had to control breathing, tongue, lips, teeth and voice box, Kyle would essentially have to learn how to talk all over. Another residual effect of the tumor was that Kyle was right-handed before the operation and became left-handed after the operation. I also learned that there are three major muscles on each side of the eye that work in unison to direct the eyes to whatever item they wanted to focus on. Since the tumor disrupted his physical coordination, Kyle had lost the ability to control his eyes. So one eye would look in one direction and the other eye in another. This wasn't pleasant to watch for a mere stranger, but for a dad it was agony. Needless to say, all of this did not set very well with me. And by this time I had received enough material on the various grades of malignant tumors, along with the life expectancy. I knew that Kyle didn't have too many years to live. That was hard to take, and many the nights, after Kyle had fallen asleep, I went into the private bathroom and broke down and cried. No, it was more than that. I broke down and sobbed and pleaded with God to spare this innocent young boy's life. I asked the Blessed Virgin to bend His ear and to ask Him to spare Kyle. I made no promises, because I felt that would be trying to tempt God, and you just didn't do that.

Seventeen days after the surgery, Dr. Hansen, the partner of Dr. Horning, came rushing by the room and asked me out into the hall. He seemed excited, if doctors can get excited. He told me that they had sent some tissue of the tumor out to a nationally renowned pathology specialist in California for further evaluation. Unfortunately, that pathologist was on a week's vacation and had just complete his pathology of the tumor. His evaluation was that the tumor was benign. *BENIGN!* My knees almost buckled under me. I asked him to repeat it. Yes, he said *BENIGN!* It's impossible to explain the waves of relief ... gratitude ... humility ... and bonding with God that washed over me. I was swept away by the euphoric elixir of renewed hope and happiness. With all those people praying for Kyle, this may have been the second miracle God had worked on Kyle. I am convinced that he listened to our prayers. I rushed to the phone and made many happy phone calls and spread the word, thanking everyone for their prayers. I felt as though we had cheated death, and was I ever glad of it.

But Kyle was still mute, and this was really bothering me. One night Richard came up to the hospital with his girlfriend. He brought with him one of those helium-filled, silver heart-shaped balloons on a string and tied it on the end of the bed. Then he tried to hand to Kyle a spring-loaded dart gun with the soft rubber suction cups at the nose of the plastic shaft, so that it stuck where you shot it. I watched Richard helping Kyle shoot this simple toy, and the most beautiful thing happened. When Kyle shot it, it made him laugh. A sound! He used his mouth to make a sound! Again and again we loaded the gun, and again and again Kyle laughed. It was music to us. This was the trigger that started Kyle out of his muteness. He gradually started talking.

Since his coordination was out of whack, he obviously couldn't feed himself. So the nurses generally helped him eat. Sometimes he let Joy or me feed him with the spoon, and it soon became obvious that Kyle felt embarrassed that he couldn't hold a spoon by himself and frequently dropped the spoon with food on himself. He also had to have a urinary catheter, since he couldn't coordinate his urinating. But he gradually overcame that. Finally, the day came when he was allowed to stand up with the help of the nurses or his family. Then he started to walk, first to the bathroom, then eventually short trips down the hall and back. Since his eyes were out of control, Kyle had to wear a black patch over his left eye, so that his right eye didn't weaken from non-use. He hated to wear it, and it was a constant give and take to keep him wearing it.

The hospital had a refrigerator out in the hall where they kept drinks and small cartons of milk, chocolate milk and juices. Kyle developed a huge taste for the chocolate milk, and many the times we'd get him a carton and a flexible straw so he could drink it. They also had small throwaway cups of pudding. Kyle liked them, and so did I. We ate a lot of those.

Through all of this, our other sons were really helpful. Don came home from college when he could, Kurt came down as well, and Richard also did his best to help Kyle. But one incident occurred that I will never forget. One night Joy, Michael and I were visiting Kyle. As usual, our focus was on Kyle. After awhile, I glanced around and Michael wasn't in the room. I thought that was odd and went looking for him. I found him just outside our room leaning against the wall, and he was crying. He was just 10 years old, and I felt so sorry for him. I asked him why he was crying, and he told me that since Kyle had his operation, it seemed that he just didn't matter to us any more. Well, of course, nothing could have been further from the truth.

I put my arm around him and told him that because we had to focus so much on Kyle, that didn't mean that we cared any less for him. I told him that if it were him in the bed with the tumor, then he would be getting the same attention. I told him that we loved him every bit as much as we loved Kyle. But right now Kyle was in a critical time of his life and needed almost all of our attention. His tears dried up, and then he came back in the room. I don't know how much this shaped Michael's personality, but he has always been the giving kind of person. He'll always volunteer to do things and is always ready to help. He was just fine after that, and from then on we tried to do little special things for Michael, just to let him know we loved him, too.

After about a month, it was obvious that Kyle was on the mend, and Dr. Hornig told us to start looking for a Rehab Hospital. He told us that Kyle would need quite a bit of rehabilitation, including speech, occupational, writing, physical, and on and on. We checked around and set up the rehab at Bethany Medical Center in Kansas City, Kansas, on an outpatient basis. This meant that Joy had to learn to drive her way clear across a different part of town again. And she did it. It's amazing how people manage to do the things that they just couldn't avoid doing. Joy drove Kyle to rehab three times a week for half-day sessions. Since Michael was so young, he had no choice but to come along. It had to be boring for him, but he never complained. Michael was truly a prince.

We had many meetings with the staff, and once there was a full meeting with all of the physical therapists and Dr. Reese, the physiatrist. A physiatrist is a physician who specializes in physical medicine. Of all the people in the meeting, he was by far the best trained, and the only doctor. During the meeting I subtly picked up on the female licensed social worker assigned to the case. Kyle was my kid, and when it comes to my kids, I am fully vocal. So I gave a good deal of input into the meeting and asked a lot of questions. I sensed that this social worker seemed to resent that. But frankly, I didn't care.

Kyle had been in rehabilitation about two weeks when Joy told me that the social worker had a number of conversations with both Michael and Kyle, asking about their home life, etc. I thought this was just the normal procedure. But was I ever wrong! Shortly after the two weeks of rehabilitation were over, I was working in my office when my phone rang. It was Joy, and she was crying, no, she was sobbing. At first I thought something dreadful had happened to Kyle. But that wasn't it. She had just received a letter from the Child Abuse section of the Division of Social and Rehabilitation Services. They said they had received a complaint that we were abusing Kyle, that they were going to have to investigate, and if necessary, they could take Kyle away from us. Joy was crying because she thought they were going to take Kyle away from us.

Well, I really didn't need this right then. I was just a few months into a new job, I had sons in college I was trying to fund, Kyle had just had critical surgery, and we were in the midst of trying to help him get back to normal, and Joy was still on medication from her nervous breakdown years ago. I really didn't need this. When was there going to be some let-up? I got her calmed down, told her that it all had to be a big mistake, and I would take care of it.

When I arrived home late that afternoon, I read the letter. It was a form letter, notifying us of the complaint. There wasn't anything I could do until the next morning. It didn't help much that child abuse had just seemed to become a popular item with the news media and the state legislature, so a lot of new legislation had recently been enacted. As soon as I got to my office the next morning, I reached the case worker (a female minority), explained to her all about the operation, the rehabilitation, and all we were doing to help Kyle. After about 15 minutes she concluded that the claim was baseless and told me she was closing the file. A few days later we received another form letter saying the case had been closed.

But how did this obvious farce happen? It was caused by that Bethany licensed social worker. During her "talks" with Michael and Kyle, she had learned that I spanked my kids, sometimes with my belt. She adamantly opposed this form of discipline, so she made the complaint to the SRS. I was furious. I confronted her with it and really unloaded on her. She was one of those typical "book" knowledge persons and really didn't know squat about raising kids, even though she had a couple of her own. (Poor kids. I wouldn't place any bets on how well they grew up). I was so mad I refused to pay the bill, and the hospital sued to be paid. During the course of the litigation, we took her deposition and learned that she was an active member in about five different environmental organizations, such as "Friends of the Earth." It fit. She was a real whacko, with very little grasp of reality.

It was extremely difficult on Joy and me after Kyle was home to stay. He presented the greatest difficulty to us in raising kids. Not that he was bad or had any glaring faults. He was just very hard to understand. For example, he would go out into the yard and come back into the house a little later. When he came back in, I'd say, "Hi, Kyle." He would drop to the floor and start crying. Joy and I would look at each other, wondering what we had done to make him cry. To this day, I still don't know. But one thing I did know. As long as Kyle knew that we loved him very much and that we were trying our best to help him, that eventually things would work out.

I've often said that Kyle has already had a lifetime of adversity. I don't doubt it a minute. Consider for a moment how he felt the years before the tumor was discovered. I'm sure he had headaches, but kids at that age tend to think that such things are normal and every kid has them. How long and how severe were his headaches? Then the operation and the complete havoc it wreaked with his coordination. The many months of wearing the eye patch. Being the center of attention, wishing he could be just an average kid, and not have people fussing over him so much. Then, four months after the operation, going back to the first grade, now in a public school in "special education." Not knowing any of the classmates. The kids pointing at his crossed eyes and laughing. Tripping and falling over nothing at all. Being in Special Education class rather than in regular, normal classes. Being unable to participate in sports when all his older brothers were exceptional athletes. Having to have four eye operations over the next two years before he could look at an object with both eyes at the same time. Tripping and falling down into a window well and having to have stitches. And all of this because of a brain tumor. Why him? Kyle has already cried enough tears to fill a pond. But we all went on.

Donald was now a sophomore at Hutchinson and had a lot more playing time. Either I, or Joy and I, went to as many games as we could. It was four and a half hours one way, but we didn't mind the trip. Late in the season his team had a game in Garden City, way out in western Kansas. There was no way I could make that game. The next day I got a call from Donald, and his left knee had been injured during the game. They sent him to a doctor in Wichita, and his injury was diagnosed as an anterior cruciate ligament tear, or an "ACL." This was the most dreaded of knee injuries. This ligament is what holds the bone below the knee against the thigh bone. It is the major factor in keeping the knee tight and stable. Without it, the knee is unstable and will flop out of control.

I wasn't comfortable with just one diagnosis, so I had Donald come home, and we had him examined by a group of orthopedic surgeons near St. Joseph Hospital. They gave us the same diagnosis. There was no choice but to schedule the surgery. Donald was extremely upset because his playing days might be over, and he had poured many, many years of 120 percent effort into playing football. But there really wasn't any choice.

The day of the surgery I went with Donald to the hospital. I stayed with him while they prepared him. The surgeon, Dr. Clymer, met with me and told me generally that they were going to do orthoscopic surgery first to confirm the diagnosis. If it was confirmed, only then would they cut it open. They sedated Donald and took him into surgery. I waited, feeling very bad for Donald. I knew how much this meant to him and how much he hated being injured. Finally Dr. Clymer came out and explained that the ACL had been completely torn. They had to open him up and repair it by using a portion of another ligament and attaching it to the thigh bone with screws. He said that Donald's chances of playing football again were very slim.

I waited until they brought Donald out of recovery and took him back to his room. The pain was excruciating, so they hooked up a special hand-held device where Donald could push a button when the pain became unbearable. He could push the button and he would receive a dose of morphine automatically. Of course, there were limits to prevent overdosing. Donald gradually came around so that he recognized me. But the pain had driven him to the point of being almost delirious. Almost out of his mind, he started venting his anger, and I was the only one there. I knew this wasn't the real Donald and he had to be delirious, so I tolerated it. But the swearing and abusive language got so blue that eventually I just couldn't take any more of it. I told him I was going to have to wait in the waiting room. I went a couple of floors down and found a nice, quiet waiting room where I could relax and my own tension eased. I wanted to be with Donald as much as possible, but the abuse just got to be too much. It was clear that he was delirious, and I didn't think badly of him. I just couldn't take any more.

After an hour or two, there was a page for me on the public address system. I wondered what the hell was going on. I picked up the phone on the wall and answered the page. Pretty soon Donald came on the line and wondered where I was. I told him I was in a waiting room, and he asked me to come back to his room. I was amazed at his ingenuity in locating me. I couldn't help but feel that he had realized he had gone too far with me and felt bad about it. When I got back, he was a little better, but was still in a lot of pain.

He floated in and out of semi-consciousness, and I tried to be as much support as I could to him. At least he knew I was there.

The next day he was much more alert, although the pain still persisted. I spent a lot of time with him, not only to help him through this physically painful experience, but also to give him some support with the long-term possibility that his football days were over. He really had his heart set on playing major college football, and, after that, who knows. I know, a lot of kids have the same dream. But with Donald, it was far more than a dream. It was an obsession, and he paid the price to try to achieve it. In mid-winter he would go up to the high school and run the steps in the stadium, and many the times as I sat in the living room, he came home dripping with sweat from running and pushing himself.

At one point he became interested in boxing. He didn't have a car at the time, so I hauled him down to the Rosedale area of Kansas City, Kansas, where there was a boxing gym, and he began training. It was a pretty rough part of town, so I felt better if I was with him. At one point he got a little training from John Brown, the trainer who brought Tommy Morrison along. Donald was cat-quick, very strong, and probably would have done well. But eventually football took all of his time and boxing died out, much to my happiness.

After Donald was released from the hospital, he recuperated at home, then returned to Hutchinson. He was to get physical therapy there with the football trainers. I got a call a couple of weeks later, and Donald said he was having a difficult time getting Dr. Clymer to set up a rehabilitation program for him to follow. The trainer could never reach Dr. Clymer, and Donald was worrying that if he didn't rehab the knee correctly, he would lose his career. I had Donald call Dr. Clymer direct to get the physical therapy straightened out.

When Donald came home for Christmas, he set an appointment with Dr. Clymer. When he came home from the appointment, Donald told me that what Dr. Clymer had told him caught him off guard. He told me that before he could even get started telling Dr. Clymer how his knee was, Dr. Clymer patted his knee and said that he had done a good operation and there was no malpractice. This stunned both of us, because neither of us had hinted anything about that. Then I began to understand. I was a lawyer, and doctors were deathly afraid a malpractice suits, thanks mostly to malpractice insurance news blitzes and activities in the legislatures. Dr. Clymer was afraid of being sued. Then it really dawned on me. Dr. Clymer was what I called a "cut and run" doctor. He billed around $4,000 for the surgery (no more than two hours actual surgery time). Follow-up office visits were $40 or $50. It was obvious he wanted to cut, cut and cut. That was where the big money was. It was all greed, pure and simple.

Eventually I persuaded the school to send me a copy of the videotape of Donald's game. I watched it from start to finish. I saw the play where he was injured late in the first half. I talked to the trainer, and he told me that, while warming up for the second half, Donald told him that his knee didn't feel right. He couldn't stop. Still, he was one of the best blocking tight ends, and this was a crucial game. The team needed it. So Donald started the second half. Sure enough, on about the fourth play from offense they called a play where Donald had to block the middle linebacker, and his knee gave out completely. He hobbled off the field, this time for good, I thought. But when the fourth quarter rolled around, and we had a slim lead and the ball and needed to run some time off the clock, guess who came in to block. That was really disgusting to see. Donald was hobbling around like a peg-legged pirate, but he was still making his blocks, and the team eventually won. I was infuriated. I even sent the tape to a big law firm in Wichita to see if there was any basis for suing the school. Unfortunately, this was a "state" school and the legislature has granted state agencies pretty wide immunity. We had to prove "gross and wanton" negligence. I thought there was, but the law firm didn't, so nothing ever came of it.

In February of '89, I got a call from Verlee, saying that Tony was in the hospital with pneumonia. I could tell that she was a little worried, but didn't think that pneumonia was serious enough for us to make the long trip out to Fort Morgan, Colorado. So I made daily calls, and Tony gradually improved. About a week after he was hospitalized, the phone rang and it was Verlee. As calmly as she could, she told me that Tony had suffered a heart attack and didn't survive it. He had passed away. This hit me hard. Tony was my closest brother. We had done everything together. We had grown up together, gone to the seminary together, worked in the oil field together, gone to college together. In fact, all our lives we called each other on our birthdays, a tradition we never missed. Mine was February 1st, his March 8th. I used to tell everyone that I was one year, one month, one week, and one day older than Tony. And Teresa was one year, one month, one week, and one day older than me.

Verlee made all the funeral arrangements, and all of Tony's family was notified. He was the first of the 12 kids to die. I recalled when Rita's son Mark was tragically killed in '84, and going to his funeral. Besides Dad, Arlon and Mark Slous, there hadn't been any other deaths to close members of our family. But this would be different. This was a brother. Joy had to stay home to take care of the kids, so I drove up to Omaha, met up with Mark and Luann, and the three of us headed for Ft. Morgan, Colorado.

There are a couple of things I should mention about this trip. I had long been dubbed the "forager" by my brothers. I never quite understood this, because I didn't see anything wrong with nosing around in the evenings in the kitchen looking for snacks. When I did this on our fishing trips, it must have caught their eye, and one thing led to another. At any rate, I liked to bring a cooler with me with my favorite cans of pop and perhaps some lunch meat. On this trip I had purchased a sliced Hormel "Cure 81" ham and had it wrapped and sitting on top of the ice in the cooler. The cooler was in the back seat with me. After we had been on the road a good while, I opened up the ham and asked Mark and Luann if they wanted some. They did, and after awhile they asked for some more, then for some more, and we eventually ate the whole ham on the way there.

About half the way there we got to talking about the funeral itself, and Mark told me that he was surprised that none of Tony's brothers were pallbearers. What? I hadn't heard that. I just naturally assumed that Verlee would want me as one of the pallbearers because she knew Tony and I were really close. But sometimes grief clouds your perception and you just don't have things in the right perspective. I made Mark get off I-80 at the next exit where there was a phone and called Verlee. I simply told Verlee that I had to be one of the pallbearers and carry Tony to the grave. She was kind enough to substitute me for a recent son-in-law. Tony had four sons, and a very close friend also wanted to be a pallbearer. So it all worked out fine.

During '89 I had been doing very well as a lawyer for Shaver. I approached each case with the question of what has to happen before the case is either settled or won. Then I went to work on making those things happen. I was making $36,000 a year plus benefits, and 25% of the fee for any cases I originated. Out of curiosity I asked Terri in bookkeeping if she kept any statistics on the financial productivity of each of the five attorneys. My annual compensation review was coming up in March of '90, so I had her start tracking the revenue performance. Much to my satisfaction, I found that in five of the last six months I had produced more fee income than any of the other attorneys, and for that six-month period I had produced almost *HALF* of the fee income for the whole firm. Terri had even supported those results with a case by case listing.

Armed with this information, I met with Dave Shaver, the sole owner of the firm, at the appropriate time to initiate discussion for the new compensation package. To me, it was a simple negotiation session. I had the results and I felt there should be a huge increase in compensation. It was almost too easy. There was some give and take in a very friendly way, and I wound up with a new base pay of $52,500 (up from $36,000), a brand new Mercury Grand Marquis, an increase in the fee participation rate on cases that I originated, along with all the usual benefits, free inside parking, paid medical benefits, vacation, etc. I went down to Bob Sight Lincoln/Mercury on Metcalf in Overland Park and specially ordered exactly the car I wanted. It was jet black with the Continental rear window, the latest in sound, and even gold-plated chrome letters and window locks. It rode like a limo. It was the car of my dreams and cost Shaver about $500 a month. I was proud of that car because I had earned it through a lot of hard work. Every now and then a man needs to have at least a teeny dream come true. Maybe now Joy and I would start reaching some financial security.

Kyle's first two years in school after his tumor surgery were very brutal and difficult for everyone, but mostly for Kyle. Before the operation he was right-handed, now he was left-handed. So he had to learn how to write all over again. His eyes were crossed, so he had a hard time seeing which, in turn, caused him to be very clumsy. He was continually tripping over nothing, especially going up and down steps. During those two years he had the four eye surgeries so that he could use both eyes. That had to bother him. Fortunately, he had a teacher at school, Mrs. Freed, who had the patience of Job and the skills of a genius in dealing with kids like Kyle who needed a lot of help and individual attention. I am convinced that she was a major factor in the recovery that Kyle made. Joy and I had many sessions at the school, always working closely with Mrs. Freed. She worked marvels with Kyle. Unfortunately, she only handled the first and second grade classes, and Kyle would have a new teacher the following school year. I had to do something special for her so she knew how much we appreciated her work. I sent her a dozen roses right before the end of Kyle's second grade, with a note telling her that of all the teachers that all five of our kids had, she was by far the very best, and Joy and I would be forever grateful to her. I just had to let her know how we felt. A simple verbal "Thank you" at the end of the year just was not enough. I heard later that when the flowers arrived at the school's office and Mrs. Freed opened and read the note, there were a lot of tears in the room. I don't like tears too much, but don't mind tears of appreciation.

15

OVERLAND PARK, KANSAS, 1990-1995

(Job Nemesis Returns, Five Kids in School, Retirement Case Bombs)

BY THE SUMMER of '90, we were riding high. I finally had a comfortable compensation package, and Joy and I could now look forward to possibly start getting the things we'd dreamed of, like buying our own house, etc. We now had excellent health coverage, I had the car of my dreams, and Kyle had dodged a tragic death, although he had a long way to go. But I could live with his situation, although it was going to take a lot of patience and love. That was far preferable to visiting a gravesite. My three oldest sons were in college, so they were on the way to being independent and able to support themselves.

To make matters even better, the Good Lord sent me what we attorneys call our "retirement" case. This client was a 32-year-old married woman who had been a front passenger in a van struck from the rear by another car. The impact caused her seat to break down toward the rear, causing her to catapult to the rear of the van. Her head hit something, causing her to have a subdural hematoma. By the time they got her to the hospital, she had suffered massive brain damage as a result of the bleeding causing pressure on the brain. For those who are not in the medical profession, one of the major causes of brain damage is damage to the brain tissue from excessive pressure caused by swelling. Her prognosis was very poor, although we all hoped and prayed that she would recover.

So things were really looking good for us. Looking back over the last 25 years, Joy and I had been through a lot. And sometimes over many years, that can get you into a rut. You get "used to" being financially strapped. You get "used to" being merely a survivor. For the first time in many years, it appeared that we now had a chance to look forward to being more than a survivor. There was now a faint glimmer of a chance to be a winner. It was a new experience for me, and it felt good. We lived in affluent Johnson County, where there were many "successful" people. Don't misunderstand me. I abhor chasing the Joneses. I just wanted to own our own home and have a decent place to live when the kids were all raised. Nothing elaborate. My kids were my fortune.

I was now an aging 53, Joy 51, Richard 23, Donald 21, Kurt 20, Michael 11, and Kyle 10. Whew! Richard was just finishing up at Kansas University, and Donald and Kurt were at Kansas State University. Richard was majoring in psychology, Donald in marketing, and Kurt in electrical engineering. Michael was going into the sixth grade and Kyle into the third grade. The boys were moving right along. I didn't have the money for college, so all three boys had to use financial aid, a combination of Pell Grants and Stafford loans. They always needed some help, but essentially they paid their own way through college.

I had made my mind up years ago that I really didn't want to finance my kids' college. Sounds crazy, doesn't it? But the reason I felt this way was that I felt if anyone gets something free, then they really don't appreciate it much. If they pay for it themselves, then they will appreciate it much more. I was going to *loan* them the money and make them pay it back after they graduated, or make a graduation present out of it. But I never had to cross that bridge, because I never really had the money to fund their college. Still, I funded each of them partially from time to time. Their loans would be late, and they needed funds to get enrolled, etc.

That summer we were finally able to go on a real vacation as a family. I mean the whole family on a real vacation, the first one in probably 15 years. All seven of us flew to Chicago, where we rented a van and checked into a local Holiday Inn. Then, for the next few days, we went all over Chicago, seeing all of the sights, the Sears Tower, the Loop, the Museum of Science and Industry, and on and on. We took a cruise out on Lake Michigan and went through Shed

Aquarium. We drove along Lake Shore Drive, saw McCormick Place and Soldier's Field. We met up with Tim, Joy's brother, and parked near the Oak Street Beach. It was a beautiful, sunny day, and the beach was crowded. Once we got there, the older boys had no desire to visit anything else in Chicago. They had found the mother lode. They had found what they wanted – girls, beautiful, exquisitely figured girls, and plenty of them. From then on, that's where they wanted to spend the rest of the vacation. I had to laugh, but who could blame them? I was young myself once. Fortunately, the whole vacation went smoothly, and we all returned in decent shape. Now, when pictures of Chicago and Soldier's Field come on TV, the kids can say they have been there.

By the fall of '90, Donald had finally let go of his dream of playing football and focused his attention on getting his degree in marketing. It was really hard on him, giving up that dream. It took 18 months for him to give it up, and that made things a little rough at times on those of us around him, but we understood and tried not to let it bother us.

Richard had already graduated, or at least I thought he did. He made the famous march down the hill in his graduation robe, etc., and Joy and I were very proud. He was the first of my sons to graduate from college. Throughout school he had been laid back about making exceptional grades, so I was really happy to see him finish. As a graduation present, I put up the money for the down payment on a car. It was an '85 Audi. Richard had a fairly selective taste as to cars, clothes, etc., so he really appreciated the car. A funny thing, though, we never saw his diploma. Finally, after a year I learned that he had graduated "provisionally." He still needed one more course in math, but always had a very hard time with algebra. Things went on this way until he started applying for jobs, and the applications asked for his degree, where, etc. Then he realized he had to finish, or his chances of getting a job were very poor.

So he finally told me the problem and wondered if I had any suggestions. I told him to drive over to Lawrence and sit down with the registrar, or advisor, or whoever the decision-maker was, and ask them if they had a solution to his problem. Sure enough, they did. They told him to take a course at the local community college, get a "C" in it, have it transferred to Kansas University, and they would send him an official graduation certificate. So he took the course, passed it, and got his "sheepskin." He was really proud of that degree. I got the impression that during high school and early college, he really didn't put much stock in a college degree. But now that he had one, he was really proud of it.

By late '90 dark clouds started appearing on the work horizon again. David Shaver had met and became totally infatuated with a very beautiful woman of either Spanish or Portuguese ancestry, who was a lawyer as well. David always had a very soft spot for the fairer sex, and some things he did were starting to get embarrassing to most of us. His judgment seemed to deteriorate dramatically, and it seemed that he was cutting some corners on his representation of clients. He had a full-page ad in the phone book, so we had a lot of business coming in the door. In fact, it was so heavy that we lawyers started timing ourselves as to how long it took us to meet with a prospective new client, get the facts, get the forms completed and have the client feeling very secure in our representation. It really became very routine to us.

The support personnel then took over and generally did a great job. They ordered all of the medical records and bills, got a copy of the police accident report, obtained verification of lost wages, scheduled medical examinations with doctors who we knew would give good reports.

Before you jump to conclusions, I don't mean doctors who would give us *phony* reports, but doctors who did thorough examinations and whose reports were perhaps somewhat biased toward the patient. The insurance company and defense attorneys had their own stock of doctors who gave reports biased against the patient. So it was somewhat of a game that just had to be played. But myself, Mike Gibbons and a couple of the other lawyers always tried to find the honest doctor. We did this because occasionally we ran into an adjuster who was just totally unreasonable, and it was going to take a lawsuit to prove him wrong. When that happened, we wanted a doctor on the witness stand who had superb credentials and excellent credibility. Make no mistake, juries collectively see through all the smoke and mirrors and together are the smartest group of people in the world.

After we had all of this information in, as well as pictures of the cars, street, and scars, casts, etc. of the client, then we evaluated what the case would be worth *at trial.* We then sent a "Demand Letter" to the insurance company who insured the negligent driver, demanding a certain dollar amount to settle the case without filing a law suit. Only about five percent of our cases resulted in a lawsuit being filed. And of those, only about five percent ever went to a jury trial. The rest were generally settled during discovery, when depositions were taken and written interrogatories or "questions" were asked and had to be answered under oath.

The concept was for the lawyers on each side to find out and establish what the true facts really were. Once that was done, then the lawyers could gauge the prospects of winning or losing at trial and how much the verdict might be. By far the majority of our clients had very little money, so we took their cases on a contingency basis, generally one-third of the recovery, if the case was settled.

With my years of private investigating, coupled with my extensive work experience, I developed an above average skill in evaluating cases and in dealing with the clients. I tried to foster trust and credibility, because that is the chief asset a lawyer has. If a client believes and trusts you and you do your job well, then you are advancing the whole legal profession. Conversely, if you're strictly money-orientated, treat clients like "inventory," and don't do a good job, then you hurt the whole profession and make it easy for the public to believe all of the jokes and horror stories they hear.

Shaver's infatuation with this woman ultimately led to a divorce from his wife, Molly, who was as sweet a person as you could ever meet. She really got the shaft from David. Soon, David's "concubine" started influencing what went on in our office. David simply went limp around her, and before long any female employee who was even slightly pretty was let go. Soon David was terminating all of the highly qualified help, who were making $10 to $15 an hour, and replacing them with completely inexperienced entry level people at $5 an hour. The productivity went to hell in a hand basket. We lawyers could no longer depend on the grunt work being done and started spending a great deal of time training these new people. The sad part of it was that after these people had been there a few months and had some experience, they found a better paying job elsewhere. The turnover rate was terrible.

David was getting involved in some other activities that really made us lawyers very nervous. We felt some of his activities were outright illegal, and we could see David getting arrested for tax fraud. He was also dealing with parties we knew had drug connections. He and his concubine took many trips to South America and cruises together. Something that still puzzles us today is that occasionally, this concubine's *husband* would drive his wife and David to the airport so they could go on these trips. And many of them were pure pleasure trips, such as 10-day cruises. We had access to the credit card slips, and I have seen billing receipts where David went to lunch on the Plaza with his concubine, then checked into a hotel room, and then bought her a mink coat for well over $5,000. And yet, he didn't want to pay his office staff more than $5 an hour. I also saw an appraisal of more than $30,000 on a diamond he was thinking of buying her.

There were very strong suspicions that David was using drugs. In fact, on one occasion, an employee walked into his office (the door was open), and she was certain he was in the act of using the powder. She called me at home that night, scared to death. Then there were occasions when everyone was certain that David was having sex with his concubine right there in the office. There was a secluded office upstairs where only one clerk worked. She went out to lunch, and while she was gone, David and his concubine went up there and used her office. In their "fun" they actually broke the desk. David's judgment was so poor that he completely forgot that one door to his office was a smoked glass door. When you stood outside that door, you could still see bodies moving around in Dave's office. On those occasions when Dave was engaged in sex in his office, the staff would watch through the glass door. And he never knew it.

By the spring of '91 all of us lawyers had really reached our limit. By staying, we were placing our own licenses in jeopardy, and if David went down, the backlash on our reputations could be disastrous. And if we confronted Dave with our concerns, his judgment was so poor, there was no way to predict his reaction. I even called a drug hotline to review all of the symptoms of someone who was using cocaine. Shaver had every one of the symptoms. They advised that the whole office staff confront him at once. Unfortunately, we couldn't get the whole staff to do it. Divided, we could accomplish nothing, so nothing was done.

Here was another sweet deal gone sour on me. And, again, it wasn't anything I had done. My performance had been stellar. I was now the chief trial lawyer for the firm on the Kansas side and also handled all the big Kansas worker's compensation cases, although we had a full-time attorney assigned to all worker's compensation cases.

But there was another factor involved. By this time it had now became obvious that the seatback case I had originated was going to be a multi-million-dollar case. This client's medical bills were now approaching $1,000,000, and she wasn't even near leaving the hospital. In fact, her brain injuries were so severe that she had to be tended to 24 hours a day at a neurological hospital at a cost of about $1,000 a day. She had a tracheotomy tube in her neck so she could breathe and a "g tube" in her stomach so they could feed her and administer medications. The sad part of it was that she wasn't expected to leave the hospital, ever.

I knew that if this case stayed with Shaver's firm, he would prostitute it, because in his mind the clients existed for his purposes. It was clear to me that he would push for settling the case for a lot less that it was potentially worth. I didn't have the "big case" experience to work this kind of products liability case, and neither did anyone else in the firm. So the protection of this client was another reason I had to leave the firm.

Mike Gibbons left the firm around June of '91, another lawyer took a job with a firm in Iowa, and soon the only lawyer or two that were left were the ones who couldn't get a decent deal. One had just bought a house and had a new baby, so he was locked into his situation. I wasn't much better off. I was driving Shaver's car, that big, beautiful Marquis dream car, and I'd have to give it up. That meant I had to scrape up funds to get a replacement car, funds I didn't have. I still had two sons in college and two in grade school.

I really needed someone to listen to me explain my situation and perhaps give me some input. I was getting tired of making decisions that looked good, and were, for a period of time, but then fizzled out. My age was becoming another factor; I was now 54. So I called my brother Mark in Omaha. About halfway between Kansas City and Omaha was a small town, Mound City, Missouri. They had a very nice nine-hole golf course that in the years before we had golfed. So I called Mark up and asked him if he'd like to meet me there on a Saturday, so we could play some golf and then I'd go over my situation with him. It's sometimes wise to get some input from others, even though you might already have a pretty good idea.

So we met and started golfing around nine or nine-thirty. I had along with me my usual cooler, full of Diet Caffeine Free Pepsi and, yes, a sliced Hormel Cure 81 ham. Mark laughed when he saw it. We really enjoyed playing 18 holes, then we hunkered down on a park bench under a huge tree by the side of the grey, crushed rock parking lot. We ate, drank some Pepsi, and then Mark pulled out a yellow writing pad, and we started talking. I told him about all of the developments, the concerns that I and the other lawyers had, and generally, what my options were. He made a line down the sheet, and we went about listing all the pros and cons.

It was during this discussion that I, for the first time in my life, realized that I had the wrong slant on life in one major area. I had always prided myself on being a "survivor." And I was proud of that. In looking back over my life, I had encountered substantial adversities, and still we managed to survive. That was something that gave me some pride. But as we talked that day, it began to dawn on me that surviving alone was just not enough. Surviving is okay on a temporary basis, and I realized that I had been making "surviving" a way of life. I began realizing that by adopting that attitude, I was limiting myself. I was putting up a barrier, at which I would slack off when I reached it. It was time to knock down that barrier and see what was on the other side. I almost blurted out that I was tired of being a "survivor"; now I wanted to be a *winner!* What a whole new concept! It was time to quit just "getting by." It was now time to try to become a winner, a winner in the sense of reaching enough financial security to ease the stress on me, which in the end would be a huge benefit for my whole family.

Mark wrote this down on the pad. Then we thought about it. We concluded that I simply had to get away from Shaver's firm as quickly as possible. That was pretty much a given. But how to do it was another thing. I needed an income to support my family. I had not been practicing law long enough to have established myself well enough within the community as an attorney, so there weren't too many openings that could match what I had been making.

The only leverage I had was the big case I've discussed that I originated and a few others that were potential big winners. I also had a number of smaller ones that I intended to work myself. I was quite certain that when I left the firm, Shaver would not give me any static over my taking these clients with me. I maintained a very close relationship with my clients, and they relied on me as their attorney. They trusted me. Even if Shaver tried to keep my clients, they would immediately terminate him and hire me. In addition, about 85 percent of the cases I was handling at Shaver's were his clients. He had to worry about me taking those clients with me.

I had maintained my office all along out in Overland Park. It was fully furnished, and I had met many clients there while I worked for Shaver. It was the Overland Park location for Shaver's firm, although the lease was in my name. So finding an office was not a problem.

The only solution I could see was to market some of my bigger cases to larger firms, with the provision that they retain me at a minimum rate per week for a year after I left Shaver. There were two firms in Kansas with the best reputations for winning multi-million-dollar verdicts and had the resources, staff and quality lawyers this case needed. One was in Overland Park and the other in Wichita. I made the same proposal to both firms, and it appeared that the one in Overland Park was most interested. I met with one of the partners twice and had a third meeting scheduled with the managing partner. Even so, I kept the firm in Wichita on my short list and continued working with them.

When I met with the Overland Park firm the third time, things did not go well. I had overestimated the stature the first partner had with his firm. In fact, in the years that followed, this same attorney got into trouble by missing a filing deadline on a large case, concealed it from his own firm and the client, set up a separate bank account in the firm's name, put thousands of dollars of his own money into it, told his client he had settled the case, and actually wrote the client a check. Somehow the client smelled a problem and blew the whistle. The ethical infractions were so severe that the attorney surrendered his license, and Lord knows what he is doing.

Fortunately, the Wichita firm was very interested in my proposal, especially the big case, and invited me to Wichita. Again, I had a formal proposal with me and had sufficient information with names, dates and other traceable information blacked out, so this firm could make an evaluation of the cases. I had to black out this information to protect the attorney/client information. We went over the four cases I had included in my package, and the founder of the firm came in to meet me. That's when I started feeling positive about the proposal.

One of the main partners came to my office in Overland Park, where I had stored the actual seat that broke back in my largest case. He personally inspected the part that broke and was very positive. He returned to Wichita and called me the next day, asking me to draft an agreement between us. I did, and we worked out a mutually acceptable written agreement. This guaranteed me $3,000 a month for a year.

The next step was to resign from Shaver. Since his judgment and temperament were so volatile, I didn't know what to expect. But it went very smoothly. The effective date was November 1, 1991, a little over a month away. I had prepared a list of the clients that I originated and agreed with Shaver that if any of his clients, whose cases I was working on wanted to come with me, I would direct them to call Shaver personally. I was not interested in a squabble with Shaver. I wasn't afraid of him, but he had been doing some almost incredible things, and I didn't want the grief. I wanted to go about my practice without wasting a lot of time in a petty fight.

Surprisingly, Shaver wanted me to stay on past that date, but I refused. I tried to transfer his cases to other attorneys and see that work in progress would continue, all the time knowing that with his completely inadequate staff, more likely than not, his clients were really going to suffer.

That $700 a week from the Wichita firm was my lifeline while I made the switch, got set back up in Overland Park and began working my own cases. I had to give up my dream car, but that was just too bad. I had just settled a case so that I had enough cash to buy a 1983 Grand Marquis that only had 62,000 miles on it and still looked like it had come right off the show room floor. (Isn't it strange how, when you really need the money, the Good Lord provides it?). Since I both couldn't afford and didn't want to hire a secretary, it now meant that I had to become computer literate. At age 54 you hate it, but as often happens, when you are forced to learn something new, it really helps you over time. I am now somewhat computer literate and am typing this myself.

The summer of '91 was probably the last year that Dave, Mark, Gery and I got together in the Ozarks for our annual fishing/golf trip. We had done this for many years, and they were really a lot of fun, and it was good for us brothers to get together. It had started many years before with just Dave and Gery camping out in tents and fishing from a very small boat. Then gradually Mark joined them, then me, and once or twice, Tony.

Dave was a very avid fisherman and taught me a great deal about fishing. As time went on, we started including playing some golf on these trips. Eventually, we got to the point where Mark, Gery and I wanted to golf, and Dave wanted to fish. He had purchased his dream bass boat with all the frills, depth finders, etc., so his focus was exclusively on fishing. This was a major source of relief for him from the pressures of his management position with a major gas pipeline company. We sort of hit an impasse over the golf versus fishing, and Dave moved to Texas, so these trips died out.

But we had a lot of good fun. One evening just before sunset, we stopped to look at one of the dams feeding the lake. We were driving my new company car, and out of force of habit I locked it when we got out. Mark and I walked over to the tall chain link fence to get a closer look at the water, and after awhile we heard Dave and Gery yelling at us. They had their camera on us, so we just bent over and mooned them. They got pictures of it, and we still laugh at that. As Mark and I reached the car, Dave and Gery were on the other side of the car with their hands on the locked door handles, looking at me like I was a complete idiot for locking the car out in the middle of nowhere with no one within miles. Oh, well!

I made the mistake of letting Gery drive the car. He decided to have some fun, speeding a little bit and taking corners in the road really fast. I thought he was going to roll the car going around one curve, so I got all over him, telling him to slow down. After all, I didn't own the car. He slammed on the brakes and jumped out of the car, and said: "Here, you drive." They have ribbed me about that for years.

Spring of '92 came and Donald graduated from Kansas State University with a degree in marketing. His last semester he had earned a straight 4.0 grade point average. I've seen letters of recommendation he received from some of his teachers, and they were very impressive. He was active in the student business management club and helped to organize a Special Olympics for the disabled. It was amazing the way he was able to channel all of his football drive into his marketing degree. For the second time Joy and I got to watch a son march across the stage and receive his degree. We were really proud of him. I scraped together a thousand dollars and gave that to him as a graduation present. Lord knows, he was just out of school and didn't have much money.

KSU is in Manhattan, Kansas, about 120 or so miles west of the Kansas City area. It's somewhat out in the middle of nowhere, and is strictly a college town. They call the main section of town where the students hang out "Aggieville." This goes back to the days when the school was named Kansas A & M, for Agriculture and Mining. I attended a few Continuing Legal Education classes there, both to meet my requirements for my license and also to visit my sons. Whenever I visited the boys, we traditionally ate at the Hibachi Hut. This was a Cajun restaurant, with the best Cajun food and steaks ever. Any time I'm there, I manage to squeeze that into my schedule.

I suppose I was dreaming, thinking that I could avoid any feuds with Shaver after I left his firm. By early '92 many of his clients, whose cases I had been handling, tracked me down and told me they wanted me to represent them. Shaver was so paranoid that after I left, he instructed the receptionist to tell these clients that I was out of the office, get their number, and Shaver himself would call them back. He didn't want the clients to know I had left the firm. Some of these were really good cases, and if I didn't have a conscience, I could have easily taken a lot of cases from Shaver. However, true to my word, I told each of them to call Shaver. This gave Shaver a chance to say whatever he wanted to try and keep the client. That seemed the fair thing to do.

But some clients, even after talking to Shaver, called me and said they didn't want Shaver. They wanted me. I could still have refused, but that meant that they would go out and find a third lawyer. And I knew all about their cases. I felt that the client was best served if I continued my representation, and, for that reason, agreed to represent about five or six of these clients. But only after they had sent a written letter to Shaver, terminating him, and gave me a copy. In this fashion I kept ethically pure, and Shaver couldn't claim any solicitation efforts on my part. None of them were huge cases, so I knew they wouldn't hurt Shaver that much.

But Shaver was furious. He called me and told me that if I agreed to take one of these cases it was like stabbing him in the back. He even asked me to agree to work on the cases on a $50-an-hour rate, and, when the case settled, Shaver would get the bulk of the fee. This wouldn't fly, because it was working a sham on the client. Again, the client's trust is the ultimate guideline, and how could I expect a client to trust me if I participated in such a sham? I listened to everything Shaver had to say, then told him I was going to represent them anyway, and I would be happy to give him a referral fee of 25%. In this way, he still got a fourth of the fee, while I did all the work. I thought that was very generous and reasonable. It still didn't satisfy him.

Not long after that, they served me with papers indicating that Shaver had sued me. I had 20 days to respond, but first I sent a long letter to Shaver, telling him that he really shouldn't continue with this, because it was going to prompt a countersuit by me against him, and I thought he had a hell of a lot more to lose than I did. To avoid that, I asked him to dismiss his suit. I received no answer. In fact, he also filed a complaint with the state ethics committee, and dragged any dirt he felt he had before them. He was actually trying to get my license to practice revoked. This was my family's livelihood.

I don't know who said that war is war, but it was now time for me to go on the offensive. No more Mr. nice guy. Those days were over. I drafted my counterclaim and included in it all of the skeletons that Shaver didn't know I had. I won't go into detail here and will explain why later. Needless to say, I served on him a set of 54 interrogatories that made it amply clear to him that he was running a huge risk, not only of losing his case against me, but also his license, and perhaps, even his freedom. He tried to hire a lawyer to defend the countersuit, but no one would take it, and he had to be careful who he took the defense to, because once they reviewed the interrogatories, they would want to have nothing to do with Shaver.

So Shaver decided to defend the case himself. Now this was a real joke. I don't think he had ever tried a jury case in his life, and I know he wasn't very familiar with the civil procedures of a suit. In fact, he missed the deadline for filing his answer to my countersuit, and I promptly filed a motion for default judgment, meaning that I won on all the claims of my countersuit. Technically, the judge could have granted it, and it would have cost Shaver a ton of money. I knew our legal system favors cases being won on their merits and not on legal technicalities, so I wasn't surprised when the judge gave Shaver permission to file an answer, although it was beyond the statutory time.

I won't bore you with the intricacies of the suit. Within a very short time, Shaver wanted to settle the suit, used a lawyer to convey that to me, and we settled the suit. Essentially he gave me everything I asked for in my countersuit and gave up everything he was suing me for. He also wanted me to agree that I would never file a bar complaint against him, but that would have been unethical and grounds for immediate suspension of my license, so that was no deal.

I did go along with his strong insistence that I agree to an order by the judge that the court's file would be sealed and not open to the public. That didn't surprise me, because I knew that if what was in my countersuit got on the street, Shaver might as well pack up and move out of the country. So I agreed to it, but insisted that I draft the settlement agreement, to which Shaver quickly agreed. In this agreement, he agreed to relinquish any claim against me of any nature, either known or unknown, or arising out of the past or the future. That was really stupid on his part. It really proved the old saying that if a lawyer represents himself, he has a fool for a client.

As to the ethics complaint that he filed, the disciplinary administrator sent it back to him, telling him that it was essentially a fee dispute and there were other methods of resolving it. In other words, they didn't want involved.

Now it was "my turn." Our profession should never tolerate such a person. In fact, there is an ethics code that says if a lawyer is aware of an ethical infraction by another attorney, then that lawyer must file an ethics complaint with the disciplinary administrator, *or he himself has committed an ethical violation.* That is some tough medicine, to "rat," so to speak on a fellow lawyer. Still, if we don't clean up our own profession, then someone else might do it for us, and we may not like it.

I had no choice. I researched the Code of Ethics and meticulously drafted a lengthy ethics complaint in both Missouri and Kansas. A long time has passed since then, and as I write this, Shaver has been disbarred in Missouri and Kansas. Shaver has closed down his practice, and I have no idea what he is doing.

I feel no shame or guilt over what has happened to Shaver. I would do it all again if I had to. He deserved everything he got and probably deserves worse. I tried to be a nice guy. I tried to be fair to him. And I didn't go on the attack until he forced me into it. You may have heard the expression, "I'm not mean, but those who are leave me alone." That's probably fitting here. But enough about Shaver.

In July of '92 I was in a sufficient financial position for Joy, Michael, Kyle and me to take a vacation by car. I had always wanted to see Mt. Rushmore and Old faithful in Yellowstone National Park. We packed up the car and headed north to Omaha, where we had lunch with Mark and Luann. After a short visit we continued north on I-29 to Sioux Falls, South Dakota, where we bedded down for the night. The next morning we started heading west. Our first stop was the famous Corn Palace in Mitchell, South Dakota. This was a very remarkable sight to see. It was a medium-sized museum with a heavy influence of American Indian and Western culture. The reason why they called it the Corn Place was because the complete exterior and interior was covered with corn cobs of different natural colors. From a distance it appeared that it was brightly painted in an appealing scheme, but when you got close, you could see that it was actually corn. The inside was the same. What was truly fascinating is that we were told that each year they completely changed the corn! And as you walked along the interior, they had large photos of the exterior for each year. Wow!

We continued west on I-90, and as we drove we listened to a Credence Clearwater Revival tape. It was good music, and we played it so much during this trip that we got to know it pretty well. Now, whenever we take a road trip, we always play that tape for the good times it calls up in us. We got off at the Highway 44 exit to see the

Prairie Settlement, then entered the northern part of the Badlands National Park. The grey, crumbly cliffs were enchanting and conjured up imaginary scenes from the old cowboy and Indian days. We could just see riders driving their horses across the plains to hide in these hills. I started getting a much better appreciation of the American Indians and their impact on our history.

After getting our fill of this enjoyment, we moved on to the small town of Wall, right off I-90. We had heard of the Wall Drug, but weren't prepared for what we found. Wall was a very small town and didn't look like it had a population of more than 750. Yet, right dab in the middle of this town was this huge tourist drugstore that took up at least two full square blocks, and that didn't include the parking areas. I said to myself, "Why? What had caused this attraction?" Soon we found the answer. It seemed that a young pharmacist around the 1920s or so went to work for the pharmacist who owned the store. After a year or two, he was offered a chance to buy the store. He and his wife agreed to give it five years to see if they could make a living. They were out in the middle of nowhere; there were very few people, and, consequently, not much demand for a pharmacy.

After about four years of struggling, in the hottest part of the summer, his wife said she was going to go upstairs and take a nap. After about a half hour later, she came downstairs saying she couldn't sleep because the cars driving by on the highway just outside of town kept waking her up. This spawned an idea in the pharmacist's head. He set about making a bunch of roadside signs, and the following weekend he went out along the highway and put these signs up at about one-mile intervals. The signs said something like: "Free ice water – Wall Drug." The next week traveling salesmen in their cars with no air conditioning saw the signs and started pulling into the Wall Drug to get a good, cool drink of ice water. And then they started buying ice cream cones, and within one year, Wall Drug had to have six or seven waitresses. And, as they say, the rest is history.

We then moved on to Rapid City, South Dakota. There were enough attractions here to spend a full week, but we just spent a few days. Mt. Rushmore was tops on our list, and we saw it first. It was really impressive, seeing those faces on the side of the mountain and reading about the struggles and the long time it took to finally finish it. This had long been a national monument, so we soaked up as much of it as we could. We drove through the Black Hills National Forest and saw the buffalo and other wild animals. Someone told us about Chief Crazy Horse, and how they were building a huge statue of him, similar to Mt. Rushmore. Well, we had to see it. We found it and discovered that it was perhaps 40% complete. We were amazed at the size of it, because when it is finished it will be about 10 times larger than Mt. Rushmore. Here we learned more about the American Indians and many of their chiefs. We learned that Chief Crazy Horse never lost a single battle and never signed a treaty with the United States. He was killed in prison, stabbed in the back by a soldier. I began to realize more and more how the Indians owned this land first, and wondered how it was that they either lost it or had it taken away from them. My respect for the Indians grew daily.

We drove over to Deadwood, where gambling was legal, and tried our hands at a little black jack and slots. This was a very old town, with meandering streets and ancient grey wood buildings. Inside were a few black jack tables and slot machines, but somehow it just seemed to be a "poor boy" casino and wasn't much fun. It was clearly a tourist trap, as there were tourists with license plates from all over the country. I like to gamble, but this just wasn't too much fun.

We spent one night in Sturgis, getting there late, because we wanted to head for Devil's Tower in Wyoming the next morning. The motel was old, but their prices sure weren't. About 10 miles from Sturgis was Spearfish, South Dakota, a small town known for its famous outdoor passion play. It looked as though it was going to be drizzling rain, so I couldn't get anyone else interested in going to the play with me. The weather proved to be a benefit because it cut down the crowd, and I got a very good seat. The play was well done, and it had the effect of adding the theme of God in our vacation, and how all of this beautiful country we had been enjoying came from Him. We enjoyed driving through the small mountains, with their narrow, winding roads and hairpin curves. Joy usually scares pretty easily in this kind of driving, but we weren't able to scare her that much. She seemed to be enjoying it as much as we did.

The next morning, we took off for Devil's Mountain National Monument in northeastern Wyoming. This was the backdrop for the movie *Close Encounters of the Third Kind,* and it is still hard for me to visualize how time and Mother Nature could have shaped this huge rock. It looked almost as though some huge being shaped this from clay and just let it stand way out in the middle of nowhere. It's truly an impressive sight. We got as close as we could, took some pictures, stopped at the general sore, then headed west.

I-90 took us west to Buffalo, Wyoming, nestled at the base of the Big Horn Mountains. Now we started seeing real mountains. We headed north along the mountains to Sheridan, then took Alternate 14 to cross the mountains. It seemed as though we went up and up forever. We started noticing stop areas where vehicles could pull over and park to let their brakes cool off. It was very steep, and a driver had to ride his brakes constantly to keep from picking up speed. We pulled into one of those stops as we were going up, just to take some pictures of the beautiful scenery, when this huge RV pulled over and stopped. The RV had to be at least 15 years old, had tandem rear wheels, and was smoking, almost burning right at each rear wheel. This short, squat old-timer, about 65, got out, stomped back to the rear wheels, took a look, then got his fire extinguisher out and sprayed both wheels. I had a lot of respect for that old-timer, because there just aren't too many men that age who would take on such a challenge.

Soon we reached the top. And I mean the top. It felt like we were on top of the world. The air was clear and we could see for miles. As we looked at the vegetation and animals, I wondered what it was like in the winter, knowing that it had to be as cold as the arctic. We then started our descent down the western side of the mountains. A good part of the way I had to be in low gear, and still had to apply the brakes. With each turn in the road we were greeted with another spectacular view. We soon became euphoric from the sheer rapture that captured our eyes. It was hard for me to keep my eyes on the road. Finally we came down into the plains and the land flattened out. We made much better time then and made it all the way to Cody, the last major town before the Shoshone National Forest and Yellowstone National Park. We bedded down here for the night.

Early the next morning we started into the forest and up the east side of the Rocky Mountains. Again we were greeted with one breathtaking view after another. We stopped at a picture-perfect cascading mountain stream and hopped along the boulders and logs out into the stream. As we sat on a log and drank in the natural beauty, I felt like never leaving. This was heaven, and it certainly took quite a God to make this. Man sure couldn't.

We kept rising until we came around a upward curve, and right before our eyes was a huge lake. I just couldn't believe it. How could such a huge lake exist way up in the top of a mountain range? Yet, there it was, and it was as quiet and peaceful as a painting. The road wound along the lake until we took the turn to Old Faithful. As we pulled into the park, the place was swarming with cars and RVs. I've never seen so many RVs in my life. And even as we were driving along, it was remarkable that almost every other vehicle was an RV. We finally located a parking space, got the camera and camcorder out, and headed for the main lodge.

We checked on the estimated time of Old Faithful's next eruption, found we had some time to kill, had some lunch, and then walked out to where the geysers were. They were something we'd never seen before. They were like giant pressure cookers, letting off steam. There were many of them, some close, some far away, and all seemed to be the precursors of the big one, Old Faithful. I was running the camcorder and thought I had a fully charged battery. We were told that it could go off at any time, so I had the camcorder on and ready. But Old Faithful picked this time not to be so faithful. We waited and waited, and I kept the camcorder on and ready. Finally, my battery light came on, and before I could replace it, sure enough, here came Old Faithful. It was majestic and powerful. It rose mightily into the air well over a hundred feet, then fell back some, gathered strength, then shot even higher. We were dumb struck with fascination. This was truly one of the wonders of the world. It gnawed on me that I had driven over a thousand miles to see this and had the camcorder conk out on me at the precise instant, but still, I got to feast on it with my naked eyes. God was both beautiful and powerful.

After the eruption, we headed south on Highway 181, headed for Jackson, Wyoming, another famous spot. We passed the Grand Tetons, huge, famous mountains, and again drank in their vastness and wonders. Snake creek, the famous trout stream, meandered along the highway as we went, and we could see fishermen angling for the catch of their dreams. Jackson was very unique. It seemed to be half-way between a very old mountain town and a new popular tourist attraction. Many of the buildings were old, but also many were new and modern. We stopped to see a play about the famous "mountain men," who were a big part of this area's history, and how they hide to fight the elements and interface with the Indians. Again, the Indians were here first. How could they let the white man take such a beautiful country from them?

The next morning we followed Highway 191 south all the way down to Rock Springs on I-80. Highway 191 was a normal two-lane asphalt highway with very shallow ditches, if any, and no fences. We were literally in the wide open space of the country. As we were driving along, I noticed a big burly animal lumber across the road and slowed down. It was much too big to be a rabbit, yet too small to be a deer or small bear. As we got right up to it, it had stopped about 20 yards from the road and stood up to look up at us. It was an enormous badger, and the way it carried itself it was just daring us to come after it. No way! We kept on going.

Once on I-80 eastbound, we made much better time and were able to make it all the way to Cheyenne, Wyoming in the extreme southeastern corner of the state. Cheyenne (another Indian name) was where they held the National Rodeo Championships, a week-long affair that was in full swing when we arrived. Cheyenne was swollen to about three times its normal population, and it was difficult getting around. We finally found a parking place outside the grandstands and were able to get into a kind of state fairgrounds, where there were various booths, shows and crafts on sale. We saw some Indian dances, looked over the booths and crafts, and I talked to an author of an Indian book I eventually bought. The sun was out, even in the late evening, and it was a pleasant time for all of us.

The next morning we were well on our way home. Just one more night on the road. We started south toward Denver, but before we got too close to the city we swung east and then south so that we could avoid the city. As we were coming south, a windstorm came up and swept dust up off the flat fields so that it almost became impossible to drive. It was slow going, and for awhile I wasn't sure that the air filter might not get clogged and kill the motor. But eventually the wind gave way to rain, and that settled the dust. We got on I-70 and made it as far east as Burlington, where we bedded down for the night, our last night. There were quite a few truckers also bedded down, so I was a little more cautious with the boys. We enjoyed a good meal that night, bedded down, then in the morning drove all the way home. It seemed like an eternity had gone by since we were here last. It was quite a trip. Over 3,000 miles and some of the most beautiful sights you could see. I had been all over Europe, and believe me, good ole USA can stand up to anything the others have to offer. What a vacation!

This was the last summer that Dave, Mark, Gery and I went on our annual fishing/golfing trip together. We returned to our usual small cabin motel on Truman Lake, complete with a full kitchen and small living area. Each unit had two individual bedrooms, so we could get some sleep without someone snoring or the TV bothering anyone. I stayed with Gery, and Mark bunked with Dave.

There were a number of important traditions that had developed over the years. Somehow, a tradition of bringing something special for the other three developed. I still have a battery-operated nasal hair trimmer that I got many years ago. Gery traditionally gave out some materials from his school, such as a golf ball marker in an elaborate case. It was actually called a Magna Mark, which had been a venture that Mark had started a few years previously, and had talked Gery into buying 500 or a thousand for his school. Dave and I already had a huge supply from Mark, so this gift was a bit of a joke.

Another tradition was the annual inspection and examination of our fishing lures. Everyone brought their tackle boxes in, and we all poured over the various lures. One year Mark surprised all of us by having a custom-made rod and reel set made for each of us, complete with our names on them. Tony was along for that trip, and Mark was just glowing. It was really a great thing for him to do.

At Oak Park Mall right across from the theater where we saw quite a few movies, there was a recording store. They had the words to all kids of music and the music to accompany it. You had the chance to practice it twice, then they recorded your singing the song. I decided to record "County Road," the John Denver song, and brought it along. Gery was driving his van when we left our cabin, and I asked him to play this song. Thinking it was a professional song I liked, he stuck it in, and it started playing. It was fortunate that we weren't out on the highway yet, because when I started singing, it was so terrible that Gery just slumped over the wheel. We laughed and laughed.

From then on I always had another song recorded, and even changed the words of the music to fit our trip. But the last one was the best. This studio had expanded to the capability of making a video of whoever was performing. I really liked the song, "Sittin' On the Dock of the Bay," but the problem was that Odis Redding was a Negro. So I went down to a costume shop, bought a ship's captain hat, a black curly wig and some make-up to color my skin a very dark brown. Then, early on a Saturday morning I headed for my office, colored myself, put on the wig and cap, took along the revised words, and was the first to the mall studio. I went through a couple of practice tries; then I cut my first video.

When we played it at the reunion, we all roared; then the others took turns putting on the wig and cap, and we took a lot of pictures. Those were really fun times for me, as I'm sure they were for all my brothers. It's too bad we're just not able to do them any more.

The summer of '92 eased into the fall. Michael was now in the eighth grade at Holy Cross, making great grades. Kyle was now in the fifth grade at Dorothy Moody and was fighting his way back from the effects of the tumor. He was making slow, but steady progress. Richard was tending bar at Studebaker's, a '50s rock 'n roll bar, where he met a sweet girl, Lisa Dallam. Kurt was closing in on his electrical engineering degree. Donald was totally consumed with trying to finding a job as a pharmaceutical salesman. He put a lot into it, including researching all the companies, keeping folders on each company, and had many interviews. But by November, he still hadn't landed anything and was getting pretty frustrated. I could tell he was beginning to wonder if pharmaceutical sales was what he was really cut out for. He decided to take a shot at law school, enrolled in a pre-LSAT course in Lawrence (paid for by me), and took the exam.

Mom's health was steadily deteriorating. She was 83 and had emphysema for many years. She now was to the point that she had to have oxygen tubes in her nose permanently and had to have an oxygen tank with her wherever she went. She had nurses come in on a regular basis to check on her and had home health care come and cook for her. Mark's mother-in-law, Louise Mitchell, lived in Great Bend also, so Mark frequently visited both of them. I got a call from Mark, and he told me that he wasn't very optimistic about Mom's condition. It wasn't critical, but still, she was in the hospital. Since I hadn't been to see her in some time, I decided to go down the next weekend without Joy and the boys. It was strictly a visit-Mom trip, down one day and back the next.

Since Manhattan was about halfway there, I stopped in to see Kurt, took him and a friend or two of his to the Hibachi Hut, and then continued on to Great Bend. I pulled into the hospital at about nine in the evening, went in, found out the floor and room number and caught the elevator up. The elevator arrived at the floor and the doors opened, and right there stood Mark. He told me that Mom had taken a drastic turn for the worse, and, in fact, she was dying. At first I couldn't believe it. Then I went in to see Mom, and she was in bed with the oxygen mask on, still trying to get the oxygen to her starved lungs. Mark said she knew her time was short. My heart went out to her as I could see she was fighting for air. Gery happened to be in town as well, and our sisters, Diane, Mary and Judy, lived close enough so that they were there, too.

Mom had half of her 12 children there to help her leave this life and go into the next. I hugged her, and I guess it was too vigorous, because she asked me not to hold her so tight. She looked at the foot of the bed where Gery was standing, and said, "My baby boy." Gery said, "What?' And she repeated it. That ornery Gery made her repeat it just because Mark was sitting right there, and Mark hated it when Mom called Gery that. We all visited with her until well past midnight. Then Judy said that she planned on staying with her through the night, so most of us left. I made sure she had the phone number of the motel where I was staying, and finally crawled into bed.

About 4 a.m. I got a call from Judy, and she said I'd better get to the hospital because Mom was going fast. I hurried up, and most of the other brothers and sisters were back. We began the "death watch." The doctor had given her a sedative to help her rest; he had held off as long as he could on giving it to her, because he knew she would never wake up. Judy explained that her liver and kidneys had ceased functioning, and Mom was obviously in a deep coma. We all went over to her one by one, kissed her on the forehead and told her we loved her. She probably couldn't hear us, but we said it anyhow. The rest of her systems started to shut down, and I studied her chest. I could see the rhythmic beat of her heart push her chest ever so slightly up and down. I watched as it became fainter and fainter. Then, almost imperceptibly, it quietly stopped completely. I knew then that she was gone. There were some tears, and then I went out into the hall to the nurse's station and told them that I thought she had died. A nurse came in, checked her and then called the doctor on duty. He came, checked her and pronounced her dead. This was a formality they had to perform.

She was the first and only person I have ever watched die. As soon as the doctor pronounced her dead, the nurses came in and started stripping away all of the tubes and equipment. Finally Mom was lying there with her mouth open, as it had been for the oxygen. It was difficult for me to comprehend at first that now this body was just a "thing." It no longer had any life to it. It was no different from the chair next to the bed or the table. It was now inanimate. I was sad that she was gone, but at the same time, happy, because she had been released from her suffering. And in the last four years of her life she suffered a lot. Spinal fusion at age 80, followed by a soft full-body cast for six months, then recovery and back home. Then a fall, and hip surgery. Then, finally, this last trip to the hospital. The years of gasping for air and oxygen were now over.

I suppose when it comes my time to pass away, I'll probably fight it just like everyone else. But right now, I firmly believe that after this life, there is a heaven. And that is where God really wants us to go. That's why he made us. I believe that more firmly than anything else I believe. So, if you try to live a good life and follow God's wishes, then when you die your reward will be waiting for you. We all know that heaven is far superior to anything on earth. There is no pain and suffering there. There is complete union with God, complete bliss. So right now, the only reluctance I have in passing away is leaving behind my loved ones, or having to go before I have my kids fully raised to the point where they can take care of themselves. Other than that, I'm ready. In fact, I welcome the thought of going on to the next life. But I also know that the good Lord will decide when that is going to be. It's not going to be my call. Until then, I'll try to do what God wants me to, and I'll try to follow His lead, wherever it takes me. Bring on heaven!

The next morning I had a lot to do. I called Joy and told her the news. Next, I talked to Donald, the oldest boy living at home, and told him the news as well and gave him some man-sized tasks. Michael and Kyle needed suits, etc., so I asked him to get them to a store quickly and get them fully outfitted for the funeral. We had been poor all our lives, but, by God, all my sons were going to be in suits at my mom's funeral. All five of them. And they were.

The older brothers and sisters were already en route, and some of them didn't learn of Mom's death until they arrived. Of course, they were sad that they didn't get to see her one more time, but again, God works in his own way. About six of us went down to the funeral home to make the final arrangements for the funeral. Now, we have a great sense of humor, and by now the initial shock was over and we started cutting up. We could see that the funeral director, who was used to a crying, grieving family making the arrangements, was fighting back laughing with all his might. But finally, someone said something funny, and he just couldn't hold it back. He busted out laughing. We didn't think less of him, and that's when we got down to business and concluded the arrangements.

The funeral itself was very sad, and Mom and all 11 of her living children were there, as well as umpteen grandkids. The procession wound out to the cemetery, and finally Mom was laid at the side of Dad, this time for the last time. After everything, we all met back at Mom's small house, and we appointed Dave the administrator to wind up Mom's affairs. And he did a good job of it. As for myself, this closed a long chapter in my life. We all knew it was coming, and now it was time to move on.

Shortly after New Year's day '93, Donald came across a job opening with a small pharmaceutical firm. There were 400 applicants. Wow! He made the first cut, then the second, and was in the final running for the position. It didn't hurt that his projected boss had graduated from K State also. And all those stellar letters of recommendation from the business school and the Special Olympics now came into play. Finally, he walked in one afternoon with a letter in his hand. It was a letter offering him the job. He was grinning from ear to ear. He had finally made it. All the work of the past years had paid off. You could tell then that he was now off and running. Isn't it funny how the good Lord lets things happen when and how He wants, and that may not always be when and how we want?

Richard and Lisa decided to get married in May of '93. This was a completely new experience for me. He was the first son of mine to marry. It was a beautiful wedding. The rehearsal dinner was at the Steak 'n Ale out in Lenexa. I had discovered a bakery in Olathe which could take a photograph and place it in a computerized cake frosting machine and duplicate the picture in color in frosting on the flat cake. I selected a nice photo portrait that we had made the previous Thanksgiving. Since all my sons had suits as result of my mom's funeral, it seemed natural to have family photo portraits done while we were all together and had suits.

I felt sure Richard would pick one of his friends, Steve Grant, perhaps, to be his best man. When he told me who he wanted as his best man, I was really knocked off my feet. It was me! At first, I didn't know what to do. I'd never heard of such a thing, and my first reaction was to decline so one of his friends could have the honor. But the more I thought about it, the more I realized it was his wedding and he should call the shots. I was *deeply* honored and felt very humble. In a way, I thought this was a way in which Richard wanted to tell me what he thought of me. Believe me, it was a very rare honor, and I will always cherish it.

The wedding was beautiful, and Lisa was stunning in her wedding dress. They were married in an Episcopalian church, which religion is probably as close as you can get to the Catholics. I was honored further when Richard asked me to do one of the readings during the ceremonies. It was a good thing that both the church and the country club where the reception and dance were held had canopies, because we were hit with a persistent heavy rain. There were many relatives from both sides of the family and many, many friends. It had to be an expensive wedding, but if you plan on marrying only once, you might as well do it first class.

For many years I had been very disturbed with Joy's sister, Evelyn. Out of pure paranoia and her own inability to earn a living, she had maneuvered her father into writing a will that permitted Evelyn to own, then sell the duplex her father had bought many years before. Not too long after that, Evelyn took her mother, Helen, and little brother, Charlie, and went into hiding. Literally. She moved, left no forwarding address, had her phone unlisted, and had her mail sent to a post office box. It didn't take a rocket scientist to know that she was simply trying to hide, to keep anyone from making a claim for her father's money. She wanted to survive on that. To her, it was simply a question of self-preservation.

But I didn't like it. It effectively cut Joy off from her side of the family. Her father had passed away, and she had only a brother, Tim, in Chicago. Everybody deserves better than that.

It wouldn't do me any good to fly up to Chicago, secretly locate her, and then get in her face. After I left, she'd just move to another hiding place. So I sent her a letter, telling her that if Joy didn't hear from her mother within two weeks, I was coming to find her, and I'd be bringing the police with me. About 10 days later, Joy got a call in the middle of the day, and her mom was on the phone. She only got a few sentences out when Evelyn took the phone from her and hung up. Well, at least Joy knew her mother was still alive.

But it bothered me that Joy had no one other than Tim who was really family. So during the summer of '93 we decided to take a week's vacation driving east into Kentucky, where not only there were some great things to see, but we could also visit Joy's Uncle Louis. We headed east just at the time of the big flood, stopping first in St. Louis to see the famous Arch. It was quite a sight and had quite a story behind it. The river was swollen, and the water had risen so close to the Arch that the police had to blockade the water to keep the tourists from any harm. We continued on I-64 to Louisville, then went on to Loretto, where Louis lived. They were gracious hosts, had a nice pool in the back, and Sunday afternoon all of Louis' kids and their kids came over to Louis' house for visiting and dinner, apparently an every Sunday ritual. We mistakenly let them talk us into spending the night there, in unique antique beds, and no air conditioning. None of us got much sleep.

The next morning Louis took us all over the area, because this was the area where Joy's father, Ralph, had been raised. He showed us the house where he had lived as a boy, the very old stone church up on a hill where Joy's grandparents and dad had attended services. Then he took us to the old graveyard, where he showed us the tombstones of many of Joy's ancestors. From there, he took us to the Sisters of Loretto convent; I had heard about the Sisters of Loretto before, and it was pleasant to visit their "home office," so to speak.

That evening we declined to spend another night at their house and went on our way sightseeing. We saw the usual tourist attractions and museums, and went by famous Fort Knox. I won't cover all of the sights, because the main purpose of the trip was for Joy to see and visit some of her family.

The summer of '93, my "retirement" case ran into a snag. Mark Hutton, a senior partner in the Wichita firm, had been lead counsel. But that firm's involvement with the breast implant cases demanded more and more of his time, so that another partner, Arden Bradshaw, was appointed lead counsel. Arden was also an electrical engineer. I tried to cooperate with him as much as possible, but it wasn't long before he started knocking the case, complaining about how much work he was going to have to do and accusing me of letting important evidence get destroyed. The defense had threatened to file a motion to dismiss the case completely, on the basis of spoliation, or that Don Hochanadel had purposely or negligently allowed critical evidence to be destroyed. Because of this, Arden wanted me to accept a lower referral fee. But that didn't bother me as much as Arden did. He was extremely arrogant, as many electrical engineers are. That bothered me more than anything. An arrogant lawyer will completely turn off and alienate a jury.

So I decided to take a closer look at Arden. He scheduled a deposition in Detroit with one of the minor witnesses in the case, and I decided to attend that deposition. I went for the sole purpose of getting a feel for Arden's abilities. The deposition was a disaster. Arden seemed more interested in showing this witness how much he knew about engineering, rather than gouging out information that we needed to win the case. When I returned, I met with the client's husband, who was her legal guardian, and went over everything, telling him of my concerns. This was a very tough decision to make. It is extremely rare to change counsel in the middle of litigation, especially civil litigation. But the concerns and welfare of the client must always remain supreme over all other considerations.

Then we got news that Arden had left the Michaud firm, and this case went with him. Now I was really concerned. I told the husband I felt we had no choice but to terminate that lawyer. It was gratifying that the husband had already formed an adverse opinion of that lawyer. So I first tried to call, then faxed a letter to Arden, telling him he was relieved of the case, and asked the husband to sign it as well, so Arden knew that this was the client's decision as well. But Arden refused to be fired. So I filed a motion to compel him to turn the file over to me and for the Court to order him to cease working on the case.

It is well known that a client can fire a lawyer at any time for any reason. It has almost never happened to me, but it did happen to the Shaver firm. All you can do is give the client his file, and the terminated attorney has a lien for his time and expenses in the case. But that didn't happen here. He knew this was potentially the biggest case of his life, and he didn't want to let go. He sent letters to Judge Kelly vilifying me and the client's husband, claiming all kinds of wild things, such as conflict of interest, and on and on. Judge Kelly was the top federal judge in the state of Kansas. This case was assigned to him.

Eventually, I got a conference call from Judge Kelly's office with Arden and the defense attorney, Tom Baker, in on the call. After the judge heard our comments and said his piece, he set a hearing in Wichita and wanted both me and the husband/legal guardian to attend. The pressure was really on me. But I knew that the interests of the client had to be supreme and knew as long as that was my motivation, I didn't think I should get into too much trouble. The hearing was set for early September. It didn't help much that Joy had experienced an emotional setback, and by the time of the hearing was back in the mental ward at Shawnee Mission Medical Center. I had purchased medical coverage for an arm and a leg, so she was covered. Kyle was in the sixth grade.

I picked up the client's husband in the parking lot of the hospital where the client was admitted, and off to Wichita we went. I was under so much pressure that I was having spontaneous nosebleeds. When we arrived at Wichita, I stopped at a convenience store and bought a small package of Kleenex just in case I got a nosebleed during the hearing, and headed for the court house. Andy Hutton was there, as well as the defense counsel, Tom Baker, and, of course, Arden. Arden immediately served me with a motion he had just filed to disqualify me from representing the client. It was again filled with venom and was dangerously close to making statements that were damaging to the client.

The hearing began with the judge narrating the development of facts as he understood them, leading up to the reason for this hearing. Then Arden got up and started vilifying me again, on the record. He made various requests, including meeting in the judge's chambers with just Arden and me. I let him go on for awhile; then I stood up and told the judge that before anything else was done, it appeared to me that the first issue to be decided was whether or not Arden was still representing the client. I told the judge that, if he was terminated, he had no more right to be a part of any further litigation. The judge agreed and addressed that issue. I told the judge that I did not expect to remain as lead counsel, but expected to name replacement lead counsel within 30 days. The judge listened to me; then said he wanted to hear from the husband, the legal guardian. The husband stood right up, told the judge that he was familiar with everything that had developed, and that he did not want Arden on the case any more. That made the judge's course of action simple. Even he didn't have any choice and told Arden that he had to be guided by the client's wish, and that Arden was no longer the attorney in the case. He told him he had a quantum meruit lien for his time and expenses, told him to file it with the court, and to turn the file over to me. Then he ended the hearing.

After the judge had left, despite the obviously personal attack on me, I decided to take the high road and offered to shake Arden's hand. He had a vengeful look on his face, called me slime and refused to shake my hand. It stunned his former partner, Andy Hutton, who flat out told Arden he wasn't being very professional.

We walked outside, where the husband and I visited with Andy for awhile. Then finally, Andy told us off the record that the firm actually had to fire Arden for the same reasons that I had to fire him.

Now they tell me! I had to go through all that anguish, using my sole judgment as a guide throughout this whole affair. It sure would have made it easier if I had known that others felt the same way I did. It was about three o'clock when we left Wichita. Joy was in the hospital, and Michael was staying after school because he was playing football, so that meant that Kyle was going to be arriving home on the school bus in about half an hour. He was going to be home alone, a thought I didn't relish. If something happened, there wasn't an adult near that could be reached until I got back from Wichita, a good two-and-a-half hour drive. It made the trip back miserable, but when I got back Kyle was okay, and I could start trying to unwind.

As a kind of an epilogue, about a week later I got a call from Tom Baker, the defense counsel, and during the course of the conversation he pointed out that I was now lone lead counsel and asked me to hold off naming new lead counsel. He wanted to try to get with the other defendants and try to get a settlement offer of $5 million on the table, pointing out that if we could settle it, I "wouldn't have to share the fee, and could keep it all myself." I've done enough fee calculations to know that this amounted to a fee for me of over a million dollars. So, in effect, he was wanting a chance to put together an offer that would make me over a million dollars. Sounds nice, doesn't it? The only problem was that I felt the case was worth substantially more than $5 million to the client, and I didn't want to sell the client down the river for my own personal gain. I just couldn't live with myself doing that. So I was non-committal and proceeded with locating new lead counsel. After lining up the top heavy-hitters, the client chose taking the case right back to the Michaud firm.

I don't hold it against Joy, but she spent almost two weeks in the hospital, and she really liked it. It was an escape for her from all her duties and responsibilities. She had arts and crafts in the afternoons, and they scheduled little outings in the afternoons she really enjoyed. She even made friends with her roommate. It was complete freedom from responsibility. I will tell you that many were the times that I wished I could take a week or two and just walk away from my responsibilities. But, so far, it has not been meant to be, and frankly,

I don't know whether I could handle it. If you get so used to it, it might be nearly impossible to let go. But maybe one of these days.

Kurt finished his degree in December of '93, and back to Manhattan we all went for another graduation and another meal at the Hibachi Hut. Occasionally, Kurt showed me some of the technical reports he had to do for his classes, and it was well beyond my comprehension. It was clear to me that Kurt was blessed with a special mathematics talent that most of us just don't have.

Like all of my sons, Kurt loved to hunt and fish. He had made good money during the summer months working for the City of Overland Park, doing street maintenance. Donald was the one who originally found this job and left management with a favorable impression. Kurt's real emphasis was on hunting. He had an old Remington shotgun and went after all the usual birds, Canadian geese, mallards, pheasants, and on and on. I now know that when hunting season came around, classes and studying came in a distant second. Still, when something was due, he'd work around the clock and get it in on time. He wasn't really concerned with getting a high grade point average. He just wanted to graduate. Knowing his great love for hunting, I bought him a very expensive Italian-made Binelli spring-loaded shotgun. It was lighter than the usual shotgun, and you could fire off five shots in under a second. His eyes really lit up when he saw that. Kurt doesn't like to telegraph his feelings very much, but I could see that I nailed just the gift for him. Since then, I've heard endless stories of his "doubles" and "trips," "trips" meaning knocking down three birds with one shot. Over the years he has accumulated a large inventory of decoys of every size and nature.

I now had three sons with college degrees. If you were to ask me to this day how we accomplished that, I couldn't answer you. I guess as time goes on, you really don't look behind to see what you have done. You're always looking forward to see what is left to do. That was the way I was raised. But still, there are times when you do pause, look back and take some pride in your accomplishments. These boys getting through college wasn't really my accomplishment, but theirs. Sure, I gave each of them a nudge of help here and there, but they are the ones who got it done. My satisfaction was the pride I had in their accomplishments.

So now Kurt set about looking for a job. Engineering jobs are very different than the type of job that Donald was after. Kurt's electrical engineering degree was in a very narrow field involving power transmission (I think). My initial concept of EE was that now he could take apart and repair anything electrical. I soon found out that is third grade EE. He was in a much more sophisticated level. His job hunting technique amounted to watching the papers, making calls, and not as aggressive as I would have hoped. But who am I? It was his life and his job to find. He wasn't interested in working for any of the large engineering firms, because he knew a number of those people and was told that they hired you for a very narrow function, and as soon as the project was finished, frequently you were laid off and starting the job hunting process all over again.

No, Kurt wanted an engineering job in technical sales. Now this floored me. Kurt had never been one to model the latest clothes and was a very husky person. His shoulders had filled out into a size 52 or 54. If he were to put on one of my suit coats, chances are he would rip off the sleeves. I often felt that his size alone would scare people into being afraid to turn him down. Nor was he the epitome of organization. But deep down he knew what he wanted and stuck to his guns, as the months rolled by.

Spring break of '94 was coming, and with just the two youngest sons left in school, I decided that it was finally time that we took a real spring break, not only for the kids, but for Joy and me. I had just settled a good case or two, so I had some funds. After a lot of discussion with the kids, we decided to go to Orlando, Florida. We booked round-trip tickets, rented a nice condominium and a new Mercury Grand Marquis. It was first class all the way, We were going to do it right. We spent a full day at Universal Studios, where we went through some very elaborate rides, like "Earthquake." We rode the boat in the "Jaws" lake, walked down the streets, catching the 1950s rock 'n roll act, and then the "Blues Brothers." Those guys were great, and people were actually asking for autographs. Their act was right out of the movie, and I really enjoyed it. There were many other Hollywood type attractions, too numerous to mention.

We also spent a full day at Sea World, seeing all of the exotic sea creatures, and had a lot of fun with the pool where the manta rays swam freely near the crowd. They were tame enough to feed and would actually come right up to you to feed and let you feel them. We had special reservations for the Hawaiian luau. This was an opulent feast of Hawaiian food, followed by a full show of Hawaiian dancers. They were phenomenal. The girls had hips that were very fluid and arms that swayed with the beautiful music. The male dancers were quite athletic and skilled, especially when they started dancing in the dark with burning staffs. We topped that day off with the famous laser show and fireworks display. I had never seen a laser show, and that was a sight I'll never forget.

We spent another full day at the Epcot Center seeing all of its attractions, such as the various foreign country sections, where you could eat their food and listen to their unique music. The AT&T section had a complete history of communications right up to the exploration of space. The I-Max theater was spectacular. We also spent a day driving over to Cocoa Beach, where we waded out into the Atlantic. Then we went to Kennedy Space Center and went through the space exhibits, where the history of our space program was shown to us. I started chatting with one of the doormen, and he told me that business was way down. I was curious as to why, and he said that the recent murders of foreigners in the Miami area had received so much international coverage, that many Europeans had dropped Florida from their vacation plans. He said that they usually had more foreigners come through there than Americans.

This turned out to be the best vacation we had ever taken. We were literally on the go every single day, getting out of the condo by nine in the morning and frequently returning well after eight in the evening. On our last evening there we ate at a famous sea food buffet that advertised all the crab legs and lobster tails you could eat. It was $20 a head, but the way Kyle and I like crab and lobster, we really got our money's worth. That Kyle – get him near shrimp, crab meat or lobster tails, and he can eat forever. A bottomless pit. After we flew back, it was great to be home again. We were totally exhausted from the sheer fun and excitement. A final touch to the vacation was the house when we returned. Kurt had given the whole house a complete cleaning while we were gone. Everything was put away where it belonged, and the house was neat as a pin. That was really a pleasant surprise.

At the end of the '93-'94 school year, Kyle was finishing up his last year at elementary school. Each member of his science class had to do a project which would be put on display during an evening's open house. The students had to stay with their projects and answer any questions the parents or visitors might have. Kurt took Kyle under his wing, and together the two of them constructed a window alarm. It included all the wiring and connections, so that when the window was raised, an alarm went off. On the night of the open house, Kyle was one of the few boys dressed in a sports coat. He really looked sharp. He had grown quite a bit and was now getting tall. All of the teachers were extremely impressed at how well Kyle understood his project and how easily and eloquently he answered all questions. I took some photos to capture this beautiful moment. I will always be grateful for the help that Kurt gave Kyle on that project. It had to be a big confidence booster for Kyle.

I had been selected the administrator of the 1994 Hochanadel family reunion. Brother Dave had put together the most extensive package I had ever seen on all of the members of the families. It not only included names, addresses, dates of birth, but the names of grandkids, great grandkids, and on and on. It was really a precious source of information, and I know he must have spent weeks on it. I sent out letters to everyone, asking them to tell me both the best location and date for the reunion. This resulted in Kansas City being picked as the location, as well as the date of the last week in June.

Gery had resigned in early '94 from his presidency of Jefferson Community College in Hillsboro, just south of St. Louis, and had moved to Grandview, Missouri, a suburb of Kansas City. This provided a great opportunity for him and me and our wives to have a good number of lunches together. We ate at all of the fine places, EBT, Tatsu's, La Mediterranee, and really enjoyed the family companionship. Gery had negotiated a good settlement of his contract, so he had plenty of time to look for another job. The stress of the Hillsboro job had caused him to gain a lot of weight, so this gave him the chance to take off a lot of it. And he did.

These lunches spawned many a prank and ideas for the reunion. Perhaps the greatest prank was the "Chester" prank we played on Mark. Mark had always been a little sensitive about losing his hair. Gery's daughter, Renee, was at Kansas State getting a degree in theater. She was in a production that came to Johnson County Community College, one that we attended and were impressed with. The night before the production Renee brought a bunch of her classmates over to Gery's house and also brought a wig from the production. This wig was worn by an actor dressed up as an old man with very thin, long hair. In fact, it made him appear almost bald. Gery put this wig on and contorted his face in some of the most grotesque ways. It was a sight to see. They took a number of pictures of him with the wig, and when Gery brought the pictures to one of our lunches, we died laughing.

Then we thought of Mark and his sensitiveness over losing hair. The wheels turned, and I got the negatives from Gery. Then I had 11 x 14 photos made of three or four of them. God, were they grotesquely funny! I brought them to the next lunch, and we laid out our prank. From time to time Mark and Luann came down from Omaha and joined us for lunch. On a previous visit we all six had dinner at EBT's, and Luann had the best steak she had ever eaten. So we suggested they come down for lunch at EBT's. They gladly accepted the invitation, so now the stage was set.

By now, Gery and I were well enough known by the staff at EBT and had made them laugh so often, we felt they would go along with this prank. I arrived early with this framed 11 x 14 portrait of "Chester," and coaxed the head waitress to hide it behind the checkout counter. Then I persuaded her to wait until we were well into our meal, then asked her to come over to our table with this "Chester" picture hidden from view and stop at Mark. At this point, she was to strike up a conversation with Mark about how much he looked like a relative of hers, known as "Chester." She was willing to go along with it. After all, we were fun repeat customers.

So we sat down and began our lunch, the food was great, and the conversation was light and fun. Then along came the head waitress with "Chester's" picture, holding it so Mark couldn't see it. Then she stopped at Mark and commented on how much he looked like her cousin, "Chester." Well, Mark had a well-developed sense of humor as well, so he said that, no, he wasn't Chester; his name was Lester. Then the head waitress said that, no, she was certain he was Chester, and she had Chester's picture right there to prove it. She then turned the portrait around and handed it to Mark. Mark had fallen for it hook, line and sinker. He tried to be gentlemanly about it. He didn't have any choice. This was a very exclusive restaurant, and Luann was laughing as well. Pretty soon his face started getting pink, then as time went on, it got completely red. You could tell that inside he was boiling, but he couldn't let it out. Later he told us that he was mad as hell, and he is still sensitive about it and doesn't like it to brought up. The next few times we called Mark we made sure his kids asked him about "Chester."

But that wasn't the end of it. I still had another framed 11" x 14" portrait of Chester. Mark and Gery were supposed to come by my office the next day. So I took this second portrait of Chester to my office and talked the receptionist into hanging it in a prominent place in the receptionist area. I had her coached so that as soon as Mark and Gery showed up, she immediately got up and shook Mark's hand, saying, "You must be Chester." Mark was stopped dead in his tracks. Then she pointed to the portrait and said, "See, I've even got a picture of you here in my office." Mark looked at it, and then his eyes closed and his head dropped forward with his chin slumping to his chest. There was nothing he could say. This was a double whammy, and it went off perfectly. I'm not sure Mark will ever forgive us for this, and now it looks like it will be perpetual.

At one of these lunches with Gery and our wives, we got to

talking about trying to come up with something to spice up the fun of the reunion. Then it dawned on me, and I blurted out, "Elvis." What a reaction it would be for all of our relatives if Elvis appeared at our reunion. The more I thought about it, the more the idea grew. I swore Joy, Gery and Joyce to total secrecy.

In my next letter on the reunion, I told everyone that there would be an international celebrity show up at the reunion. I told them he was a very well-known celebrity and insisted on secrecy. Everyone was advised to bring cameras, pens for autographs and camcorders. Then I set about getting ready. I couldn't find a costume shop that had the Elvis outfit I wanted. But there was one on Troost that wanted to add another Elvis outfit to their inventory, but couldn't find a good picture of Elvis. They wanted to duplicate the "Aloha from Hawaii" outfit, but couldn't find it. I had bought that video a year or two earlier, so I loaned it to them, and they made the uniform to fit me. That is quite a chore, because I was six foot tall, 260. So I wasn't your typical scarecrow. They had the wig, shoes, everything. I had sunglasses, but I had a mustache. I knew the mustache had to go for the surprise to be complete.

I had rented the dining hall next to Holy Cross School. It had enough chairs, tables and even a kitchen, so the location was great. It even had a private parking lot out front. We were expecting about a hundred relatives, literally from coast to coast and border to border. But best of all, my law office was only about four blocks away on 95th Street. Then I reserved a long white stretch limousine to meet me at a specified time at my office. I had also previously purchased the CD of Elvis on the "Aloha" show. I had a five-disc CD player at my office with double tape capabilities, so I put together an entrance tape for Elvis, consisting of the "Star Wars" introduction, followed by the awesome drums and orchestra entrance music. This latter part I repeated on the tape about 10 times, because I expected to do some pretty fancy prancing when I got out of the limo.

I had Elvis' outfit at my office the day before the reunion, shaving equipment, a boom box with the tape set so all the driver of the limo had to do was hit the "play" button, and a towel to set the boom box on, and a set of sunglasses. I had made arrangements for Gery to bring Renee to my office to apply the make-up. So we were all set. I even rented a fake wireless microphone for $10 and had a white silk scarf. Then I started practicing Elvis' moves during his song, "Suspicious Minds" on the video down in our basement. It was one of my all-time favorites, and I intended to sing that song at the reunion, so I wanted the moves down pat.

The mystery of who the celebrity was, was driving some of my brothers and sisters crazy. They all wanted to know who it was going to be. Dianne even attempted to bribe Michael and Kyle with money to get them to tell, but they wouldn't give in. I got word that Daisy Lancaster, the last living sibling of my dad, was going to celebrate her 80th birthday, so Elvis planned on singing happy birthday to her. None of her five kids knew anything about this.

I had obtained special rates at a Holiday Inn not far from the hall, and many of the out-of-town relatives stayed there. Fortunately, Dave and Lyla came up from Texas a few days before the reunion, and we met at the hall to set up. Largely through their help, we decided to set up a buffet so everyone could eat at the hall and not have to go out to eat. They were a very big help. I was just trying to handle too much, and thank God they picked up on that and pitched in. That night many of us met at the Holiday Inn to meet and break the ice with those we hadn't seen in a long time. That's really when the reunion started.

Then the day of the reunion came, and everything was in place. We all arrived at the hall and started visiting. There were relatives from California and Illinois that most of us hadn't seen in decades. People kept arriving as time went on, and then we set up the buffet, and everyone went through the line and sat down to eat. Toward the end of the meal, Dave had a great suggestion that we start at the back of the hall and have everyone introduce themselves, so everyone knew everyone. There were a lot of humorous quips made while all this was going on. The Hochanadel sense of humor was funning rampant.

At the appointed time I casually slipped out to my car and quietly headed to my office. I went into the bathroom and shaved off my mustache. I changed into the Elvis outfit, just as Gery and Renee arrived. Gery took one look at me and almost fell on the floor laughing. He knew this was going to be great. Then they left and my limousine arrived at my office. I had rented him for two hours, so we didn't have to push things. I carefully went over what we were going to do, and even he started getting into the spirit. I had him put the towel and boom box where he could get it, and then we took off.

We pulled into the private parking lot, and I told him to drive very slowly around the parking lot a couple of times to give those inside the chance to see the limo. People started pouring out of the hall, armed with cameras, camcorders, pens and paper. They couldn't see inside the limo, and the looks of expectation were just unbelievable. The driver stopped the limo just in front of the hall, calmly placed the towel on top of the limo, took out the boom box and punched the "play" button. The "Star Wars" introduction started picking up steam, and the crowd was braced with anticipation. The driver had his handle on the door, and as soon as the drums and orchestra part came, he pulled open the door, and *out stepped Elvis!* The relatives roared, cameras clicked everywhere, and camcorders were whirling. Everyone had the biggest smiles on their faces. I took a few strutting steps, and damned if my belt didn't drop around my ankles. I quickly pulled it up and went on. That just added more laughs.

I pranced back and forth to the music and swaggered like Elvis, stopping every now and then to strike an Elvis prose. Finally, we went inside. Now came the surprises I had planned. I set up the boom box, got the microphone, and had Daisy step forward in front of everyone. I asked her to sit on a chair, told her I had heard she had just turned 80. I then knelt down and sang "Happy Birthday" to her, giving her my white silk scarf. Her five kids, who hadn't been to many reunions didn't know this was coming and were really beaming. Then I told everyone I had a tight schedule, but I could do one song for them. I punched the tape for "Suspicious Minds" and started mimicking and imitating Elvis. The crowd roared at some of the moves, and I think I managed to kiss every girl and sister in the hall. Cameras flashed right and left. God, was everyone having a great time!

But I wasn't done yet. After that song I invited Daisy and her five kids to a limo ride around Overland Park. None of them knew this was coming either. I took them through Corporate Woods, showing them the many modernistic office buildings along College Boulevard, and then stopped in front of Dick Clark's American Bandstand and posed for pictures with them. We returned, and then I took all my family on a limo ride. The limo was costing some good bucks, so I wanted them to get something out of it. At 91st and Lowell, some kids had set up a lemonade stand, so I had the driver pull over, and Elvis got out and bought some lemonade. This was a five-way stop intersection, with a fair amount of traffic. Cars started stopping and gawking at Elvis and his white limo. It was way out of place. At the stop sign next to us there was a cute blond in a convertible who stopped, taking all this in. Soon cars started honking, and I looked over at her. She blew me a kiss, and I blew one back, and then she took off. We got back in, and then I had the driver take us back.

Elvis stayed around the hall for pictures with different groups, and Daisy made him autograph the silk scarf so she could show it to her girlfriends back in Wichita. Then I had Gery take me down to my office, where I changed back into my clothes and returned to the reunion. One of the oddest things about the Elvis act was that for a little while, Joy wasn't sure it was me. Shaving my mustache had thrown her off. All in all, everyone had a great time. But the truth is, I probably had more fun than anyone else. It was the best reunion ever. A few weeks later, I received a large envelope in the mail from Linda Hochanadel in Palm Springs, and she sent me an authentic French silk scarf, with a sweet message. I also received a lot of thank you cards from Daisy's kids, and one of the relatives from Illinois even sent me a couple of small sofa pillows that had sunflowers all over them.

Kurt's efforts to find a job weren't producing a job. I know this was pretty frustrating to him, as it was to me. I knew exactly how he felt. Nothing is more frustrating than to have a lot of talent and ability, *but nowhere to use it.* Kurt had this impressive degree and was a hard worker, but he just didn't have the job. He had been looking for a job for over a year and still hadn't found anything, when he ran across an opening right smack in his field. It even turned out that the person who was going to be his boss had gone to school with Richard, and also knew Donald. He was English, as was his father who also worked with this firm. This gave Kurt the inside track, and he had the remaining credentials, so he finally got the job in his field, starting February 1, 1995. His stubbornness had proven out. He had to wait for the job that was in his field or give up his whole college education. Fortunately, his judgment was right, and he is still working there today. Once again, the good Lord sometimes gives you what you want, but not always when you want it. I was really glad, because now, not only did I have three sons through college, but they also had jobs in their fields. Now the three oldest sons were completely self-sufficient.

Getting back to my retirement case, after firing Arden Bradshaw and new lead counsel was appointed, the first step was to get the court to deny the defense motion to dismiss the case on the basis of spoliation of evidence. I took a lot of flak from the defense counsel, even during formal pleadings, and they took my deposition for a full day. But there was nothing there for them, because I simply hadn't done anything wrong. A year and a half later, and after reams of pleadings and affidavits, the judge summarily denied the defense's motion, and the case was set for trial in June of '95.

I had been working on this case for five and a half years. I had left Shaver's firm partly to protect it. I went through the hell of terminating Arden Bradshaw. A lot of my soul was in this case. I had seen the client in the neurological hospital many times, and especially because she had no concept of what was happening, that heightened my sense of duty and responsibility to her. Arrangements had to be made and approved by the Johnson County probate court to rent a furnished apartment for the client's husband to stay during the trial, something that I had to do. I even got the probate court to allow an expenditure of literally thousands of dollars to fly the client by helicopter ambulance down to Wichita for the trial, even though at the last minute lead counsel decided not to take her to Wichita, feeling that the jury might feel it was a effort at sympathy.

We had about three hours of videotape of a typical day in the life of the client in the hospital. Lead counsel asked me to put together a "Day in the Life" video of the client to introduce into evidence and show to the jury. I spent a whole day at the video shop working with their technologist, and produced a one-hour tape of the most important aspects of her care, starting with her being awakened, then getting food, medications, cleaning of the trach tube, her different therapies, physical, speech, occupation, etc., and then to bed at night. It was a very accurate description of her life as it was right before trial.

In June of 95 the trial started. The courtroom was as big as a cathedral; after all, this was the courtroom of the top federal judge in Kansas. There were actually three levels. The first level was our level, and we had close to 60 boxes of documents and exhibits, all categorized so that if our lawyer wanted a document, the paralegal could pull up the location on the computer and go right to the box, retrieve it, and have it in the hands of the lawyer literally in seconds. The next level was right in front of the judge where the witness stand and court reporter sat. The third level was where the judge's bench rested. It certainly placed the judge in the highest position of prominence in the whole room.

There were damn good lawyers on both sides. We had Chris Christian, Mark Hutton and Chan Townsley from the Michaud firm, as well as myself. Baker had about four lawyers on his side, not including the senior corporate counsel for the van manufacturer. Jury selection started, and the defense succeeded in showing our "Day in the Life" film to the prospective jurors. This was a good move on the defense's part, because it eliminated those jurors who said they just couldn't cast a vote against that poor woman after they had seen the video.

We then started with our fact witnesses, then moved through our expert witnesses. And we had a ton of them. Our seat expert testified for three days, our biomechanical expert for two days, and our glass expert, with a doctorate from MIT, completely blew away the defense's contention that our client had somehow banged her head on the front windshield. Mark Hutton put on the appropriate medical experts to testify that she had a normal life expectancy and that the future medical costs would be well above $15,000,000. We finally rested our case, seeking damages around $20,000,000.

I didn't stay around for much of the defense's case, which was fairly short compared to the length of our case. The bulk of their case was one expert, who had testified hundreds of times for the automotive industry. The defense brought into court an actual van, even though it was cut down and not on wheels. This expert had the jurors sit in the van and explained his theories of the movement of our client's body during the accident. He was very smooth and had been asked every possible question a hundred times, so he was extremely well prepared and smooth.

We countered that testimony by bringing an actual identical van to the courthouse, and the judge allowed the jurors to go out, sit in it, look around, see where the seats were, etc. Our lead counsel thought this effectively countered their experts' testimony.

Finally, the defense rested, and closing arguments were set for a Friday morning. I made the trip down to Wichita, hopefully for the last time. We had worked hard for a very long time, and I prayed that the jury would respond to us favorably. The closing arguments were well done by both sides, and we broke for lunch. The husband and I had already checked out from his apartment because it was a Friday, and if jury deliberations were going to continue, they would go into the following week. We had lunch with the lawyers from the Michaud firm. We tried to be loose and optimistic, but inside out stomachs were churning.

After lunch, the husband and I went back to the firm's office to wait for whatever was going to happen. It was now in the hands of the jury. That woman's fate was now their call. We had done everything we could. The firm had spent almost $250,000 in litigation expenses on this case, a record, I think, for them. Surely, the Lord would smile on her. I know, we all had a vested dollar interest in the case, but to us that was secondary to the client's. Some cynics will sneer at that, but it is true. All our motives were right. We should win.

About three that afternoon a call came through that the jury had reached a verdict. That was too quick. We all knew right then that we had lost. If we had won, they would have taken a lot longer, especially in calculating the damages. The trip to the courthouse was made with very heavy hearts. The judge brought in the jury, and yes, the verdict was for the defense. We had lost. I turned to the client's husband, and told him I was sorry. Then, as a gentleman, I walked over and congratulated the defense attorneys. That was difficult, especially after their personal attacks on me claiming that I had willfully destroyed evidence. But I was determined to retain my integrity and class, regardless of all that. We returned to the firm's office in a state of shock. There wasn't much any of us could say right then, the disappointment was so great. The husband and I said good-bye to the firm and started the long road home, each in our own vehicles. I pulled into our driveway and sat in the car for a few minutes before going in. It was not going to be any fun telling the family that we lost, that our "retirement" case was gone. They took it very well, and it was a source of consolation to look into their eyes and see the hurt that they were also feeling over my loss. There was a lot of empathy there, and it meant a lot to me.

As I write this, I don't really know if I'll ever really get over losing that case. I know it left me stunned for a very long time, and to this day I am still stunned. I suppose there is a healing process that has set in and the wounds are slowly scarring over. That was one of the hardest jolts I've ever taken, especially since I went through so much hell for that woman. But no matter how much it hurts, life goes on ....

16

OVERLAND PARK, KANSAS, 1995-1996
(End of First Life, Start of Second Life)

I ORIGINALLY NAMED the book *One Of Lonk's Kids.* My dad's nickname was "Lonk," and in a way I felt I was an extension of him, so he should have the honor. I startedthis book in July of '95 and wrote when I had time. There were some faint monetary motives, so I went to the library and reviewed *The Writer's Market* and other resource books. After I had written the first three or four chapters, I started sending out copies to various publishers and editors. Soon the stack of rejections made it clear that unless you were *SOMEBODY,* they were just not interested. I did get a few positive responses along the lines that I had lived an interesting life, but from a marketing viewpoint there wasn't much value. Still, that didn't stop me. I guess I'm too stubborn to give up easily. I continued writing and slacked off on marketing the book. As I wrote on, things started happening to me.

On March 13, 1996, Kyle was confirmed at Holy Cross Church. Donald was his sponsor, and Archbishop James P. Keleher, S.T.D. performed the confirmation. As I sat there in the pew with Joy, Michael and Richard, I was really proud of Kyle, because I could remember his tumor days when we thought his years were few. I was also proud of Donald, because he came over to our house around 4 p.m., helped Kyle get ready, took him out to eat, and saw to it that both of them arrived at the church by the appointed time. This was the last son to be confirmed, and I could sense that this was a subtle reminder that the last of our kids was growing up. It gave me a twinge of regret, but that was followed by a sea of pride.

During the fall of '95 there was an announcement at mass that it was the "chain of life" day, and we were asked to join in the human chain of people lining up along both sides of 95th street, the major east-west street in our city. I decided to participate and arrived at our designated parking area, picked up our pro-life signs and proceeded to the area we were asked to stand. It was a very uplifting experience. Both sides of the street for miles was lined with all these people of all ages, holding up signs for the passing cars to read and encouraging them to respect life. I was strangely exhilarated. I felt a rush of goodness. I hadn't ever felt that feeling in my life before. I was outwardly and openly doing something for the Lord. Now I had a slight glimpse of how the apostles must have felt.

After the allotted time elapsed, we returned home. But something was stirring in my heart. I even talked to Joy later about the chain and asked her how she felt while standing on the side of the street. She said she felt different, too. The stirring in my soul eventually led me to the realization that for all these many years since the *Roe v. Wade* decision, I had been sitting in the stands and casually watching the battle between pro-abortion and pro-life opponents. In October of '95 our pastor gave a full sermon on the March '95 encyclical of Pope John Paul on the "Gospel of Life." I was literally thrilled by what he said, to the point that I asked him for a copy of the sermon. All he had were his notes, but he was willing to give them to me, and I still have them. After glancing over them, I stuck them in a file at my office.

Over the past 30 years or so, I had been aware of the deterioration of the family unit. I knew the divorce rate had escalated to the extent that marriage was now no more than a formal "tryout." I also knew that if there were children involved, then they were the ones who suffered the most. To me, the greatest tragedy in any family situation was a young child whose parents got divorced. Generally, the kid had to be confused, was torn between his mother and father, both of whom were competing for the child or else trying to convince the child that he or she was the "good parent." I feel very sorry for these children, because they grow up learning to be suspicious of, or in virtual fear of most adults, reluctant to fully give their affection to any adults, and lacked the examples of all the important things like commitment, love, dedication, self-giving and caring. Children are the true victims of any divorce.

When Clinton was elected President, I felt the nation's morals had hit an all-time low. I had avoided deep involvement in politics and still avoid them as much as possible. But watching this man in office, I realize that it took a sick nation to allow him to be elected. He was pro-abortion, and that was something I disagreed with strongly. I felt the true reason he was pro-abortion was simply because he felt that he would get more votes with that position. I was convinced that he had no personal morals, no personal principles that he stuck to, come hell or high water. His character and credibility were zero. He was the antithesis of a true leader; everything he did was dictated by the number of votes he could get. He was a pure political animal.

After the first of the year in '96, a number of things started happening to me that drew me closer to the pro-life struggle. While I was writing this autobiography, I came to the part where I included the essay that my dad wrote in 1952, "(No) More Than One To a Customer." Only this time I read it with a lot more understanding. When I compared the thoughts my dad had in this 1952 essay to the present condition of the world, regarding children and life, only then did I begin to realize just how great a man my dad was. My love and respect for him zoomed. I was at the same time even more saddened that I had not known him better and hadn't had the chance to spend more time with him, one on one. I now knew that he had been a very great man, born before his time, and that his ideals were exactly the ideals that this country really needed today. They were values of the sanctity of life and true family values. This experience nudged me even closer to the pro-life conflict.

While this was kicking around in my mind, someone approached me to participate in a golf marathon to raise funds for the pro-life movement. I attended a meeting at the "Kansans For Life" office for the golfers and got all the usual information. But what I didn't expect to get was a feeling that these people had been fighting this battle for many years, while I had been sitting up in the stands, watching. Why wasn't I at the front, fighting with all my strength for what I knew to be right? It was only then that I started to realize the heritage that Dad and Mom left me. The call to arms was now getting much stronger.

As a golfer in the marathon, I had to solicit sponsors who would agree to contribute so much per hole for each hole I golfed. We were told we had to golf 100 holes. At first I laughed at this, because that amount of holes was virtually impossible for me. The most I had ever done was 27 back in '89, when Mom had her operation. But they explained that we would all ride carts, that we had the entire course to ourselves for the whole day, and there were some "special" rules that applied. For example, you never looked for lost balls, and if your ball was within a yard of the cup, it was considered in the cup, and you played through as much as possible.

So now my work was really cut out for me. I had to start looking for sponsors. This didn't bother me too much, because back when my kids were in the various little leagues, I had done a lot of soliciting for sponsors for their teams. It didn't bother me to ask for money. I had been accustomed all my life to being turned down and had encountered so many personal adversities that a refusal to sponsor me didn't phase me at all. We were told that they wanted each of us to raise $2,500. Wow $2,500! Were these people crazy? That's a lot of money. But who knows until you try, so I started.

I've never been one to do anything halfway. Michael was a junior at Aquinas, a Catholic high school, and I knew many of these people had quite a bit of money. So I called the new president and asked if she would let me have a set of labels for all the families with students at Aquinas, and she was very happy to give them to me. I then drafted a letter to them, had envelopes printed, as well as return envelopes and pledge slips. My whole family pitched in and helped me stuff the envelopes, and Kansans For Life handled the postage.

Then I thought about the parish and asked the pastor if he would give me a set of labels, too. I was disappointed when he declined. I couldn't understand it. Here was a very legitimate cause. I fully expected him to be all for it. But he wasn't. He explained that he frequently got requests from realtors and other such commercial or mercenary entities, with promises of sharing the "profits" with the parish, and he just had a policy of refusing to give the labels out for any reason. I told him that this was for pro-life, but it didn't make any difference. Then I asked him if he had any problem with me hiring someone to address the envelopes, using the addresses in our parish directory, and he was even against that. He said that such a thing was not the purpose of the directory. Now I was really confused. Hearing this, I started questioning just how pro-life he really was and started suspecting that maybe pro-abortion Catholics were getting to him, and he was afraid of lower Sunday collections. But that really wasn't my problem. My job was to raise funds to stop abortions, and if it ruffled the pastor's feathers somewhat, tough.

I had periodically used an outside typist for a couple of years to do work for me, and she was set up to do the addressing through her computer system. The secretarial service at my office was just a few months old, and their receptionist had quite a bit of free time. I know that some people just hate sitting and doing nothing, so her boss said it was okay if she addressed envelopes to make the time go faster. Between the two of them, they addressed over 2,000 envelopes. I had to draft a different letter to the parishioners and print both envelopes and return envelopes. All in all, before I knew it, I had about $400 of my own money invested in it. We were struggling financially, but I felt the Lord would see to it that we were taken care of; after all, He had done so for well over 30 years. We forged ahead and got another 2,000 letters out to the parishioners.

About the same time as all this was going on, I had been attending noon meetings of the juvenile bench/bar at the county courthouse. I wanted to get involved to see what I could do to help the plight of today's kids and to get a better handle on what was really going on in the juvenile court system. The juvenile courts are closed to the public, so you just can't walk in and watch. An old friend, whose son I had coached one year in little league basketball, was the chairman. I learned that this committee had been providing speakers to the various high schools to meet with the detention students and try to help them avoid more serious problems. This intrigued me for many reasons. First, it was a captive audience, and secondly, I felt the best way to prevent youths from getting into trouble with the law was to get to them before they broke the law and let them know what the law could and would do to them if they broke it.

So my friend gave me the names of some of the high school liaisons, and I started calling them. This was new turf for me, and I was starting virtually from scratch. I decided to try to contrast the world they were growing up in with the one I grew up in. My presentation was to contrast such things as music, cars, forms of entertainment, sexually transmitted diseases, now versus then, and things of that nature. I rented some old radio show tapes from the library and made copies of Red Skelton, the Lone Ranger, the Whistler and others. I had some 30-year-old LP albums that I brought along, a copy of the latest *Sports Illustrated* swimsuit edition, and some newspaper advertising of men's and women's underwear.

I let the students know that at any time, if any of them had any questions, they were to just raise their hands and I would try to answer them. The whole thrust of my presentation was that my age group had allowed the morals of our society to erode to the point that these kids were growing up in a very dangerous minefield of moral danger. I apologized to them for the atmosphere that my generation had created for them, and stated that I was there to help them through the years ahead of them. I told them they ran the risk of AIDS, a disease that didn't even exist when I was their age. I told them about my family and read my father's essay, trying to emphasize the concept of two-parent families. I gave them a heavy emphasis on morals, showed them the *Sports Illustrated* swimsuit edition, pointing out today's preoccupation with sex. I covered the beer commercials which seemed to say that the only way to have fun is by drinking.

I drafted a questionnaire for them to complete, because I wanted to start compiling my own data as to what really made these kids tick. The questions focused on what was important to them, where they wanted to be five years from now, what they liked the most, what they hated the most, and similar questions. Many of them were sincere in their answers, but there were still the few who openly rebelled against everything.

What I started finding out was both gratifying and shocking. Many of the kids were level-headed, and their responses on the questionnaire showed that they had the right priorities. Others did not, or gave answers that were obviously crazy. I told them that abstinence is the only true way to avoid pregnancy, and I beat that drum very hard. Occasionally, I had young girls come up to me after the sessions and thank me, telling me that they appreciated my time, and that I had made a definite impression on them. Some of my presentations lasted three hours, but none less than an hour. Occasionally, I had to tolerate complete disinterest from some of the students, but I didn't let that hold me back. If I could help just one kid, it was worth it.

The most shocking incident occurred at Blue Valley Northwest High School. There were only about six students on detention. One was openly rebellious, and the monitor had to constantly go over and wake him up. Finally, they had to take him from the room. He looked as though he had either been up all night or was on some kind of drugs. But what shocked me the most was a young girl, very attractive, and probably a junior, maybe 16 or 17 years old. I told the group about one evening at home when Joy and I were watching TV, surfing the channels, and stumbled on this channel that showed from a full frontal view of the actual birth of a baby. I told them that we were both shocked to see that. This young girl put up her hand, and in an almost defiant tone asked what was wrong with that. She said it was perfectly natural. I agreed with her, but told her that it was shown around eight o'clock in the evening, and asked her if she would want her six-year-old child to watch that. She didn't see any problem with that either.

That's when I started realizing that there just weren't too many things sacred anymore with some of today's youth. I made about four of these presentations, and despite opening with a disclaimer that everything I told them was my own personal opinion and information and in no way reflected the thinking or opinions of their school's administration, I think the schools may have thought that I might be a bit too controversial, because I haven't been invited back. Oh, well. I tried.

This Kansans For Life, or "KFL," Golf Marathon caused me to come in touch with the Wichita office of the same organization. I had a number of conversations with the staff in that office and sent them a copy of my dad's essay. Through them and their local office, I started getting an education as to which politicians in the state were pro-life and pro-choice. I was told that probably the most hard-core pro-abortion politician was my own state senator, Dick Bond. They also told me about a pro-life day at the legislature where pro-life proponents were going to assemble in January of 1995 at the state capitol and get a chance to meet with their legislators to try and persuade them to vote along pro-life lines.

I had a conflict, but I made an appointment with Senator Bond the following week to meet with him in Topeka. I asked Richard to come with me, since he was adopted, and who I believe was the catalyst in our being able to have four more sons. We arrived at the appointed time, and Senator Bond was gracious enough to meet us. He was very polite and listened intently to what I had to say. I left with him a copy of my dad's essay and an 8" x 10" photo of our family. I told him about Joy and I losing our first two babies, that Richard was adopted, and the whole story. He then told me that he himself had two adopted sons. That jarred me. He admitted that abortion was a very sensitive issue, and he was concerned about it. He said that he opposed third trimester abortions and would try to enact legislation that would ban them. I was happy to hear that. He asked Richard where he went to school and where he worked. When he heard that Richard worked at Kaw Valley home for troubled youths, he told Richard that he had put together the $3,500,000 to start that home and was actually Richard's board chairman. What a surprise! He spent a good 30 minutes with us, and we left. We may not have influenced him enough to change his political stance, but maybe we did plant the seed.

Another golf meeting was scheduled at Kansans For Life out in

Shawnee. Pat Adair was the local director, and I got to know her and her crew pretty well. They were good people, hard workers, and not radical. They simply believed deeply in an ideal and worked relentlessly to reach it. It seems more and more that if you are strongly for something such as pro-life, you tend to get branded a "radical." That is a misnomer, because literally all of the pro-life people I know are very calm, determined and well-mannered. They are simply dedicated to an ideal and are willing to give of themselves and their time to further that cause. I don't think anyone will argue with me that when Jesus was alive, he was considered a "radical."

At any rate, I learned at the meeting that the fund-raisers were not only offering a three-day paid vacation for all those who were able to raise $2,500 in sponsor funds, but whoever raised the most funds also received free air transportation to the three-day vacation spots. That changed the whole game for me. I found out that I was at about $2,300, and another golfer was already at $4,000. The letters from the parish and Aquinas had long ago went out, and there were still funds dribbling in from them. I was really disappointed in our parish, though. I had sent out 2,000 letters to them and 950 to Aquinas parents. You'd think they would contribute at a rate of about twice that of Aquinas. Not so. It was the other way around. Aquinas parents doubled the contributions of Holy Cross. I have often wondered if that was the result of a vacancy in the pro-life committee chairperson for almost a year. It was curious to me why there was a vacancy for so long, and found out that almost a year ago the previous chairperson had been very upset over something that the assistant pastor did. He had made her so mad that both she and her husband quit the parish. Hmmmm ... could there be something wrong with the assistant pastor?

But back to the marathon. I decided to raise my pledge solicitation efforts to a completely new zone. I calculated that my chief opponent would top $5,000, and would think he had won top honors. So I set a goal for myself of $6,000. That meant I needed another $3,700. I commenced a telephone blitz of the legal field using the various bar directories. No one was too sacred for me to call up for sponsorship. The cause was absolutely worth any hurt feelings or bruised relationships. After that, I started calling on old little league acquaintances, and businessmen. The money started rolling in. I was now working almost half of each day on this project. Still, you can't put a dollar value on a baby's life.

The day of the marathon finally arrived. It was a Monday. On both the previous Saturdays and Sundays I went down to my office and called for more pledges. I was so tired of the push that the actual marathon was going to be a relief. I pulled my son Michael out of school to be my caddie, and we arrived at the Club of the Country course by seven a.m. I had a huge wad of pledges and checks that I turned in, and the staff told us it would be late morning before they would have a final tally.

The tournament itself was really a lot of fun. After the first 18 holes, quite a few golfers left, and that really opened up the course. Now Michael and I had a wide open course in front of us, so Michael started playing every hole as well. When we came to a par three hole, I'd hit four balls, play each one of them, and count that as four holes. On the par four and par five holes, I played two balls, and that helped me to get closer to my hundred holes. The girls brought us sack lunches, and we ate them on the fly. It was great fun for me to be spending almost the whole day with one of my sons, and Michael seemed to be having a helluva good time, too.

I finished my hundred holes around 3:30 p.m., and we headed for the club house. I was amazed at how well I had stood up physically. In fact, it would have been easy for me to get more holes in, but I told my pledgers that I would stop at 100 holes, and stop I did. Now the only question was, did I the raise the most funds? Pat Adair met me as I walked in the door and congratulated me. My opponent had topped $5,300, but I had squeezed past him with just under $5,600. It was a great feeling to win, but I can tell you this, I don't think anyone worked harder on it than I did. The ride home was really pleasant. It was a great feeling to set a very difficult objective and then achieve it. I had won a short vacation for Joy and me, and we deserved it. Our cash was tight, so it looked as though we wouldn't have a vacation this year other than our family reunion in June. When the time was right, we would take off.

By now, I was knee-deep in pro-life activities. I had called Stella, the church secretary, a few weeks previous to this about the vacancy on the pro-life committee, not so much because I was interested in it, but because I wanted to help in that area. I found out that another person had just been appointed to that committee, and we are now working hand in hand to move the parish along in the fight for life.

So where has all of this brought me? What am I doing here? When I started this book, all I wanted to do was to tell a true story about one of my dad's kids. But as the pages and chapters and months of reflection came and went, a completely unexpected realization developed. The first ember of this flame was when I took out my dad's essay and thought about it with a lot more maturity. I now realized that he was 45 when he wrote that essay. I also realized that he wrote it *over 50 years ago! 50 years!* That was when life was simple and national morals were high. If he placed such a high value on life way back then, what would his reaction be if he were living today and found out that 40 million babies had been killed through government approved abortions? Yes, "government approved" abortions. The *Roe v. Wade* ruling made abortions legal, and the legislature did nothing to make them illegal. So the government had approved each one of them.

That brought me to this question: What would my dad do if he were suddenly brought back to life today? Assuming he physically survived the shock of this horrendous outrage, and further, assuming that he managed to keep his sanity, he would roar with just rage over the slaughter of these poor, defenseless babies. I am certain that he would dedicate his every breath to ending the abortion plague as we know it today. I am sure that he would spend every second to stop this terrible national and world-wide insult to God and the Blessed Virgin.

I remember how excited Dad was when World War II was finally over. He came out of the back door of our house in Olmitz and yelled to us at the top of his voice with a happy grin on his face that the war was over. I have never, ever seen him that excited. I now realize that part of his excitement was because now his sons wouldn't have to go into the military and perhaps get killed. Sure, that was the biggest thing. But as I write this now, I think I understand Dad better, and I think a good part of his joy was that there would be no more sons and daughters killed by the war, causing sorrow to their moms and dads. I'm certain of it.

It was only during the writing of the last two chapters of this book that I decided to change the name of the book. I chose the word "odyssey," because Lord knows my life has been one wild odyssey up to now. In looking back, I now feel that everything the good Lord let happen to me was part of some kind of plan he had for me. Everything that has happened to me so far in my life has been "training." I've tasted the sweet successes of life and have had a lion's share of adversities. But why? And why is it that, just as my youngest son has reached high school and is showing more signs of independence, I suddenly wake up to the terrors of abortion? Has everything up to this point simply been stage one of my life, and is it now time to start into phase two?

As I thought more and more about the abortion issue, I started to learn more and more statistics. Uppermost is the statistic that there are about 1,500,000 abortions a year in the United States, and that we have surpassed 40,000,000. *40,000,000!* Let's focus on that number. How many wars must we add together to reach that number? I've not researched that yet, but I'll bet that all the wars this century wouldn't even come close to that number. In wars, many have lost their lives fighting, because they were drafted into the military. Their mothers didn't want them to die. They died for the most part defending an ideal.

Other statistics from the *Alan Guttmacher Institute* are very astounding. More than 50 percent of the pregnancies in America are unintended, and half of these are terminated by abortion. Self-gratifying sex reigns supreme. Each year nearly three out of 100 women aged 15-45 have an abortion. Forty-six percent have had at least one previous abortion, and 53 percent have had a previous birth. The United States has one of the highest abortion rates among the developed nations. Fifty-five percent of the women seeking abortions are *under age 25!* Where was our parenting? *Catholic women are about as likely as to obtain an abortion as are all women nationally, while Protestants and Jews are less likely! Catholic women are 30 percent more likely than Protestants to have abortions!*

Then there's the rape, incest and deformity arguments. *Guttmacher* statistics show that of the women having abortions, only one percent have been advised that the fetus has a defect, and an additional 12 percent fear that the fetus may have been harmed by medications or other conditions. Only about 15,000 women have abortions each year because they become pregnant as a result of rape or incest. Sixty-one percent of minors have abortions *with a parent's knowledge!* How deep do we have to sink before the good Lord declares Sodom and Gomorrah II?

What is most excruciating is the intentional factor. If these deaths were the result of a terrible disease, such as the famous black plague, that would be easier to stomach, although still a tragedy. But here, these mothers are ***intentionally*** *killing their own babies!* There is no war or disease that is claiming these lives. No. These are ruthless, intentional killings of the most defenseless of human beings. What kind of amoral society are we, that we tolerate this mass infanticide? Sure, some say it must be done to "save" or "preserve" the life of the mother. As a lawyer, and having to deal with many, many doctors, I can tell you that anyone who wants to can find a doctor who will give her the medical opinion she wants. Abortion has now become a form of birth control, or an accepted method of correcting an error of judgment in the heat of sexual satisfaction, or a perverted outgrowth of the so-called woman's liberation movement.

Somehow, we must stop this volcanic eruption of unborn blood that is flowing down the mountainside of mankind. Somehow, we must restore the sanctity of life and the traditional morals for which Christ himself gave his life thousands of years ago. Have we really learned anything from that? Can we truly be called Christians and still do nothing to end this, the worse blight on mankind's history since the crucifixion of Christ? Do we expect Christ to come back a second time and rescue us again from ourselves?

Although I will never presume to know what God wants me to do, it does seem clear that I am living my life in two sections. The first section ended around February of '96, when I first started getting involved in the pro-life cause. It just seems to make sense. I lost my "retirement" case and had a great deal of time on my hands. Why? Was it because God wanted me to write this book? Was it to bring me to a much fuller appreciation of the horror of abortions, and to make me ask myself how my dad would react to the abortion scourge? Maybe being born into a large family with the special father I had, the years in the seminary, the years in the military, my marriage and the loss of our first two babies, the adoption of Richard, and then having four sons the traditional way, the denial of wealth, and Kyle's brain tumor were all just part of God's boot camp for me. Lisa and Richard gave us our first grandchild on January 19, 1995. Maybe he was just getting me ready for the real war – the fight for the lives of the unborn.

I don't know the answer to that. But I do know this. God has given me some good talents. I'm smart enough to know that. At the same time, I am also smart enough to know that these talents are just gifts from Him, so I myself personally am really nothing special. I do believe that God now wants me on the front lines. The kids are essentially raised, and they are good kids. Not perfect, but I'm certainly proud of them *for the right reasons.* Sure, there might be some things I might like to change with each one of them, but what dad doesn't have the same feelings? I'm happy with them, and feel that as time goes on they will mature and maybe see God more as I do.

After choosing the word "odyssey," the rest was easy. I was headed toward life, toward trying to save the lives of the unborn. That is how I arrived at the title to the book. I have journeyed to the realization that we must eliminate the abortion blight on our society. Don't get me wrong. I don't consider myself the next great leader, the person God has selected to lead man from the brink of this terror. No, I'm just one of his little tools, and I really don't yet know how he wants to use me. I do feel him calling me, and I am ready for whatever he wants me to do. I'm sure he will lead me the way he wants. All he wants is for me to be willing to go with him. And I am certainly willing.

So the door is now open to the second phase of my life, and I am stepping through. I don't know how God expects me to have much influence in this war. But mine is not to know, but to follow. So I'm dedicating the rest of my life to rid the world of abortion. I don't know if I'll even dent it, but I'm going to try. I don't expect to conquer it overnight. I know that wars are won by winning one battle at a time. And we are going to lose some battles. That's just part of the turf, and we can't let that slow down our resolve. Life itself is at stake here. And nothing is more worthy of our highest efforts.

Before I step all the way through the door into the second stage of my life, I should pause and be grateful for my wife, Joy. This woman has had a very difficult life, as I've already covered. Losing two babies, surgeries, being dragged all over the country by a husband who eventually sank into alcoholism, struck by emotional problems, endured many lengthy periods of unemployment by her husband, was frequently being forced beyond her ability to cope, and yet, still being there for me and her five sons, all of the meals, housecleaning, laundry, and frequently not getting the respect she deserved, not knowing where her mother and younger brother are – this adds up. I hope the good Lord eases her load as I move into this new life of dedication. She certainly has earned it.

17

BUMPS IN ROAD FOR KYLE, THE "ANGEL," AND MONTREAL

(Kyle's Second Tumor, a Miraculous Little Angel, and Montreal Trip)

I ORIGINALLY FINISHED the book in early August of 1996, ending with Chapter 16. It is now August 2005. Much has happened in the last nine years so that I could easily write practically a whole new book. However, I decided to cap it all off with these last two chapters.

First, I forgot to mention in the *Odyssey To Life* that Richard found a gem of a wife and they were married on May 7, 1993. And naturally they started having kids. Their first was Morgan, born January 19, 1995. As I write this, she is 10 years old and a pretty young lady. She must have inherited Rich and Lisa's athletic abilities, because she can really run fast, in long powerful strides. She usually starts on offense in soccer, scores three or four goals, and then the coach puts her on defense to keep the score down. The problem for the other team is that she's also a great defensive player. She gets to the ball very quickly, gets it away from the offensive player and boots it down the field. Our goalie has to be bored as the dickens when Morgan is on defense.

Their second baby, Hailey, was born on October 16, 1996. She is now eight and has a lot of natural agility that I think could develop into many different things. She also plays soccer and does a good job of it. She has a smile that will knock your socks off. Both have been invited to "The Academy," which is a year-around soccer group of players chosen by invitation only. They have already been taking out-of-town trips.

Then there is Hunter, who is now five. He is a real challenge. He has a lightning quick mind which, when he makes it up, will not be deterred. He is so quick and determined that I call him the Tasmanian devil. When he gets into sports, look out!

About mid-1996 Michael was getting ready for his senior year at Aquinas, lifting weights and in training every morning. Kyle had completed middle school and was going to start high school next year. High school. A whole new atmosphere for him. He had worked through middle school and gradually reduced the special ed classes he had to attend. So this was going to be a whole new step for him – and Joy and me.

After Michael had injured his left elbow during wrestling in the spring of 1995, I felt there was no way that I was going to let him play both football and wrestling without some kind of medical coverage. So I applied for both him and Kyle with Blue Cross and Blue Shield. I really wanted Kyle to have coverage, too, because of his brain tumor and the slight clumsiness that ensued. I answered all the medical history questions as truthfully as possible and thought there was no way that Kyle would be accepted for insurance. But again, we all know Who is really running the show. I got the response, and Kyle was accepted in the "preferred" category, but Michael had to pay higher rates in a lower category of coverage. Who would have thought?

On both policies pre-existing conditions were not waived until after one year. The effective date of Kyle's policy was 8/1/95. So one year later, or 8/1/96, he would be covered for anything relating to his brain tumor. I recalled Dr. Hornig saying that every few years Kyle should have a precautionary MRI. So I scheduled it, guess where, at Children's Mercy Outpatient Center, Nall and College, the same place where his first one was discovered. And guess what, we had the same pediatric neurologist. Kyle was hinting heavily that he wanted to play football and was hoping that this MRI would clear him for that. Deep down, I knew there was no way the doctors were going to allow this, given his previous tumor.

At any rate, the doctor brought the MRIs in and hung them in the light box so they could be read. Kyle, the doctor and I looked at them. They didn't look like the ones that I had seen in 1988, so I asked the doctor how they looked, and would he allow Kyle to play football? He said that decision was up to Dr. Hornig, and we should take the MRIs to him so he could see them. So the next day or so we took them down to Dr. Hornig's office. We turned them in at the desk and waited.

We had a long wait, because Dr. Hornig is always on call and frequently has to even cancel appointments. But finally he showed up and went back into his office. He put the MRIs on his light screen. Then, in a very matter-of-fact tone, said Kyle had another tumor and it had to come out. The shock was shattering, but I had to focus on Kyle. I could see his eyes were teary, and I could sense his deep disappointment. But Dr. Hornig said that fortunately we caught this one before it got as big as the first one. This one was "only" ping ball sized. He said it should come out soon, but there was no real crisis. I was wondering just how much the good Lord was going to give Kyle to handle.

Surgery was scheduled to be done a week after high school started. Kyle was a freshman. What a way to start high school! The school week went by, and Sunday night we headed for Children's Mercy Hospital.

Michael was now a senior at St. Thomas High School and was on the varsity football team. The season had started. He had a teammate, Jeff Ohmes, and word got around that Mike's younger brother was going to have brain tumor surgery. Jeff's grandmother made a cone-shaped angel, and they got it to me before the surgery. Mind you, I had bad visions of the havoc that the first tumor had ravaged Kyle. God, did I ever hate that Monday morning. We followed Kyle to the doors to the operating room. Then the long wait started.

While we were waiting in the surgery waiting room, I noticed what looked like about a two-year-old boy who seemed a bit cranky. I've always been fond of little kids because they haven't yet been smeared with all the trash that had grown into the bilge of our society. His parents explained that he was there to have his tonsils removed. That was a relief! This was one of the very few boys that I couldn't make smile and get friendly with me. The parents seemed like good people, though you could see some hurt in their eyes. Eventually, the nurses came and got the poor little boy.

About three hours after Kyle went into the surgery room, Dr. Hornig came out and told us that the surgery went extremely well and Kyle should never have to worry about this again. He said that soon they would be taking Kyle up the fifth floor to Pediatric Intensive Care. So Joy and I took the elevator up to the fifth floor and began waiting. Soon the elevator came up with Kyle on the hospital bed. He was pretty much still out of it. They only allowed one parent at a time in ICU, so Joy went first. She had with her this crude little angel that been made by Jeff Ohmes' grandmother. When Joy went in, she put the angel on a shelf above Kyle. Then I took my turn, and Kyle was still out of it. I stood at the foot of his bed and stared at him, praying as hard as I could that he would be all right. Then it was Joy's turn, and I went out to the ICU waiting room.

While I was waiting, the mother of the little boy with the tonsil surgery came up and asked me how Kyle was doing. I told her that I thought he was okay. Then I thanked her for being so considerate in coming up to the fifth floor just to see how Kyle was doing. Then she hit me with a bomb shell. She told me that the doctors ran into a problem with their son. They found that the tonsils had cancer, and so they were going to put him in ICU also. I tried to be as sympathetic as I could under the circumstances, but then the nurses brought the little boy up and the mother disappeared into ICU with her son.

Finally, I got to go in again and found that the little boy was placed in a kid's crib, typical for that aged boy, and they had placed him **right next to Kyle**. While I was standing by Kyle, he started coming out of it. I was hoping and praying that he would be okay. He opened his eyes, and he wasn't cross -eyed. That was a great relief as it told me he wouldn't have to go through eye surgeries again. Then he looked over at me and said something. I don't remember what he said, but this was heavenly music to me because it told me that he wasn't mute. Another bullet dodged. After a little more time passed, Kyle moved his feet and his arms. He had good coordination. Another bullet dodged. Finally Kyle was awake to the point that he could carry on a conversation. That's when I knew he had come through the operation with no residual effects. My level of relief and gratitude was very, very high. Kyle was going to be okay. What a blessing God had bestowed on him and us.

It was about this time that I looked over to the parents of the little boy in the crib next to us. They were sitting next to the bed and took turns holding their son who was cranky from the operation. I'll never forget the blank stare of deep sadness they both had. You could tell this was almost the end of the world for them. I then looked back at Kyle. He had gone through his surgery perfectly, and apparently there were no residual effects.

Eventually, I looked above Kyle's bed, and my gaze seemed to settle on the little angel doll that we had been given. Then it struck me that since Kyle was okay, we really didn't need the angel any more. So why not give the angel to the parents of the little boy? I thought about it a little more and then decided to give it a try. So I took the angel down and walked over to them. I explained the history of the angel doll to them and told them Kyle was fine. I told them I didn't know how they felt about these kinds of things, but I told them that with it Kyle came out fine. I felt a little silly, but nevertheless I took a chance and asked if them if they wanted it. Without hesitation, they literally grabbed it and put it on the shelf above their boy.

We were informed early the next morning that they were going to move Kyle down to a regular recovery floor. I couldn't get to the hospital until noon. I was walking along the hall to Kyle's nurses' station when I saw the mother of that little boy coming the opposite way. Only this time there was no sullen sadness; no blank, dismal stare. Her face was radiant with an exciting smile like I've never seen. When we met, she told me that the doctors had taken another look at the results on her son and determined that their son did not have cancer. In fact, they were going home that afternoon! I congratulated her, but told her that I'd like the angel back before they left. Later, as I was sitting in Kyle's room, they both came into Kyle's room with the angel. They cradled that angel like it was the most precious thing in the world, thanked me, and took their son home.

I'm not claiming that a miracle happened here. But I know this. No doctor is going to tell the parents of a little boy that he had cancer unless they were 99 percent sure that he actually did have cancer. I guess we'll never know.

Eventually word of the angel got around. I got a call from Pat Adair, a Kansans For Life worker, who said that a friend of hers had a little girl who had an inoperable brain tumor, located right in the center of her head. The doctors said she had only a five percent chance of coming through surgery on that tumor, so they refused to operate. But when the little girl started having seizures, that left them no choice. They had to operate. So I gave the little angel to Pat, who got it to the mother of the little girl. I had insisted that I wanted the angel back after the surgery. I was quite surprised to learn that the brain tumor surgery was a complete success. Some time later when we were in Topeka on the *Roe v. Wade* debacle, standing outside with quite a crowd of pro-lifers, Pat pointed out the little girl to me. It was obvious that she was a completely normal girl. It was a very heart-warming experience. Again, I guess we'll never know.

Kyle by this time was out of the hospital. He had a six-inch scar down the shaven back of his head which was the traditional "zipper." He told me that kids at school would come up to him and ask him what happened. He just told them he had a brain tumor removed. And they usually responded with, "Cool," and went on.

Eventually there was some swelling on the surgery in the back of the head which slowly got bigger. So back to Dr. Hornig we went. He told us that Kyle was slowly leaking cerebral spinal fluid. The only way to correct it was to put Kyle back in the hospital, insert a small shunt into his lumbar spine and let the leaking gradually heal over and stop. This meant that Kyle had to lie on his back in the hospital for six straight days in October.

So back to the hospital we went for the new surgery, and back to the operating room waiting area. While waiting there, I noticed a mother with a cranky little two or three-year-old boy. The mother hand her hands full in keeping him calm. Being a nosy fella, I got her to tell me why she was there. She said they were up from Oklahoma for treatment for the boy's eyes. She said they had discovered terminal cancer in his retinas. Naturally, I felt very sorry for this woman. I really had no choice but to tell her about the angel. She wanted it immediately. Unfortunately, it was still with the little Lawrence girl. But the mother said she had regular visits at Children's Mercy Hospital and would keep checking with me.

About three weeks went by, and the angel was returned to me. A week or so passed, and I got a call from this mother. It was a Sunday afternoon. She wanted to know if I had the angel and could I bring it up to Children's Mercy Hospital. Of course, I agreed and headed to the hospital. I went to the room where her boy was asleep and gave her the angel. She was very happy to get it, and we talked for a time. Before I left, I told her she was free to use it, but when she finished with it, I really wanted it back. And then I left. Months later, I got a call from this mother, and she was very, very happy. She said that her son was getting his last treatment and then he was going home *completely healed!* She said she would send the angel to me, but never did.

Even though I've never had the angel returned to me, I look back at the three young kids who had serious ailments and were somehow healed, and I guess I'll never know if somehow that little angel was instrumental for at least thee "happenings" that may be miracles. To this day, I still wonder where that little angel is and whether it is still curing little kids.

While Kyle was in the hospital, I had one of the most heart-warming experiences of my life. This was in October and we got an early wet snow. It was the kind that made huge drifts and big, soft flakes came straight down. The problem was that the wetness made the snow stick to whatever it fell on. Then the new snow stuck until soon we had at least eight inches of snow covering everything.

Kyle couldn't get out of bed, so I stood at the window and tried to verbally describe to Kyle how beautiful the snow was. Eventually, we turned out the lights, but I still lingered with Kyle while he went to sleep. I somehow guessed that just being close to Kyle was a little more help in healing him. After a long while, I thought Kyle was asleep. So I tried to leave as quietly as I could and had stepped half-way into the hall. While I stood there with the door partially open, I whispered to Kyle, "I love you, Kyle." However, before I could close the door, Kyle replied in a very soft voice, "I love you, too, Dad." That really stopped me in my tracks and filled me with a warm feeling of togetherness and true affection. I slowly closed the door and left, almost crying.

When I got to the car, it was covered with about eight inches of wet snow. It was the kind that stuck to everything rather than falling to the ground. As I started driving, the radio said there was a severe winter storm and we should all stay off the road. But I had to get home. I could see limbs loaded with the beautiful white snow and bending way down. As I came down Metcalf Avenue, tall trees had bent over and broke. Many huge branches had fallen into the street, literally blocking traffic. The only way I could get through was by driving way over in the opposite lane, then drive around the fallen limbs, and then get back into my lane. Fortunately, there weren't any other cars, so I was able to do it safely.

This was happening in 1996, an election year. At that time I was deeply into trying to get pro-life legislators elected. With the permission of the home owners, I had placed yard signs along 103rd street, which was one of the main traffic arteries. When I got to that area on my way home from the hospital, I noticed that all my signs were taken down. That was really dirty pool. I am a conservative Republican, so I surmised that it either had to be Democrats or "moderate" Republicans. What really amazed me is that they had to pull all of these signs out during the heavy snowstorm. But I was one step ahead of them. I had a large supply of yard signs in my garage. So right in the middle of the storm I went out with more signs and completely covered the area with replacement signs. In fact, there were now more than there had been before.

But I took it a step further. The next day I eased up one of the side streets and parked along the street so that I could see if anyone was going to do it again. I had positioned my car close to 103rd Street so that I could watch literally all the signs that covered almost three blocks. One sign after another. I had my video camera with me and waited. I was there for a couple of hours and nothing happened, so I left. But apparently I had made my point and the replacement signs stayed up right up to the election.

Kyle's hospitalization was successful, the leak healed over, and the bag at the back of his head began dwindling until it was gone. He returned to school and started the long road back. By virtue of everything that had happened to Kyle, I'd not spent much time on Michael. Michael was a real blessing. He had such a good nature that he handled all of the attention Kyle was getting exactly as you would like him to. I was really proud of him.

Michael was doing well at Saint Thomas Aquinas High school. He was now a senior and was at the top of the heap. He was also a starting lineman on STA's football team. The road to the state championship had a unique format. The teams had a regular season in which they played some non-conference teams and all of the conference teams. Then every team in the league went into a four-team sub-state play off. The rationale was that your team could have a bad season for most of the regular season, but could still go all the way to State. STA won their sub-state. The next step was to play the winner of another sub-state champion. They were now one of eight teams vying for state champion. This game was played at STA's field, and we won! That meant that we were in the FINAL FOUR!

This meant that we had to drive to Salina and play a team called Salina Central. Salina Central was located off I-70 about 150 miles west of Overland Park. It was a night game, and it seems like the whole high school made the trip. We started filling the stands and then started reading the game brochure. What we saw had to be multiple misprints. Mike was our heaviest lineman, coming in at about 285. That's pretty big for any high school player. But when we read the roster of Salina Central, it listed six players over 300 lbs.! And only three of them were seniors.

Soon the game started, and it was readily apparent that the other team could out-muscle us. All those big linemen opened up big holes for this very quick back to get into the secondary. Once there, he was gone. And then they shot cannon off after every touchdown. I've got to handle it to Mike. In that game he gave it all he had. He threw his body around with reckless abandon and probably had the best game of his career. I think the score was 40 to zip when we finally got the ball into their end zone. At least, we saved enough face to avoid a shut-out. Then for some reason, the cannon shot off. It seems that an STA fan or cheer leader simply walked down to the cannon and shot it off after our score. That really upset the home team, but we didn't care, as that would give them something to remember us by. We lost, but we had made it to the final four in the state.

The year 1996 slipped into 1997, and we were still renting a house at 10240 Woodson. Had been since the early '80s. This was Mike's final year, and he was knocking down some very good grades. Every year STA put on a huge fund-raising event that was really impressive. It was called the "Extravaganza." They had a pretty stiff charge just to get in. There was a very good buffet line with top-of-the-line catering. There were black jack tables and many, many other exhibits and booths.

I ran into Bill McHale at some function, and he told me that he and his wife had accepted the position of heading up the next Extravaganza. Then he told me they really needed a new computer dedicated just to this event. He told me that IBM had agreed to an 80 percent discount on a $2,100 computer and they were looking for someone to donate the remaining $420 so they could buy the computer. I thought about it for awhile, and it was Mike's last year, so in gratitude to the school, I agreed to donate the first $420 so the school could get the computer. The first thing next morning Joan McHale came to my office to get the check. As she was sitting in front of my desk, she was smiling from ear to hear and I could see the greed oozing from her eyes. I wrote the check and she swiftly left.

I thought that they might send Joy and me free tickets to the event and might perhaps thank me for the donation for the computer. However, no free tickets came. Actually, the only other communication we ever received on this was an invitation to purchase tickets to the affair! I was really hurt over this. We were not wealthy at the time and never have been. Even so, I had made the donation, and as soon as they got the money, they were gone. And they apparently completely forgot about who made the donation, because I never heard from them again.

There is another story I should tell you about Bill McHale. Holy Cross had some Knights of Columbus function where there were two tables side by side where the people coming in paid for whatever it was. As luck would have it, Bill McHale and I sat next to each other at the two tables.

At times there were no people coming by, so we had a lot of time to talk. All during this time I had to listen to McHale virtually rant and rave about all the material things he had. He talked about how he and his wife were in a pool in Phoenix, I think, and they enjoyed it so much that he said he told his wife: "Let's just buy a home here." Then he talked about how he could do it and had a renter ready to rent it for two years until Bill was ready.

I have never seen anybody as wrapped up in themselves as much as I did that evening. So at the end I got up, leaned down on Bill's table, held my face close to him, and told him: "Bill, I had to sit here all during the time we were here and had to listen to you talk about all the material things you had. I just think you might like to know that I am renting the house we live in, that I was nearly broke most of the time, and it's nice to see you enjoying all the material things you have." This made me think of the Bible reading where it says: "It is easier for a camel to pass through the eye of a needle than it is for a rich man to enter My Father's house." He didn't have much to say.

Not long after that I was heavily involved in the first Kansan's For Life golf tournament. All profits went to various entities that tried to help keep young mothers from getting abortions. I mailed donation requests to the parents of St. Thomas Aquinas High School and to the members in the church directories. I made calls to people I knew, including lawyers. There was one in particular who listened to my spiel, then said "Hell, I sent $500 to Planned Parenthood, so I will also send you $500." I almost fell off my chair. The hard work paid off as I won a four-day, three-night paid vacation as the top money producer.

One of the people I called was good ole Bill McHale. After one of the masses, I hit him up for a contribution for the tournament. He said he would. A week went by and I hadn't heard from him, so two weeks later I hit him up again. To me it was "payback time." I had written a $420 check for his computer, so I thought he would match that. Eventually I got a check from him … for $100. Big deal! $100! What a cheap #%@^! I almost sent the check back, but kept it for the sake of the babies. There must be something wrong with Mr. McHale, because whenever I accidentally bump into him, he usually tells me he just opened up another fast food restaurant in Puerto Rico. Who the hell cares about that? All he is doing is bragging about his material things. But enough of this garbage.

Mike graduated from STA in May of 1997. His grades were very good. He was accepted in Kansas State School of Engineering to study computer science. Graduation was very rewarding. It was held outside on the football field with all the parents, relatives and friends sitting in the bleachers. As they introduced each senior, they listed the scholarships they had won and the schools they were going to attend. Then I knew that all of the tuition we had paid to send him to a Catholic grade school, then to a Catholic high school, had given him a good education and was worth every penny. I was really proud of him when he walked across the stage.

He landed some very good scholarships and moved into one of the bigger school apartments. "Apartments" is too kind. The rooms barely had space for two small beds, a little studying space, and not room for much more. But he met a lot of people, some of whom have become good friends.

I think it was during the summer of 1997 that Joy and I took advantage of the free vacation that I won. We decided to get out of the country and ultimately chose Montreal. The trip was fabulous. We stayed at the St. Elizabeth Hotel that had 1,000 rooms. There was a small fruit basket on the table. The room was spacious and had the French flavor. We were a little tired from the trip, so we turned in for the night.

The next morning we were full-fledged tourists and took off around nine o'clock. The first thing we wanted to see was the Notre Dame church. We had heard that it was unbelievably exquisite, but we hardly could believe what we saw when we entered. I had been to Notre Dame in Paris, but this Notre Dame was actually more impressive. As we walked down the wide center aisle, on each side were meticulously carved wood bench seats. As we looked to each side from the center of the church, we saw an additional two tiers along both sides of the church where additional visitors could sit and watch mass. The sheer elegance of virtually everything was astounding. I could almost write a book on this church alone, but that would invade the concept of an autobiography. Suffice it to say that this is the most beautiful church in North America.

We strolled down one of the side aisles and admired the beautifully carved wood that was set into the walls and wrapped around the large pillars that extended from the floor up to the tops of the walls and supported the arches of the roof. A huge altar was in the center of the sanctuary. In the half-circle that went from the left of the altar to the right of the altar was a high wooden wall, about 20 feet high, that was filled with more ornate carvings. Above these were many more of the carved pillars. There were also eight recessed areas in the mid-level of the wall that contained beautiful statues of various saints. About 20 or 30 yards behind the altar were six to eight enclaves that contained large statues of some of the saints of the church. Also behind the altar were castle-like pillars that were again very ornate and reached almost to the interior dome. Here there were more intricate statues and then slender steeples that extended upward almost to the ceiling.

We stood and drank in the pure beauty of this church. It had so much to look at that one could easily spend the entire day there and still not see it all. Then we walked down one of the side aisles approaching the altar. The communion rail was more of the intricately carved dark wood. When we got to the communion rail, we discovered that there was a narrow hallway that went completely around the back of the altar and on around to the other side of the church. Since this was also open to the public, we followed it.

When we reached a point directly behind the altar, we discovered a large set of doors. We thought this was a strange place for the doors, so we tried to open them. They easily swung open. What we saw then was truly beyond any words. These doors opened into yet another chapel that was so large that it would match most churches in size. It had even more ornately carved wood. As we walked down the long center aisles, we learned that this was the chapel that was used for marriages. And there was a waiting list so long that it was a year and a half before your wedding could be scheduled. Truly amazing.

We then went to the market area which was located on the St. Lawrence Seaway. The waterway was so wide at this point that it looked more like a lake than a wide river. There was a combination of antique stores and an open market, along with other shops. It was a tourist attraction, and but had many, many shops and people trying to sell their wares. Occasionally, we came upon some musicians and listened to the music. We walked around and eventually ran across a police van that was parked as one of the exhibits. The police officers explained the van and their equipment to anyone who stopped and showed some interest. I should tell you that in the three full days that we were there, we saw only three police vehicles, and one of them was the van down by the sea market area.

It began to get late and the sun was going down. Rather than take a cab, we decided to walk to our hotel. We walked leisurely and talked and took in the sights as we were going along. As we went, we felt oddly safe. We were in a section of the city that in any other city no one would ever dare walk at this time of the evening. We didn't see any police cars or the slightest thing that could or should have alarmed us to some danger. The sun was setting when we started walking the 17 blocks to our hotel. By the time we arrived, it was almost completely dark outside. We cleaned up and then walked a few blocks to this great restaurant. There can be no doubt that the French know how to cook. I don't recall exactly what we had, but it was certainly delicious.

The next day we decided to take an excursion boat up and down the St. Lawrence waterway. We got fairly close to some huge ocean-going ships that were docked. The captain took us in closer at one point so we could see some really unique apartments. This was a huge apartment complex ,and the main attraction was that there was a private entrance into each apartment. This meant that the building looked like a stack of blocks loosely stacked together. There were even open spaces where you could look through huge spaces and see the sky and waterway on the other side. It was a real oddity and surely worth the trip.

From there we took a cab to the Brother AndrE complex. Brother Bassette was born in 1845 to a family of 12 and was orphaned at a very early age. He was plagued by bad health ,and for the first 25 years of his life he worked on farms and in factories in both Canada and the United States. In 1870 he joined the Congregation of the Holy Cross in Montreal. Brother AndrE was given the menial job of janitor and doorkeeper at Holy Cross School. After performing his work duties, he would sneak up in the woods on top of this very high hill, Mount Royale. Brother AndrE would find a small clearing, then get down on his knees, place on the ground some holy pictures and then start praying rosaries. He prayed long and deeply.

In 1904 he asked the Archbishop of Montreal if he could build a chapel to Saint Joseph on the mountain, and was given permission. With the few hundred dollars that he had, he built a small wooden shelter 15 x 18 feet. Eventually, he started to build the larger church, dedicated it to the foster father of Jesus, the Oratory of St. Joseph on Mount Royale.

Then somehow Brother AndrE healed a very sick child. Then it happened again. Then again. Then word spread all over Canada about this holy brother to whom God had given the power of healing. Thousands of people visited him. This disturbed the college where he worked. So they moved him to a train station. The crowds got even bigger. But he still continued taking care of the sick and sometimes working miracles.

As Brother AndrE's reputation grew, so did the surroundings.

When we got off the bus, we immediately saw two sets of very wide steps ascending the small mountain. There were at least 200 of them. They were separated by flowers and small bushes which streamed gently down the hill. It was really breathtaking. As we walked around the bottom, we saw many people kneeing at various steps, praying. The people were spread all the way to the top of the steps. Then it dawned on me that they would kneel down on the bottom step, say some prayers, and then kneel on the next higher step, then say some prayers, and on and on until they reached the top. It was an impressive sight to watch.

On January 6, 1937, over a million people gathered for the funeral services of Brother AndrE. By this time he was known as the "Miracle Man" of Montreal, has been beatified by the church and is expected to be canonized as a saint.

To continue, we began the long walk up the steps to the top. We had to stop periodically to catch our breath. When we reached the top of the steps, we entered the basilica, named St. Joseph's Oratory. Once we entered, we were stunned by the size of it. It had a 97-meter dome that made it second only to St. Peter's in Rome. And to think that this was the result of a simple uneducated brother whom God used to build this beautiful church to honor St. Joseph.

We had heard a lot about their famous casino, so we caught a cab, rode across the main bridge and stopped at the casino. This was the ultimate of elaborate. The lush lawn and flower gardens were perfectly cut and cared for. There were benches so you could just sit and watch the beautiful scenery. We entered the casino and looked around. There were various levels where black jack was being played, and it seemed that the higher the level you went up, the higher the stakes were in the games. As I got to the upper level, the players at each table I approached sized me up. By simply looking at their steely eyes, I could see that these people not only played for big money, but they were dead serious about it. They didn't want just any hick to sit down at their table and disrupt their pace of play. I was primarily interested in black jack, so I returned to the first floor where the stakes were a lot lower and played a little. After a while it got boring, so I went looking for Joy.

We met and decided to get some lunch and went to a small café portion of the casino. We ordered and sat there and just enjoyed the plush atmosphere and just plain being on vacation. We had enjoyed almost three full days of great fun. It was as close as I knew how to enjoy a fantastic, though short vacation. I was really happy that all my hard work on the Kansans For Life golf tournament had won us this vacation. I had literally spent months of time in winning this vacation because I knew that I could never talk Joy into going to Montreal. I wanted her to see how some foreign cities and countries compare to those in the USA. I was proud of what I had accomplished.

18

WHILE SEXUALLY ABUSED VICTIMS ARE BEING PAID BILLIONS BY THE CHURCH, THE SOULS OF ABORTED BABIES ARE GOING TO HELL BY THE MILLIONS EACH YEAR BECAUSE OUR CARDINALS, ARCHBISHOPS, AND BISHOPS HAVE MADE SECULARISM AND MONEY THEIR PRIMARY GOALS, LETTING THE SOULS OF ABORTED BABIES PERISH

(Is Money the New God of the Catholic Church?)

BUT IT IS time to address perhaps the most important purpose of this book. The autobiographical part of this book was finished in 1996 and was intended as entertainment. But for some reason it ended in my conviction that abortion must be stopped and I should do all I could do to end it. A lot has happened between then and now. I will capsulate it, as it tells you about my odyssey to life and the experiences and discoveries of the past nine years regarding the war on abortion.

The year 1996 was a very active one with many happenings, some happy, some sad. Starting with the pro-life activities, I got on the "Respect Life" committee at Holy Cross. The pastor told our chairman that the word "pro-life" was too "harsh." We were disturbed by this watering down of this major issue "so we wouldn't offend some members of the parish." I suppose this should have warned us about the difficulties we would later encounter from our own pastors.

Our "Respect Life" committee at Holy Cross was very active. We didn't meet once a month; we met twice a month. And we addressed the abortion issue head on. In the long run, we realize now that our pastor gave us a lot more latitude than most other pastors did. Over the years we were able to put up the white crosses on the school grounds so that it looked like Arlington National Cemetery. Each cross was for one abortion. However, the following year we were not allowed to do that because many of the parents of the students complained too much. This was the beginning of the gradual realization that there were many Catholic mothers who had abortions. We also started learning that there actually were some priests who would leave the decision of abortion to the "mother" to decide, rather than strongly urging her not to have an abortion.

Perhaps I should cover why I am so pro-life. As you know, we lost our first baby in Chicago in 1964 and our second one in Tulsa in 1966. This led us to applying for adoption in November 1966, and we were able to adopt Richard in May of 1967. Our cost was $700, and it took us only seven months. Today adoptions cost between $20,000 and $30,000 and may take two years to finish the adoption. And couples may have to adopt babies (or children) from outside the U.S. Why? Because in this country we are killing about a million babies a year in abortions! We just shouldn't have allowed it. And who really wants a Russian or Chinese baby? I'm not putting China and Russia down. It's just that if a mother doesn't want to keep her baby, she should then put it up for adoption. All her bills will be paid and she won't suffer the lifetime of guilt of killing her baby. It really pains me that a loving couple, who would be properly investigated, can't adopt a baby.

But getting back to the pro-life involvement, every year I went over to Topeka, the State Capitol, on the January anniversary of *Roe v. Wade,* and met with many legislators. One of the most powerful was Senator Dick Bond. I took Richard with me and introduced him to Senator Bond. Now Richard had grown into an impressive young man, about 6'7" tall, and rather good-looking. But even that didn't have any effect on the senator. We also managed to get our pastor to allow members of our committee to address the parish after Communion, and we all did well, actually getting applause from the parish when we were done.

Our Respect Life Committee had been so active that our pastor told us we were the most active committee in the parish. The Archdiocese had a Respect life coordinator who asked us to put together an all-day Respect Life Day at the pastoral center in western Kansas City, Kansas. So we accepted the extra challenge and put it all together. We had some very capable speakers. I arranged for the author of *Lime Five,* Mark Crutcher, to fly up from Dallas. He had written a very gutsy book revealing what the abortion industry is really doing. I also got Phil Kline, our present attorney general; Dave Gittrich, executive director of Kansans For Life; the president of the state's Right to Life; a state senator from western Kansas, and many others to give speeches. We had display booths such as Advice and Aid, Kansans For Life, and the like. It was attended by 100 to 150 dedicated pro-lifers in the audience, but no priests and no bishop.

Soon after joining the Respect Life committee, I was asked to write a one-page insert for the Sunday bulletin. This was dedicated to the *Evangelium Vitae,* or *The Gospel of Life.* I started at the front and just started paraphrasing the book, inserting comments as I went along. I had to clear each of them through the pastor. The Archdiocese coordinator got wind of this and started asking me for copies, which she put into mail-outs to the entire archdiocese. We were rocking along pretty well until we got down to the first hard issue, abortion and contraception. Our pastor would not allow us to insert that in the bulletin. I realized then that our pastor was soft. He wanted everyone to "feel good." That is when I started understanding what was going on. The pastors in our archdiocese were intimidated by the people and didn't want to offend them. I can't say for sure why, but I wouldn't be surprised if it wasn't related to the collection boxes. The pastors may have been afraid of losing collections if they got too tough.

Then I started realizing it wasn't the people who weren't following God's laws and principles. The real problem was the priests! They were afraid of getting tough on this issue. Maybe they were getting mean calls from pro-abortion people in the parish. I don't know if that was the reason, but it was very clear that in all the years and efforts I had made on abortion gained very little. *We only got about one inch in a thousand-mile journey.* In other words, we were getting no return on all our hard work. So I bowed out of the committee work and started a new mission.

I decided that I was going to work on the priests. To me at that time, they were the ones clogging the pipeline of preventing abortion. I got the addresses of all the priests in the archdiocese and started sending them a letter that never exceeded the front and back. I called it "THE BABY PULPIT." One letter was on pink paper, the next on blue paper. I even had pink and blue envelopes printed with THE BABY PULPIT as the return address. And for the next year and a half I sent these out to the priests. I paid for the postage myself. Some were angrily returned, and some priests applauded it. But with the usual change in priests, my addresses changed. And by now the Archdiocese was "somewhat" upset with me, so I could not get a new list of addresses.

Some time later the sexual abuse scandal hit the news. Then there was this meeting of the almighty National Council of Catholic Bishops (NCCB) in Dallas. What a waste of time! They beat their chests and said "mea culpa." But all they did was talk. Oh, they came up with some guidelines to deal with the sexual abuse issue, but that whole meeting opened my eyes to the Catholic Church in the United States. The NCCB never really showed any solid leadership of the priests. About this time the book, *Good-bye, Good Men,* came out. It was a true expose of how the seminaries were actually driving good men out of the seminaries or else attempting to get them to participate in gay and lesbian activities. By far the worst area was the Boston area with Cardinal Law. It just seems that once a cleric reaches the level of Bishop, he cannot resist the adulation of everyone. So I guess the adulation leads the bishops to a sense of being invulnerable. We have U.S. senators and representatives who call themselves Catholic, but they are staunchly pro-abortion. It almost looks like they have sold their souls for the power of their political offices.

But the final crushing blow to me was the November 2002 elections. For governor we had a pro-life candidate and an avid *pro-abortion* "Catholic" woman, Sebelius. She had a huge war chest, and it was an uphill battle for our guy. But it was going to be close enough that with the right things done, it was winnable. To do so, it was going to take some courage of our Archbishop Keleher. So, two months before the election, I called his office, got his secretary and asked if she would ask the archbishop to allow me 15 minutes of his time to talk about abortion. Two weeks went by and no word. So then I wrote the Archbishop a letter, again asking for the 15 minutes. Again, no reply. I knew he was going to be at the October 11th Pro-Life banquet. I attended it also and managed to get him one on one for a brief moment and handed him an envelope containing a full page ad that I wanted him to put in the *Leaven.* It has a circulation of over 21,000 Catholic families in the eastern one-third of Kansas. The remaining two-thirds had their own weekly newspaper and their combined circulation of a little over 15,000. So you can see that our newspaper would be received by at least one-half of the Catholics in the state. Keep in mind that it was to be a full page ad, and I face-to-face told the archbishop that I would pay for the whole ad. Here it is on pages 408 and 409.

This ad mentions no political party, nor any candidate by name. All it does is clearly tell Catholics what moral values they should seek in a candidate. It does not cross the boundary between church and state.

I never heard another word from Archbishop Keleher. I looked forward with hope when the last issue before the election came out. But when it came out, I was sadly disappointed that the ad never appeared. The pro-abortion "Catholic" governor was elected, and we now have serious problems for the next four years. This was the final blow for me. It taught me that our own Catholic hierarchy, for the most part, didn't have the guts to stand up in the pulpit for this core belief, telling "Catholics" legislators that they must legislate according to their faith and that the Archbishop must insist that his priests *repeatedly* preach against abortion.

It was either the Sunday before the elections or shortly thereafter that we were shown at all masses a video of Archbishop Keleher asking for support for his $50,000,000 Capital Campaign.

VOTERS!

The Catholic Church cannot engage in politics. However, we have a moral and religious duty to inform all Catholics of the church's position on certain important issues that are related to some of the issues that appear in elections.

FIRST, YOU HAVE A MORAL DUTY TO VOTE

Section 2240 of the Catechism of the Catholic Church under the DUTIES OF CITIZENS section states:

> **"The duty of citizens includes: *"Submission to authority and co-responsibility for the common good make it morally obligatory to pay taxes, to exercise the right to vote, and to defend one's own country."***

THEREFORE, ALL CATHOLICS MUST VOTE.

SECOND, ALL HUMAN LIFE MUST BE RESPECTED.

Section 2270 of the Catechism under the section on abortion says:

> **"Human life must be respected and protected absolutely from the moment of conception. From the first moment of his existence, a human being must be recognized as having the rights of a person — among which is the inviolable right of every innocent being to life."**

THEREFORE, CATHOLICS ABSOLUTELY CANNOT SUPPORT ABORTION.

THIRD, "THOU SHALL NOT KILL" IS A COMMANDMENT.

Section 2258 states:

"Human life is sacred because from its beginning it involves the creative action of God, and it remains forever in a special relationship with the Creator, who is its sole end. God alone is the Lord of life from its beginning until its end; no one can under any circumstance claim for himself the right directly to destroy an innocent human being."

Therefore all abortions are directly contrary to the Catholic faith.

THAT MEANS CATHOLICS CANNOT SUPPORT ABORTION IN ANY FORM.

This includes voting for a candidate who supports abortion.

For the upcoming election all Catholics must determine those candidates who are for abortion and those that are Pro-Life.

CATHOLICS MUST THEN VOTE FOR THAT PRO-LIFE CANDIDATE.

There are many other very important issues that we all know about, but no issue is more important than the issue of abortion. There are 10,000 abortions a year in this state. That must be stopped, and the way to do it is at the ballot box.

CATHOLICS MUST VOTE PRO-LIFE!

Unbelievable! Could it be that he was too concerned that my "Voters" ad would upset too many Catholics and his Capital Campaign would suffer? Lord, I hope not, or this Archbishop will have a lot to answer for when he meets his Maker. I never received a call or letter from the archbishop or even from a subordinate explaining why they chose not to run the ad.

This is covered here to put you in the context of the *Odyssey To Life* and carry that forward. As you can see from all of this, in my opinion, the Catholic faith is in the lowest and worst shape I have seen in my life, and I am now working on 69. My final comment on this issue is that it took me about six years to realize that I can't convince even one parish priest, let alone the Catholic Church, that abortion is the number one problem.

But I can't quit. I will continue to work to save babies, primarily by giving presentations on adoptions as an alternative to abortion. I will also begin a presentation to couples preparing for marriage. I want them to know that when they say "in sickness and in health, for richer and for poorer ..." I will tell them they had better mean it. Then I will relate the events of our marriage so they know their marriage will not be all roses. The objective is to help them bond so that when they have kids, those kids will always have two parents. Hopefully, this will lead to the benefit of the kids. Kids. That's what it is all about. If we can raise good kids, then our future is much brighter. It's really that simple.

BUT THE SADDEST THING ABOUT ABORTION IS THE RISK OF LOSING THE BABIES' SOULS TO HELL.

Having been in the seminary for six years and then all the college, two degrees, and finally being admitted to the bar, I know how to search out the facts. The starting point is our own Catechism of the Catholic Church, the 1994 Interdicasterial Commission of the Catechism of the Catholic Church, whose chief authority was the Council of Trent. I will use the Catechism for research as to what happens to the souls of the aborted babies. Here are my results:

1. I have found **no *absolute* confirmation** that the souls of aborted

babies somehow go to heaven for eternity if they die without baptism.

2. I have found **no *absolute* repudiation** that the souls of aborted babies go ultimately to hell for eternity if they die without baptism.

Instead, the Bible commences with the history of man, Adam and Eve, and how they enjoyed the Garden of Eden, committed original sin, and embedded original sin on the souls of every single baby conceived. After that first (original) sin, the world is virtually inundated by sin. The following specific sections give us further direction:

> *404. How did the sin of Adam become the sin of all descendents? The whole human race is in Adam as "one body of one man." By this "unity of the human race" all men are implicated in Adam's sin, as all are implicated in Christ's justice.* ***Still, the transmission of original sin is a mystery that we cannot fully understand*** *... It is a sin which will be transmitted by propagation to all mankind, that is, by the transmission of a human nature* ***deprived*** *of original holiness and justice. And that is why original sin is called "sin" only in an analogical sense. It is a sin "contracted" and not "committed" – a state and not an act.* (Portions omitted).

It is encouraging that the church is forthright enough to openly admit to a mystery it cannot fully understand. I don't understand it either. But the most important catechetical edict that we get from 404 is that ***the transmission of original sin is a mystery that we cannot fully understand.*** So we can reasonably rely on the belief that we were born with original sin on our souls.

But now we come to the real crux of the matter. What happens to the souls of those babies that have been killed in the womb? Are they sent directly to hell? Section 405 in part states, ***Baptism, by imparting the life of Christ's grace, erases original sin and turns***

a man back toward God ... This clearly suggests that only Baptism can cleanse the soul of original sin. **BUT ABORTED BABIES DON'T GET BAPTISM!** So the natural conclusion is that the baby's soul is denied heaven and is sent to hell.!

The very life of Christ also indirectly supports the conclusion that these babies' souls lose heaven and suffer in hell. When Christ came, he brought the seven sacraments. The very first sacrament is Baptism, and is conventionally done **after the baby is born or as an adult.** I have never heard of a Baptism of a baby while it is still in the womb. So during that nine-month gestation period the baby doesn't even have a chance at Baptism. Still, we have shown above that the baby has original sin on its soul during that nine-month period.

The urgency of Baptism for infants is further emphasized in Section 1262 of the Catechism which states:

> As regards children who have died without Baptism, the Church can only entrust them to the mercy of God, as she does in her funeral rites for them. Indeed, the great mercy of God, who desires that all men should be saved, and Jesus' tenderness toward children which caused him to say: "Let the children come to me; do not hinder them," allow us **TO HOPE** that there is salvation for children who have died without Baptism. **All the more urgent is the Church's call not to prevent little children coming to Christ through the gift of holy Baptism.** *(Emphasis added.)*

This issue has been studied in great detail, and for a thorough analysis I suggest you read the Vatican City December 16, 2004 article by Father Peter Gumpel, "What The Church Has Said About Children Who Die Without Baptism." In this article Father Gumpel relates that St. Augustine believed that original sin existed, and that unbaptized babies are destined to hell, saying that they are subject to the flames of hell, although adding that they are "very mitigated flames." Fr. Gumpel's ultimate conclusion is that all we can do is hope.

But I don't like living with just hope, as the unborn are completely pure except for original sin. That original sin must be removed so their souls can go to heaven and be with Jesus.

So the only conclusion I can draw from all of this is that the souls of aborted babies are simply doomed to hell. That being true, WHERE ARE OUR CARDINALS, ARCHBISHOPS AND BISHOPS?